Religion and American Politics

INTERNATIONAL RELATIONS IN ASIA, AFRICA AND THE AMERICAS

The series International Relations in Asia, Africa and the Americas is edited by the Centre for International Studies and Development of the Jagiellonian University in Kraków.

Edited by Andrzej Mania & Marcin Grabowski

Vol. 19

Paulina Napierała (ed.)

Religion and American Politics

Domestic and International Contexts

PETER LANG

Berlin - Bruxelles - Chennai - Lausanne - New York – Oxford

Bibliographic Information published by the Deutsche Nationalbibliothek
The Deutsche Nationalbibliothek lists this publication in the Deutsche Nationalbibliografie; detailed bibliographic data is available in the internet at http://dnb.d-nb.de.

Library of Congress Cataloging-in-Publication Data
A CIP catalog record for this book has been applied for
at the Library of Congress

This publication was financially supported by the Institute of American Studies and Polish Diaspora, Jagiellonian University and the Centre for International Studies and Development.

The cover image courtesy of Paulina Napierała.

ISSN 2511-588X
ISBN 978-3-631-86596-5 (Print)
E-ISBN 978-3-631-91194-5 (E-PDF)
E-ISBN 978-3-631-91195-2 (E-PUB)
DOI 10.3726/b21390

© 2024 Peter Lang Group AG, Lausanne
Published by Peter Lang GmbH, Berlin, Germany

info@peterlang.com - www.peterlang.com

All rights reserved.

All parts of this publication are protected by copyright. Any utilisation outside the strict limits of the copyright law, without the permission of the publisher, is forbidden and liable to prosecution. This applies in particular to reproductions, translations, microfilming, and storage and processing in electronic retrieval systems.

This publication has been peer reviewed.

Contents

Paulina Napierała
Introduction 7

Paulina Napierała
The Role of Religion in American Politics: Research Approaches 11

Evolving Relations Between Religion and American Politics 29

Károly Pintér
American Civil Religion After Trump: Twilight or Rebirth? 31

James L. Guth and Lyman A. Kellstedt
Religious Influences on American Conservative Populism 71

Constitutional Dimensions of Religious and Political Debates in the United States 93

Sebastian Kubas
The Exploitation of Religious Passions in the U.S. Constitutional
Practice: The Christian Right and the Judicial Review 95

Jerold L. Waltman
The Legal and Political Context of Contemporary Free Exercise
Jurisprudence 129

Emily R. Gill
Religion, Liberty, and Marriage Equality 143

Elad Ben David
Religious Clauses of the First Amendment in the Concept of
"American Islam" of Post-9/11 Era: The Case of Yasir Qadhi 167

Religion, Race, and Politics: The Political Role of the Black Church 187

Paulina Napierała
The Ebenezer Baptist Church in Atlanta and the Activist Tradition of the Black Church 189

Cristóbal Serrán-Pagán y Fuentes
Martin Luther King, Jr. on the Three Social Evils in the United States: Racism, Poverty, and Militarism 241

Michael McLaughlin
Cooking Up the Revolution: The Black Panthers, Church Kitchens, and the Place of Religion in the Black Power Movement 263

Jajuan S. Johnson
The Fire This Time: Black Church Burnings in the Era of Obama and Black Lives Matter 279

Religion, International Politics, and Global Issues 301

James L. Guth and Brent F. Nelsen
Religion and Support for the "Trump Doctrine" 303

Husam Mohamad
Evangelicals' Influence on U.S. Policy on Israel and the Palestinians in Recent Decades 327

Lyman A. Kellstedt and James L. Guth
Religion and American Public Attitudes on Global Warming, 2020 353

Notes on Contributors 373

Index 377

Paulina Napierała

Introduction

The idea behind this volume is to present a broad international and interdisciplinary perspective on the role of religion in American politics (both domestic and international). The United States is remarkably religious and secular at the same time. While it is a pluralist democracy, known for its multicultural identity, the role of religion has been crucial in the formation of the nation's identity and history as well as in American politics. The relations between religion and U.S. politics are complex and delicate, and while the United States remains a world power, they also influence its foreign policy and international relations. Therefore, researchers continue their efforts to analyze and understand these dynamics.

This volume is a result of cooperation between Jagiellonian University scholars and an international group of academics, including renowned American specialists, who study a variety of topics surrounding the interactions between religion and American politics. Coming not only from the United States but also from Israel, Spain, Hungary, Poland, and the Palestinian territories, they provide a unique international perspective on how the United States deals with issues at the intersection of religion and politics and how American solutions concerning the interactions between the two spheres are perceived around the world. As one aspect of this cooperation, the contributors to this book also had the opportunity to meet and discuss these topics at the international "Religion and Politics in the United States" conference organized in 2021 by Paulina Napierała and the GIRES Institute (which during the pandemic served as a commodious forum for online academic events).

The authors of the following chapters represent several academic fields. Therefore, they examine how religion and politics in the United States conflict, collaborate, or otherwise influence each other, taking various perspectives. The majority of us are political scientists, but others represent theology, religious studies, law, history, and cultural studies. The topic of religion and politics is interdisciplinary in its nature, but a (recently actively developing) sub-field of political science—the politology of religion (or political science of religion)—while often drawing on different perspectives, also adds its own prism and offers new models, concepts, and other theoretical and methodological tools useful in analyzing religious influences in the political sphere. Therefore, in the introductory chapter, I explain the research approaches taken in this volume as well as the new concepts.

The book explores the intersections between religion and American politics in many contexts, historical and contemporary, domestic and international. It is divided into four parts: *Evolving Relations Between Religion and American Politics*; *Constitutional Dimensions of Religious and Political Debates in the United States*; *Religion, Race, and Politics: The Political Role of the Black Church*; and *Religion,*

International Politics, and Global Issues. Each part starts with a slightly longer chapter that takes a broader perspective and considers historical background, and thus introduces readers to the particular topics discussed in the following chapters.

The first part starts with Károly Pintér's chapter, where he analyzes the evolution and condition of American civil religion as well as its prospects after Donald Trump's controversial and divisive use of it. The author places the recent transformation of civil religion in a historical and theoretical perspective. In the second chapter, James L. Guth and Lyman A. Kellstedt examine the role of religion in creating support for recently rising populist movements, paying special attention to conservative populism in the United States. Using quantitative methods, they analyze how different ethnoreligious traditions respond to populist themes and to what extent theological traditionalism influences attitudes toward American conservative populism.

In the second part of the book, the authors analyze constitutional dimensions of various religious debates in the United States. It starts with Sebastian Kubas' text concerning the relations between the modern liberal constitutional state and religious organizations. Kubas examines the attempts of the Christian Right to institutionalize their cultural preferences through decisions of the U.S. Supreme Court. His chapter introduces a broader perspective of the evolution of the Christian Right's legal strategies and then discusses cases concerning both the Free Exercise and the Establishment Clauses. In the next chapter, Jerold L. Waltman focuses specifically on contemporary free exercise jurisprudence, putting it into legal and political context. He carefully examines three major cases from the last few terms of the Court, presenting arguments and perspectives of both sides of the "religious freedom" debate. He also distinguishes between regulations that might apply to religious organizations and to commercial enterprises that invoke religious reasons. Emily R. Gill's chapter concentrates on the debate focused strictly on the issues of religion, liberty, and marriage equality. She starts with discussing differences between negative and positive liberty, and then analyzes *Obergefell v. Hodges*, describing four different positions concerning marriage equality and referring to prior U.S. Supreme Court decisions. The last chapter of this part also discusses religious clauses of the First Amendment, concentrating, however, on how they influence a "foreign" non-Christian (immigrant) group in the United States. Elad Ben David shows how the clauses are being incorporated in the concept of "American Islam," particularly by Yasir Quadhi. This chapter, while generally discussing domestic issues, also touches upon the international contexts and events that have influenced the situation of Islam in the United States.

The third part of the book is dedicated to the role of the Black Church in American history and politics—a topic usually discussed separately although it is deeply connected to the relations between religion and politics in the United States. The chapters here describe the complicated relations among religion, race, and American politics, concentrating on a particular ethnic minority church but also depicting the role that minority churches can play in democratic pluralistic societies (despite or against the systemic flaws). In the introductory chapter,

Paulina Napierała, focusing on the Ebenezer Baptist Church in Atlanta, analyzes a comprehensive topic of the activist tradition of the Black Church. She places her study in a broader historical and theoretical perspective and provides a background for specific themes discussed in the following chapters. The next topic, analyzed by Cristóbal Serrán-Pagán y Fuentes, concerns the life and the writings of Dr. Martin Luther King Jr.—one of the most famous figures in the Black Church. The author pays special attention to King's stance on the "triplet social evils" in the United States: racism, poverty, and militarism. While racism and poverty are mostly seen as domestic problems, in discussing King's attitude toward the Vietnam War Pagán also touches upon the international context. Michael McLaughlin, on the other hand, focuses on a lesser known aspect of history, the role of churches in the Black Panther Party's Free Breakfast for Schoolchildren Program, showing how—despite ideological differences—they provided a sanctuary for the Black Panthers and gave the Party a chance to influence communities through caring for the hungry. In the last chapter of this part, Jajuan Johnson presents the consequences of Black churches' continuous engagement on the side of their communities. He examines the evolution of racialized violence against Black churches in the post-Civil War era and presents cases of violence against this symbol of Black independence in the era of Barack Obama and the Black Lives Matter movement.

The final part of the volume discusses religious influences on American international policies and on public attitudes toward global issues, including militarism and global warming. In the first chapter, James L. Guth and Brent F. Nelsen analyze how religion shapes public attitudes toward the "Trump Doctrine." They begin with the broader context, commenting on how the "return to religion" in international relations has sparked interest in the role of religion in shaping attitudes toward foreign affairs—one channel through which faith can influence a nation's policy. They define the "Trump Doctrine" as a "distinctive blend of nationalism, militarism and unilateralism" and find it important that religion significantly influences public attitudes toward Trump's policies. In the next chapter, Husam Mohamad puts the focus on a specific narrower topic: how the beliefs of evangelical groups such as dispensationalists and Christian Zionists have been influencing U.S. policies in the Middle East. He also investigates how these groups promote their vision of Israel's relations with the Palestinian territories. In the last chapter, Lyman A. Kellstedt and James L. Guth examine how religion shapes American attitudes toward global warming, finding considerable differences among members of American religious groups. The global issue of environmentalism turns out to be highly influenced by religion, especially by theological traditionalism that usually results in skeptical attitudes toward global warming.

The publication of this volume would not have been possible without a grant from the Institute of American Studies and Polish Diaspora at Jagiellonian University and additional funds provided by the Centre for International Studies and Development, which I acknowledge and greatly appreciate. I would also like to thank the Kosciuszko Foundation and the Advanced Research Collaborative for the grants that allowed me to work on the last stages of the editing process at the

City University of New York. I am grateful for academic support from scholars representing various Polish and American universities who agreed to review particular chapters of the book, and especially for the work of the reviewer of the whole volume. Mostly, however, I want to thank all the scholars who agreed to participate in this publication.

Paulina Napierała

The Role of Religion in American Politics: Research Approaches

Regardless of secularization processes taking place in the modern world, especially in terms of institutional or functional differentiation,[1] and against the predictions of the early proponents of secularization theory, including Karl Marx, Max Weber, and Émile Durkheim, who expected that with modernization religion would disappear (at least from the public life), it still plays an important role in the public and political sphere[2] of many countries, including the highly modernized United States. Because religion's constant presence attracts new research, some scholars argue that secularization theories were wrong. Others, on the other hand, explain that such theories usually comprised several levels, claims, and assumptions, including structural differentiation, decline of religious practices and beliefs, and marginalization or privatization of religion. As they argue, while the general historical structural trend of secular differentiation has been taking place, religions have reacted to it in different ways—not only by marginalization and retreat to the private sphere (as previous theories would suggest) but also by what Jose Casanova calls the "deprivatization" of religion. In this perspective, privatization and deprivatization are simply different historical options for religions in the modern world.[3] Both of these processes have been taking place in the United States as

---

1 Understood as the differentiation of the secular spheres from religious institutions and norms. More in: Casanova, Jose: *Public Religions in the Modern World.* The University of Chicago Press: Chicago 1994, p. 211.
2 More about levels of the public sphere, including the strictly political level in: Calhoun, Craig (ed.): *Habermas and the Public Sphere.* MIT Press: Cambridge 1993; Rawls, John: *Teoria sprawiedliwości.* PWN: Warszaw 1994; Buksiński, Tadeusz: *Publiczne sfery i religie.* Wydawnictwo Naukowe Instytutu Filozofii UAM: Poznań 2011.
3 Casanova, Jose: *op. cit.*, pp. 211–214. See also: Beyer, Peter: *Globalization and Religion.* SAGE Publications: London 1994. Beyer suggests that "the globalization of society, while structurally favoring privatization in religion, also provides fertile ground for renewed public influence of religion" (p. 71). Religion for him can be understood as a "mode of communication" and globalization as "a situation in which the revitalization of religion is a way of asserting a particular (group) identity [...]" (p. 4). Beyer, who based his theory on Niklas Luhmann's systemic concept, claims that religions try to maintain their influence in the public sphere in various ways. Some of them choose the liberal option and some the conservative one. The conservative option means "a reassertion of the traditional view of transcendence, often explicitly as a

well—and as a result of the dominance of one option or the other, over the past few decades, "the study of religion and politics has gone from being ignored by the scholarly community to being a major focus of research."[4]

Secularization theories have had a similar effect on studying international relations, and despite the recent "return to religion" in international relations, it is important to remember that the religious factor "stayed on the backburner in the study of international relations for a long time,"[5] which has been especially evident in theoretical approaches. Currently, one group of academics suggests that religion's return poses a fundamental challenge to international relations theory and therefore new and alternative paradigms should be developed, while another group has argued that the study of religion in international relations does not require a revolution, but rather evolution of the theoretical frameworks currently at our disposal.[6]

Because religion continues to be an important force in American domestic and international politics, as well as in international relations in general, in this volume scholars focus on how it influences various policies and public attitudes, including those toward foreign affairs, and how—through that—it also influences U.S. foreign policy. They further examine how American religious groups can act as social movements, political actors, and interest groups (in both domestic and international contexts).

This chapter provides an overview of different perspectives and approaches taken by the authors to examine and explain the complicated relations between religion and American politics. It also presents the attempts undertaken by the representatives of the political science of religion to structure the way the new sub-discipline draws on different fields and approaches, adding its own prism

---

normative response to a society ("the world") that is seemingly heading in a different and evil direction" (p. 90).

4 Smidt, Corwin/Kellstedt, Lyman/Guth, James (eds.): *The Oxford Handbook of Religion and American Politics*. Oxford University Press: New York 2009, introduction.

5 Sandal, Nukhet A./James, Patrick: "Religion and International Relations Theory: Towards a Mutual Understanding." *European Journal of International Relations* 17 (1), 2010, p. 3. More in: Fox, Jonathan: "Religion as an Overlooked Element of International Relations." *The International Studies Review* 3 (3), 2001, pp. 53–73.

6 More in: Sandal, Nukhet A./James, Patrick: *op. cit.*; Hatzopoulos, Pavlos/Petito Fabio: "The Return from Exile: An Introduction." In: Hatzopoulos, Pavlos/Petito Fabio (eds.): *Religion in International Relations: The Return from Exile*. Palgrave Macmillan: Basingstoke and New York 2003, p. 3; Kubalkova, Vidulka: "Toward an International Political Theology." In: Hatzopoulos, Pavlos/Petito (eds.): *Ibid.*, pp. 79–105; Thomas, Scott: *The Global Resurgence of Religion and the Transformation of International Relations: The Struggle for the Soul of the Twenty-First Century*. Palgrave Macmillan: New York and Basingstoke 2005, pp. 72–77.

and methodology and trying to develop a separate theoretical framework. It is thus necessary to begin this discussion with a brief presentation of how scholars researching the relations between religion and politics conceptualize religion.

There are many definitions of religion, including theological, non-theological, inclusive, exclusive, substantive, functional, sociological, and psychological ones.[7] Theological definitions are useful mostly for theologians, but not so much for social scientists. Substantive definitions focus on the presence of a set of items (the content) associated with religion, such as God, gods, other supernatural beings, or the Absolute.[8] Functional definitions concentrate on the role that beliefs and rituals play for a community (sociological) or an individual (psychological).[9] Many scholars researching religion and politics have adopted a substantive rather than a functional approach, viewing religion as related to the supernatural.[10] One of the most general substantive definitions is that authored by Edward Burnett Tylor which simply states that religion is a belief in spiritual beings.[11] The reason for choosing substantive definitions in political studies has been explained by the authors of the *Oxford Handbook of Religion and American Politics*:

> Although the core of religion—the realm of the transcendent, supreme beings, and direct communication with the divine—is beyond the realm of social science [...], research can show how the beliefs and behaviors and organizations associated with religion shape individual political attitudes and behavior, as well as institutional structures and processes.[12]

On the other hand, some of the most well-known definitions often contain both levels: substantial and functional—for example, Durkheim's famous definition that states, "[R]eligion is a unified system of beliefs and practices relative to sacred things, that is to say, things set apart and forbidden—beliefs and practices which unite into one single moral community called a Church, all those who adhere to them."[13] Some authors argue that both functional and substantive approaches can be useful in political science, depending on the research purpose.[14] As Maciej

---

7   More in: Adamski, Franciszek (ed.): *Socjologia religii. Wybór tekstów*. WAM: Kraków 1983; I analyze it in more detail in: Napierała, Paulina: *In God We Trust. Religia w sferze publicznej USA*. Księgarnia Akademicka: Kraków 2015, pp. 21–25.
8   Depending on how inclusive the definition is. More in: Potz, Maciej: *Political Science of Religion. Theorising the Political Role of Religion*. Palgrave Macmillan: Cham, Switzerland 2020, p. 23.
9   *Ibid.*
10 Smidt, Corwin/Kellstedt, Lyman/Guth, James (eds.): *op. cit.*, p. 4.
11 More in: Tylor, Edward Burnett: *Religion in Primitive Culture*. Harper: New York 1958.
12 Smidt, Corwin/Kellstedt, Lyman/Guth, James (eds.): *op. cit.*, p. 4.
13 Dukheim, Émile: *The Elementary Forms of Religious Life*. Free Press: New York 1995, p. 44.
14 Potz, Maciej: *op. cit.*, p. 23.

Potz stresses, if scholars want to "explain general mechanisms by which various beliefs and ideas translate into political action, the functional approach will enable generalizations," showing similarities between "religious" and "secular" ideas.[15] However, if the purpose of the study is to understand the difference that religion makes in politics (which the political science of religion is mostly interested in), then "substantive definitions will better serve this purpose." Focusing on these ideas, beliefs, and practices, "which refer to the supernatural," substantive definitions allow investigation into their political impact.[16] In the end, for his own studies he chooses a broad substantive understanding of religion that combines sociological and psychological approaches, according to which "religion is a system of beliefs and practices related to the supernatural, held and practiced individually or collectively."[17]

As the authors of *The Oxford Handbook of Religion and American Politics* stress, however, no matter how religion is defined, it is a multidimensional phenomenon and scholars do not always agree on the number and character of its dimensions. Nevertheless, a number of social scientists have accepted the view that there are at least "three major components of religion that are potentially important for politics: believing, behaving, and belonging."[18] In this perspective, "the substantive content of a faith is embodied in religious beliefs, the practice of a faith is reflected in behavior, and belonging is revealed by affiliation with a religious community."[19] While all of these dimensions provide a useful scheme for analyzing the political influence of religion, different theoretical approaches put varying emphases on these three dimensions.

Theoretical perspectives that consider these dimensions are often applied by political scientists researching the American religious context, and they have been carefully analyzed by Corwin Smidt, Lyman Kellstedt, and James Guth in *The Oxford Handbook of Religion and American Politics*. I will briefly present these perspectives before discussing other approaches and different propositions of theoretical frameworks. As the authors explain, since the 1980s American political scientists have been looking at the influence of religion on politics through two most common competing perspectives. More recently, another perspective was added—one that attempted to provide a kind of synthesis of the previous two. Importantly, the first of these, the *ethnoreligious perspective*, is closer to Durkheim's

---

15 Potz, Maciej: *op. cit.*, p. 25.
16 Potz, Maciej: *op. cit.*, pp. 25–26. As he admits, in political science of religion, psychological approaches can also be sometimes useful.
17 *Ibid.*
18 Layman, Geoffrey: *The Great Divide: Religious and Cultural Conflict in American Party Politics*. Columbia University Press: New York 2001—qtd. In: Smidt, Corwin E./Kellstedt, Lyman A./Guth, James L. (eds.): *op. cit.*, p. 4.
19 Smidt, Corwin E./Kellstedt, Lyman A./Guth, James L. (eds.): *op. cit.*, p. 5.

notion of religion as a social phenomenon where the affiliation with a religious group shapes political responses, and the second, the *theological restructuring perspective*, more reflects Max Weber's view that religion is embodied in beliefs which shape political attitudes and behavior. The third one, the *synthetic perspective*, views religion as embodying belonging, beliefs, and behavior, all of which influence political life.

As the experts explain, the *ethnocultural perspective* was formulated primarily by historians, and it focuses on the different ethnoreligious groups that migrated to America. According to this view, these groups held differing worldviews, cultural preferences, and religious reference groups, all of which shaped their political and partisan views and preferences.[20] And although, as sociologists of religion argue, these ethnoreligious attachments have been recently weakened by assimilation and other processes, many American political analysts continue to apply this scheme, finding it still, at least partially, relevant.

The second perspective, also known as *religious restructuring theory*, was introduced in the 1980s to explain the growing divisions within American faith traditions and was further developed in the 1990s.[21] The scholars behind it argued that growing theological divisions within different traditions had affected political divides. "Orthodox" believers who adhered to traditional doctrines tended to support the political right, while religious "progressives," who argued for a compromise with science, tended to move toward the left. Within this theory, theological divisions are more important than ethnoreligious divisions.[22]

The third perspective built on the previous two, arguing that both religious affiliations and religious beliefs, along with religious behavior, help to explain how religion shapes American politics. According to this approach, some groups behave as the ethnoreligious model would suggest and others respond on the basis of contemporary divisions over beliefs.[23]

These models, often used by American researchers including political scientists and sociologists (usually in their quantitative analyses), have been applied in several studies included in this volume. In the following chapters, they are extensively used particularly by F. Nelsen, James L. Guth, and Lyman A. Kellstedt. However, elements of these perspectives, especially of restructuring theory, also appear,

---

20 All the explanations here are based on: Smidt, Corwin E./ Kellstedt, Lyman A./ Guth, James L. (eds.): op. cit., pp. 3-42; 69– 94.
21 Introduced by: Wuthnow, Robert: *The Restructuring of American Religion*. Princeton University Press: Princeton 1988 and developed by: Hunter, James D.: *Culture Wars: The Struggle to Define America*. Basic Books: New York 1991.
22 More in: Smidt, Corwin E./Kellstedt, Lyman A./Guth, James L. (eds.): *op. cit.*, pp. 6–7. James Guth, Lyman Kellstedt and Brent F. Nelsen use these schemes in their following chapters and explain them in more detail.
23 More in: Smidt, Corwin E./Kellstedt, Lyman A./Guth, James L. (eds.): *op. cit.*, pp. 7–8.

while not always explicitly, in other analyses, including the chapters authored by Pintér, Kubas, Gill, Napierała, and Mohamad. In a similar vein, the elements and certain assumptions of the ethnoreligious model can be traced in the articles concerning Black churches.

As the aim of this volume was to include interdisciplinary research on religion and politics in the United States, as well as both qualitative and quantitative analyses, the authors—representing different disciplines—have also taken theoretical and methodological approaches characteristic of their various fields of studies. Moreover, some of them, apart from using a particular perspective, draw widely from other fields as well. A number of the contributors, including the political scientists, employ legal, sociological, historical, theological, religious, and cultural studies approaches, as well as politological.

Károly Pintér, for example, as a specialist in language, literature, history, and culture, not only examines the historical development of certain concepts studied by sociologists of religion, but he also employs elements of content analysis and discourse analysis, focusing on linguistic and rhetorical aspects of the researched phenomenon while placing it in a political context. Cristóbal Serrán-Pagán y Fuentes, on the other hand, while strongly concentrating on the theological perspective and theological interpretations, also applies elements of historical, biographical, and comparative religions approaches, especially when he explains the influences of certain Christian and non-Christian theologies on Martin Luther King's political views. Michael McLaughlin largely uses a historical framework, building on social historical work and historiography related to the Black Panthers and their partnership with churches. Additionally, however, he draws from social movement theories and research perspectives common in the Black Church studies and sociology of religion, especially when examining the role of religion in Black political organizing. Jajuan Johnson while looking through the prism of heritage studies, adds elements of cultural and religious studies theories as well as elements of theological analysis when approaching Black liberation theology. Generally, however, he places the topic of Black church burnings in the political context of Barack Obama's election. Focusing on political mobilization of Black churches and using an interpretative model developed within political science, Napierała additionally places her analysis in a historical perspective and discusses previous sociological approaches to the topic of Black Church activism. She concentrates on theology as well, and touches upon the potential applicability of certain elements of the restructuring model in analyzing the levels and forms of political behavior of Black churches. The legal scholar Sebastian Kubas extensively applies his legal perspective in focusing on church-state relations and constitutional law. He stresses, however, that the legal disputes that he describes concern the socio-political realm. He also pays attention to sociological and political studies on the Christian Right. Elad Ben David applies a legal perspective in his chapter as well, while his knowledge of Islamic studies and references to international politics play an important role in his analysis. Jerold L. Waltman and Emily R. Gill are political scientists who analyze constitutional dimensions of religious and political debates in the

United States, widely drawing from both the legal framework and political philosophy. Husam Mohamad, also a political scientist, employs a broad theological analysis, and while concentrating on the role of interest and lobbying groups in the policymaking processes, he also touches upon social movements theories.

All these analyses, in result, provide a truly interdisciplinary picture of the intersection between religion and politics in the United States. The variety of perspectives, which the authors (representing different fields) have employed, undoubtedly contributes to the understanding of the political role of religion and to the general topic of religion and politics. Moreover, a number of these approaches have sometimes been applied by some political scientists who postulate the development of a new separate sub-discipline of political science: the politology of religion or political science of religion.[24] While they generally see the new subfield as "a specific discipline due to its research of political science themes, in the context of religion,"[25] they do not always agree on details in methodology. Therefore, the use of the above-mentioned approaches would be possible mostly for those scholars who, while seeing the politology of religion as a specific sub-field of political science (rather than religious or other studies), treat it broadly and interdisciplinary in terms of methodology.[26] Not all political scientists favoring the development of the politology of religion, however, agree with such an approach. Some postulate a narrower definition of the sub-field along with a set of separate analytical models and theoretical tools emerging strictly from political science. Therefore, it is useful to take a closer look at different approaches to the politology of religion and their evolution.

---

24 It is important to note that not all political scientists who research relations between religion and politics support the idea of creating a new sub-discipline within political science. Steven Kettell, for example, argues "that such an enterprise would create more difficulties than benefits." He encourages political scientists to engage more with religious issues, but stresses that "the tools of political science should be committed to a broader, more interdisciplinary and holistic approach to the academic study of religion in general." Kettell, Steven: "Do we need a 'political science of religion'?" *Political Studies Review* 14 (2), 2014, p. 210.
25 Jevtić, Miroljub: "25 Years of Politology of Religion." *Christianity World. Politics* 23, 2019, pp. 151–158, 151. More about the development of this sub-discipline in Europe in: *ibid.*
26 In Poland, the politology of religion was first regarded by some religious studies scholars as a sub-discipline of their field. With time, however, Polish political scientists initiated attempts to conceptualize it as a sub-discipline of political science—in the way that sociology of religion is considered a sub-field of sociology. More about it: Michalak, Ryszard: "History of Politology of Religion in Poland. A Research Overview." *Politics and Religion Journal* 14, 2020, pp. 219–262.

Michalak who in 2016 defined the politology of religion quite broadly—as "interdisciplinary exploration within subject matters, where religious and political factors intersect and interact with each other"[27]—later decided to analyze, classify, and specify several different understandings of this term that had developed over the years.[28] As he explained, the first understanding is the most popular and commonly used interpretation. It sees the politology of religion as whole research that takes into consideration all combinations of phenomena that are specific to the worlds of religion and politics. It also encompasses methods of many disciplines, especially political science, religious studies, theology, sociology, philosophy, anthropology, cultural studies, history, and law. As a result, the specific findings of these disciplines "will be an inherent part of the politology of religion." In this sense, however, the politology of religion will be their sub-discipline or auxiliary science. In the second understanding, the politology of religion is defined specifically as a sub-discipline of political science. In this case, its essential interest is the political analysis of the phenomenon of religion (including its components, such as doctrine, worship, and religious organization). The basic assumption here is to see religion as a political phenomenon, similarly to how sociology of religion sees religion as a social phenomenon. The third understanding of the politology of religion also sees it as a sub-discipline of political science, but "assumes that its content includes issues of the permeability of interplay of religious phenomena and political phenomena," while "the obligatory starting point for research is the assumptions of political science with reference to methods and achievements of other scientific disciplines." The fourth understanding is narrower, seeing the politology of religion "as political research on religion based on the paradigm of the function of the political factor in religion."[29]

Apart from these four understandings, Polish political scientist Maciej Potz developed another, even narrower, understanding of this sub-discipline, publishing his suggestions in 2019[30] and 2020.[31] The scope of his definition of the politology

---

27 Michalak, Ryszard (ed.): *Implementacja zasad religijnych w sferze politycznej*. Morpho: Zielona Góra 2016, p. 5. Originally: "interdyscyplinarna eksploracja w obszarze spraw, w których krzyżują się i wzajemnie oddziałują na siebie czynniki religijne i polityczne."
28 Efforts to define the politology of religion were undertaken at several conferences attended by Polish and international scholars, whose contribution to the field Michalak describes in his article. The list is too long to include here, but it should be acknowledged. More in: Michalak, Ryszard: "History...," *op. cit.*, pp. 235–236.
29 Michalak, Ryszard: "History...," *op. cit.*, pp. 235–236. The author himself remains committed to "the validity of exploring the relationship between religion and politics based on the tools of many scientific disciplines," p. 252.
30 Potz, Maciej: "Perspektywy badawcze w politologii religii." *Studia Religiologica* 52 (4), 2019, pp. 277–291.
31 Potz, Maciej: *Political...*, *op. cit.*

of religion was a result of setting strict boundaries to political science, understood as "empirical science about the mechanisms of political power." From this perspective, the task of the politology of religion as a sub-discipline of political science would be to find the answer to the question about the importance of religion for the relations of political power.[32]

In his writings, Potz has stressed that research on the relationship between religion and politics was long outside of the mainstream of political science. It was often dominated by the legal approach, with the main focus on church-and-state relations and constitutional law. There was also research within religious studies (the field that considered the politology of religion its own sub-field), but apart from that, as he argues, the relations between religion and politics were either analyzed from confessional positions (e.g., in Poland—in connection with Catholic social teachings) or from the perspective of political philosophy (or political theology). On the other hand, as he points out, in many English-speaking countries the topic of religion and politics has been regarded as inherently interdisciplinary (i.e., studied by scholars representing different disciplines, who would discuss any interactions between religion and politics).[33]

In his view, all these perspectives have not been sufficient, especially from the point of view of political science. Therefore, not only does he advocate seeing "political science of religion as an explanatory framework of the political role of religion, grounded in political science," but he also formulates a multilevel theoretical approach to the study of the political role of religion.[34] While doing so, he criticizes previous approaches, especially the prevailing legal and theological ones, not only as insufficient but also as "being normatively overloaded and failing to grasp the actual impact of religion on power relations."[35] At the same time, he acknowledges and values the theoretical perspective discussed and applied by the authors of *The Oxford Handbook of Religion and American Politics*[36] but stresses that "it is for the most part applicable only to the United States,"[37] while his aim has been to develop a more broadly applicable concept. Therefore, he offers an approach that

> consists of three distinct—but integrated—theoretical perspectives: the economic or transactional approach, grounded in rational choice theory and economic theories of religion; the social movements theory (SMT) approach, looking at the internal assets,

---

32 This vision seems too narrow to some Polish scholars. Michalak mentions controversies around it. Michalak, Ryszard: "History...," *op. cit.*, p. 236.
33 Potz, Maciej: "Perspektywy...," *op. cit.*, pp. 277–278. Some scholars have also stressed that political scientists should apply an eclectic and multi-disciplinary approach to religious issues. More in: Kettell, Steven, *op. cit.*
34 Potz, Maciej: "Perspektywy...," *op. cit.*, p. 277.
35 *Ibid.*, More in: Potz, Maciej: *Political...*, *op. cit.*, pp. 9–13.
36 Smidt, Corwin E./Kellstedt, Lyman A./Guth, James L. (eds.): *op. cit.*, pp. 3–12.
37 Potz, Maciej: *Political...*, *op. cit.*, p. 8.

organization and dynamics of religious actors; and the cultural/humanistic approach, exploring evolutionary, psychological and sociological determinants behind individual propensity to religion-inspired political mobilization.[38]

What is important in his concept of the politology of religion and its research approach is that religious organizations (churches, sects, cults, etc.) are seen as political actors (either as organizations or communities), while religion is considered a system of beliefs and practices (related to the supernatural) that motivates people to social and political behavior. Therefore, in his view, these religious-political actors should be analyzed in the same way as secular political actors (e.g., political parties, social movements, or interest groups). Even religious organizations themselves are seen here as political systems—"the arenas of power relations." The author stresses that while politics is secondary to their "supernatural goals," their political activity should be still analyzed from the political science perspective because "they share a lot with other political actors in terms of their short-term objectives and strategies of political action."[39] As he explains, they use "mimicry strategies," taking the roles of social movements or interest groups while additionally holding specifically religious instruments.[40] As such they can act either as stakeholders or as veto players.[41] Religious actors still play an important role not only in theocracies but also in democratic political systems, bargaining with political parties, lobbying decision-makers and mobilizing their members into political action, all while providing religious ideas that motivate political attitudes.[42] The fact that religion claims special status among other systems of beliefs, as well as the fact that religious organizations behave like political actors, contribute, according to the author, to the sustained presence of religion in the public arena of the contemporary world.[43] Therefore, in his view, their engagement in politics should be analyzed at the three levels connected to the three above-mentioned theoretical perspectives.

The economic or transactional approach which (most) generally looks at how religious actors interact with other actors within a political system should be applied at the macro level—when analyzing the interaction among actors within an entire political market/system. The social movements theory, which focuses on collective mobilization, can be used at the mezzo level to analyze a particular organization and research communication mechanisms, resources, and other elements influencing its mobilization potential. The cultural/humanistic perspective which

---

38 Potz, Maciej: "Perspektywy...," *op. cit.*, p. 277.
39 Potz, Maciej: *Political...*, *op. cit.*, pp. 20–21.
40 Potz, Maciej: *Political...*, *op. cit.*, pp. 126–132.
41 Potz, Maciej: *Political...*, *op. cit.*, pp. 34–40.
42 Potz, Maciej: *Political...*, *op. cit.*, p. 118.
43 Potz, Maciej: *Political...*, *op. cit.*, p. 121.

aims at explaining relations between religion and politics in the context of individual motivations is useful at the micro (individual) level.[44]

As Potz explains, the economic perspective or transactional approach might actually be relevant in explaining two spheres—not only the behavior of religious organizations as entrepreneurs competing with other actors on a political market but also the relations between individuals as consumers and religious organizations as producers or suppliers of religious goods.[45] He thinks, however, that it is better suited for macro-level analyses concerning competition among actors.[46] The basic assumption behind this approach is that religious organizations are seen as economic entities operating within a market (understood as either a society at large in a "religious economy" or a political system in political science of religion). They produce and sell goods to their members, such as the promise of salvation, but they also sell and exchange goods with other political actors (such as political parties or governments). This second kind of goods includes their members' votes and mass actions that they are able to organize for or against these other political actors.[47] Moreover, as economic actors, religious organizations can also engage in various profit-maximizing behaviors, including subcontracting, vertical integration, monopolistic practices, and fierce market competition.[48] Therefore, this perspective is most useful for macro analyses that look at religious organizations from the outside.

The social movement theory, on the other hand, as the author points out, reveals more of the internal operations within religious organizations, and it can be useful for the analysis of the collective mobilization of religious actors. It bridges the gap between culturally shaped individual dispositions and institutionalized political action,[49] and allows to study the mechanisms by which available resources (e.g., communication networks, internal power structures, culture) and emergent collective qualities (common identity, shared normative commitments) are utilized to "convert critical dispositions to political action."[50] Generally, it explains motives, means, and opportunities that allow religious organizations to take actions.[51] Motives might be shaped by religion (which is helpful in creating group identities, legitimizing norms, and upholding worldviews). Means, such as symbols, money,

---

44 Potz, Maciej: "Perspektywy...," *op. cit.*, pp. 284–289.
45 Potz, Maciej: *Political...*, *op. cit.*, p. 42.
46 He also stresses that it has to be treated as a metaphor and cannot be pushed too far. Potz, Maciej: *Political...*, *op. cit.*, p. 43.
47 Potz, Maciej: *Political...*, *op. cit.*, p. 42.
48 Potz, Maciej: *Political...*, *op. cit.*, p. 43.
49 Potz, Maciej: *Political...*, *op. cit.*, p. 45.
50 Potz, Maciej: *Political...*, *op. cit.*, p. 46.
51 More in: Wald, Kenneth D./Silverman, Adam L./Fridy Kevin: "Making Sense of Religion in Political Life." *Annual Review or Political Science* 8, 2005, pp. 121–141.

ideas, leadership, communication, or political space might also be provided by religious organizations. Political opportunity structure, on the other hand, includes legal environments for the activities of non-state actors.[52] Importantly, as the author notices, one great advantage of this approach is that "it helps integrate the church-state paradigm into political science of religion," which happens "through the notion of political opportunity structure which contains much of what the church-state studies are concerned with [...]."[53]

The cultural perspective, which in his approach is useful at a micro level, helps determine individual motivations and social mechanisms behind the religiously inspired political behavior of individuals and religious organizations. While exploring evolutionary, psychological, and sociological predispositions toward religion-inspired political mobilization, it might focus on religious mechanisms of the religious legitimation of power, religious doctrines that either make people obedient or inspire their (political) behavior, as well as on the political role of religious leaders and the mechanisms of political control within religious organizations.[54] As such it encompasses many aspects of research characteristic of such fields as psychology, sociology of religion, and religious studies.[55]

Potz argues it would be best to integrate all these perspectives, but he acknowledges that it is often difficult, especially for a single researcher.[56] A scholar might thus concentrate on one of the levels, applying appropriate theoretical concepts. Potz also admits that "[n]one of these perspectives is predisposed to become *the* theory of politics and religion. They have their own territories and the aspects of the relationship they are best at explaining." At the same time, their territories sometimes overlap.[57]

His proposition is both interesting and useful, as it might help organize and structure research on topics strictly connected with political science. He discloses, however, that he does not offer "a single, coherent theory for studying all instances of the religion's influence on the sphere of politics." As he acknowledges, "[p]olitical science of religion is too vast an area to be approached with a single method or model." Therefore, what he proposes is "[...] a structured selection of conceptions, models and other theoretical tools potentially useful for the analysis of religion-related political phenomena [...]"[58]—within the narrowly defined

---

52 Potz, Maciej: *Political...*, *op. cit.*, p. 46.
53 Potz, Maciej: *Political...*, *op. cit.*, p. 48.
54 Potz, Maciej: *Political...*, *op. cit.*, pp. 48–51. He also stresses that while religion may play a vital role in shaping various elements of cultural repertoire, the relation between culture and political behavior is not deterministic.
55 Potz, Maciej: "Perspektywy...," *op. cit.*, p. 289.
56 *Ibid.*
57 Potz, Maciej: *Political...*, *op. cit.*, p. 53.
58 Potz, Maciej: *Political...*, *op. cit.*, p. 6.

sub-field of political science. He also adds that even such a narrowly defined politology of religion and its approach to studying the relations between religion and politics does not exclude the use of other disciplines, such as psychology, sociology, religious studies, or theology, as long as they help in understanding the influence of religion on power relations.[59]

There is no doubt that the authors of this volume use a number of approaches characteristic of many of the above-mentioned disciplines. Some of them also analyze their particular topics from an interdisciplinary perspective. While they all contribute to the topic of religion and politics (often considered as inherently multi-disciplinary), they do not necessarily represent the politology of religion (understood narrowly). This volume, in turn, offers a broad approach to the topic of religion and politics. Nevertheless, although not all of the authors are political scientists and not all of their analyses can fall in the category of political science of religion—unless it is defined in the broadest sense—the book might still be considered as contributing to the field of the politology of religion (understood in both the broader and narrower senses). For those who stress "the validity of exploring the relationship between religion and politics based on the tools of many scientific disciplines,"[60] it will deliver several new perspectives, topics, and approaches. Those who prefer a narrower understanding of this new sub-field of political science will not only find several analyses that can be classified as representing the politology of religion in the narrowest sense but also studies which, despite drawing on approaches from other fields, do concentrate on the influence of religion on power relations. Other analyses in this volume might contribute to further politological research.

In many chapters, including some interdisciplinary ones, the authors touch upon certain elements of the analytical framework proposed by political scientists, including some concepts and theoretical tools postulated in the politology of religion (although not always in a structured way). They also analyze the political engagement of religious organizations at various levels, including the suggested micro, mezzo, and macro levels. And while a number of them might not represent a fully developed political science approach to the study of religion in politics, they can certainly contribute to further politological analyses, providing additional details (more carefully examined in their respective fields). Therefore, their analyses serve an important subsidiary role, as their findings can be interpreted in the light of theoretical frameworks applied by political scientists. Moreover, if we look at this volume as a whole, it can provide a multilevel analysis (suggested by Potz) of religion-related political processes taking place in the United States (although not every process and not every phenomenon will be analyzed at each level).

---

59 Potz, Maciej: "Perspektywy...," *op. cit.*, p. 288.
60 Michalak, Ryszard: "History...," *op. cit.*, p. 252.

The first part of the book, which comprises contributions by Károly Pintér, James L. Guth, and Lyman A. Kellstedt, might be considered as representing the microlevel and the cultural perspective. Both chapters focus on individual motivations and social mechanisms influencing religiously inspired behavior. Guth and Kellstedt, while applying the ethnoreligious and restructuring theories characteristic in American studies on religion and politics, focus on how belonging and believing influence political behavior and individual attitudes, in this case toward American conservative populism. And while the restructuring perspective concentrates most directly on beliefs, and the ethnoreligious perspective focuses more on religious affiliation and identity (rather than theologies and beliefs themselves), they all influence individual motivations, which are analyzed here. Pintér, on the other hand, concentrates on civil religion and its social function, touching upon the specific role political-religious leaders play in civil religion, examining how they use specifically understood religious doctrine/ideology to influence certain political attitudes of Americans.

The second part of the book, which concentrates on constitutional dimensions of religious and political debates in the United States, might be considered by the proponents of the very narrow interpretation of the politology of religion as being outside its scope. As Potz argues, "[e]valuating the existing relations between state institutions and religious institutions from the perspective of normative assumptions about the proper model of 'church-state relations' is the job of a political philosopher, not a political scientist."[61] On the other hand, however, he admits that through one part of the social movement theory, the church-state paradigm can be integrated into the political science of religion (even narrowly understood). This is made possible thanks to the notion of political opportunity structure, which includes legal and constitutional solutions concerning possible activity of religious actors.[62] Kubas, Waltman, Gill, and David discuss this structure, which, alongside motives and means, allows religious organizations to take actions or prohibits/constrains them from doing so. When church-state relations are perceived through this prism, it can be assumed that this part of the book concerns the mezzo level. Several topics discussed in the chapters of this part, however, might actually suggest the macro level of analysis. David, for example, analyzes negotiations of a certain group's status within constitutional law, while Kubas, apart from discussing the political and legal strategies the Christian Right has used to mobilize a specific group of voters, also focuses on their attempts to, as he puts it, institutionalize their cultural preferences by translating them "into legal obligations or exemptions." By presenting legal battles fought in competition against other groups, he seems to be touching upon the transactional perspective. Religious actors competing on a political market, employing various strategies, including legal (also described herein

---

61 Potz, Maciej: *Political...*, op. cit., p. 21.
62 Potz, Maciej: *Political...*, op. cit., p. 48.

by Gill and Waltman), advocating "for policies that promote their own desired outcomes,"[63] and offering other political actors (e.g., parties) their members' votes and protest actions (also concerning legal solutions), can most likely be examined within the economic perspective. This is especially so if their engagement in profit-maximizing strategies, such as subcontracting and integration (e.g., evangelicals and conservative Catholics united within the Religious Right and in some court battles), is also taken into consideration. And although it is true that legal analyses might be narrow or may contain a "normative overload," they seem to contribute to both mezzo and microlevel analyses of strictly politological research.[64]

The chapters of the third part of the volume generally contribute to the mezzo level, concentrating on the role of churches in collective mobilization. They analyze how Black churches encourage social action, create or participate in social movements, and what resources they provide. Most of the texts refer to (or touch upon) elements of social movement theory and provide an overview of the mobilization processes that take place within Black religious institutions. They try to explain the motives, means, and opportunities that influence the ability of Black churches to take socio-political actions. While some authors concentrate more on churches' resources and opportunity structures (McLaughlin, Johnson), others pay special attention to religious and theological motives that influence their stance on activism (Napierała) or the attitudes of their leaders to particular political issues (Pagán). Jajuan Johnson additionally analyzes the consequences of the political and social engagement of Black churches. Most authors in this part discuss the various means that churches can use for social mobilization, such as symbols, ideas, leadership, material resources, and social spaces. Johnson and McLaughlin especially focus on buildings as safe havens. They all agree on the important role of Black churches in Black social mobilization and Black political organizing, especially during the civil rights movement, and they acknowledge the significance of applying religious ideas to shape socio-political movements. Napierała and Pagán further stress the role of Black religious leaders and the theological ideas that shaped them. While Pagán concentrates explicitly on theological influence, Napierała puts it in the context of a political mobilization model that sees theology as one of the factors shaping political behavior, next to other resources and opportunities. Nonetheless, both of them (as well as Johnson, who addresses the role of Black theology) touch upon the cultural perspective and the microlevel analysis. And although theology as one of the motives can be analyzed within social movements theory, when stressing its influence on individual dispositions and its effects on people's attitudes, the micro perspective seems to overlap.

---

63 More in: Emily R. Gill's chapter.
64 In fact, Potz also admits that the notion of opportunity structure can be a link between social movements theory and economic approach. More in: Potz, Maciej: "Perspektywy...," *op. cit.*, p. 286.

The last part of the book can also be considered as generally contributing to microlevel analysis. In the contributions by James L. Guth and Brent F. Nelsen, and Lyman A. Kellstedt and James L. Guth, who again use the ethnoreligious and restructuring models, the cultural perspective seems to dominate. In the first chapter, Guth and Nelsen present strong evidence that both ethnoreligious affiliation and religious beliefs (conservative or liberal) influence individual (and public) attitudes toward foreign policy. In the final chapter, Kellstedt and Guth, using the same theories, analyze public attitudes toward global warming to find that "ethnoreligious affiliation, religiosity, and religious beliefs all have substantial relationships with environmental views" (while theological traditionalism has the strongest). The middle chapter authored by Husam Mohamad's also contains many elements of the cultural perspective, especially in its approach to analyzing the effects of religious beliefs of premillennialists and Christian Zionists. At the same time, however, there are elements of social movement theory, especially in the part presenting the development of the Christian Right as a social movement. Moreover, elements of macro analysis are detectable when the author describes how specific movements and interest groups compete with other actors over Middle East policy. Consequently, the micro, mezzo, and macro perspectives overlap here.

Therefore, we hope that all the analyses presented in this volume contribute not only to the broad topic of religion and politics and to studies on religion in American politics but also to the politology of religion.

References

Adamski, Franciszek (ed.): *Socjologia religii. Wybór tekstów*. WAM: Kraków 1983.

Beyer, Peter: *Globalization and Religion*. SAGE Publications: London 1994.

Buksiński, Tadeusz: *Publiczne sfery i religie*. Wydawnictwo Naukowe Instytutu Filozofii UAM: Poznań 2011.

Calhoun, Craig (ed.): *Habermas and the Public Sphere*. MIT Press: Cambridge 1993.

Casanova, Jose: *Public Religions in the Modern World*. The University of Chicago Press: Chicago 1994.

Dukheim, Émile: *The Elementary Forms of Religious Life*. Free Press: New York 1995.

Fox, Jonathan: "Religion as an Overlooked Element of International Relations." *The International Studies Review* 3 (3), 2001, pp. 53–72.

Hatzopoulos, Pavlos/Petito Fabio: "The Return from Exile: An Introduction." In: Hatzopoulos, Pavlos/Petito Fabio (eds.): *Religion in International Relations: The Return from Exile*, Palgrave Macmillan: Basingstoke and New York 2003, pp. 1–20.

Hunter, James D.: *Culture Wars: The Struggle to Define America*. Basic Books: New York 1991.

Jevtić, Miroljub: "25 Years of Politology of Religion." *Christianity World. Politics* 23, 2019, pp. 151–158.

Kettell, Steven: "Do we need a 'political science of religion'?" *Political Studies Review* 14 (2), 2014, pp. 210-222.

Kubalkova, Vidulka: "Toward an International Political Theology." In: Hatzopoulos, Pavlos/Petito (eds.): *Religion in International Relations: The Return from Exile*. Palgrave Macmillan: New York 2003, pp. 79–105.

Michalak, Ryszard: "History of Politology of Religion in Poland. A Research Overview." *Politics and Religion Journal* 14, 2020, pp. 219–262.

Michalak, Ryszard (ed.): *Implementacja zasad religijnych w sferze politycznej*. Morpho: Zielona Góra 2016.

Napierała, Paulina: *In God We Trust. Religia w sferze publicznej USA*. Księgarnia Akademicka: Kraków 2015.

Potz, Maciej: "Perspektywy badawcze w politologii religii." *Studia Religiologica* 52 (4), 2019, pp. 277–291.

Potz, Maciej: *Political Science of Religion. Theorising the Political Role of Religion*. Palgrave Macmillan: Cham, Switzerland 2020.

Rawls, John: *Teoria sprawiedliwości*. PWN: Warszaw 1994.

Sandal, Nukhet A./James, Patrick: "Religion and International Relations Theory: Towards a Mutual Understanding." *European Journal of International Relations* 17 (1), 2010, pp. 3–25.

Smidt, Corwin/Kellstedt, Lyman/Guth, James (eds.): *The Oxford Handbook of Religion and American Politics*. Oxford University Press: New York 2009.

Thomas, Scott: *The Global Resurgence of Religion and the Transformation of International Relations: The Struggle for the Soul of the Twenty-First Century*. Palgrave Macmillan: New York and Basingstoke 2005.

Wald, Kenneth D./Silverman, Adam L./Fridy Kevin: "Making Sense of Religion in Political Life." *Annual Review or Political Science* 8, 2005, pp. 121–141.

Wuthnow, Robert: *The Restructuring of American Religion*. Princeton University Press: Princeton 1988.

Evolving Relations Between Religion and American Politics

Károly Pintér

American Civil Religion After Trump: Twilight or Rebirth?

Abstract: In this chapter, I propose to examine the prospects of American civil religion in the 2020s after its foundational notions have been subverted by Donald Trump as well as his allies and enablers. Can we still meaningfully talk about an American Creed that is accepted and adhered to on both sides of the political aisle and across a broad ideological spectrum? Or is the storming of the Capitol by a bunch of self-styled "patriots" the harbinger of a new era in American history in which even the idea of what constitutes patriotism, who stand for "the people," and what the common principles and norms of the republic are will degenerate into tribal concepts? Are we on the brink of a major paradigm shift in the history of American civil religion?

Keywords: American civil religion, Trump Donald, white evangelicals, white nationalism, presidential rhetoric

Introduction

The following chapter is undertaking an examination of the future prospects of American civil religion (ACR) after Donald Trump's presidency. In the section "Understanding Civil Religion in the 1970s and in the 2010s," I present a brief overview of the conceptual problems surrounding civil religion and examine rivaling interpretations of ACR through the examples of two recent books. In the section "The Role of the President in American Civil Religion," I focus on the relationship of the American presidency and ACR and scrutinize the crucial role of presidential rhetoric. In the section "Donald Trump and His Clash with American Civil Religion," I concentrate on Trump's relationship with the civil religious tradition and the significant negative impact he has left behind.

Understanding Civil Religion in the 1970s and in the 2010s

The claim that a certain "civil religion" exists in the United States of America—and the further claim that it has existed at least since the foundation of the republic—was first proposed by Robert N. Bellah in a now-famous essay in 1967. In Bellah's original interpretation, which was inspired partly by Jean-Jacques Rousseau's original concept but perhaps more significantly by Emile Durkheim's idea of religion as an essential cohesive force of social groups, American civil religion was a "set of beliefs, symbols, and rituals"[1] related to American political institutions that the overwhelming majority of American citizens shared and affirmed. His specific examples included the presidential inauguration, the oath of office taken (so far by each and every president) on the Bible while ad-libbing the phrase "so help me God"; the inevitable references in the inaugural address to God, divine Providence or some other transcendental influence guiding the United States through its difficult times and imparting a sense of higher purpose and destiny to national life; the rituals of such national holidays as Independence Day, Thanksgiving or Memorial Day; and the careful and consistent separation of such religious behavior and utterances from the speaker's personal faith and denomination, in other words, a consistent distinction between personal religion and "civil religion." In Bellah's summary, "civil religion at its best is a genuine apprehension of universal and transcendent religious reality as seen in or, one could almost say, as revealed through the experience of the American people."[2]

Bellah's essay triggered a decade-long debate about American civil religion among scholars of various disciplines: sociologists, historians, religious scholars, and political scientists all entered the fray, but the debate soon got bogged down in rivaling definitions and a variety of disparate interpretations, and ultimately ended without any consensus about what exactly civil religion is or whether it exists at all as a distinct and distinguishable phenomenon.[3] Looking back on the debate itself, however, one can hardly miss the conspicuous fact that the publication of Bellah's essay coincided with a particularly turbulent period of American history, the late 1960s, and Bellah himself made it clear in the closing part of his essay that his motivations were far from merely academic.[4] He was clearly worried about the descent of the United States into the Vietnam maelstrom, but he also warned about an unfolding theological crisis concerning the central symbolism of God in American civil religion:

---

1 Bellah, Robert N.: "Civil Religion in America." *Daedalus* 96 (1), 1967, p. 4.
2 Bellah, Robert N.: *op. cit.*, p. 12.
3 For details, see Pintér, Károly: "American Civil Religion: Revisiting a Concept after 50 Years." *Americana: E-Journal of American Studies in Hungary* 12 (2), Fall 2016.
4 Bellah's later contributions to the civil religion debate revealed his distress about the state of the contemporary American polity even more explicitly: his most extensive exploration of the history of American civil religion, *The Broken Covenant* (1975), was written after the Watergate scandal and exposes the deep pessimism of its author, who in conclusion declares, "Today the American civil religion is an empty and broken shell." Bellah ultimately abandoned any use of the term 'civil religion' after 1980. Bellah, Robert N.: *The Broken Covenant. American Civil Religion in Time of Trial.* 2nd ed. The University of Chicago Press: Chicago and London, 1992, p. 142.

If the whole God symbolism requires reformulation, there will be obvious consequences for the civil religion, consequences perhaps of *liberal alienation and of fundamentalist ossification* that have not so far been prominent in this realm. The civil religion has been a point of articulation between the profoundest commitments of the Western religious and philosophical tradition and the common beliefs of ordinary Americans. It is not too soon to consider how the deepening theological crisis may affect the future of this articulation.[5]

Bellah's remark quoted above has proven particularly prophetic: the polarization of American political parties along the conservative religious—secular liberal axis has been widely discussed in American political science as among the most significant changes in American politics since the 1970s. The prominent entry of the "religious right" (based predominantly on evangelical Protestant groups) into party politics from the late 1970s and early 1980s cemented the ties between religious conservatives and the Republican Party to such an extent that by the early 2000s, a whole cottage industry had developed for the study of the role and use of religion in conservative American politics.[6] On the other hand, American liberals and progressives in the past half-century have become much more secular in their overall outlook, occasionally even outright hostile to organized religion and its influence in public life. The Democratic Party's "God problem" or "religion gap" became a particularly popular topic after the 2004 presidential election, which was widely perceived to have been decided by certain "moral issues" (especially gay marriage) and the mobilization of conservative religious voters.[7] As a parallel and related development, America has been engulfed by a series of increasingly bitter "culture wars" between the two ideological camps since the 1980s, in which the advocates of religious values typically congregated on the conservative side, further embroiling religion in partisan political conflicts.[8]

---

5 Bellah, Robert N.: "Civil Religion in America," pp. 15–16, italics added.
6 See, e.g., Heineman, Kenneth J.: *God Is a Conservative. Religion, Politics, and Morality in Contemporary America.* New York University Press: New York and London 1998; Layman, Geoffrey C.: *The Great Divide. Religious and Cultural Conflict in American Party Politics.* Columbia University Press: New York 2001; Domke, David/Coe, Kevin: *The God Strategy. How Religion Became a Political Weapon in America.* Oxford University Press: Oxford and New York et al. 2008; Williams, Daniel K.: *God's Own Party. The Making of the Christian Right.* Oxford University Press: Oxford and New York 2010.
7 Campbell, David E. (ed.): *A Matter of Faith. Religion in the 2004 Presidential Election.* Brookings Institution Press: Washington, DC 2007; Green, John C. et al (eds.): *The Values Campaign? The Christian Right and the 2004 Elections.* Georgetown University Press: Washington, DC 2006; Green, John C.: *The Faith Factor: How Religion Influences American Elections.* Praeger: Westport, CT 2007.
8 The original definition of "culture wars" comes from Hunter, James Davison: *Culture Wars. The Struggle to Define America.* Basic Books: New York 1991. Since then, lots of

What chance is left for a nationwide patriotic civil religion among all these cultural and political circumstances? The instinctive answer of several scholars has been in the negative,[9] yet the polarization of American politics and culture has recently generated a renewed interest in civil religion, no doubt exactly because of its integrative potential. When I first "discovered" the idea of ACR in the early 2000s, there was hardly any contemporary secondary literature on the subject: most scholars seemed to regard it as a thing of the past, an outdated concept from an era when the overwhelming majority of Americans were theists, and certain American principles and values still stood above party politics and ideology. Yet in the 2010s, a new wave of scholarly publications began to reconsider civil religion, with the obvious intention of salvaging it from the past and proposing it as a foundation for bridging the deep chasms dividing the nation.

Examples of such reassessments of civil religion include Peter Gardella's *American Civil Religion: What Americans Hold Sacred* (2014), which is not simply one more theoretical examination of ACR but rather a kind of consensus-building effort by example. As the author summed it up in his concluding chapter, his volume is "an outline and guide to American civil religion, including its sacred places and symbolic dimensions as well as its texts and values."[10] In the brief introductory chapter, Gardella simply takes the existence of American civil religion for granted, declaring that it is centered around four values: personal freedom, political democracy, world peace, and cultural tolerance.[11] He incidentally also distinguishes seven historical phases in the development of American civil religion (borrowing partly from earlier authors) and illustrates these phases in the history of the Liberty Bell in Philadelphia,[12] but he does not insist on this historical framework during the rest of his book. He selects and surveys the cultural history of more than thirty items (phrases, objects, buildings, locations, historical events and documents, poems and songs, etc.) that have acquired a "sacred" quality during the course of the history of the United States. The oldest of these is the very name and

---

publications have dealt with various aspects of the culture wars, including McGough, Michael: *A Field Guide to the Culture Wars. The Battle over Values from the Campaign Trail to the Classroom*. Praeger: Westport, CT 2009; and Hartman, Andrew: *A War for the Soul of America: A History of the Culture Wars*. The University of Chicago Press: Chicago and London 2015. The culture war thesis has been questioned by some authors, e.g., Fiorina, Morris P. et al: *Culture War? The Myth of a Polarized America*. 3rd ed. Longman: Boston et al. 2011.

9   See, e.g., Gedicks, Frederick: "American Civil Religion. An Idea Whose Time is Past." *George Washington International Law Review* 41 (4), 2010, pp. 891–908.
10 Gardella, Peter: *American Civil Religion: What Americans Hold Sacred*. Oxford University Press: New York and Oxford, 2014, p. 367.
11 Gardella, Peter: *op. cit.*, p. 3.
12 Gardella, Peter: *op. cit.*, pp. 4–5.

adjective "America(n)" as well as the two oldest English settlements, Jamestown and the Mayflower Puritans, while the most recent is Ground Zero in New York City. In his closing chapter, he expresses his hope that "a survey of this pattern may give hope ... [and] may also provide a sense of direction." However, in his survey of the events of the early 2000s, he also admits that "there are times when it seems that no political or cultural leader can be heard by all Americans."[13] Throughout his book, he insists on the obvious reality of American civil religion: "[B]oth for good and for ill, American civil religion is now a concrete reality and a vital force, one of the most influential religions in the world."[14]

Gardella's approach to ACR exemplifies one characteristic understanding of the concept which departs from Bellah's original definition and uncouples the cult of the American nation from any traditional belief in a deity or a higher power. During the civil religion debate in the 1970s, this interpretation was labeled by Richey and Jones as religious nationalism or, alternatively, the religion of patriotism.[15] The obvious advantage of this approach is that it opens up ACR to all patriotic Americans without regard to their religious convictions; in other words, it makes no further demands on potential participants than subscribing to the traditional and time-honored symbolism of American patriotism, from the Declaration of Independence and the Constitution to the National Mall and the national pantheon of American heroes. Its obvious drawback, on the other hand, is that its conspicuous lack of transcendental reference and support exposes it to the charge of idolatry from the perspective of the theologically orthodox observers: for instance, this was the criticism leveled against ACR by Will Herberg, who, while acknowledging ACR as a "genuine religion" and applying to it his earlier term—the religion of the American Way of Life—warned that it should not assume "any claim to ultimacy and absoluteness on the part of any thing or any idea or any system short of God, [...] it is still human, man's own construction, and not God himself."[16]

A very different kind of project was undertaken by Philip Gorski in his 2017 volume *American Covenant: History of Civil Religion from the Puritans to the Present*. Although presented as a historical overview, it is actually a rather impassioned plea for the reinforcement of a "vital center" in American public life, and he sees American civil religion, alternatively defined as "prophetic republicanism," as the best source of such a moderate political middle ground that would provide a

---

13 Gardella, Peter: *op. cit.*, pp. 359, 362.
14 Gardella, Peter: *op. cit.*, p. 367.
15 Jones, Donald G./Richey, Russell E.: "The Civil Religion Debate." In: Jones, Donald G./Richey, Russell E. (eds.): *American Civil Religion*. Harper & Row: New York 1974, pp. 16–17.
16 Herberg, Will: "America's Civil Religion: What It Is and Whence It Comes." In: Jones, Donald G./Richey, Russell E. (eds.): *American Civil Religion*. Harper & Row: New York 1974, pp. 86–87.

common basis for rational debate and intelligent compromise on the major political issues of the day.[17] In Gorski's scheme, civil religion has two rival ideologies, or rather ways of thinking about the nation: religious nationalism and radical secularism, which have diametrically opposed views on the role of religion in public life. Religious nationalists insist that the United States is "God's favored nation" and believe in a radical form of American exceptionalism which Gorski defines simply as "national self-worship."[18] They also tend to believe that a conservative interpretation of the Bible and the Judeo-Christian tradition should serve as the primary moral compass for American politics. Radical secularists, on the other hand, are militant liberal individualists who consider religion a threat to public life and strive for a comprehensive and consistent separation between the two by insisting on religious "neutrality," which in practice means the total exclusion of religiously informed views from the "public square." Gorski considers both views a threat to crucial American republican values like individual freedom and civic equality, and he wishes to demonstrate the vitality and relevance of the civil religious tradition, predominantly in Bellah's vein. He emphasizes that ACR has a canon (a set of crucial texts, a kind of sacred scripture, including the Declaration of Independence, the Constitution, and certain writings of the Founders), a pantheon (the founders, heroes, saints, and martyrs of American public life, including such twentieth-century figures as Martin Luther King or John F. Kennedy), a narrative ("an interpretation of the past that generates a vision of the future"[19]), and an archive (or a potential pool of further historical figures, texts and stories that can be canonized into the tradition).

Gorski's understanding of ACR, unlike Gardella's, presupposes a positive disposition or at least an openness to traditional religious language and symbolism applied to the nation, which has been handed down by generations of Americans. Gorski's emphasis on two particularly crucial sources for these traditions—New England Puritanism and the intellectual heritage of the Founders' generation—is essentially in line with the assessments of several other historians, beginning with Bellah himself.[20] But Gorski contends that secularists may interpret the "religiousness" of civil religion "in a historical or literary sense," as a biblical tradition that

---

17 Gorski, Philip: *American Covenant: History of Civil Religion from the Puritans to the Present*. Princeton University Press: Princeton 2017, pp. 1–3.
18 Gorski, Philip: *op. cit.*, p. 3.
19 Gorski, Philip: *op. cit.*, p. 31.
20 See, e.g., Bellah, Robert N.: *The Broken Covenant, op. cit.*; Albanese, Catherine L.: *Sons of the Fathers. The Civil Religion of the American Revolution*. Temple University Press: Philadelphia 1976; McKenna, George: *The Puritan Origins of American Patriotism*. Yale University Press: New Haven, CT and London, 2007; Meacham, Jon: *American Gospel. God, the Founding Fathers, and the Making of a Nation*. Random House: New York 2007.

emphasizes individual righteousness and social justice, while religionists can consider the "ethical and even theological sense" of civil religion. His way of marking off the civil religious approach from its two rivals is summed up in their differing attitudes to the "proper relationship between the religious and the political realms [...] Religious nationalists advocate total fusion; radical secularists advocate total separation; civil religionists accept partial overlap."[21]

Both Gardella's and Gorski's attempts to present an integrative version of ACR reveal some of the inherent contradictions of the concept. Gardella essentially considers ACR a cult of the American nation, accessible to anybody without regard to individual religious views, but deliberately neglects the inescapable connotations of the very words "religion" and "sacred," which point to the predominantly Judeo-Christian roots of the cult, its language, and symbolism. Gardella's idea of ACR is a collection of handy symbols of American history and traditional values that have provided a sense of unity to the nation, but without the transcendent background, it easily degenerates into a shallow worship of "Americanness." Gorski's historical approach foregrounds the religious, or in his preferred term, "prophetic," tradition behind ACR. However, he considers it primarily as a national political philosophy most suitable to cherish and preserve the values of the American republic by offering the most inclusive and tolerant view of the American nation. His struggles to demarcate ACR from both religious nationalism and radical secularism do reveal the limits of the consensus-building potential of the idea: while ACR might be too little or too lukewarm for religious conservatives, it can easily become too much and too "transcendental" for nonreligious fellow citizens who view the Christianity-inspired terminology of ACR with distrust or even suspicion.

While representing two parallel but different strains of the ACR tradition, Gardella and Gorski obviously share the conviction that ACR is an integrative tradition capable of bridging cultural and political chasms or at least offers a shared set of national values for a common starting point. Incidentally, both authors devote considerable attention to their contemporary president of the United States, Barack Obama, who—as the first Black president in the history of the United States with a Muslim African father and a white mother—embodied the triumph of the most progressive values of ACR, and who also consciously articulated this tradition in his most influential speeches.[22]

The Role of the President in American Civil Religion

The focus of these ACR authors on Obama is obviously justifiable on the grounds that American presidents from Washington onward have played an outsized role in

---

21 Gorski, Philip: *op. cit.*, pp. 15, 17.
22 See Gardella, Peter: *op. cit.*, pp. 360–362; and Gorski, Philip: *op. cit.*, pp. 191–201. Obama's civil religious views will be discussed in more detail below.

civil religion as "high priests" of the national cult. Bellah in his first essay launched his entire discussion of civil religion based on a rhetorical analysis of Kennedy's inaugural speech, and in the following, he cited Franklin, Washington, Jefferson, Lincoln, Reinhold Niebuhr, Lyndon Johnson, and William Fulbright: five of his eight references were former or current presidents. One of the most insightful early commentators on Bellah's theory, religious scholar Martin E. Marty, distinguished between a "priestly" and a "prophetic" mode in the civil religious tradition and set up two further attitudes under each mode (without giving them proper names, unfortunately[23]): one that sees the nation "under God," in other words, considers social and political life to be directed or guided by some kind of deity, while the other focuses on the nation itself as a "self-transcendent entity" and only habitually employs references to God (the practice of such routine and ritualistic mentions of God was subsequently named "ceremonial deism" by Supreme Court Justice William J. Brennan[24]). The former attitude corresponds more closely to Bellah's (or Gorski's) understanding of civil religion, since he emphasized the necessity of belief in a transcendental higher power as an essential and indispensable part of ACR, whereas the latter is a variety of religious nationalism, in which the idea of the nation itself becomes the heart and focus of religious worship (similarly to Gardella's understanding). Marty singled out presidents—with the notable exception of Abraham Lincoln—as the normative representatives of the "priestly" mode, whose main function is to "be celebrative, affirmative, culture-building."[25] Michael Novak carried the idea a step further by declaring the presidency "the nation's most central religious symbol" and the president "the one pontiff bridging all" of the political religions of the land, uniting the symbolic roles of an elected king, "a high priest and a prophet."[26] Charles Henderson argued that it is precisely the presidency that provides an institutional base for an otherwise rather loose and incoherent set of cultural phenomena brought under the heading of "civil religion": "[T]he presidency is the stage on which the nation's leaders play their parts, acting out their priestly and prophetic functions ... It is not the nation which is the focal point of civil religion, but the presidency."[27]

---

23 "I shall eschew neologisms—let me disappoint those who are seeking novel designations." Marty, Martin E.: "Two Kinds of Two Kinds of Civil Religion." In: Jones, Donald G./Richey, Russell E. (eds.): *American Civil Religion*. Harper & Row: New York 1974, p. 144.
24 *Lynch v. Donnelly*, 465 U.S. 668 (1984), p. 716. https://supreme.justia.com/cases/federal/us/465/668/#T2/24.
25 Marty, Martin E.: *op. cit.*, pp. 144–147, 151–152.
26 Novak, Michael: *Choosing Presidents: Symbols of Political Leadership*. 2nd ed. Transaction Publishers: New Brunswick and London 1992, pp. xxviii–xxix, 3.
27 Henderson, Charles P.: "Civil Religion and the American Presidency." *Religious Education*, 70 (5), (1975), p. 484.

Following up on these insights, Richard V. Pierard and Robert D. Linder devoted a whole book to the relationship of American civil religion and the presidency in 1988, which is still the most extensive treatment of the topic. Some of their observations about the interaction between civil religion and the presidency have lost none of their validity since:

> The truth is that most Americans regard the office with a measure of religious awe and that certain presidents down through history have used the position with great success in playing the role of prophet and/or priest in America's public religion. [...] As the high priest of the civil faith, he leads the people in affirming and celebrating the nation, and at the same time he glorifies the national culture and strokes his political flock. [...] Most presidents have been a mixture of prophet, priest, preacher, and pastor, and any president can be any or all of these, if he chooses.[28]

Pierard and Linder selected nine presidents for closer scrutiny: besides the self-evident choices of Washington and Lincoln, they devoted a chapter each to McKinley, Wilson, Franklin D. Roosevelt, Eisenhower, Nixon, Carter, and Reagan. Employing Marty's model to various presidents, they found that post-war presidents, especially Nixon and Reagan, shifted from the pastoral role, and increasingly to the priestly mode of "the second kind," which means that they tended to equate God's work with the self-transcendent American nation, the "promise of America," as Marty summed it up.[29] Their discussion ended with Reagan, whose crucial role in the civil religious tradition will be discussed in more detail below.

Presidents' attitude to ACR is mostly revealed by their political oratory. Political scientist Roderick P. Hart already argued in 1977 that ACR is essentially nothing more than a certain kind of public rhetoric; as he put it, "Bellah discovered not 'religion,' but interesting rhetorical assertions," and built a flawed construct on it. Hart contends that "there are other methods for interpreting the religious refrains found in presidential discourse, methods which appear to be aligned closely with the observed realities themselves."[30]

Hart prefers to apply the term "civic piety" to the phenomena he discusses, relying on John F. Wilson's argument, who claimed that Bellah's ACR does not pass muster if one applies the strict criteria characterizing sophisticated and differentiated religions. Absent are such essential features as regular and frequent ceremonies, recognized leaders with effective authority, clear grounds for membership and ways of participation, and prescribed rules of behavior for believers.

---

28 Pierard, Richard V./Linder, Robert D.: *Civil Religion and the Presidency*. Academie Books: Grand Rapids, MI 1988, pp. 20, 24–25, 26.
29 Pierard, Richard V./Linder, Robert D.: *op. cit.*, pp. 291–293; Marty, Martin E.: *op. cit.*, pp. 151–152.
30 Hart, Roderick P./Pauley, John L.: *The Political Pulpit Revisited*. Purdue University Press: West Lafayette, IN 2005, pp. 39, 41.

It was Wilson's proposal that the phenomena described by Bellah should rather be denoted by the phrase "civic piety," describing certain forms of behavior rather than an institutionalized religion.[31] Wilson's proposed term, although it never gained wide currency in scholarly circles, certainly eliminates the most problematic aspect of Bellah's conceptualization, which suggests a full-blown alternative cult to established churches, with a faint idolatrous whiff never far away.

In Hart's interpretation, civil religion or civic piety is essentially an unwritten rhetorical contract between the government and organized religion that has governed the public religious attitude of politicians with regard to utterances concerning God and faith. Instead of a true separation of church and state, Hart describes the situation largely as a convenient and expedient cooperation, in which the churches lend their spiritual influence to mobilize people for national and patriotic goals, while government officials pay lip service to God and religious ideals in general. While government is legally and financially separated from organized religion, there are a number of instances in which the government rhetorically approves religious faith and various activities related to it.[32]

Hart considers the civil religious rhetoric essentially conservative and repetitive in character, while its function is largely ceremonial, typically embellishing the opening and closing sections of speeches. Examining the inaugural addresses of presidents, he has found that certain features of God are notably absent from official civic piety: there are no references to God's vengeance or punishment; neither do presidents try to divine His purposes or foretell the future. "A receptive God, an inactive God, a 'font of wisdom' God may well be on its way to becoming America's most popular God. [...] At least as presented rhetorically, America's God is an expedient God, one who watches over His people as they set about their various tasks."[33]

Beyond representations of the civic deity, Hart describes civil religious rhetoric as predominantly non-existential, that is, not concerned with everyday practical matters. It deals mostly with the past and the future and prefers to employ symbolic language. He considers it an essential part of the unwritten contract that churches typically avoid activist, mobilizing rhetoric, celebrating America's religious history and heritage instead. He characterizes the bulk of civil religious rhetoric as quiescent, nostalgic, and ritualistic.[34]

Scholars of political rhetoric disagree whether Hart's "unwritten contract" is still valid today: Martin Medhurst, for instance, argues that the 1980s and their aftermath represented a radical change. In the 1970s, "organized religion" was

---

31 Wilson, John F.: "The Status of 'Civil Religion' in America." In: Smith, Elwyn A. (ed.): *The Religion of the Republic*. Fortress Press: Philadelphia 1971, pp. 10–13.
32 Hart, Roderick P./Pauley, John L.: *op. cit.*, pp. 50–53.
33 Hart, Roderick P./Pauley, John L.: *op. cit.*, p. 67.
34 Hart, Roderick P./Pauley, John L.: *op. cit.*, pp. 68–85.

represented mostly by liberal mainline Protestant churches, the Catholic hierarchy, and Reform Judaism. Since then, however, evangelical and fundamentalist Protestants have entered the "public square" in massive numbers, and they have superseded mainline denominations not only in the number of their adherents but in their public cultural and political influence as well, while a significant proportion of blue-collar Catholics have become much more conservative in their political views, primarily due to their opposition to abortion, a central debate of the culture wars.[35] Presidents responded to these developments by beginning to talk more openly about their personal faith, brandishing their religious bona fides to a crucial part of the political audience that was receptive to such messaging.[36]

The election of Jimmy Carter in 1976 is considered a fundamental turning point in the earlier convention that drew a firm line of separation between personal faith and public religious rhetoric. Carter, who declared emphatically at the outset of his presidential campaign that "I am a farmer, an engineer, a businessman, a planner, a scientist, a governor and a Christian,"[37] carefully cultivated not only his image as a Washington outsider but also his upright and trustworthy character, including his born-again evangelical Christian faith, during his bid for the White House.[38] His success heralded a new era regarding the public religious attitude of future presidents, as well as a new expectation by at least some of the public that candidates should come clean about their religious convictions and act upon their principles as presidents. As Brian T. Kaylor observes:

> Beginning especially with Carter's campaign in 1976 and continuing through the 2008 contest, presidential candidates have employed religious-political rhetoric in their campaign appeals by talking openly about their personal faith and how their religious beliefs inspire and inform their public policy decisions.[39]

The 1980 election is often considered a watershed in American political history since Carter's example was successfully imitated by Ronald Reagan, who had been remarkably restrained in his "God talk" during his 1976 bid for the Republican nomination but focused energetically on religious conservatives in the 1980 campaign.[40] This decision may have seemed unwise at first sight since Reagan was

---

35 Medhurst, Martin J.: "Forging a Civil-Religious Construct for the Twenty-First Century. Should Hart's 'Contract' Be Renewed?" In: Hart, Roderick P./Pauley, John L.: *The Political Pulpit Revisited.* Purdue University Press: West Lafayette, IN 2005, pp. 154–155.
36 Medhurst, Martin J.: *op. cit.*, pp. 156–157.
37 Quoted in Hogue, Andrew P.: *Stumping God. Reagan, Carter, and the Invention of a Political Faith.* Baylor University Press: Waco, TX 2012, p. 101.
38 Hogue, Andrew P.: *op. cit.*, pp. 120–131.
39 Kaylor, Brian T.: *Presidential Campaign Rhetoric in an Age of Confessional Politics.* Lexington Books: Lanham, MD 2012, p. 37.
40 Hogue, Andrew P.: *op. cit.*, pp. 107–110, 169–205.

running against Carter, the self-described "born-again" Southern Baptist, while Reagan, who had been raised by a pious mother as a member of the Disciples of Christ in Illinois, also had a solid faith in God but rarely attended church in his adult life before his political career, and received criticism for his infrequent church attendance even as president.[41] Nonetheless, the "self-taught Christian," as his former staffer Pat Buchanan characterized Reagan,[42] who was the only other divorcee before Trump in the White House,[43] managed to gain the approval and enthusiastic support of the overwhelming majority of evangelical leaders, especially after his famous declaration at a Religious Roundtable meeting in Dallas, Texas, on August 22, 1980: "I know this group can't endorse me, but I want you to know that I endorse you and what you are doing."[44] Reagan's resounding victory brought about a lasting realignment of religious conservatives in the South, who had been a loyal constituency of the Democratic Party for over a century. Reagan ultimately received an estimated 65% of the white evangelical vote, which increased to 74% in 1984 and such a proportion was not achieved again by any candidate until George W. Bush in 2000 and 2004.[45] The decisive political entry of the Religious Right on the side of the Republicans permanently altered the character of both parties.[46]

Political scientists have long debated whether the mostly happy "marriage" between Reagan and white evangelicals was a practical alliance based on ideological closeness and perceived common interests, or it was born out of a genuine appreciation felt by evangelical leaders for Reagan's rather simple but straightforward and apparently heartfelt approvals of Christian faith and morality, the Bible as a unique source of wisdom and guidance, and his emphasis on the necessity of

---

41 Hutcheson, Richard G.: *God in the White House. How Religion Has Changed the Modern Presidency*. Macmillan: New York and London 1988, pp. 161–172; and Smith, Gary Scott: *Faith and the Presidency. From George Washington to George W. Bush*. Oxford University Press: Oxford and New York 2006, pp. 325–326, 331–332.
42 Hutcheson, Richard G.: *op. cit.*, p. 168.
43 Divorce was considered a far more reprehensible moral issue in the eyes of religious conservatives in the late 1970s than in the 2010s. For the softening up of evangelical views on divorce, see Balmer, Randall Herbert: *God in the White House. A History. How Faith Shaped the Presidency from John F. Kennedy to George W. Bush*. HarperCollins e-books: New York 2008, pp. 112–113.
44 Balmer, Randall Herbert: *op. cit.*, pp. 118–119.
45 Kellstedt, Lyman et al.: "Faith Transformed. Religion and American Politics from FDR to George W. Bush." In: Noll, Mark A./Harlow, Luke E. (eds.): *Religion and American Politics. From the Colonial Period to the Present*. 2nd ed. Oxford University Press: Oxford and New York 2007, pp. 271–273.
46 For details, see Williams, Daniel K.: *God's Own Party. The Making of the Christian Right*. Oxford University Press: Oxford and New York, 2010, pp. 187–211.

God's grace for earthly undertakings, including his own presidency. Reagan repeatedly emphasized the need for a spiritual awakening or renewal for America to strengthen the moral foundations of the nation, especially in its fight against communism.[47] While consistently avoiding a public revelation about his own personal faith, Reagan spoke from the viewpoint of a nondenominational Protestant Christian, essentially reaffirming the classic civil religious tradition based on exactly this generalized Protestant piety.[48]

Since Reagan's presidency, the most controversial practitioner of public religious rhetoric was, beyond doubt, George W. Bush, who campaigned from the start as a proud born-again Christian and declared "Christ" to be his favorite political philosopher in one of the Republican primary debates.[49] After the terror attacks on September 11, 2001, he repeatedly framed the War on Terror as a worldwide battle between "freedom and fear," and at least on one occasion, in a televised speech on September 12, 2001, as "a monumental struggle of good versus evil, but good will prevail."[50] He followed that with constructing or rather inventing an "axis of evil" of enemy nations in his 2002 State of the Union address[51] and repeatedly expressed

---

47 Pierard, Richard V./Linder, Robert D.: *op. cit.*, pp. 276–279.
48 See Catherine Albanese's argument about public Protestantism as "the one religion of the country." Albanese, Catherine L.: *America. Religions and Religion.* 3rd ed. Wadsworth Publishing: Belmont, CA 1999, pp. 396–431.
49 Several scholars single out this episode as a powerful message to evangelical voters, e.g., Balmer, Randall Herbert: *op. cit.*, p. 145; and Rozell, Mark J.: "Introduction: Religion and the Bush Presidency." In: Rozell, Mark J./Whitney, Gleaves (eds.): *Religion and the Bush Presidency.* Palgrave Macmillan: New York and Basingstoke 2007, p. 1.
50 Bush, George W.: "Address to the Joint Session of the 107th Congress on September 20, 2001." In: Bush, George W.: *Selected Speeches of President George W. Bush 2001–2008*, p. 72, retrieved 11.06.2021, from https://georgewbush-whitehouse.archives.gov/infocus/bushrecord/; Bush, George W.: "Televised Speech on September 12, 2001," retrieved 11.06.2021, from https://www.pbs.org/newshour/world/terrorism-july-dec01-bush_speech_9-12.
51 Bush, George W.: "State of the Union Address to the 107th Congress on January 29, 2002." In: Bush, George W.: *Selected Speeches of President George W. Bush 2001–2008*, p. 106, retrieved 11.06.2021, from https://georgewbush-whitehouse.archives.gov/infocus/bushrecord/. The apparently random selection of three very different autocratic regimes dumbfounded observers at the time, since one of them—North Korea—was a Communist dictatorship unrelated to Islamic terrorism, while the two others—Iraq and Iran—had no proven connection to Osama bin Laden or Al-Qaeda, while they were in a notoriously hostile relationship with each other. The only similarities that connected these countries were the oppressive character of their political regimes and their sharp antagonism to the United States.

his understanding that the United States had a mission to "rid the world of evil."[52] Peter Singer, who devoted a whole book to the examination of Bush's ethical views and utterances, observed in 2004 that "[n]o other president in living memory has spoken so much about good and evil, right and wrong." In his assessment, Bush used the word "evil" almost 1,100 times in over 300 separate speeches in a period of about eighteen months (between his inauguration and June 2003), and in the overwhelming majority of cases (over 900 times) he used the word as a noun, "as a *thing*, or a force, something that has a real existence ... His readiness to talk about evil in this manner raises the question of what meaning evil can have in a secular modern world."[53]

Such apocalyptic language was arguably Bush's greatest deviation from the traditional and standardized rhetoric of American civil religion, or in Gorski's assessment, his "stumble down the slippery slope from civil religion to religious nationalism."[54] The rhetorical arsenal of civil religion predominantly focuses on positive and unifying principles and values; even when it veers toward what critics describe as American exceptionalism, suggesting or explicitly claiming that the United States enjoys the unique favor of God and therefore fulfills a divine purpose on Earth,[55] it emphasizes the uniqueness of American history, institutions, and values rather than singling out and stigmatizing other nations or regimes as "evil." Yet Bush did not invent anything new: he essentially revived a widely practiced

---

52 Bush, George W.: "National Day of Prayer and Remembrance Service on September 14, 2001." In: Bush, George W.: *Selected Speeches of President George W. Bush 2001–2008*, p. 59, retrieved 11.06.2021, from https://georgewbush-whitehouse.archives.gov/infocus/bushrecord/.

53 Singer, Peter. *The President of Good and Evil: Taking George W. Bush Seriously*. Granta Books: London 2004, pp. 1–2.

54 Gorski, Philip: *op. cit.*, p. 186.

55 This is not the only possible interpretation of the expression: one scholarly tradition argues that the United States differs significantly from other Western nations in several key aspects of its political institutions, cultural values, and social attitudes, and they summarize these untypical or singular aspects of the United States under the heading of "American exceptionalism." See, e.g., Lipset, Seymour Martin: *American Exceptionalism: A Double-Edged Sword*. Norton: New York and London 1996. The most widespread use of the term, however, is less descriptive and more evaluative in its implication: it suggests that the uniqueness of the United States stems from its pioneering role in the history of humanity and the example it sets to other nations with its unwavering devotion to freedom and democracy. A typical summary of this view of American exceptionalism can be found in Berns, Walter. *Making Patriots*. The University of Chicago Press: Chicago 2001, pp. ix–x.; for its thorough-going criticism, see Hodgson, Godfrey. *The Myth of American Exceptionalism*. Yale University Press 2009, pp. 1–29.

nineteenth-century American rhetorical tradition, commonly known under the name of "manifest destiny," which relied on the same claim of divine support and preference to justify current policies that were often aggressive or imperialist in character.

In my view, Bush's greatest failure as a civil religious orator was his inability to recognize that his twenty-first-century version of American exceptionalist rhetoric fails to achieve the most important purpose of civil religion: the unification of the American nation behind vital national goals. Despite his careful nods to the formal conventions of civil religion and messages of inclusion, his rhetoric bore all the hallmarks of traditional Protestant Christian vocabulary, imagery, and references. A devout born-again Christian himself, Bush was obviously convinced that such language is the most suitable to communicate his vision and policy objectives to the American audience, but he did not realize that a significant part of the nation no longer shares his religious background or speaks the same language. As a result, the tireless repetition of his conviction that exporting freedom by military means to the Middle East is a divine mission that will bring about some sort of miraculous salvation and the elimination of the threat of terror worldwide rang as an increasingly hollow cant to an ever-larger part of the public audience. In a very significant sense, Bush's reckless overuse of "freedom" led to a rhetorical inflation and debasement of the term which is indeed at the heart of the American civil religious tradition.

Bush's successor, Barack Obama, made a clear-cut attempt to return to the orthodox civil religious tradition. As Philip Gorski explains, Obama was an uncommon candidate to posit himself as an authentic spokesman of civil religion since he had a very special personal background story,

> deeply and even uniquely American, a blend not only of black and white but of native-born and immigrant, city and country, the heartland and the coasts. "I stand here knowing that my story is part of the larger American story," he proclaimed in 2004, "and that, in no other country on earth, is my story even possible."[56]

Gorski further insists that Obama's unusual personal background and career made him stand out of the common racial, ethnic, and class stereotypes, which forced him to develop "a coherent personal identity [that] necessarily involved reflections on America's collective identity."[57] This search for an authentic self included coming to grips with his relationship with religion, and ultimately led to his adult baptism in a historically Black church in Chicago; as he describes it in *The Audacity of Hope*, "it came about as a choice, and not an epiphany; the questions I had did not magically disappear."[58] His decision to join seems to be at least partly

---

56 Gorski, Philip: *op. cit.*, p. 191.
57 Gorski, Philip: *op. cit.*, p. 192.
58 Obama, Barack: *The Audacity of Hope. Thoughts on Reclaiming the American Dream.* Crown Publishers: New York 2006, p. 208.

motivated by his desire to belong to a community, and also his determination to take a side in America's racial divide to which he had long been an outsider, raised by his white mother and maternal grandparents.

However, his relatively new-found personal faith may have shaped his views about the role of religion in American public life. In his book, he cogently argues that contemporary American liberalism generally tries to avoid discussing religious values in the name of church-state separation, which is a poor political choice because it deprives left-leaning politicians of the rhetorical means to communicate their moral ideas to a large segment of the American population: "Scrub language of all religious content and we forfeit the imagery and terminology through which millions of Americans understand both their personal morality and social justice."[59] On the other hand, the religious neutrality of government is a time-honored idea of the Founding Fathers that the growing religious diversity of the United States makes more compelling than ever: "we are no longer just a Christian nation; we are also a Jewish nation, a Muslim nation, a Buddhist nation, a Hindu nation, and a nation of nonbelievers."[60] As a result, while devout people may not be required to abandon their religious convictions when they enter the public arena to discuss political issues, they cannot make absolute claims based on their faith alone. "What our deliberative, pluralistic democracy does demand is that the religiously motivated translate their concerns into universal, rather than religion-specific, values. It requires that their proposals must be subject to argument and amenable to reason."[61]

Armed with these convictions, Obama seemed perfectly positioned to advocate an American civil religion of the kind Bellah circumscribed, which does not shy away from mentioning God in relation to the United States or employing the language of faith in public, but it would not demand a special place or priority for religious values in political decision-making. However, few people would claim that he was successful in his attempts to rhetorically unify the nation. One reason, according to Gorski, was his willingness to admit America's historic failures as well as recognize its achievements, which exposed him to charges from conservatives that he did not believe in American exceptionalism. Instead, he was practicing the "prophetic" version of the civil religious tradition, voicing criticism next to admiration about the nation's history. Gorski argues that Obama, an avid reader of Reinhold Niebuhr, is a deep believer in original sin both in the individual and in the collective sense, which makes him wary of nationalistic excess and biased arguments about America's greatness.[62]

---

59 Obama, Barack: *op. cit.*, p. 214.
60 Obama, Barack: *op. cit.*, p. 218.
61 Obama, Barack: *op. cit.*, p. 219.
62 Gorski, Philip: *op. cit.*, pp. 195–197.

Following in the footsteps of a president of conservative personal faith and religious nationalist affections, and another one with liberal religious views practicing a traditional but occasionally prophetically self-critical civil religious rhetoric, the question arises: how do we assess the role of Donald Trump as the "pontifex maximus" of American civil religion?

Donald Trump and His Clash with American Civil Religion

Most students of the presidency doubtlessly agree that the electoral victory of Donald Trump in 2016 broke many unwritten rules that had been considered "musts" for a prospective presidential candidate: he was the first president with no prior political or military experience, who launched his political career with the presidency as his first elected office; he was the first president who had gained most of his fame (and notoriety) as the host and leading figure of a long-running television reality show; he was the first twice-divorced president whose private life had provided plenty of material for tabloids, including his extramarital affairs and his well-documented attraction to pretty young models. Trump was arguably also the first president who had very limited background in religion, yet he enjoyed the overwhelming support of conservative evangelical Christian voters both at the election and throughout his presidency.[63]

Among the post-1945 presidents, Trump has arguably had the most tenuous connection with organized religion, with the possible exception of Barack Obama, who converted to Christianity as an adult. Trump does not come from a strongly religious family despite having been confirmed at a Presbyterian church in Queens in 1959, at the age of 13. In the 1960s, his millionaire father, Fred Trump, chose to attend the Marble Collegiate Church (originally part of the Reformed Church of America, but later a nondenominational church) on Fifth Avenue, due to the preaching of Norman Vincent Peale, the local pastor, who was also the author of enormously successful self-help books in the 1950s. Donald Trump was, by his own admission, impressed by Peale's sermons, married both his first and second wife at Marble Collegiate Church, and apparently attended Sunday services there

---

63 See Smith, Gregory A.: "Among White Evangelicals, Regular Churchgoers Are the Most Supportive of Trump." *Pew Research Center*, April 26, 2017, retrieved 11.04.2021, from https://www.pewresearch.org/fact-tank/2017/04/26/among-white-evangelicals-regular-churchgoers-are-the-most-supportive-of-trump/; and Nortey, Justin: "Most White Americans Who Regularly Attend Worship Services Voted for Trump in 2020." *Pew Research Center*, August 30, 2021, retrieved 11.04.2021, from https://www.pewresearch.org/fact-tank/2021/08/30/most-white-americans-who-regularly-attend-worship-services-voted-for-trump-in-2020/.

for decades, but the church announced that he was no longer an active member during his presidential campaign in 2016.[64]

Beyond his former membership in a church congregation famous for attracting wealthy New Yorkers, Trump's attachment to organized religion seems to be minimal. During his presidential campaign, Trump described himself as a Presbyterian and brandished his confirmation picture on his Facebook page, but his repeated gaffes when attempting to speak the language of faith exposed him to ridicule. For instance, he referred to a New Testament quote as "Two Corinthians 3:17, that's the whole ballgame,"[65] or he described his Holy Communion as "I drink my little wine [...] and have my little cracker."[66] Perhaps more significant as these less-than-pious utterances is his admission in an interview that he had never asked for God's forgiveness.[67] According to a Pew Research survey published in February 2020, the majority of Americans do not believe that Trump is a religious man: 63% of all respondents said he is "not too religious" or "not at all religious," only a majority of white evangelicals and Republican supporters were convinced that Trump is "somewhat religious," but even among them, only 12% considered him "very religious."[68] This is clear evidence that most Americans have not been persuaded by Trump's "God talk" very much.

This fact is not particularly significant in itself, as deep and sincere religious faith is not an official requirement of any resident of the White House; but it is all the more remarkable when juxtaposed with Trump's sky-high approval ratings among white evangelical Protestants, who have traditionally had rigorous moral and confessional expectations of their favored politicians. Trump achieved greater support among white evangelical voters than either of their previous conservative favorites, Ronald Reagan and George W. Bush, when he netted an estimated 81% of

---

64 Barron, James: "Overlooked Influences on Donald Trump. A Famous Minister and His Church." *The New York Times*, September 5, 2016, retrieved 11.06.2021, from https://www.nytimes.com/2016/09/06/nyregion/donald-trump-marble-collegiate-church-norman-vincent-peale.html.

65 Taylor, Jessica: "Citing 'Two Corinthians,' Trump struggles to make the sale to Evangelicals." *NPR*, January 18, 2016, retrieved 11.06.2021, from https://www.npr.org/2016/01/18/463528847/citing-two-corinthians-trump-struggles-to-make-the-sale-to-evangelicals?t=1636217257439.

66 Scott, Eugene: "Trump believes in God, but hasn't sought forgiveness." *CNN*, July 19, 2015, retrieved 11.06.2021, from https://edition.cnn.com/2015/07/18/politics/trump-has-never-sought-forgiveness/index.html.

67 *Ibid.*

68 Fahmy, Dalia: "Most Americans Don't See Trump as Religious; Fewer Than Half Say They Think He's Christian." *Pew Research Center*, March 25, 2020, retrieved 11.06.2021, from https://www.pewresearch.org/fact-tank/2020/03/25/most-americans-dont-see-trump-as-religious/.

the evangelical vote during the 2016 presidential election.[69] Why did they not reject Trump and favor a genuinely religious and conservative presidential nominee?

Many American political and religious scholars are vexed by this glaring contradiction, which has proved not merely a fleeting phenomenon of the 2016 election, since Trump once again reaped an estimated 76% of the white evangelical vote in 2020, suggesting that the overwhelming majority of his conservative religious supporters were satisfied enough with his performance to give him another four-year mandate.[70] Various answers have been proposed to account for the mystery, which may all offer partial explanations for a complex phenomenon.

According to the most conventional views often floated in the mainstream media, many white evangelical voters have let go of their exacting moral standards and become pragmatic voters like the majority of the American public: although they had personal reservations about Trump's moral character, they voted for him because he promised to appoint conservative (and therefore pro-life) justices to the Supreme Court, or because they were concerned about the fragile economic recovery and believed that Trump would indeed bring back American jobs,[71] or simply strongly disliked Hillary Clinton and opted for the less repugnant alternative. While any or all of these considerations may have played a role, they do not seem to adequately justify the astonishing compromise evangelicals made between their moral convictions and their favored presidential candidate.

A far more sophisticated explanation was proposed by Michael Gerson, former speechwriter of George W. Bush and an evangelical Christian himself, who subjected the unwavering and occasionally pusillanimous support of several well-known evangelical leaders for Trump to a devastating critique in his 2018 analysis. Gerson argues that modern evangelicalism has lost the confidence and postmillennialist social activism that characterized it back in the mid-nineteenth century, and instead retired from the social and cultural mainstream during most of the twentieth century, only to return in the 1970s and 1980s as a reaction to seismic cultural shifts (the sexual revolution, the growing social acceptance of divorce,

---

69 As I mentioned before, Reagan collected an estimated 74% of Evangelical Protestant votes during his 1984 reelection, while the younger Bush achieved a 78% share in 2004 (see Kellstedt, Lyman et al.: *op. cit.*, pp. 272–273.). Regarding Trump's performance among Evangelicals, see Renaud, Myriam: "Myths Debunked: Why Did White Evangelical Christians Vote for Trump?" *Sightings*, Divinity School of the University of Chicago, January 19, 2017, retrieved 11.07.2021, from https://divinity.uchicago.edu/sightings/articles/myths-debunked-why-did-white-evangelical-christians-vote-trump.

70 Newport, Frank: "Religious Group Voting and the 2020 Election." *Gallup*, November 13, 2020, retrieved 11.07.2021, from https://news.gallup.com/opinion/polling-matters/324410/religious-group-voting-2020-election.aspx.

71 Renaud, Myriam: *op. cit.*

nontraditional families and sexual minorities, the legalization of early term abortion), which they predominantly rejected and continue to oppose. As a result, evangelicals feel alienated and threatened by mainstream American social and cultural norms, and see themselves as a beleaguered minority who are safeguarding the traditional values of the United States[72]:

> the primary evangelical political narrative is adversarial, an angry tale about the aggression of evangelicalism's cultural rivals. In a remarkably free country, many evangelicals view their rights as fragile, their institutions as threatened, and their dignity as assailed. The single largest religious demographic in the United States—representing about half the Republican political coalition—sees itself as a besieged and disrespected minority. [...] The overall political disposition of evangelical politics has remained decidedly conservative, and also decidedly reactive.[73]

Gerson also castigates the evangelical political agenda as narrowly focused on a few symbolic issues that are either irrelevant (e.g., the restitution of school prayer), impossible to achieve (e.g., a nationwide abortion ban) or contrary to the accomplishments of modern science and reason (primarily the repudiation of the theory of evolution), and this limited agenda has created a prevalent impression in the majority of the American public that "evangelical political engagement is negative, censorious, and oppositional. This funneled focus has also created the damaging impression that Christians are obsessed with sex."[74] Their predominant public rhetoric also tends to be pessimistic and apocalyptic in tone, constantly reproaching America's cultural decline and envisioning an impending catastrophe, essentially in line with modern evangelicals' premillennial persuasions, which expect Christ's Second Coming to put an end to earthly chaos and moral degeneration.

Gerson pinpoints this prevalent cultural and political outlook among white evangelicals as a primary reason why most of them fell for Trump's populist rhetoric:

> [...] evangelicals would prove highly vulnerable to a message of resentful, declinist populism. [...] when the candidate talked of an America in decline and headed toward destruction, which could be returned to greatness only by recovering the certainties of the past, he was strumming resonant chords of evangelical conviction. Trump consistently depicts evangelicals as they depict themselves: a mistreated minority, in need of a defender who plays by worldly rules. [...] Protecting Christianity, Trump essentially argues, is a job for a bully.[75]

---

72 Gerson, Michael: "The Last Temptation." *The Atlantic*, April 2018, retrieved 11.06.2021, from https://www.theatlantic.com/magazine/archive/2018/04/the-last-temptation/554066/.
73 *Ibid.*
74 *Ibid.*
75 *Ibid.*

By publicly approving Trump's divisive rhetoric, morally reprehensible utterances, and proven lies, Gerson argues that evangelicals commit themselves to more than a political compromise: they closely link their faith and moral convictions to deplorable causes like racism, nativism, misogyny, and deception.

Gerson's sweeping excoriation of evangelicals is based on his perception of a tragic mistake they have made by committing themselves to Trump. Another widely shared view, however, sees less of a contradiction and more of an organic development in white evangelicals' infatuation with Trump, which is based not so much on their religious views but rather on their positive reception of Trump's rhetoric on race.

Trump's racial rhetoric is perhaps the most contentious aspect of a distinctly controversial president. Liberal or progressive scholars often describe him simply as a "racist" without much hesitation, pointing at a few select examples from his campaign and presidency, such as his unusually harsh anti-immigration statements directed primarily against Mexicans and Hispanics in general,[76] his ban on immigration from several Muslim majority countries,[77] his (private) description of Third-World nations as "shithole countries,"[78] and his equivocation to condemn the outspoken white-supremacist rally at Charlottesville, Virginia, in August 2017, declaring that "I think there is blame on both sides. [...] you had some very bad people in that group. But you also had people that were very fine people on both sides."[79]

---

76 See his infamous campaign-opening speech on June 16, 2015, in Trump Tower: "When Mexico sends its people, they're not sending their best. They're not sending you. They're not sending you. They're sending people that have lots of problems, and they're bringing those problems with us. They're bringing drugs. They're bringing crime. They're rapists. And some, I assume, are good people." And later: "I would build a great wall, and nobody builds walls better than me, believe me, and I'll build them very inexpensively, I will build a great, great wall on our southern border. And I will have Mexico pay for that wall." Trump, Donald: "Here's Trump's Presidential Announcement Speech." *TIME*, June 16, 2015, retrieved 21.11.2021, from https://time.com/3923128/donald-trump-announcement-speech/.
77 See Cainkar, Louise: "The Muslim Ban and Trump's War on Immigration." *Middle East Report*, 294 (Spring 2020), retrieved 28.11.2021, from https://merip.org/2020/06/the-muslim-ban-and-trumps-war-on-immigration-2/; and Niayesh, Vahid: "What Trump's Travel Ban Really Looks Like, Almost Two Years in." *The Conversation*, October 18, 2019, retrieved 28.11.2021, from https://theconversation.com/what-trumps-travel-ban-really-looks-like-almost-two-years-in-123564.
78 Watkins, Eli/Phillip, Abby: "Trump Decries Immigrants from 'Shithole Countries' Coming to the US." *CNN*, January 12, 2018, retrieved 28.11.2021, from https://edition.cnn.com/2018/01/11/politics/immigrants-shithole-countries-trump/index.html.
79 Trump, Donald: "Full text: Trump's Comments on White Supremacists, 'Alt-Left' in Charlottesville." *Politico*, August 15, 2017, retrieved 28.11.2021, from https://www.

Despite these well-known examples, I think the indiscriminate application of the label "racist" to Trump does not do full justice to his inconsistent and occasionally contradictory but often politically expedient utterances on racial matters. He cannot be described simply as a "white nationalist" or an "alt-right" sympathizer as some hostile commentators have done, despite the vocal support he has received from white nationalist and alt-right circles and the presence of some well-known personalities with alt-right connections in his administration, such as Steve Bannon and Stephen Miller. In my opinion, Matthew Wilson has come closest to the truth when he observes that Trump is no ideologue, not even a theoretical and consistent thinker on social or cultural issues, so his public comments reflect his muddled and confused way of thinking more than the promotion of any specific political ideology. On the other hand, his predominantly narcissistic personality cannot resist praise and flattery, so he typically speaks positively of those who offer verbal support—including people of right-wing extremist views.[80]

Yet the very fact that Trump refused to consistently repudiate explicitly racist or racially dubious political views that had been considered "far-right" or "extreme" by the political mainstream—including the Republican mainstream—since the 1970s was in itself a taboo-breaking gesture by a president, who is expected to represent and voice a kind of national political consensus on fundamental political values. Quite often, Trump appeared to revel in his role of a national political taboo-breaker which was an integral element of his electoral victory in 2016: his harsh language on immigration, foreign trade, and other issues, his mocking nicknames and offensive remarks addressed to his rivals, his wholesale condemnation of the entire American political elite coupled with blatant self-glorification may have alienated many moderate voters but sent a signal to the far right that a new kind of politician appeared on the conservative side of American politics, who is willing to challenge political orthodoxies and may offer a chance for radical views to enter the mainstream.

The term "white nationalism" has a relatively recent history in American political discourse: it originates from the 1990s and received its first academic treatment by Carol M. Swain in 2002. Swain argued that white nationalism represented a new stage in the development of racialist white thinking, primarily a reaction to social and cultural changes in the previous three decades: the success of the civil rights movement in providing equal rights for African Americans, the introduction of affirmative action programs to compensate for historic inequalities in employment and higher education, the widespread acceptance of political correctness

---

politico.com/story/2017/08/15/full-text-trump-comments-white-supremacists-alt-left-transcript-241662.

80 Wilson, Matthew: "Donald Trump and the 'Alt-Right': How Much Connection Is There?" *ISPI*, July 17, 2020, retrieved 28.11.2021, from https://www.ispionline.it/it/pubblicazione/donald-trump-and-alt-right-how-much-connection-there-26990.

in public communication, and the intensifying immigration of nonwhite ethnic groups into the United States. White nationalists observed all these new trends with alarm and fear, as they thought these transformations would ultimately lead to the destruction of traditional American culture and values, which they predominantly equated with white European cultural heritage. They did not believe in the longevity of a multiracial, socially and culturally diverse American nation, and envisioned a racially separatist "white America," with a few authors even drawing up maps to divide the United States into racially homogeneous enclaves.[81]

Swain was one of the first authors to single out some novel features of this new form of racist white thinking: they uniformly denied that they would promote white supremacy, arguing that they simply wanted to protect white civil rights and white culture the same way as Blacks defended and promoted theirs. Instead of aggressive, extremist rhetoric and symbolism employed by the Ku Klux Klan and other organizations in the mid-twentieth century, white nationalists employed rational discourse and persuasion, targeting more educated, middle-class voters, and taking up some mainstream conservative political positions to make themselves more acceptable for people who shy away from radicalism.[82] Swain also pointed out the outstanding importance of the internet in the dissemination of white nationalist ideas, although her book was written before the explosive popularity of social media platforms.[83]

Since the early 2000s, white nationalism has been able to reach a much wider audience with the help of a few popular internet sites, particularly Breitbart News under the leadership of Steven Bannon, who publicly described the site as "the platform for the alt-right" in 2016.[84] By hiring Bannon as his campaign chief and adviser, Trump—intentionally or not—gave a clear signal to the predominantly white, male, anti-Muslim, anti-immigration, and anti-political-correctness followers of the site and its promoted ideologies that he volunteered to be their champion. Trump's populist rhetoric blended in well with several priorities of alt-right: his isolationist foreign policy stances (ending foreign wars, criticizing American commitment to NATO), his economic nationalism, and his anti-immigration tirades, but above all his sweeping and successful attacks on the political establishment, were all music to the ears of alt-right enthusiasts, who had harbored long-standing ambitions to displace establishment conservatives from their dominant position

---

81 Swain, Carol M.: *The New White Nationalism in America: Its Challenge to Integration.* Cambridge University Press: Cambridge and New York 2002, pp. 15–22.
82 Swain, Carol M.: *op. cit.*, pp. 25–30.
83 Swain, Carol M.: *op. cit.*, pp. 30–33.
84 Posner, Sarah: "How Donald Trump's New Campaign Chief Created an Online Haven for White Nationalists." *Mother Jones*, August 22, 2016, retrieved 28.11.2021, from https://www.motherjones.com/politics/2016/08/stephen-bannon-donald-trump-alt-right-breitbart-news/.

on the right side of American politics. The meteoric rise of Trump within the GOP seemed to offer exactly this chance for the alt-right: to raise their profile above a network of obscure extremist websites and to a position from which they would be able to shape national political agendas and priorities. While it is open to debate to what extent their ambitions have been fulfilled by Trump's presidency, Trump himself has definitely become a unifying figure for the otherwise fragmented, constantly rivaling and bickering alt-right groups: as J.M. Berger observed in 2018, after studying some 30,000 alt-right Twitter accounts, their hashtags, and posts, "Trump is the rising tide that lifts all boats in the sea of right-wing extremism. [...] Trump is holding the rickety structure of the alt-right together, for now and probably for the foreseeable future."[85]

In light of his broad popularity among white nationalists and alt-right circles, it may come as a surprise that there is limited evidence for Trump's verbal support of racially divisive ideas and policies in his official public rhetoric during his presidency. For instance, his inaugural address was dominated by classic populist tropes, depicting his takeover as a victory for ordinary Americans over entrenched Washington elites: "January 20th, 2017 will be remembered as the day the people became the rulers of this nation again. The forgotten men and women of our country, will be forgotten no longer."[86] Trump painted a gloomy picture of the recent American past, characterized by economic decline, the impoverishment of the middle and working classes, the loss of jobs to foreign competition, and the lack of good public education and public safety, and blamed previous governments that neglected the plight and concerns of everyday Americans for too long, as well as other countries who have skillfully taken advantage of American magnanimity and the lack of protectionist policies. He presented himself as the champion of narrowly defined American interests: "A new vision will govern our land, from this day forward, it's going to be only America first, America first. Every decision on trade, on taxes, on immigration, on foreign affairs will be made to benefit American workers and American families."[87] While employing the customary inclusive statements about American patriotism and solidarity unifying the people regardless of race or background, and invoking the traditional civil religious image of a nation enjoying divine protection ("most importantly, we will be protected by God"), his speech is dominated by the message of a new beginning, a "new millennium" during which "America will start winning again, winning like never

---

85 Berger, J.M.: "Trump Is the Glue that Binds the Far Right." *The Atlantic*, October 29, 2018, retrieved 28.11.2021, from https://www.theatlantic.com/ideas/archive/2018/10/trump-alt-right-twitter/574219/.
86 Trump, Donald: "Full Text: 2017 Donald Trump Inauguration Speech Transcript." *Politico*, January 20, 2017, retrieved 21.11.2021, from https://www.politico.com/story/2017/01/full-text-donald-trump-inauguration-speech-transcript-233907.
87 *Ibid.*

before."[88] These characteristic examples of Trumpian hyperbole aside, his inaugural address can hardly be described as racially or socially divisive (except in its scornful treatment of self-serving political and economic elites) and the promise of a bright future was not restricted to any specific group of Americans.

This primary impression is significantly qualified by a survey conducted in December 2016 by YouGov and published by *Huffington Post*, in which people were asked whether they agree with the statement, "Over the past few years, average Americans have gotten less than they deserve," and with a similar statement in which the phrase "average Americans" was substituted with "Blacks." Overall, the majority (57%) of respondents concurred with the first statement, but only about a third (32%) accepted the second. Among Trump voters, however, the difference was much more pronounced: while almost two-thirds (64%) believed that "average Americans" were the victims of recent American policies and developments, only a fraction (12%) saw Blacks in a similar light. In contrast, Clinton voters approved both statements in equal proportions.[89] The author of the article, political scientist Michael Tesler, explained the glaring difference by arguing that Trump supporters, who were predominantly white, translated the term "average American" as "white" in their mind and contrasted it with African Americans, whom they considered much less deserving. In Tesler's interpretation, whites tend to explain their own difficulties and lack of success with external factors, such as unfavorable economic and social conditions, while in the case of Blacks, they tend to cite problems of moral character and disposition, like the lack of work ethic or propensity for crime, as the ultimate causes.[90]

If Tesler's inferences are correct, then Trump's apparently color-blind populist message put forward in his inaugural address could similarly be interpreted by a substantial part of his base as a veiled promise that finally a champion has arrived in the White House to fight for "average Americans," that is, ordinary whites abandoned by callous Washington elites. This interpretation may have been founded on the spectacular contrast presented by Trump and his predecessor, the first Black president Barack Obama, who was seen by racist right-wingers not as the symbol of a multicultural America but as an alarming premonition of a future takeover of the country by nonwhites. In their eyes, Trump's long-standing and vocal support for the "birther" conspiracy theory that questioned Obama's eligibility as a "natural-born" American president because he was allegedly born outside the United States

---

88 *Ibid.*
89 Tesler, Michael: "Trump Voters Think African Americans Are Much Less Deserving than 'Average Americans.'" *Huffington Post*, December 12, 2016, retrieved 21.11.2021, from https://www.huffpost.com/entry/trump-voters-think-africa_b_13732500.
90 *Ibid.*

offered proof that Trump was the "right president" for American whites.[91] In fact, political scientist Philip Klinkner proved on a representative sample already in 2014 that believers of the "birther" theory are overwhelmingly white, Republican supporters, and they harbor views of racial resentment toward African Americans. Klinker also observed (two years before the presidential election) that Trump's spread of the malicious libel had elevated him to a potent presidential candidate on the Republican side.[92]

Based on the evidence above, we can declare with some confidence that Trump's electoral success, at least to some extent, can be attributed to his deliberately provocative, racially and socially divisive campaign rhetoric, which stood in diametrical opposition to the core values of American civil religion. However, as the saying goes, presidents campaign in poetry but govern in prose. Did Trump's rhetoric change substantially once he occupied the White House?

If one examines Trump's major, scripted speeches during his presidency, exemplified for our purposes by his State of the Union (SoU) addresses, a few dominant themes recur with predictable regularity in each one. Each speech typically begins with a victorious list of economic achievements (increasing number of jobs, low unemployment figures, stock market growth, new factories and investments, etc.) attributing every positive development in the national economy to his administration and the tax cut the Republican majority pushed through Congress in 2017. Special emphasis is placed on the number of new blue-collar jobs and the record low level of unemployment among Blacks and Hispanics. Together with another constant theme, the elimination of earlier free trade deals like NAFTA and the introduction of punitive tariffs to force international trading partners—primarily China—to play fairly, Trump wishes to drive home that he has worked miracles with the American economy, thanks to his "America first" nationalism, benefiting all Americans but particularly the lower-income groups, who are the unmistakable targets of his populist messaging.

The other obligatory part of Trump's SoU addresses is the castigation of illegal immigration and the lack of security at the southern border, illustrated with graphic examples of violent crime committed by illegal aliens (which potentially lend themselves to the interpretation of being veiled messages with racist overtones, even if some of these crime stories have been carefully selected to feature victims from minority groups). He routinely praises the heroic work of the ICE in fighting illegal immigration, urges Congress to fund his border wall (which, despite being

---

91 Serwer, Adam: "Birtherism of a Nation." *The Atlantic*, May 14, 2020, retrieved 29.11.2021, from https://www.theatlantic.com/ideas/archive/2020/05/birtherism-and-trump/610978/.
92 Klinkner, Philip: "The Causes and Consequences of 'Birtherism.'" Paper presented at the 2014 Annual Meeting of the Western Political Science Association. Retrieved 29.11.2021, from http://www.wpsanet.org/papers/docs/Birthers.pdf.

Trump's favorite rhetorical ploy, remained mostly a plan) and pass a comprehensive immigration reform which would involve a crackdown on illegal immigrants and prioritize a merit-based system of legal immigration. While the economic success reports could be interpreted as positive messages of national unification, the consistent equation of illegal immigrants with crime, drugs, and harmful economic impact undoubtedly remained a strongly partisan issue throughout Trump's presidency, intended to fire up his conservative base.

Other recurring features of his speeches were calls for a large-scale infrastructure bill to invest in decaying roads and bridges (a campaign promise that Trump essentially did nothing to keep beyond such rhetorical gestures during his four years in office); promises to make prescription drugs cheaper and replace Obamacare with a superior but strictly private health insurance system (another unfulfilled pledge); declarations about ending unnecessary military commitments in Afghanistan (eventually carried out by his successor, Joe Biden), while Islamic terrorism should be relentlessly fought, among other means by specific restrictions against immigrants from predominantly Muslim countries; and tough foreign policy stances against Iran, Cuba, and Venezuela, while alternating between threats and negotiations vis-à-vis North Korea, and defiantly supporting Jerusalem as the capital of Israel. Few of these positions (except for the need for infrastructure development and ending unpopular wars) could be described as non-partisan, and Trump carefully added a few more targeted messages for his supporters: he repeatedly expressed his opposition to late-term abortion, brandished his record of appointing federal judges who "uphold our Constitution as written"[93] (in other words, originalist conservative jurists), repeatedly lashed out against "socialism in the United States," promoted school choice as the solution to "failing public schools," and made rhetorical declarations to defend religious liberty and the Second Amendment.

All of these items were sandwiched in impeccably civil religious opening and closing statements in each SoU address: anniversaries of great events in American history (e.g., D-day in Normandy or the Moon landing[94]) were recalled in glowing terms, the sacrifices of American veterans were dutifully evoked, and members of Congress were repeatedly called on to set aside partisan differences and unite their efforts to achieve the glorious purposes outlined by the president. Each address ended with an almost hymnic evocation of American exceptionalism, as if to versify Trump's campaign slogan, "Make America Great Again":

---

93 Trump, Donald: "Address Before a Joint Session of Congress on the State of the Union." February 4, 2020, retrieved 05.12.2021, from https://www.presidency.ucsb.edu/documents/address-before-joint-session-the-congress-the-state-the-union-27.

94 Trump, Donald: "Address Before a Joint Session of Congress on the State of the Union." February 5, 2019, retrieved 05.12.2021, from https://www.presidency.ucsb.edu/documents/address-before-joint-session-the-congress-the-state-the-union-26.

> We are Americans. We are pioneers. We are the pathfinders. We settled the New World, we built the modern world, and we changed history forever by embracing the eternal truth that everyone is made equal by the hand of Almighty God.
> America is the place where anything can happen. America is the place where anyone can rise. And here, on this land, on this soil, on this continent, the most incredible dreams come true.
> This Nation is our canvas, and this country is our masterpiece. We look at tomorrow and see unlimited frontiers just waiting to be explored. Our brightest discoveries are not yet known. Our most thrilling stories are not yet told. Our grandest journeys are not yet made. The American age, the American epic, the American adventure has only just begun.
> Our spirit is still young, the Sun is still rising, God's grace is still shining, and, my fellow Americans, the best is yet to come.[95]

These soaring words, thoroughly alien to Trump's spontaneous speaking style and undoubtedly the product of his scriptwriters, were in conspicuous contradiction to the everyday communication of the president, especially his Twitter feed, which revealed a characteristically narcissistic personality,[96] preoccupied with glorifying himself while repeatedly and harshly attacking his critics and political opponents, giving an entirely new meaning to the term "bully pulpit." All previous presidents, or at least all presidents since FDR who occupied the office since the advent of modern telecommunication, have aspired to the role of a national leader transcending party allegiances and ethnic, racial, social, or ideological fault lines. Beyond his scripted and carefully rehearsed major speeches, Donald Trump appeared to be uninterested in such a leadership role: his very limited tolerance for criticism, an indispensable skill of public political figures, may be due to his lack of political experience before the presidency, but he explicitly refused to conform to the expectations of the nation's figurehead. He continued to behave as if he were still on the campaign trail or running his own reality show, quick to retort to the slightest perceived offense but never admitting to any error or apologizing for his behavior.[97]

---

95 Trump, Donald: "Address Before a Joint Session of Congress on the State of the Union." February 4, 2020, *op. cit.*

96 "For psychologists, it is almost impossible to talk about Donald Trump without using the word *narcissism*" (McAdams, Dan P.: "The Mind of Donald Trump." *The Atlantic*, June 2016, retrieved 01.10.2023, from https://www.theatlantic.com/magazine/archive/2016/06/the-mind-of-donald-trump/480771/).

97 This article offers a broad selection of Trump's characteristically rude, offensive, or insensitive tweets, which also commonly contained factually false statements: Coles, Amy: "US Election: Donald Trump's 45 Most Controversial Tweets." *Sky News*, October 12, 2020, retrieved 07.10.2023, from https://news.sky.com/story/us-election-donald-trumps-45-most-controversial-tweets-12098204.

His occasionally astounding lack of civility and explicit refusal to conform to the conventional rules of acceptable public behavior was, however, not seen as a moral failure or lapse in the eyes of his many supporters but rather a sign of strength and determination. The detrimental impact of years of public taboo-breaking culminated in the instigation of the siege of the Capitol on January 6, 2021. After dropping hints that he might be cheated out of a victory at the presidential election by a nationwide Democratic conspiracy months before November,[98] he refused to concede defeat and encouraged his faithful devotees to mount legal challenges against the legitimate outcome in all the swing states won by his Democratic opponent, Joe Biden. After these efforts failed in state and federal courts due to the lack of credible evidence,[99] Trump made a desperate last-ditch attempt to stop the certification of state electoral votes—a normally routine and formal process in accordance with constitutional requirements—on January 6, 2021. Trump organized a rally outside the White House on the occasion, and his speech was stylistically consistent with his tweets as well as his unscripted interviews; therefore, it can reasonably be considered a demonstration of his authentic personality. While making a lot of baseless claims about his overwhelming victory and unprecedented voter fraud, he presented a lot of wild accusations at the "fake news media" that suppressed the truth, the Democrats who engineered a nationwide electoral deception, the "weak Republicans" and the Supreme Court failing to come to his aid when they should show loyalty and gratitude—and so forth. Yet in this apparently unfocused stream-of-consciousness rant about his greatness and his opponents' vileness, he displayed a remarkable instinct to stop just short of explicit incitement to violence and law-breaking to ensure he can plausibly deny responsibility. Here are a few examples:

> Our country has had enough. We will not take it anymore and that's what this is all about. And to use a favorite term that all of you people really came up with: We will stop the steal. [...] We will not let them silence your voices. We're not going to let it happen, I'm not going to let it happen.[100]

---

98 Kessler, Glenn/Rizzo, Salvador: "President Trump's False Claims of Voter Fraud: A Chronology." *The Washington Post*, November 5, 2020, retrieved 06.12.2021, from https://www.washingtonpost.com/politics/2020/11/05/president-trumps-false-claims-vote-fraud-chronology/.

99 For a summary, see the following article: Shamsian, Jacob/Sheth, Sonam: "Trump and His Allies Filed More Than 40 Lawsuits Challenging the 2020 Election Results. All of Them Failed." *Business Insider*, February 22, 2021, retrieved 07.10.2023, from https://www.businessinsider.com/trump-campaign-lawsuits-election-results-2020-11.

100 Trump, Donald: "Transcript of Trump's Speech at Rally before US Capitol Riot." *AP News*, January 14, 2021, retrieved 06.12.2021, from https://apnews.com/article/election-2020-joe-biden-donald-trump-capitol-siege-media-e79eb5164613d6718e9f4502eb471f27.

Trump employs the first person plural personal pronoun very often in this speech, suggesting a unity of opinion, will, and purpose with his audience. When he declares "We're not going to let it happen," he issues an implied command to his supporters that they should do something against it—yet he remains conveniently vague about what and how they should do to "not let it happen."

In another part of his speech, he puts strong verbal pressure on Vice President Mike Pence, who, in his capacity as the president of the Senate, officially oversees the certification process of state electoral votes:

> I hope Mike is going to do the right thing. I hope so. I hope so. Because if Mike Pence does the right thing, we win the election. [...] He has the absolute right to do it. We're supposed to protect our country, support our country, support our Constitution, and protect our constitution. [...] All Vice President Pence has to do is send it back to the states to recertify and we become president and you are the happiest people.[101]

It is a characteristic example of Trump's enormous capacity for hyperbole and the inversion of truth that he presents an unconstitutional overruling of state electoral votes by the Vice President as protection of the Constitution,[102] or that he equates his victory at the election (note the use of "we" again: "we become president") with national happiness. But the most infamous utterance of the whole speech consisted of urging his supporters to march on the Capitol to intimidate Congress into breaking the law:

> Now, it is up to Congress to confront this egregious assault on our democracy. And after this, we're going to walk down, and I'll be there with you, we're going to walk down, we're going to walk down.
> Anyone you want, but I think right here, we're going to walk down to the Capitol, and we're going to cheer on our brave senators and congressmen and women, and we're probably not going to be cheering so much for some of them.

---

101 *Ibid.*

102 Section 1 of Article II of the U.S. Constitution merely states, "The President of the Senate shall, in the presence of the Senate and the House of Representatives, open all the Certificates, and the Votes shall then be counted." Nothing in the text of the Constitution suggests that the Vice President, in his capacity as president of the Senate, has any right to arbitrarily reject the validity of the certified electoral votes of the states; therefore, what Trump expected of Mike Pence was clearly unconstitutional. In the two previous disputed presidential elections, those of 1876 and 2000, the outcome turned on the states that had close and contested popular vote results, but never on the Senate or its president, who is expected to accept certified electoral votes without question. For relevant constitutional and legal details, see Nagle, John Copeland: "How Not to Count Votes." *Columbia Law Review* 104 (6), 2004, pp. 1732–1763.

Because you'll never take back our country with weakness. You have to show strength and you have to be strong. We have come to demand that Congress do the right thing and only count the electors who have been lawfully slated, lawfully slated.
I know that everyone here will soon be marching over to the Capitol building to peacefully and patriotically make your voices heard.[103]

Americans as well as millions of viewers all over the world watched in shock and disbelief how this "peaceful and patriotic march" ended later the same day—without the presence of the president, despite his promise to accompany them. Reading Trump's speech in its entirety, an objective observer may justifiably come to the conclusion that he fomented the ensuing attack on the Capitol by stirring up the passions of his most fanatic supporters with wildly inaccurate accusations and urging them to "do the right thing" and "defend the Constitution." While he never actually instructed them to violently break into the building of the federal legislature, his rhetoric ever since Election Day—and even before—amplified the same spurious message: that the opposing party and their shady allies are committing all they can to illegally remove the American people's champion from power, and all true patriots have a duty to "stop the steal."

It is an alarming sign of the present dysfunction of American democracy that such a blatantly unconstitutional and criminal deed—the first clear-cut case in the history of the United States when a president was impeached for a profoundly illegal act rather than due to partisan rancor—was not followed by a successful impeachment procedure, and Trump was never held constitutionally accountable for instigating an open attack on another branch of the federal government. While a number of Republican senators, above all minority leader Mitch McConnell, refused to convict the President by arguing that he could no longer be impeached after he had left office,[104] it is a credible assumption that their reluctance to vote against Trump was motivated by more pragmatic considerations: the majority of the Republican base did not turn against their former president following the events on January 6, 2021; in fact, a year after the Capitol riot the majority of Republican voters believe that Trump bears no responsibility for the January 6 attack, and roughly two-thirds of them consider him the definite (33%) or probable (33%) winner of the 2020 presidential election.[105] Perceiving the continued popularity of

---

103 Trump, Donald: "Transcript of Trump's Speech at Rally before US Capitol Riot." *AP News*, January 14, 2021, *op. cit.*
104 McLeod, Paul: "Republicans Voted to Acquit Trump for the Deadly Capitol Attack, Tying Their Party to His Violence for Years to Come." *BuzzFeed News*, February 13, 2021, retrieved 14.02.2022, from https://www.buzzfeednews.com/article/paulmcleod/donald-trump-impeachment-trial-2021-acquitted.
105 Jones, Bradley: "Fewer Americans Now Say Trump Bears a Lot of Responsibility for the Jan. 6 Riot." *Pew Research*, February 8, 2022, retrieved 14.02.2022, from https://

Trump and concerned about their own future electoral prospects if they openly confront the notoriously vindictive ex-president, most Republican Congressmen refused to uphold the principles of the Constitution.

Conclusion

How can we assess Trump's legacy from a civil religious perspective? By degrading the traditional role of the president as the high priest of civil religion and refusing to act as a national leader above partisan politics, I believe that he has done serious damage to the civil religious tradition. His frequent ad hominem attacks especially in his tweets, his unabashed partisanship in almost all public situations (except in his scripted State of the Union addresses), and his flagrant disregard for factuality and truth all worked to undermine the presidency as a putatively respectable institution, even when the scandals of other presidents before him—from Richard Nixon to Bill Clinton—have undoubtedly contributed to the decline of its prestige. I think that Trump's total lack of political experience also played a part: as a complete novice in politicking on any level, he neither understood nor appreciated a fundamental feature of the American political system which it has inherited from the Founders: the need for pragmatic compromises to get things done. The constitutional system of checks and balances between the separated branches of power, as well as partisan divisions within and between the two chambers of Congress, make it manifestly impossible for any president to unilaterally carry out his political program or even make his wishes come true—from the erection of the wall along the Mexican border to the reform of NATO or trade battles with China. Unable or unwilling to accept that fundamental fact, Trump chose to bully the other political side into compliance (mostly unsuccessfully), rail at all real or perceived political enemies or blame others for his lack of success—or even more simply, denied existing facts and realities, claiming success and celebrating his fantastic leadership without justification. Political rhetoric is inseparable from selective and biased argumentation and sugarcoating unfavorable data or developments—but Trump's persistent denial of fundamental facts (most spectacularly, the fact that he lost the presidential election of 2020) carried this politically motivated bending of reality to a whole new level, into the realm of alternative reality and conspiracy theories.

One of the core axioms of American civil religion is the existence of a common denominator of shared national symbols, values, and principles which are beyond political arguments and partisan rancor, as Peter Gardella's book, discussed in the section "Understanding Civil Religion in the 1970s and in the 2010s" of this chapter, has also demonstrated. While it is missing from Gardella's list, one such

---

www.pewresearch.org/fact-tank/2022/02/08/fewer-americans-now-say-trump-bears-a-lot-of-responsibility-for-the-jan-6-riot/.

crucial conviction is the acceptance of one's political opposition as equally patriotic Americans who also want the best for the country, even when there is little agreement about the specific ways and methods of how to proceed. I fear that Trump's potentially most detrimental impact on the civil religious tradition was his reckless abuse of the rhetoric of American patriotism: his equation of himself with the American people and his ceaseless castigation of Democrats, the mainstream media, technological companies, political elites, and other "enemies of America." There is a long-standing tradition for such divisive rhetoric in the history of American politics when certain groups deliberately exclude others from the symbolic community of the nation, from the racist, anti-Semitic, and anti-Catholic platform of the Ku Klux Klan in the early twentieth century through deportations of ethnic Japanese citizens during World War II to the McCarthy era of anti-Communist witch hunts in the early 1950s, but they were either voiced by isolated fringe groups beyond the political mainstream or represented limited periods followed by self-correction—and they never directly involved the active political role of the president. By his norm-breaking behavior, Trump has created a new standard for viewing all public debates or conflicts on entirely and exclusively partisan terms, or even on purely personal terms. Trump's ego turns every political matter into a personal issue; other people's moral and intellectual worth is determined by their positive or negative attitude toward him. There is a long series of examples during his presidency for how he insulted respectable members of his own party apparently out of personal spite (e.g., Senator and former presidential candidate John McCain) or radically reversed and publicly aired his judgment about his own staff and cabinet members as soon as they disagreed with him in any major or minor issue (well-known examples include Vice President Mike Pence, Attorneys General Jeff Sessions and William Barr, Defense Secretary Jim Mattis or National Security Adviser John Bolton). Such behavior goes radically against the normative expectations of the nation's highest office, yet it did not result in the marginalization and the bipartisan rejection of Donald Trump, as opposed to Richard Nixon following the Watergate scandal, for instance. Trump has never been officially branded as a political transgressor, which doubtless contributed to his enduring popularity among voters of the American right and to the normalization of his political behavior among his loyal followers, commonly referred to as MAGA-Republicans.

This exceedingly corrosive and divisive public attitude of the nation's putative "high priest," the living symbol of national unity and patriotism, has left deep scars behind and dramatically increased the already existing political polarization in the American polity. If such a flagrantly illegal and unpatriotic deed as storming the nation's legitimately elected legislation by an angry mob egged on by the president has not led to a national soul-searching and an attempt on both sides of the political aisle to look for a new, non-partisan redefinition of what the core values of American civil religion are, it is very difficult to imagine what needs to happen to produce a similar nationwide self-reflection. In the early 2020s, American civil religion seems to be in a more profound crisis than anything Robert N. Bellah was able to imagine.

References

Albanese, Catherine L.: *America. Religions and Religion.* 3rd ed. Wadsworth Publishing: Belmont, CA 1999.

Albanese, Catherine L.: *Sons of the Fathers. The Civil Religion of the American Revolution.* Temple University Press: Philadelphia 1976.

Balmer, Randall Herbert: *God in the White House. A History. How Faith Shaped the Presidency from John F. Kennedy to George W. Bush.* HarperCollins e-books: New York 2008.

Barron, James: "Overlooked Influences on Donald Trump. A Famous Minister and His Church." *The New York Times*, September 5, 2016, retrieved 11.06.2021, from https://www.nytimes.com/2016/09/06/nyregion/donald-trump-marble-collegiate-church-norman-vincent-peale.html.

Bellah, Robert N.: "Civil Religion in America." *Daedalus* 96 (1), 1967.

Bellah, Robert N.: *The Broken Covenant. American Civil Religion in Time of Trial.* 2nd ed. The University of Chicago Press: Chicago and London 1992.

Berger, J.M.: "Trump Is the Glue that Binds the Far Right." *The Atlantic*, October 29, 2018, retrieved 28.11.2021, from https://www.theatlantic.com/ideas/archive/2018/10/trump-alt-right-twitter/574219/.

Berns, Walter: *Making Patriots.* The University of Chicago Press: Chicago 2001.

Bush, George W.: "Address to the Joint Session of the 107th Congress on September 20, 2001." In: Bush, George W.: *Selected Speeches of President George W. Bush 2001–2008*, pp. 65–73, retrieved 11.06.2021, from https://georgewbush-whitehouse.archives.gov/infocus/bushrecord/.

Bush, George W.: "National Day of Prayer and Remembrance Service on September 14, 2001." In: Bush, George W.: *Selected Speeches of President George W. Bush 2001–2008*, pp. 59–61, retrieved 11.06.2021, from https://georgewbush-whitehouse.archives.gov/infocus/bushrecord/.

Bush, George W.: "State of the Union Address to the 107th Congress on January 29, 2002." In: Bush, George W.: *Selected Speeches of President George W. Bush 2001–2008*, pp. 103–113, retrieved 11.06.2021, from https://georgewbush-whitehouse.archives.gov/infocus/bushrecord/.

Bush, George W.: "Televised Speech on September 12, 2001," retrieved 11.06.2021, from https://www.pbs.org/newshour/world/terrorism-july-dec01-bush_speech_9-12.

Cainkar, Louise: "The Muslim Ban and Trump's War on Immigration." *Middle East Report*, 294 (Spring 2020), retrieved 28.11.2021, from https://merip.org/2020/06/the-muslim-ban-and-trumps-war-on-immigration-2/.

Campbell, David E. (ed.): *A Matter of Faith. Religion in the 2004 Presidential Election.* Brookings Institution Press: Washington, DC 2007.

Coles, Amy: "US Election: Donald Trump's 45 Most Controversial Tweets." *Sky News*, October 12, 2020, retrieved 07.10.2023, from https://news.sky.com/story/us-election-donald-trumps-45-most-controversial-tweets-12098204.

Domke, David/Coe, Kevin: *The God Strategy. How Religion Became a Political Weapon in America*. Oxford University Press: Oxford, New York et al. 2008.

Fahmy, Dalia: "Most Americans Don't See Trump as Religious; Fewer than Half Say They Think He's Christian." *Pew Research Center*, March 25, 2020, retrieved 11.06.2021, from https://www.pewresearch.org/fact-tank/2020/03/25/most-americans-dont-see-trump-as-religious/.

Fiorina, Morris P. et al.: *Culture War? The Myth of a Polarized America*. 3rd ed. Longman: Boston et al. 2011.

Gardella, Peter: *American Civil Religion: What Americans Hold Sacred*. Oxford University Press: New York and Oxford 2014.

Gedicks, Frederick: "American Civil Religion. An Idea Whose Time is Past." *George Washington International Law Review* 41 (4), 2010, pp. 891–908.

Gerson, Michael: "The Last Temptation." *The Atlantic*, April 2018, retrieved 11.06.2021, from https://www.theatlantic.com/magazine/archive/2018/04/the-last-temptation/554066/.

Green, John C.: *The Faith Factor: How Religion Influences American Elections*. Praeger: Westport, CT 2007.

Green, John C. et al. (eds.): *The Values Campaign? The Christian Right and the 2004 Elections*. Georgetown University Press: Washington, DC 2006.

Hart, Roderick P./Pauley, John L.: *The Political Pulpit Revisited*. Purdue University Press: West Lafayette, IN 2005.

Hartman, Andrew: *A War for the Soul of America: A History of the Culture Wars*. The University of Chicago Press: Chicago and London 2015.

Heineman, Kenneth J.: *God Is a Conservative. Religion, Politics, and Morality in Contemporary America*. New York University Press: New York and London 1998.

Herberg, Will: "America's Civil Religion: What It Is and Whence It Comes." In: Jones, Donald G./Richey, Russell E. (eds.): *American Civil Religion*. Harper & Row: New York 1974, pp. 76–88.

Henderson, Charles P.: "Civil Religion and the American Presidency." *Religious Education* 70 (5), 1975, pp. 473–485.

Hodgson, Godfrey. *The Myth of American Exceptionalism*. Yale University Press: New Haven, CT 2009, pp. 1–29.

Hogue, Andrew P.: *Stumping God. Reagan, Carter, and the Invention of a Political Faith*. Baylor University Press: Waco, TX 2012.

Hunter, James Davison: *Culture Wars. The Struggle to Define America*. Basic Books: New York 1991.

Hutcheson, Richard G.: *God in the White House. How Religion Has Changed the Modern Presidency.* Macmillan: New York and London 1988.

Jones, Bradley: "Fewer Americans Now Say Trump Bears a Lot of Responsibility for the Jan. 6 Riot." *Pew Research,* February 8, 2022, retrieved 14.02.2022, from https://www.pewresearch.org/fact-tank/2022/02/08/fewer-americans-now-say-trump-bears-a-lot-of-responsibility-for-the-jan-6-riot/.

Jones, Donald G./Richey, Russell E.: "The Civil Religion Debate." In: Jones, Donald G./Richey, Russell E. (eds.): *American Civil Religion.* Harper & Row: New York 1974, pp. 3–18.

Kellstedt, Lyman, et al.: "Faith Transformed. Religion and American Politics from FDR to George W. Bush." In: Noll, Mark A./Harlow, Luke E. (eds.): *Religion and American Politics. From the Colonial Period to the Present.* 2nd ed. Oxford University Press: Oxford and New York 2007, pp. 269–295.

Kessler, Glenn/Rizzo, Salvador: "President Trump's False Claims of Voter Fraud: A Chronology." *The Washington Post,* November 5, 2020, retrieved 06.12.2021, from https://www.washingtonpost.com/politics/2020/11/05/president-trumps-false-claims-vote-fraud-chronology/.

Klinkner, Philip: "The Causes and Consequences of 'Birtherism.'" Paper presented at the 2014 Annual Meeting of the Western Political Science Association, retrieved 29.11.2021, from http://www.wpsanet.org/papers/docs/Birthers.pdf.

Layman, Geoffrey C.: *The Great Divide. Religious and Cultural Conflict in American Party Politics.* Columbia University Press: New York 2001.

Lynch v. Donnelly, 465 U.S. 668 (1984). https://supreme.justia.com/cases/federal/us/465/668/#T2/24.

Marty, Martin E.: "Two Kinds of Two Kinds of Civil Religion." In: Jones, Donald G./Richey, Russell E. (eds.): *American Civil Religion.* Harper & Row: New York 1974, pp. 139–157.

McAdams, Dan P.: "The Mind of Donald Trump." *The Atlantic,* June 2016, retrieved 01.10.2023, from https://www.theatlantic.com/magazine/archive/2016/06/the-mind-of-donald-trump/480771/.

McGough, Michael: *A Field Guide to the Culture Wars. The Battle over Values from the Campaign Trail to the Classroom.* Praeger: Westport, CT 2009.

McKenna, George: *The Puritan Origins of American Patriotism.* Yale University Press: New Haven, CT and London 2007.

Meacham, Jon: *American Gospel. God, the Founding Fathers, and the Making of a Nation.* Random House: New York 2007.

Medhurst, Martin J.: "Forging a Civil-Religious Construct for the Twenty-First Century. Should Hart's 'Contract' Be Renewed?" In: Hart, Roderick P./Pauley, John L. (eds.): *The Political Pulpit Revisited.* Purdue University Press: West Lafayette, IN 2005, pp. 151–160.

Nagle, John Copeland: "How Not to Count Votes." *Columbia Law Review* 104 (6), 2004, pp. 1732–1763.

Newport, Frank: "Religious Group Voting and the 2020 Election." *Gallup*, November 13, 2020, retrieved 11.07.2021, from https://news.gallup.com/opinion/polling-matters/324410/religious-group-voting-2020-election.aspx.

Niayesh, Vahid: "What Trump's Travel Ban Really Looks Like, Almost Two Years in." *The Conversation*, October 18, 2019, retrieved 28.11.2021, from https://theconversation.com/what-trumps-travel-ban-really-looks-like-almost-two-years-in-123564.

Nortey, Justin: "Most White Americans Who Regularly Attend Worship Services Voted for Trump in 2020." *Pew Research Center*, August 30, 2021, retrieved 11.04.2021, from https://www.pewresearch.org/fact-tank/2021/08/30/most-white-americans-who-regularly-attend-worship-services-voted-for-trump-in-2020/.

Novak, Michael: *Choosing Presidents: Symbols of Political Leadership.* 2nd ed. Transaction Publishers: New Brunswick and London 1992.

Obama, Barack: *The Audacity of Hope. Thoughts on Reclaiming the American Dream.* Crown Publishers: New York 2006.

Pierard, Richard V./Linder, Robert D.: *Civil Religion and the Presidency.* Academie Books: Grand Rapids, MI 1988.

Pintér, Károly: "American Civil Religion: Revisiting a Concept after 50 Years." *Americana: E-Journal of American Studies in Hungary* 12 (2), Fall 2016.

Posner, Sarah: "How Donald Trump's New Campaign Chief Created an Online Haven for White Nationalists." *Mother Jones*, August 22, 2016, retrieved 28.11.2021, from https://www.motherjones.com/politics/2016/08/stephen-bannon-donald-trump-alt-right-breitbart-news/.

Renaud, Myriam: "Myths Debunked: Why Did White Evangelical Christians Vote for Trump?" *Sightings*, Divinity School of the University of Chicago, January 19, 2017, retrieved 11.07.2021, from https://divinity.uchicago.edu/sightings/articles/myths-debunked-why-did-white-evangelical-christians-vote-trump.

Rozell, Mark J.: "Introduction: Religion and the Bush Presidency." In: Rozell, Mark J./Whitney, Gleaves (eds.): *Religion and the Bush Presidency.* Palgrave Macmillan: New York and Basingstoke 2007, pp. 1–10.

Scott, Eugene: "Trump Believes in God, but Hasn't Sought Forgiveness." *CNN*, July 19, 2015, retrieved 11.06.2021, from https://edition.cnn.com/2015/07/18/politics/trump-has-never-sought-forgiveness/index.html.

Serwer, Adam: "Birtherism of a Nation." *The Atlantic*, May 14, 2020, retrieved 29.11.2021, from https://www.theatlantic.com/ideas/archive/2020/05/birtherism-and-trump/610978/.

Shamsian, Jacob/Sheth, Sonam: "Trump and His Allies Filed More Than 40 Lawsuits Challenging the 2020 Election Results. All of Them Failed." *Business Insider*, February 22, 2021, retrieved 07.10.2023, from https://www.businessinsider.com/trump-campaign-lawsuits-election-results-2020-11.

Singer, Peter: *The President of Good and Evil: Taking George W. Bush Seriously*. Granta Books: London 2004.

Smith, Gary Scott: *Faith and the Presidency. From George Washington to George W. Bush*. Oxford University Press: Oxford and New York 2006.

Smith, Gregory A.: "Among White Evangelicals, Regular Churchgoers Are the Most Supportive of Trump." *Pew Research Center*, April 26, 2017, retrieved 11.04.2021, from https://www.pewresearch.org/fact-tank/2017/04/26/among-white-evangelicals-regular-churchgoers-are-the-most-supportive-of-trump/.

Swain, Carol M.: *The New White Nationalism in America: Its Challenge to Integration*. Cambridge University Press: Cambridge and New York 2002.

Taylor, Jessica: "Citing 'Two Corinthians,' Trump Struggles to Make the Sale to Evangelicals." *NPR*, January 18, 2016, retrieved 11.06.2021, from https://www.npr.org/2016/01/18/463528847/citing-two-corinthians-trump-struggles-to-make-the-sale-to-evangelicals?t=1636217257439.

Tesler, Michael: "Trump Voters Think African Americans Are Much Less Deserving than 'Average Americans.'" *Huffington Post*, December 12, 2016, retrieved 21.11.2021, from https://www.huffpost.com/entry/trump-voters-think-africa_b_13732500.

Trump, Donald: "Address Before a Joint Session of Congress on the State of the Union." January 30, 2018, retrieved 05.12.2021, from https://www.presidency.ucsb.edu/documents/address-before-joint-session-the-congress-the-state-the-union-25.

Trump, Donald: "Address Before a Joint Session of Congress on the State of the Union." February 5, 2019, retrieved 05.12.2021, from https://www.presidency.ucsb.edu/documents/address-before-joint-session-the-congress-the-state-the-union-26.

Trump, Donald: "Address Before a Joint Session of Congress on the State of the Union." February 4, 2020, retrieved 05.12.2021, from https://www.presidency.ucsb.edu/documents/address-before-joint-session-the-congress-the-state-the-union-27.

Trump, Donald: "Full Text: 2017 Donald Trump inauguration speech transcript." *Politico*, January 20, 2017, retrieved 21.11.2021, from https://www.politico.com/story/2017/01/full-text-donald-trump-inauguration-speech-transcript-233907.

Trump, Donald: "Full text: Trump's Comments on White Supremacists, 'Alt-Left' in Charlottesville." *Politico*, August 15, 2017, retrieved 28.11.2021, from https://www.politico.com/story/2017/08/15/full-text-trump-comments-white-supremacists-alt-left-transcript-241662.

Trump, Donald: "Here's Trump's Presidential Announcement Speech." *TIME*, June 16, 2015, retrieved 21.11.2021, from https://time.com/3923128/donald-trump-announcement-speech/.

Trump, Donald: "Transcript of Trump's Speech at Rally before US Capitol Riot." *AP News*, January 14, 2021, retrieved 06.12.2021, from https://apnews.com/article/election-2020-joe-biden-donald-trump-capitol-siege-media-e79eb5164613d6718e9f4502eb471f27.

Watkins, Eli/Phillip, Abby: "Trump Decries Immigrants from 'Shithole Countries' Coming to the US." *CNN*, January 12, 2018, retrieved 28.11.2021, from https://edition.cnn.com/2018/01/11/politics/immigrants-shithole-countries-trump/index.html.

Weiss, David: "Civil Religion or Mere Religion? The Debate over Presidential Religious Rhetoric." In: Edwards, Jason A./Valenzano, Joseph M. (eds.): *The Rhetoric of American Civil Religion: Symbols, Sinners, and Saints*. Lexington Books: Lanham, MD and London 2016, pp. 143–164.

Williams, Daniel K.: *God's Own Party. The Making of the Christian Right*. Oxford University Press: Oxford and New York 2010.

Wilson, John F.: "The Status of 'Civil Religion' in America." In: Smith, Elwyn A. (ed.): *The Religion of the Republic*. Fortress Press: Philadelphia 1971, pp. 1–21.

Wilson, Matthew: "Donald Trump and the 'Alt-Right': How Much Connection Is There?" *ISPI*, July 17, 2020, retrieved 28.11.2021, from https://www.ispionline.it/it/pubblicazione/donald-trump-and-alt-right-how-much-connection-there-26990.

James L. Guth and Lyman A. Kellstedt

Religious Influences on American Conservative Populism

Abstract: Although the rise of right-wing populism in Western democracies has received enormous attention from social scientists, there has been much less research directed at the role of religion in creating support for populist movements. In this chapter, we consider the influence of religious factors in the development of conservative populism in the United States. We find that ethnoreligious traditions have very different responses to populist themes, with evangelical Protestants quite supportive of most populist attitudes and atheists and agnostics spearheading the opposition. Many, but not all, of these differences are explained by theological traditionalism, with the religiously orthodox in almost all ethnoreligious groups more prone to take populist stances.

Keywords: conservative populism, ethnoreligious tradition, theological traditionalism, "thin" populism

Introduction

In recent years, the rise of conservative populism has attracted enormous attention from students of comparative politics. Although American scholars were slow to assess populist tendencies at home,[1] recent presidential elections have ended that neglect, as Donald Trump exploited typical populist anxieties, mimicked the style of populist leaders across the developed world, and was soon emulated by many other Republican politicians.

Despite a rapidly expanding literature, however, explanations for this American populism have failed to "converge."[2] Most theories about populism's causes fall into two distinct categories, focusing on either *cultural resentment* or *economic stress*, although some scholars have sought to connect the two.[3] Each view has

---

1 Lee, Frances: "Populism and the American Party System: Opportunities and Constraints." *Perspectives on Politics* 18 (2), 2020, pp. 370–388.
2 Norris, Pippa: "Measuring Populism Worldwide." *Party Politics* (online), 2020, https://journals.sagepub.com/doi/10.1177/1354068820927686.
3 Rodrik, Dani: "Why Does Globalization Fuel Populism: Economics, Culture and the Rise of Right-Wing Populism?." Working Paper 27526. National Bureau of Economic Research: Cambridge, MA 2020.

distinguished proponents, but cultural interpretations have dominated accounts of European and American populism on the political right, dubbed "right-wing populism,"[4] "authoritarian populism,"[5] "national populism"[6]—or our own preference, "conservative populism."[7] And in the Western political context, at least, such parties constitute a large majority of all "populist" parties.

Despite the emphasis on culture, relatively little attention has been paid to religion. Cultural explanations do often entail cursory discussions of the topic, albeit in different ways. Scholars in Western Europe have noted a recent turn toward religious discourse by conservative populists, but usually as culture or identity markers against outsiders—especially Muslims—rather than as reassertions of active faith.[8] In fact, such European populists tend to be *less* traditionally religious than constituents of other conservative parties.[9] Some analysts do see some connection between conventional religiosity and conservative populism, especially in Eastern Europe and the United States, mediated by religion's strong ties to social traditionalism, at least a minor feature of these movements.[10] But few studies address conservative populism's attraction for different ethnoreligious groups. This question may be irrelevant in Europe, where secularization has often eroded any influence of what was often a single national religious tradition, but the varying appeals of populism may be crucial in the United States, with its persisting religious vitality and significantly greater religious diversity.

In previous work on the 2016 American presidential election, we found distinctive religious contributions to the "Populist Syndrome," an attitudinal complex comprising support for strong leaders, "rough politics," nativism, white nationalism, and other populist themes.[11] All these emphases echoed strongly among

---

4   Kaufmann, Eric: *Whiteshift: Populism, Immigration, and the Future of White Majorities.* Abrams Press: New York 2019.
5   Norris, Pippa/Inglehart, Ronald: *Cultural Backlash: Trump, Brexit, and Authoritarian Populism.* Cambridge University Press: Cambridge 2019.
6   Eatwell, Roger/Goodwin, Matthew: *National Populism: The Revolt Against Liberal Democracy.* Penguin Random House: London 2018.
7   Guth, James L.: "Are White Evangelicals Populists? The View from the 2016 American National Election Study." *Review of Faith and International Affairs* 17 (3), 2019, pp. 20–35.
8   Marzouki, Nadia/McDonnell, Duncan/Roy, Olivier (eds.): *Saving the People: How Populists Hijack Religion.* Oxford University Press: New York 2016.
9   Guth, James L./Nelsen, Brent F.: "Party Choice in Europe: Social Cleavages and the Rise of Populist Parties." *Party Politics* 27 (3), 2021, pp. 453–464.
10 Norris, Pippa/Inglehart, Ronald: *op. cit.*
11 Guth, James L.: "Are White Evangelicals Populists? The View from the 2016 American National Election Study." *Review of Faith and International Affairs* 17 (3), 2019, pp. 20–35.

white evangelical Protestants, the largest religious constituency in Trump's 2016 electoral coalition[12] and, subsequently, his most steadfast supporters. Our findings confirmed Bonikowski's claim that evangelicals were "ardent" populists and "central" to any analysis of Trumpist populism.[13] In addition, we showed that orthodox religiosity also supported populist attitudes, even beyond the evangelical community. Conversely, ethnoreligious minorities and the growing cohort of secular citizens, especially atheists and agnostics, were arrayed on the anti-populist ramparts, with other religious communities distributed along a continuum, less strongly committed on either side.

Our present purpose is quite simple: to revisit the "religious" location of American conservative populism after four years of the Trump administration. During that period, religious appeals were a prominent feature of the Republican political strategy, as the notoriously nonreligious president surpassed even his GOP predecessors in cultivating religious conservatives. Other religious groups (and secularist organizations) mobilized to oppose administration policies. As a result, we expect that the Populist Syndrome has persisted, but think that four years of populist leadership in Washington might well have changed some of its features, suggesting possible fluidity in key attitudes.

The analysis proceeds as follows: First, we provide a brief overview of prominent themes in the literature on conservative populism, focusing on its "cultural" side. Then, using the American National Election Study of 2020, we derive empirical measures tapping those themes and examine the religious connections with each dimension of populist politics, assessing the effects of membership in ethnoreligious traditions and the influence of other religious variables. Then, we test whether the traits attributed to conservative populists "hang together," confirming that a Populist Syndrome still exists, but with some interesting modifications since 2016. Finally, we assess the interaction of religious, socioeconomic, and political factors on the Syndrome and speculate about the future of "religious" populism.

Theory: Populist Themes

Although efforts to confirm or reconcile competing theories about the origins of conservative populism continue,[14] we bypass these controversies by focusing on

---

12 Kellstedt, Lyman A./Guth, James L.: "Religion and Electoral Behavior in the United States, 1936–2016." In: Malici, Akan/Smith, Elizabeth (eds.): *Political Science Research in Practice*. 2nd ed. Routledge: New York 2019, pp. 117–136.
13 Bonikowski, Bart: "Trump's Populism: The Mobilization of Nationalist Cleavages and the Future of US Democracy." In: Weyland, Kurt/Madrid, Raúl (eds.): *When Democracy Trumps Populism: European and Latin American Lessons for the United States*. Cambridge University Press: Cambridge 2019, p. 119.
14 Rodrik, Dani: *op. cit.*

universally acknowledged themes of conservative populist rhetoric and ideology.[15] Despite significant disputes over conservative populism's origins, a broad consensus exists on certain characteristic attitudes and traits. In previous work, we examined many aspects of populist style and politics in great detail, but those traits coalesce in larger configurations, combined both in theory and empirically. In the next few paragraphs, we delineate those configurations.

Many theorists argue that populism is a "thin" ideology stressing a few central themes on the nature of the political system.[16] The crucial one might be summarized as "majoritarian anti-pluralism." Populists see the remedy for national and personal ills in a return to rule by "the [true] people," even if that means excluding minorities from the political process—or perhaps from the nation itself. This populist revival requires a strong leader to take unconventional, unconstitutional, or even illegal action to restore national greatness. Thus, populism has "inherent tendencies toward authoritarianism."[17] "Thin populism" rejects both pluralism and procedural safeguards in favor of majoritarian popular sovereignty, expressed through a charismatic leader.[18] We summarize this package as *majoritarian rough politics*.

Other "thin" traits involve antagonism toward traditional political elites and other cultural authorities. First of all, populists distrust politicians and share a sense of national decline, feeling that both their country and its citizens have seen better days. The nation has been betrayed by political leaders and institutions, explaining both its declining fortunes—and the faltering prospects of its citizens. Economic opportunity is gone, and populists often see themselves as victims of economic globalization and other international forces beyond their control. Not only do they lack confidence in conventional political leaders, but they also distrust specialized expertise, preferring to rely on the superior judgment of ordinary people, rather than that of scientists, journalists, or bureaucratic professionals.[19] Here we consider three additional attitudinal structures: *distrust of politicians, declinism,* and *distrust of experts*.

All these "thin" perspectives are shared by populists left and right, but conservative populists add specific "second-order" themes to their worldview, themes

---

15 Weyland, Kurt/Madrid, Raúl (eds.): *When Democracy Trumps Populism: European and Latin American Lessons for the United States*. Cambridge University Press: Cambridge 2019.

16 Mudde, Cas: *Populism: A Very Short Introduction*. 2nd ed. Oxford University Press: New York 2017.

17 Weyland, Kurt: "Populism's Threat to Democracy: Comparative Lessons for the United States." *Perspectives on Politics* 18 (2), 2020, pp. 389–406.

18 Norris, Pippa: *op. cit.*, p. 6.

19 Collins, Harry/Evans, Robert/Durant, Darrin/Weinel, Martin: *Experts and the Will of the People: Society, Populism and Science*. Palgrave Macmillan: London 2020.

more directly related to public policies. One universal component is the reassertion of national identity. Indeed, as Jan-Werner Müller puts it, "populism is always a form of identity politics."[20] At one level, this reassertion usually entails the rejection of limits to national sovereignty posed by multilateral commitments, whether in the form of the European Union, the UN, World Health Organization, World Trade Organization, or NATO. National identity politics also valorizes "traditional" or majority ethnic culture and norms, sometimes including historic religious traditions, against "newer" or minority entrants to the society, often giving rise to anti-immigrant sentiments, nativism, preference for white ethnic power, and (in both Europe and America) anti-Muslim sentiment.[21] In the American case, Theda Skocpol sees "ethno-nationalism" and "Christian conservatism" as the twin pillars of Trump's populist appeal.[22] Whitehead and Perry combine these pillars in "Christian nationalism,"[23] which they see as a distinct movement but is better viewed as one component of American conservative populism. We call this American variant of national identity politics *white nationalism*.

As populism is always a "moralistic interpretation of politics," other cultural accounts posit the reassertion of traditional morality as a key feature. Even those who see populism as a rejection of globalization or neo-liberal economics concede that this reaction is often expressed as moral traditionalism, sexual chauvinism, anti-feminism, or demands for law and order.[24] Capturing these tendencies in a broader framework, Norris and Inglehart argue that conservative populists reject new *postmaterialist* values in favor of older *materialist* ones.[25] Or in Hooghe and Marks' formulation, populists oppose "green-alternative-libertarian" values in favor of "traditional-authoritarian-nationalist" ones.[26] Whatever the terminology,

---

20 Müller, Jan-Werner: *What Is Populism?* University of Pennsylvania Press: Philadelphia 2016, p. 3.
21 For discussions of these features in the United States and Europe, see: Sides, John/Tesler, Michael/Vavreck, Lynn: *Identity Crisis: The 2016 Presidential Campaign and the Battle for the Meaning of America*. Princeton University Press: Princeton 2018; Jardina, Ashley: *White Identity Politics*. Cambridge University Press: Cambridge 2019; Eatwell, Roger/Goodwin, Matthew: *op. cit.*; Kaufmann, Eric: *op. cit.*
22 Skocpol, Theda: "The Elite and Popular Roots of Contemporary Republican Extremism." In: Skocpol, Theda/Tervo, Caroline (eds.) *Upending American Politics*. Oxford University Press: New York 2020, pp. 3–27.
23 Whitehead, Andrew/Perry, Samuel: *Taking America Back for God: Christian Nationalism in the United States*. Oxford University Press: New York 2020.
24 Rodrik, Dani: *op. cit.*
25 Norris, Pippa/Inglehart, Ronald: *op. cit.*
26 Hooghe, Liesbet/Marks, Gary: "A Postfunctionalist Theory of European Integration: From Permissive Consensus to Constraining Dissensus." *British Journal of Political Science* 39 (1), 2008, pp. 1–23.

conservative populists are uncomfortable with new moral frameworks and their advocates, lamenting the legalization of abortion, gay marriage, and LGBTQ+ rights, and rejecting new gender roles. Thus, American conservative populists should score highly on *social traditionalism*.

A final value dimension that may draw on nationalist and traditionalist sentiments but can also feed off economic stress is *welfare chauvinism*.[27] Ennser-Jedenastik sees this as "an important element in the agenda of the populist radical right" everywhere.[28] Welfare chauvinists want public benefits confined to "worthy" members of society—primarily "hard-working" native citizens—and denied to "lazy" and "unworthy" immigrants, aliens, or minority groups. Such attitudes fester when ethnic and cultural diversity increases in a society,[29] and often become racialized.[30] Although American analysts have not usually employed this term, they have often described the same phenomenon in public opinion.[31]

Although scholars debate the relative weight of these "cultural" dimensions, most would concede that they all play some role in fostering conservative populism. We find that these dimensions are tightly knit in a broader Populist Syndrome, although one with some interesting modifications since 2016. Despite these changes, religious variables still make a distinctive contribution to our understanding of American conservative populism.

Theory: Religion

In examining religion, our concepts are drawn from the insights of two theoretical frameworks. The first is *ethnocultural* theory, used primarily by historians, who contend that competing ethnoreligious groups have constituted the building blocks of American political party coalitions.[32] Thus, the older British and Western

---

27 Kros, Mathijs/Coenders, Marcel: 'Explaining Differences in Welfare Chauvinism between and with Individuals Over Time'. *European Sociological Review* 35 (6), 2019, pp. 860–873.
28 Ennser-Jedenastik, Laurenz: "Welfare Chauvinism in Populist Radical Right Platforms." *Social Policy and Administration* 52 (1), 2018, pp. 293–314.
29 Van der Meer, Tom/Reeskens, Tim: "Welfare Chauvinism in the Face of Ethnic Diversity." *European Sociological Review* 37 (1), 2021, pp. 89–103.
30 Harell, Alison/Soroka, Stuart/Ladner, Kiera: "Public Opinion, Prejudice and the Racialization of Welfare in Canada." *Ethnic and Racial Studies* 14 (37), 2014, pp. 2580–2597.
31 Edsall, Tom: "The Rise of 'Welfare Chauvinism' in the United States." *New York Times*, December 17, 2014. https://www.nytimes.com/2014/12/17/opinion/the-rise-of-welfare-chauvinism.html.
32 For a review and summary, see: Swierenga, Robert P.: "Religion and American Voting Behavior, 1830s to 1930s." In: Smidt, Corwin E./Kellstedt, Lyman A./Guth, James L.

European Protestant traditions have usually been the core of the GOP, and ethnoreligious minorities, such as Catholics, Jews, and Black Protestants have preferred the Democrats. A more recent competing perspective is the *religious restructuring* or *culture wars* theory, drawn from the sociology of religion, which posits that most ethnoreligious traditions are now divided along *theological* lines between the "orthodox" (sometimes "traditionalists" or "conservatives") and religious "progressives" (sometimes "liberals"). These new theological tendencies, rather than the historic traditions, are now the primary factor shaping religious politics, with the orthodox favoring the GOP, and the progressives, the Democrats.[33] Finally, the growing inroads of secularization have added the religiously unaffiliated ("Nones") to the Democratic side—especially if they claim a consciously "secular" or "secularist" identity.[34]

We expect that both perspectives should provide some insight into the religious location of conservative populist attitudes. The historic white American ethnoreligious traditions might well be more susceptible to several populist themes, while ethnoreligious minorities should be more resistant. At the same time, religious traditionalists may find more to like in populist politics than their more progressive religious counterparts—or secular citizens—do.

Data and Methods

We use the 2020 American National Election Study (ANES) to analyze conservative populism and examine its religious nexus. As the "gold standard" for political science surveys, the ANES provides several tested religious measures and a large N (7,453) in the post-election sample, allowing us to include many ethnoreligious groups in the analysis. And the survey has multiple items tapping the dimensions of conservative populism. Almost all the variables used here are highly reliable scores derived from principal components analyses (PCA), facilitating multivariate analysis and giving us considerable confidence in the robustness of our results. Indeed, alternative specifications using fewer or more variables produce very similar results.[35]

(eds.): *The Oxford Handbook of Religion and American Politics.* Oxford University Press: New York 2009, pp. 69–94.

33 See: Wuthnow, Robert: *The Restructuring of American Religion.* Princeton University Press: Princeton 1988; Hunter, James D.: *Culture Wars: The Struggle to Define America.* Basic Books: New York 1991; Kellstedt, Lyman A./Guth, James L.: *op. cit.*

34 Campbell, David E./Layman, Geoffrey C./Green, John C.: *Secular Surge: A New Fault Line in American Politics.* Cambridge University Press: Cambridge 2021.

35 We briefly describe the items included in each measure of populism traits here, but for more detailed information on their construction, see: Guth, James L.: "Religion and American Populism: The View from the 2020 American National Election Study."

Although lacking a full range of religious measures, ANES 2020 has enough items to evaluate the insights of the ethnocultural and religious restructuring theories. First, detailed questions on religious affiliation, ethnicity, and race allow us to assign respondents into specific ethnoreligious traditions, following the RELTRAD scheme used by most political scientists and sociologists.[36] Testing the restructuring approach is a little more complicated, as the ANES has several items that allow us to operationalize "orthodox" or "progressive" religious worldviews more or less directly. In previous work, we used these measures individually as predictors of populist attitudes, but here we use a summary measure, a principal components analysis (PCA) score combining several measures: view of the Bible; thermometer ratings for "Christian fundamentalists" and "Christians"; a summary of religious identifications[37]; and status as a "born-again Christian."[38] Although we might have preferred items such as belief in God, the afterlife, etc. that might be more appropriate to religious traditionalists of all faiths, this measure clearly differentiates among Americans from broadly Christian backgrounds, producing a continuum from the most secular to the most traditionalist. In addition, we tap *religiosity*, combining religious service attendance and the importance of religion in one's life (*theta* = .77). Although not a direct measure of traditionalism, the "orthodox" predominate among the highly observant, and "progressives" among the less faithful. Although religiosity might be added to the traditionalism measure, we kept it separate, as religious participation sometimes produces different results than theological orientation, especially in multivariate analysis.

Paper presented at the annual meeting of the American Political Science Association, Seattle, 30.09.2021–03.10.2021.

36 See: Smidt, Corwin E./Kellstedt, Lyman A./Guth, James L. (eds.): *The Oxford Handbook of Religion and American Politics*. Oxford University Press: New York 2009; Steensland, Brian/Park, Jerry/Regnerus, Mark/Robinson, Lynn/Wilcox, Bradford/Woodberry, Robert: "The Measure of American Religion." *Social Forces* 79 (1), 2000, pp. 291–318.

37 The identification scale was created from ANES items as follows: (3) "Traditionalists" include anyone taking "evangelical," "fundamentalist," "Pentecostal/charismatic," or "traditional" identities; (2) "None" includes all not responding or choosing "none" as a response; (1) *Progressive* includes "progressive," "spiritual but not religious," or "nontraditional"; and (0) *Secular* includes all choosing that identity.

38 The four "restructuring" items produced a single PCA component with an eigenvalue of 2.849 and these loadings: views of the Bible (.81), "Christian fundamentalist" thermometer (.81), "Christian" thermometer (.78), religious identification scale (.70), and "born-again" status (.67). *Theta* reliability = .81.

Religion and "Thin" Populism: Political System Beliefs

To examine the impact of religious factors on each "thin" dimension of conservative populism, in the following tables, we report their bivariate correlations and then turn to OLS regression to assess the direct influences of ethnoreligious traditions and theology on each dimension. (We include controls for age, gender, income, and education in the analyses but do not report the results except for occasional observations in the text.)

Majoritarian Rough Politics

We begin with majoritarian rough politics, a key feature of the populist "style." This score is derived from items tapping beliefs that majorities should rule and minorities adapt to that rule; that a strong leader is necessary, unconstrained by Congress or the courts; that force should be used to stop civil protests; that people are "too sensitive" in political discussions; that compromising leaders are "selling out" their followers; and that firearms should be more easily available to citizens. The score also includes the standard authoritarianism scale (*theta* = .77).

We might expect that religious factors play an important role here. Cynthia Burack found that "imprecatory prayers" expressing many themes of rough politics were characteristic of "right-wing" clerical leaders (almost all from the evangelical tradition) and might well influence their followers[39] (as might the language of populist politicians). As the first column in Table 1 shows, ethnoreligious traditions have distinctive positions: white evangelicals indeed are the most "populist," followed at a distance by white Catholics, Latino evangelicals, Eastern Orthodox, Latter-day Saints, and Mainline Protestants, who are very near the sample mean. Atheists and agnostics occupy the anti-populist pole, the counterpart to white evangelicals. Jews, the unaffiliated ("Nothing in Particular"), Black Protestants, members of World Religions (Muslims, Hindus, Buddhists, Sikhs, Baha'is), and Latino Catholics follow in decreasing levels of opposition. Finally, religious restructuring variables also have clear ties to this majoritarian bent: conservative theology has a very strong correlation and religiosity, usually another marker of orthodox belief, and has a solid positive tie as well.

Of course, these religious variables are interrelated in complex ways: Black Protestants and white evangelicals tend to be more religiously committed than mainline Protestants, for example, and secular citizens are unlikely to hold conservative theological views. To ascertain the relative influence of ethnoreligious affiliation and religious restructuring variables, we ran an OLS regression. As the second column shows, the ethnoreligious coefficients drop considerably from the bivariate level, but those for evangelicals and white Catholics still point toward

---

39 Burack, Cynthia: "Let Death Seize Upon Them: Populism in Political Prayers of Imprecation." *Politics and Religion* 13 (3), 2020, pp. 492–516.

greater populism, and those for Black Protestants, atheists, and agnostics, and Jews still contribute to opposition. But conservative theology retains all its power, suggesting that the large bivariate correlations for evangelicals and atheists/agnostics are partly an artifact of their traditional religious beliefs (or lack of them). Note, however, that anti-populism *increases* among Black Protestants once the effects of their conservative theology are held constant. Even in that ethnoreligious community, then, conservative belief has populist implications.

One restructuring measure behaves strangely, however. Although conservative theology and religiosity are highly correlated ($r = .70$), the religiosity coefficient "flips signs" in the regression and predicts *less* support for majoritarian rough politics. This suggests that (atypical) "liberal" religiosity produces anti-populist sentiments, *not* that religiosity has a moderating effect on orthodox believers. (In fact, bivariate data shows that the populism score rises with each increase in both religiosity and traditional theology.) Altogether, religious variables explain an impressive 30% of the variance. And these effects are independent of demographic influences: including education, income, age, and gender in the analysis ha virtually no effect on the religious coefficients and adds only 4% to the variance explained (data not shown).[40]

Distrust of Government

Distrust of government and government officials is a trait universally ascribed to populists. Our score is derived from nine standard items asking how often the government in Washington can be trusted to do what's right, whether government is run for the benefit of a few big interests, how much tax money is wasted, how many politicians are corrupt (two items), whether politicians care about people, whether they are trustworthy, or whether they only care about the rich (*theta* = .78). Even with this robust measure our analysis produces ambivalent results for the theory, showing little religious impact. This is primarily due to the pervasive political distrust characterizing Americans: when everyone is cynical about politicians, few variables explain the extent of that cynicism.

Despite this limitation, in 2016 we found weak tendencies for evangelicals to be more distrustful, and religious minorities of all sorts somewhat more positive, but the effect of other religious variables was small and inconsistent, with religious variables explaining only 6% of the variance.[41] By 2020 the influence of religion was even more attenuated. As Table 1 shows, evangelicals were mildly more cynical and some religious minorities a little less so, but the ethnoreligious picture is very mixed. Conservative theology pointed to a little *more* trust, and religiosity,

---

40 Although the impact of the demographic factors varies, higher education tends to reduce all populist traits and women are less populist, but age and income have only a few very modest effects.

41 Guth, James L.: "Are White Evangelicals Populists?," *op. cit.*, p. 23.

Table 1. Religion and Process Traits of Conservative Populism: (Pearson's *r and OLS betas*)

	Majoritarian Rough Politics		Distrust Government		Declinism		Distrust Experts	
	r=	*b=*	*r=*	*b=*	*r=*	*b=*	*r=*	*b=*
Ethnoreligious Tradition								
White Evangelical	.27***	.06***	.05***	.05**	−.18***	−.05***	.28***	.13***
White Catholic	.08***	.08***	−.04***	−.04*	−.07***	−.06**	−.00	.03*
Latter-day Saints	.03*	.01	−.01	−.02	−.06***	−.04***	.05***	.03*
Latino Evangelical	.07***	−.02	−.01	−.01	−.06*	.00	.06***	−.01
Mainline Protestant	.02*	.02	−.08***	−.07***	−.05*	−.05***	.00	.03*
Eastern Orthodox	.04***	.00	−.04***	−.04*	−.03*	.00	.03**	−.00
Latino Catholic	−.02	−.01	−.01	−.02	.03*	.03*	−.03**	−.05***
Nothing in Particular	−.08***	.02	.07***	−.01	.05***	−.03	−.01	.06***
World Religions	−.04***	.02	−.04***	−.05***	−.01	−.04***	−.06***	−.02
Jews	−.10***	−.02*	−.04***	−.06***	.06***	.01	−.09***	−.03**
Black Protestant	−.06***	−.14***	.02*	.01	.13***	.18***	−.04***	−.12***
Atheist/Agnostic	−.28***	−.05**	.01	−.04*	.18***	.03	−.25***	−.06***
Conservative Theology	.51***	.51***	−.03*	−.05**	−.33***	−.39***	.42***	.36***
Religiosity	.30***	−.07***	.03*	.03	−.20***	.05**	.25***	−.01
R squared= *Religion*		**.30**		**.02**		**.16**		**.22**
R squared= *Controls*		**.34**		**.04**		**.18**		**.26**

Source: American National Election Study 2020.

***p <. 001; **p <. 01; *p <.05.

a little less. Perhaps the finding for conservative theology reflects the impact of Trump's appeal to conservative believers, although his constant attack on the "deep state" may have limited that effect. Nevertheless, the variance explained by religion is even less than in 2016—only 2%. Clearly, religion was even less of a contributor to political cynicism than it had been four years earlier.

Declinism

Speculation about the possible impact of the Trump regime seems more warranted on another "populist" dimension: declinism, a central feature of populist ideology. In 2016, evangelicals and other religious traditionalists saw the country on the "wrong track" and suffering economically, attitudes bolstered by evangelical identification and conservative theology.[42] Do we still find this attitude among American religious populists? Or are they more optimistic after four years of a congenial administration? Our declinism score comes from thirteen items on respondents' sentiments about the national situation: whether they felt hopeful, afraid, outraged, angry, happy, worried, proud, irritated, or nervous; whether the country was on the wrong track; whether the economy was worse; whether the income gap was larger; and whether opportunity for mobility had declined (*theta* = .91). A much more elaborate measure than the one we used in 2016, it taps even more effectively sentiments about national fortunes.

But here we find a dramatic religious change. In Table 1 all the signs have "flipped" from their direction in 2016, as the religion variables fostering declinism then now work against it. Evangelicals (and to a much lesser extent, other white traditions), theological conservatives, and the observant are all more *positive* about the "state of the union" than are ethnoreligious minorities, theological progressives, and secularists. Once again, conservative theology proves most potent in the regression, but ethnoreligious tradition retains some influence, with Black Protestants again becoming *more* anti-populist when theology and religiosity are controlled, although atheists and agnostics are not more pessimistic than their "theology"—or rather, their lack of one—would predict.

The key to this religious conversion, of course, is that a populist occupied the White House after 2017, producing sentiments among his followers at odds with characterizations by theories of populism. Obviously, not all features of conservative populist ideology are constants: some are situational, shaped by the dictates of oppositional politics. Once populists are in power, the incentives for emphasizing themes useful in opposition may diminish or even reverse, creating a different configuration of attitudes. The evidence here shows that the religious impact on populists' sentiment about their nation's future had thoroughly reversed from 2016. "Populist" and anti-populist religious groups had traded places on this "core" feature of populist ideology.

---

42 *Ibid.*, pp. 23–28.

Distrust of Experts

One populist "thin" trait that has received much scholarly and journalistic attention has been distrust of expertise and trust in the judgment of ordinary people. This trait takes various forms, depending on whether the "expert" is scientific, academic, journalistic, or even bureaucratic. The populist propensity is to prefer the judgment of common folks to that of any knowledge elite. Among American populists—and those elsewhere—this has recently been exhibited in antagonism toward expert judgments on evolution, global warming, and the COVID-19 pandemic, whether issued by scientists or government officials. Similarly, populists distrust the "mainstream" media and journalistic expertise, echoing their leaders' complaints about "fake news," and preferring "alternative facts." Although we initially expected some differences in the assessment of scientific expertise and evaluation of the media, we found that two separate measures were highly correlated. Thus we have created a global *distrust of experts* score from twelve individual ANES items: seven assessing trust in science and scientists and five eliciting confidence in journalists and the media (*theta* = .85).

Religion has a substantial impact on regard for expertise. As the last section of Table 1 shows, white evangelicals and atheists/agnostics once more occupy polar positions. Latter-day Saints and Latino evangelicals are less skeptical, while religious minorities are generally somewhat more trusting. As expected, conservative theology and religiosity point strongly against respect for expertise. The regression reveals the power of conservative theology but does not eliminate the impact of membership in many ethnoreligious traditions, especially evangelicals' greater distrust and Black Protestants' more positive response to expertise. The inclusion of demographic variables modestly increases the variance explained (most of this is from education's effects) from 22% to 26%, but it does not alter the religious coefficients, except for several that actually *increase* under controls (data not shown).

To summarize: examination of religious influences on the "thin" traits of conservative populism reveals both continuity and change. On majoritarian rough politics, religious patterns look remarkably similar to those in 2016: evangelicals and those adhering to conservative theology are still prone to adopt this facet of populist politics, while ethnoreligious minorities, religious progressives, and secularists form the opposition. Almost identical patterns appear on another feature of conservative populism: distrust of professional expertise. But on two putative marks of conservative populism, distrust of politicians and declinism, the weight of religion has shifted: the "conservative" religious variables no longer point consistently toward political distrust, while on declinism, they push in a distinctly more *optimistic* direction. Just as public economic assessments are increasingly determined by partisanship, rather than real conditions,[43] declinism may rise and fall with transitions in the White House.

---

43 Gerber, Alan/Huber, Gregory: "Partisanship, Political Control and Economic

Religion and Populist Policy Beliefs

Perhaps it is not surprising that assessments of political processes and participants should change with the identity of those in charge, but policy preferences of conservative populists should exhibit greater stability. Indeed, these aspects of the ideology should have even stronger connections to religion. And that is just what we see. Table 2 reports on the influence of religion on white nationalism, traditional social values, and welfare chauvinism.

White Nationalism

In the massive literature on recent American electoral politics, an array of theories has argued for the centrality of "identity" factors. Many focus on ethnic identity, whether expressed as a "positive" identification with "whites"[44] or, more frequently, as anti-immigrant sentiment, nativism, "white power" ideologies, or Islamophobia.[45] Although some approaches reference "white Christian" or "white Protestant" as part of the phenomenon, religion seldom plays any direct role in the analysis. Others see a larger role for religion, as in Whitehead and Perry's work on "Christian Nationalism."[46] Despite these different foci, we may have a case of the blind men and the elephant: all these "identity" variables are powerfully related.

We created a white nationalism score from scales and individual items tapping several attitudes stressed in the literature cited above: toward immigration and immigrants (12 items); preference for white political power (four items); whether discrimination exists against minorities (seven items); whether diversity is good or bad for America; a preference for the United States to shun international commitments (four items); nativist sentiments (four items); a belief that all Americans must speak English; and finally, a thermometer rating for "Muslims," capturing attitudes toward that important religious reference group (*theta reliability* = .93).

Once again, white evangelicals are the most adamant adherents of white nationalism, with atheists and agnostics on the other end. Both conservative theology and religiosity are strongly related to this score, and the regression results show that conservative theology is the driving force among religious variables, while religiosity drops and once more "flips signs." Membership in many ethnoreligious groups retains significance, perhaps reflecting the "ethnic" part of identity. Once

---

Assessments." *American Journal of Political Science* 54 (1), 2010, pp. 153–173.
44 Jardina, Ashley: *op. cit.*
45 Sides, John/Tesler, Michael/Vavreck, Lynn: *op. cit.*; Skocpol, Theda: *op. cit.*
46 Whitehead, Andrew/Perry, Samuel: *op. cit.* See also: Guth, James L.: "Protestant Clergy and Christian Nationalism." *Perspectives in Religious Studies* 48 (2), 2021, pp. 135–147.

more demographic variables are largely independent of religious measures—but add only 4% to the variance explained by religion.

Table 2. Religion and the Ideology of Conservative Populism: (Pearson's r and OLS betas)

	White Nationalism		Social Traditionalism		Welfare Chauvinism	
	$r=$	$b=$	$r=$	$b=$	$r=$	$b=$
Ethnoreligious Tradition						
White Evangelical	.29***	.10***	.34***	.11***	.29***	.13***
White Catholic	.10***	.11***	.06***	.06***	.14***	.12***
Latter-day Saints	.03***	.02	.08***	.05***	.06***	.05***
Latino Evangelical	.02	−.04***	.07***	−.02	.01	−.04***
Mainline Protestant	.06***	.06***	.02*	.02	.07***	.10***
Eastern Orthodox	.02	.00	.03*	.00	.03	.01
Latino Catholic	−.06***	−.06***	−.00	−.01	−.05***	−.05***
Nothing in Particular	−.07***	.05***	−.10***	.08***	.01	.07***
World Religions	−.06***	−.01	−.05***	−.01	−.04**	−.00
Jews	−.07***	−.00	−.09***	−.01	−.07***	−.03*
Black Protestant	−.04***	−.10***	−.04**	−.13***	−.24***	−.26***
Atheist/Agnostic	−.29***	−.05***	−.32***	−.02	−.22***	−.03*
Conservative Theology	.50***	.46***	.54***	.50***	.38***	.41***
Religiosity	.31***	−.04**	.44***	.08***	.22***	−.06***
R squared=	Religion	.30		.40		.28
R squared=	Controls	.34		.43		.30

Source: American National Election Study 2020.

***p <. 001; **p <. 01; *p<. 05.

This analysis shows that most of the theories related to nationalist explanations of populism have a good bit of validity. The American populist version of white nationalism has not only been evident in Trump administration policies but is imbedded in grassroots sentiment. And religion plays a significant role, as evangelicals and other religious conservatives are the chief proponents of this dimension of populist ideology, with ethnoreligious minorities, religious liberals, and secularists aligned on the other side.

Social Traditionalism

As we observed earlier, most analysts of conservative populism concede some role for social traditionalism in its development. For some, traditionalism is simply a marker for those disadvantaged by the globalized economy: the modestly educated, rural residents, or the blue-collar population—who inevitably hold traditionalist attitudes because of their social position. Other scholars, however, join Norris and Inglehart[47] in positing a causal role for the persisting value conflict between *materialist* (and socially traditionalist) populations and the *post-materialist* (and socially liberal) vanguard as central to the rise of populism. However described, social traditionalism usually has deep religious roots.

Our social traditionalism score is derived from eighteen items tapping attitudes on gay rights, abortion, feminism, "postmaterialist" values, and the death penalty (*theta* = .87). The second section of Table 2 shows the impact of religious variables. The correlations reveal a yawning gap between evangelicals and the atheist/agnostic camp, with most ethnoreligious groups taking their accustomed positions: the predominantly white groups modestly on the traditionalist side, and ethnoreligious minorities, on the other. Social conservatism is also powerfully linked to conservative theology and religiosity, confirmed by the regression, which shows that conservative theology is buttressed by religiosity—which does not change signs in this analysis, unlike in earlier cases. With both theology and religiosity included, coefficients for most ethnoreligious minorities drop out, except for Black Protestants, for whom it increases once again. On the other side, coefficients for evangelicals, white Catholics, Latter-day Saints, and non-affiliates remain significant and positive. Religion explains two-fifths of the variance, an impressive result. Once again, sociodemographics have little impact on the religious coefficients and add only 3% to the overall variance explained.

Welfare Chauvinism

Finally, we examine welfare chauvinism, based on thirteen ANES items, with seven asking about affirmative action or other assistance to Blacks and six items on support for greater social welfare spending (*theta* = .91). In a "racialized" American context, this measure gets at the heart of welfare chauvinism. How does religion influence such attitudes?

To borrow from the New York Yankee catcher and political sage Yogi Berra, the results are "*déjà vu* all over again," replicating those for white nationalism and social traditionalism, albeit with a slightly smaller gap between evangelical and atheist/agnostic camps. Ethnoreligious minorities—especially Black Protestants—oppose chauvinism, perhaps unremarkably. At the bivariate level, both conservative theology and religiosity are associated with chauvinism. Once more, the regression reveals the

---

47 Norris, Pippa/Inglehart, Ronald: *op. cit.*

strength of conservative theology, but membership in most ethnoreligious traditions retains significant influence in the expected directions. Religious variables explain 28% of the variance, and demographic factors add only 2%.

For the "policy" dimensions, several conclusions are warranted. First, the impact of religious variables on all three dimensions is quite similar. True, religiosity does not "flip signs" on social traditionalism, and Black Protestants are especially distinctive on welfare chauvinism, but overall the patterns are much alike. Second, all the policy dimensions not only reveal the powerful influence of conservative theology but also exhibit some continuing distinctiveness of ethnoreligious traditions. Evangelicals' populism, for example, is clearly due to something more than their conservative theology. Third, the impact of ethnoreligious tradition is sometimes changed when controls for theology and religiosity are introduced. Black Protestants often become *more distinct*, once their conservative theology and high religiosity are accounted for, while the dramatic effects of identifying as atheist/agnostic are largely eliminated.

Putting It All Together: Religion and the "Populist Syndrome"

The strong similarity of religious responses to these putative conservative populist dimensions suggests that they are related. To confirm this, we ran a secondary principal components analysis (PCA) of the dimension scores, producing two factors, with all dimensions except distrust of government loading strongly on the first, confirming that distrust was not a distinguishing feature of conservative populism during the Trump years. The other six scores formed a remarkably "tight" dimension, with very high loadings for white nationalism (.91), social traditionalism (.90), welfare chauvinism (.88), majoritarian rough politics (.89), and distrust of expertise (.83)—but also optimism about the nation's condition (−.69 for declinism), a major shift from 2016. And the resulting score has very impressive reliability (*theta* = .90). We think this measure aptly captures the conservative populism described by most observers.[48]

To conclude, we put conservative populism in a broader political context, examining the influence of religion as mediated by political factors. Table 3 reports bivariate correlations of the Populist Syndrome with religious and political variables, as well as two OLS regressions: the first with religious variables only (again with demographic controls), and the second incorporating partisanship and ideology. The correlations show a very familiar pattern, with Syndrome scores ranging from the very populist

---

48 This finding also suggests caution about efforts to pinpoint which of these factors is the "most" powerful in influencing particular religious groups, given their extremely high intercorrelations (cf. Marsh, Wayde Z.C.: "Putting US First: How Outgroup Hostilities and Defense of the Status Quo Motivate White Evangelical Affect toward Candidates in U.S. Elections 2004–2016." *American Politics Research* 49 (5), 2021, pp. 534–547).

evangelicals to the strongly anti-populist atheists and agnostics, with the historic white traditions mildly on the Populist side and the ethnoreligious minorities arrayed on the other. Conservative theology and religiosity have strong positive correlations with the Syndrome. (Demographic variables again have a modest impact: education works against populism and women are marginally less populist.) Politics, naturally, is connected, with Republicans and conservatives adopting populist ideology.

Table 3. Religion, Politics and the Populist Syndrome (Pearson's *r* and OLS *betas*)

	Pearson's r=	Model 1 Religious Variables (with controls) b=	Model 2 + Political Variables b=
Ethnoreligious Tradition			
Evangelical	.32***	.11***	.02*
White Catholic	.09***	.09***	.02
Latter-day Saints	.06***	.04***	.00
Latino Evangelical	.05***	−.03*	−.00
Mainline Protestant	.02**	.05***	.01
Eastern Orthodox	.04**	−.00	.01
Latino Catholic	−.03*	−.04***	.01
Nothing in Particular	−.05*	.05***	.03***
World Religions	−.05***	.00	.02**
Jewish	−.09***	−.02*	.00
Black Protestant	−.09***	−.18***	−.01
Atheist/Agnostic	−.31***	−.05***	−.02
Conservative Theology	.54**	.42***	.18***
Religiosity	.34**	−.03*	−.03**
Political Factors			
Party ID (GOP)	.76***		.41***
Ideology (Conservative)	.74***		.37***
Adj. R squared=	Religion	**.36**	**.36**
Adj. R squared=	All Variables	**.39**	**.71**

Source: American National Election Study 2020.

***p <. 001; **p <. 01; *p <. 05.

Model 1 shows that religious variables are powerful predictors of conservative populism, with conservative theology again leading the way, while many of the ethnoreligious traditions retain significant influence in expected directions. Indeed, religion alone explains well over a third of the variance in Syndrome scores. And Model 2 shows that most ethnoreligious influences are mediated by partisanship and ideology, as their coefficients are reduced to insignificance. This should not be a surprise: ethnicity and religion are now dominant features of American party coalitions,[49] and populist styles and attitudes have been assiduously adopted by Republicans. But note that religious restructuring variables still *add* to the explanation, even when partisanship and ideology are in the equation: conservative theology retains a significantly added "punch," while religiosity once more reverses signs and has a modest negative effect on populist attitudes. In all, Model 3 explains 71% of the variance.

Summary and Conclusions

Our exploration of the way religion shapes key dimensions of conservative populism reveals considerable continuity since 2016, as well as significant changes. Most attitudes constituting populism then were still present four years later: majoritarian rough politics, disdain for expertise, white nationalism, social traditionalism, and welfare chauvinism were, if anything, more tightly integrated in a populist belief system than in 2016. On the other hand, declinist perceptions had given way to optimism about the national condition. Both the features of continuity and change may reflect the impact of the Trump presidency, constantly emphasizing central populist themes, on the one hand, but providing hope to supporters, on the other.

Similarly, the religious contributions to conservative populism in 2020 look much like those in 2016. Evangelicals still formed the religious vanguard of conservative populism, with atheists, agnostics, and "secular" citizens leading the resistance. The older "white" mainline Protestant, Catholic, and LDS traditions provided some populist support, while most ethnoreligious "minorities" were on the other side. Within many of these communities (especially among mainline Protestants and white Catholics), the religiously orthodox and observant were more tempted by populism than their progressive and generally less observant brethren.[50]

All these tendencies fed into the party system, with the strongest Republican religious constituencies exhibiting the most pronounced populist tendencies, not

---

49 Margolis, Michele: "Who Wants to Make America Great Again? Evangelical Support for Donald Trump." *Politics and Religion* 13 (1), 2020, pp. 89–118.
50 This was true even in the Jewish community, where Orthodox and Conservative Jews fell on the populist side of the national mean, while Reform and unaffiliated Jews were strongly anti-populist.

only on substantive policy but also on political process and style, contributing to what we have called the "rough politics" element of the party. Still, the populism measure may capture a powerful political force not entirely encapsulated in traditional partisanship and ideology. If, for example, we include it with partisanship and ideology in a stepwise binary logistic regression of the 2020 presidential vote, it enters the equation *first*, before the traditional partisan and ideological identities, suggesting that it adds something new to the electoral equation.

What does all this augur for the future of conservative populist politics? To the extent that populist preferences are influenced by religious developments, we might foresee two different scenarios. For optimists on the left, the declining evangelical population and faltering American religiosity, combined with burgeoning numbers of ethnoreligious minorities and unaffiliated Americans, might seem to augur well for a more civil, moderate, or even "progressive" political process. On the other hand, those very trends might well exacerbate the "culture wars" confronting American society, with the Republican party increasingly embodying populist people (and a "populist style" of rough politics) and the Democrats capturing the opposition, perhaps demanding a return to "the regular order," but often tempted to emulate the approach of their opponents if necessary to win. Indeed, if recent events are any indication, this latter possibility seems more likely, albeit much less auspicious for the future of the United States.

References

Bonikowski, Bart: "Trump's Populism: The Mobilization of Nationalist Cleavages and the Future of US Democracy." In: Weyland, Kurt/Madrid, Raúl (eds.): *When Democracy Trumps Populism: European and Latin American Lessons for the United States*. Cambridge University Press: Cambridge 2019, pp. 110–131.

Burack, Cynthia: "Let Death Seize Upon Them: Populism in Political Prayers of Imprecation." *Politics and Religion* 13 (3), 2020, pp. 492–516.

Campbell, David E./Layman, Geoffrey C./Green, John C.: *Secular Surge: A New Fault Line in American Politics*. Cambridge University Press: Cambridge 2021.

Collins, Harry/Evans, Robert/Durant, Darrin/Weinel, Martin: *Experts and the Will of the People: Society, Populism and Science*. Palgrave Macmillan: London 2020.

Eatwell, Roger/Goodwin, Matthew: *National Populism: The Revolt Against Liberal Democracy*. Penguin Random House: London 2018.

Edsall, Tom: "The Rise of 'Welfare Chauvinism' in the United States." *New York Times*, December 17, 2014. https://www.nytimes.com/2014/12/17/opinion/the-rise-of-welfare-chauvinism.html.

Ennser-Jedenastik, Laurenz: "Welfare Chauvinism in Populist Radical Right Platforms." *Social Policy and Administration* 52 (1), 2018, pp. 293–314.

Gerber, Alan/Huber, Gregory: "Partisanship, Political Control and Economic Assessments." *American Journal of Political Science* 54 (1), 2010, pp. 153–173.

Guth, James L.: "Are White Evangelicals Populists? The View from the 2016 American National Election Study." *Review of Faith and International Affairs* 17 (3), 2019, pp. 20–35.

Guth, James L.: "Protestant Clergy and Christian Nationalism." *Perspectives in Religious Studies* 48 (2), 2021, pp. 135–147.

Guth, James L.: "Religion and American Populism: The View from the 2020 American National Election Study." Paper presented at the annual meeting of the American Political Science Association, Seattle, 30.09.2021–03.10.2021.

Guth, James L./Nelsen, Brent F.: "Party Choice in Europe: Social Cleavages and the Rise of Populist Parties." *Party Politics* 27 (3), 2021, pp. 453–464.

Harell, Alison/Soroka, Stuart/Ladner, Kiera: "Public Opinion, Prejudice and the Racialization of Welfare in Canada." *Ethnic and Racial Studies* 14 (37), 2014, pp. 2580–2597.

Hooghe, Liesbet/Marks, Gary: "A Postfunctionalist Theory of European Integration: From Permissive Consensus to Constraining Dissensus." *British Journal of Political Science* 39 (1), 2008, pp. 1–23.

Hunter, James D.: *Culture Wars: The Struggle to Define America*. Basic Books: New York 1991.

Jardina, Ashley: *White Identity Politics*. Cambridge University Press: Cambridge 2019.

Kaufmann, Eric: *Whiteshift: Populism, Immigration, and the Future of White Majorities*. Abrams Press: New York 2019.

Kellstedt, Lyman A./Guth, James L.: "Religion and Electoral Behavior in the United States, 1936–2016." In: Malici, Akan/Smith, Elizabeth (eds.): *Political Science Research in Practice*. 2nd ed. Routledge: New York 2019, pp. 117–136.

Kros, Mathijs/Coenders, Marcel: "Explaining Differences in Welfare Chauvinism between and with Individuals Over Time." *European Sociological Review* 35 (6), 2019, pp. 860–873.

Lee, Frances: "Populism and the American Party System: Opportunities and Constraints." *Perspectives on Politics* 18 (2), 2020, pp. 370–388.

Margolis, Michele: "Who Wants to Make America Great Again? Evangelical Support for Donald Trump." *Politics and Religion* 13 (1), 2020, pp. 89–118.

Marsh, Wayde Z.C.: "Putting US First: How Outgroup Hostilities and Defense of the Status Quo Motivate White Evangelical Affect Toward Candidates in U.S. Elections 2004–2016." *American Politics Research* 49 (5), 2021, pp. 534–547.

Marzouki, Nadia/McDonnell, Duncan/Roy, Olivier (eds.): *Saving the People: How Populists Hijack Religion*. Oxford University Press: New York 2016.

Mudde, Cas: *Populism: A Very Short Introduction*. 2nd ed. Oxford University Press: New York 2017.

Müller, Jan-Werner: *What Is Populism?* University of Pennsylvania Press: Philadelphia 2016.

Norris, Pippa: "Measuring Populism Worldwide." *Party Politics* (online). 2020. https://journals.sagepub.com/doi/10.1177/1354068820927686.

Norris, Pippa/Inglehart, Ronald: *Cultural Backlash: Trump, Brexit, and Authoritarian Populism.* Cambridge University Press: Cambridge 2019.

Rodrik, Dani: "Why Does Globalization Fuel Populism: Economics, Culture and the Rise of Right-Wing Populism?" Working Paper 27526. National Bureau of Economic Research: Cambridge, MA 2020.

Sides, John/Tesler, Michael/Vavreck, Lynn: *Identity Crisis: The 2016 Presidential Campaign and the Battle for the Meaning of America.* Princeton University Press: Princeton 2018.

Skocpol, Theda: "The Elite and Popular Roots of Contemporary Republican Extremism." In: Skocpol, Theda/Tervo, Caroline (eds.): *Upending American Politics.* Oxford University Press: New York 2020, pp. 3–27.

Smidt, Corwin E./Kellstedt, Lyman A./Guth, James L. (eds.): *The Oxford Handbook of Religion and American Politics.* Oxford University Press: New York 2009.

Steensland, Brian/Park, Jerry/Regnerus, Mark/Robinson, Lynn/Wilcox, Bradford/Woodberry, Robert: "The Measure of American Religion." *Social Forces* 79 (1), 2000, pp. 291–318.

Swierenga, Robert P.: "Religion and American Voting Behavior, 1830s to 1930s." In: Smidt, Corwin E./Kellstedt, Lyman A./Guth, James L. (eds.): *The Oxford Handbook of Religion and American Politics.* Oxford University Press: New York 2009, pp. 69–94.

Van der Meer, Tom/Reeskens, Tim: "Welfare Chauvinism in the Face of Ethnic Diversity." *European Sociological Review* 37 (1), 2021, pp. 89–103.

Weyland, Kurt: "Populism's Threat to Democracy: Comparative Lessons for the United States." *Perspectives on Politics* 18 (2), 2020, pp. 389–406.

Weyland, Kurt/Madrid, Raúl (eds.): *When Democracy Trumps Populism: European and Latin American Lessons for the United States.* Cambridge University Press: Cambridge 2019.

Whitehead, Andrew/Perry, Samuel: *Taking America Back for God: Christian Nationalism in the United States.* Oxford University Press: New York 2020.

Wuthnow, Robert: *The Restructuring of American Religion.* Princeton University Press: Princeton 1988.

Constitutional Dimensions of Religious and Political Debates in the United States

Sebastian Kubas

The Exploitation of Religious Passions in the U.S. Constitutional Practice: The Christian Right and the Judicial Review

Abstract: This chapter seeks to examine the uneasy relations between the modern liberal constitutional state and religious organizations, and the role a constitutional court can play in this regard. Attempts to institutionalize Christian cultural preferences required translating these demands into legal obligations or exemptions and, by extension, into Supreme Court decisions, which are discussed in more detail. In the area of Establishment Clause jurisprudence, the Supreme Court of the United States moved to a regime that requires direct funding of religious enterprises, while in the current Free Establishment Clause jurisprudence the Court practically abandoned the *Employment Division v. Smith* decision which means that the government needs to demonstrate a compelling interest in targeting a religious practice. This stance proved very consequential during the COVID-19 pandemic when the Court blocked some governmental regulations protecting public health. I argue that this is the Scopes Monkey Trial revisited and a feigned problem-solving.

Keywords: judicial review, religion clauses, First Amendment, accommodation of religion, religious exemptions

Introduction

The political successes of the so-called Christian Right in the last half-century and the profound transformation of American constitutional law triggered by these successes are legitimately the subject of great interest to constitutional scholars and political pundits. Recently, two sets of issues in particular have emphasized the need to critically examine the uneasy relations between the modern liberal constitutional state and religious organizations, and the role a constitutional court can play in this regard. The first is the Christian Right's staunch support for Donald Trump's presidency, which drew criticism for reinforcing authoritarian tendencies[1] and culminated in the mob attack on the U.S. Capitol on January 6, 2021, that for

---

1 See: Sunstein, Cass R. (ed.): *Can It Happen Here? Authoritarianism in America.* HarperCollins: New York 2018.

some "was a kind of Christian revolt."² According to Andrew L. Whitehead and Samuel L. Perry, Americans who sensed a threat in the form of ethnic and religious outsiders encroaching on their privileged position most likely envisioned a Trump presidency as a "return" to a better time.³ This is a cultural vision captured by Christian nationalism, that the United States is a country belonging to white Christians from roughly the 1950s, a time when "[t]o their delight, evangelicals found themselves securely within the political and cultural mainstream."⁴ The second issue is the Christian Right's resistance to health orders and restrictions imposed by authorities due to the COVID-19 pandemic. According to a recent report: "The Covid-19 crisis has largely affirmed the power government officials have to set restrictions to protect public health in almost all respects except one: religion."⁵

From an irreligious perspective, it could be argued that the issues described here have no bearing on purely religious matters. Ellis West aptly noted in 1990 that ironically, the laws involved in free exercise cases are almost never ones whose primary purpose or primary effect is to harm religion; instead, their general purpose or effect is to protect or promote the health, safety, property, morals, or general welfare of the people.⁶ This observation still holds true. We are not dealing with governmental interference with religious doctrine. Federal and state officials do not claim the authority to supervise ordinations, nor do they monitor whether the liturgy conforms to the current scientific knowledge. The legal disputes described here concern the socio-political realm: the governmental regulatory authority over social behavior, particularly with regard to the conduct of members of society, including in the commercial or educational spheres. One possible response is that such behavior of the faithful is a direct manifestation of their religious beliefs. Therefore, any governmental attempts to regulate such behavior (for instance, teaching evolution and not creationism, bans on racial segregation, or public health mandates concerning social gatherings during the pandemic) infringe on

---

2   Boorstein, Michelle: "A Horn-Wearing 'Shaman.' A Cowboy Evangelist. For Some, the Capitol Attack was a Kind of Christian Revolt." *The Washington Post*, June 6, 2021, retrieved 07.01.2022, from https://www.washingtonpost.com/religion/2021/07/06/capitol-insurrection-trump-christian-nationalism-shaman/.
3   Whitehead, Andrew L./Perry, Samuel L.: *Taking America Back for God. Christian Nationalism in the United States*. Oxford University Press: New York 2020, p. 63.
4   Kobes Du Mez, Kristin: *Jesus and John Wayne. How White Evangelicals Corrupted a Faith and Fractured a Nation*. W.W. Norton: New York 2021, p. 36.
5   Wheeler, Lydia: "Religious Objections Stand in Path of Mask, Vaccine Mandates." *Bloomberg Law*, June 29, 2021, retrieved 07.01.2022, from https://news.bloomberglaw.com/health-law-and-business/religious-objections-stand-in-path-of-mask-vaccine-mandates.
6   West, Ellis: "The Case Against a Right to Religion-Based Exemptions." *Notre Dame Journal of Law, Ethics & Public Policy* 4 (3), 1990, p. 592.

the free exercise of religion. This means that the distinction between the religious domain and the nonreligious domain in the contemporary state is unworkable. As Ran Hirschl and Ayelet Shachar note, all constitutions address the issue of religion head-on.

> With the exception of the concrete organizing principles and prerogatives of a polity's governing institutions, the only substantive domain addressed by all modern constitutions is religion. What could be a more telling illustration of religion's omnipresence in today's world, or a stronger testament to constitutionalism's entanglement with, if not existential fear of, religion?[7]

Developments in the United States, and especially the rise of "Christian nationalism" and its influence on American politics, prove that this existential fear is well-grounded. In both these issues—the condition of democracy in the United States and the preservation of public health—it can be argued that what is at stake is the preservation of the community, in the political and biological sense.

Two Socio-Political Trajectories Raising the Importance of Religious Voters

One preliminary caveat at the outset is required here. The term "the Christian Right," describing the contemporary political activity within the American Right may be both useful and deceiving. L. Benjamin Rolsky points out:

> From its very beginnings, "the Christian Right" gave disparate but related events and phenomenon [sic] a coherence often far removed from the experiences of conservative evangelicals, fundamentalists, and Pentecostals on the ground.[8]

He then argues that the narrative of "the rise of the Christian Right" and white support of Donald Trump led to an analytical "whitening" of American evangelicalism, with scholars and journalists accusing white evangelicals of corrupting a faith and fracturing the nation, but scholars do not realize that such "whitening" is largely the product of their own analyses, which are based on a particular set of assumptions about evangelicals.[9] It is also striking that the authors of a study about "Christian nationalism" in the United States claim that there is a considerable overlap between Christian nationalism and white evangelicalism, but they attempt to show that Christian nationalism is not "Christianity" or even "religion" properly

---

7   Hirschl, Ran/Shachar, Ayelet: "'Religious Talk' in Narratives of Membership." In: Graber, Mark A./Levinson, Sanford/Tushnet, Mark (eds.): *Constitutional Democracy in Crisis?* Oxford University Press: New York 2018, p. 531.
8   Rolsky, Benjamin L.: "Producing the Christian Right: Conservative Evangelicalism, Representation, and the Recent Religious Past." *Religions* 12 (3), 2021, p. 4.
9   Rolsky, Benjamin L.: *op. cit., passim.*

speaking but that Christian nationalism often influences Americans' opinions and behaviors in the exact opposite direction than traditional religious commitment does.[10] After all, even with the explosive issue of abortion, this religious commitment led to creating organizations like the Religious Coalition for Abortion Rights (currently the Religious Coalition for Reproductive Choice) and Catholics for Free Choice, who argued that leaving the abortion choice in private hands is the best solution in a religiously pluralistic society.[11] The process that began in 1979 called the fundamentalist takeover or the "Conservative Resurgence" in the Southern Baptist Convention, during which SBC fundamentalists purged moderate Baptists from their ranks, also shows clearly that "there were moderates who fought valiantly (but failed) to protect the SBC from what they saw as deeply politicized extremism."[12] It is not uncommon in the social sciences that vague or fuzzy concepts that are open to interpretation may usefully direct the attention of researchers, as in this case. Although the term "the Christian Right" and the related term "Christian nationalism" may not accurately denote millions of followers with worldviews that are not uniform, it seems justified to use these terms for a distinct faction within white American Christians that is rooted in a cultural attitude cultivated in the South since at least the nineteenth century. What is currently described as the Christian Right is the bloc of conservative Christians or fundamentalists (who dubbed themselves "evangelicals") closely attached to the Republican Party whose ancestors were politically active since the early twentieth century and who were committed, as Daniel K. Williams put it, to the idea of a Christian nation with a Protestant-based moral code (defending the "fundamentals" of the faith against cultural liberalism).[13]

Despite the complexity of these issues, they may be presented as two sociopolitical trajectories which converged in the 1970s and by the 1990s had formed into a formidable electoral coalition that affects significantly, if not overwhelmingly, the U.S. political system and the law. The first one is the reaction of white Southerners to social changes and upheavals stemming from at least three major developments: the abolition of slavery in the wake of the Civil War, the modernization and secularization processes of the late nineteenth and early twentieth centuries, and the cultural revolution of the Long Sixties. The outcome is neatly summarized by Andrew Hartman: "All of a sudden, viewing obscene material in

---

10 Whitehead, Andrew L./Perry, Samuel L.: *op. cit.*, p. 20.
11 Tribe, Laurence H.: *Abortion. The Clash of Absolutes.* W.W. Norton: New York 1992, p. 166.
12 Maxwell, Angie/Shields, Todd: *The Long Southern Strategy. How Chasing White Voters in the South Changed American Politics.* Oxford University Press: New York 2019, p. 270.
13 This story is detailed in Williams, Daniel K.: *God's Own Party: The Making of the Christian Right.* Oxford University Press: New York 2012.

private was legal, but organized prayer and Bible reading in school were not."[14] The second trajectory was a conscious and diligent effort of the Republican Party to create an effective coalition, a new voting bloc that could destroy the New Deal coalition "by emphasizing race and culture war issues that appealed to white working-class voters."[15]

One way to look at this effort is to call it "the Long Southern Strategy." Angie Maxwell and Todd Shields have used this expression to describe a series of decisions the Republican Party made on race, feminism, and religion to target alienated and angry white Southerners, finding issues that would set southern hearts and minds aflame, and thus relentlessly fishing for southern white voters with racial, gendered, and religious bait, starting with Barry Goldwater in 1961 urging fellow Republicans "to go hunting where the ducks are."[16] From this perspective, religious voters were "foot soldiers" serving the Republican Party and its big-business sponsors. Kevin Kruse has demonstrated that as early as the 1930s corporate leaders were attempting to use clergymen in order to regain the upper hand in their war with Franklin Delano Roosevelt's New Deal revolution.[17] In Michael J. Klarman's concise narrative, wealthy conservative industrialists supported radical libertarians ("neo-Ayn Randians") who, since the 1960s, had come to dominate the Republican Party and who, in the 1970s, found willing foot soldiers in the Christian Right:

> [I]n exchange for Republican opposition to abortion and gay rights, leaders of the religious right promoted libertarian economics to their followers, even though many of the neo-Ayn Randians were themselves irreligious and often disparaging of people of faith.[18]

Fears of conservative Christians being reduced to a cultural minority were masterfully stoked. Tom Nichols observes that citizens now elevate political differences to existential struggles because doing so makes for a more interesting and all-consuming confrontation between good and evil. He then quotes the conservative evangelical writer Erick Erickson, who admitted:

---

14 Hartman, Andrew: *A War for the Soul of America. A History of the Culture Wars.* The University of Chicago Press: Chicago 2019, p. 79.
15 Balkin, Jack M.: *The Cycles of Constitutional Time.* Oxford University Press: New York 2020, p. 166.
16 See: Maxwell, Angie/Shields, Todd: *op. cit.*
17 Kruse, Kevin M.: *One Nation Under God. How Corporate America Invented Christian America.* Basic Books: New York 2016.
18 Klarman, Michael J.: "Foreword: The Degradation of American Democracy—and the Court." *Harvard Law Review* 134 (1), 2020, p. 141.

I really was one of those people who believed every election was an existential crisis and we were on the verge of destruction. [...] I used to really believe the nation would collapse if Obama or Clinton or Biden got elected.[19]

As deliberate as this Republican strategy was, it arguably succeeded beyond expectations, transforming American politics and the Republican Party along with it. In 1998 evangelical leader James Dobson began a campaign to change the relationship between the Christian Right and the Republican Party, accusing Republican leaders of passivity and defying God's law. Even before the 1996 presidential election, Dobson threatened Republicans that evangelicals might launch a third-party candidacy against Bob Dole.[20] This was because Republicans initially employed a calculated "God strategy"—a direct response to the rising prominence of religious voters involving the use of religious signals while avoiding alienating moderate voters.[21] According to Anne Nelson, the aforementioned "Conservative Resurgence" of the Southern Baptist Convention was a success that was replicated when the archconservatives who formed the Council for National Policy in 1981 set their sights on the Republican Party, "conducting a decades-long crusade to promote right-wing extremists and drive moderates out of office."[22]

Among the important consequences of this union between the Republican Party and the Religious Right was the convergence of Christian ideology and a whole set of political issues. The authors of "The Long Southern Strategy" explain that the Christian Right expanded its vision beyond moral issues into policy battles over other issues like the environment, the economy, and immigration. In fact, "every issue becomes part of the evangelical cosmology in a spirit of Christian nationalism,"[23] and over the stretch of three decades the Christian Right would inject religion into virtually every domestic and international policy issue[24] while, accordingly, the Republicans repackaged "secular" issues regarding the economy and even war as issues of religious-political concern to maintain the loyalty of these voters.[25]

It is worth emphasizing here that it would be a mistake to focus solely on political strategies. Surely, there was a lot of what Jacob S. Hacker and Paul Pierson

---

19 Nichols, Tom: *Our Own Worst Enemy. The Assault from within on Modern Democracy.* Oxford University Press: New York 2021, p. 103.
20 FitzGerald, Frances: *The Evangelicals. The Struggle to Shape America.* Simon & Schuster: New York 2018, pp. 446–454.
21 See: Domke, David/Coe, Kevin. *The God Strategy. How Religion Became a Political Weapon in America.* Oxford University Press: New York 2010.
22 Nelson, Anne: *Shadow Network. Media, Money, and the Secret Hub of the Radical Right.* Bloomsbury Publishing: New York 2021, pp. xviii–xix.
23 Maxwell, Angie/Shields, Todd: *op. cit.*, p. 224.
24 Maxwell, Angie/Shields, Todd: *op. cit.*, p. 287.
25 Maxwell, Angie/Shields, Todd: *op. cit.*, pp. 289–290.

call "outrage-stoking." It is always tempting for political parties to seek to mobilize voters on the basis of race, ethnicity, religion, or citizenship. As the two authors argue:

> Decades of research suggest that these spirals of extremism do not bubble up from below; they emerge when elites capitalize on preexisting prejudices in pursuit of political gain, forcing citizens and leaders to take sides in an intensifying battle of competing identity claims. In the absence of such elite outrage-stoking, citizens may well be receptive to more moderate party stances and strategies.[26]

The vigor of the Religious Right suggests, however, that these preexisting prejudices and needs are very deeply rooted. Frances FitzGerald claims that the decline of the Christian Right began earlier than assumed, in the 1990s, and generations who had not lived through the Long Sixties were less fearful and angry about social changes.[27] Yet the recent study shows that the cultural framework of Christian nationalism supporting a wish to institutionalize conservative "Christian" cultural preferences in America's policies and self-identity is still most prevalent among white evangelicals. As A.L. Whitehead and Samuel L. Perry claim, Christian nationalism has thoroughly permeated American society and culture. In their view, this framework provides "a lens through which all Americans experience and interpret the social world, and the rejection or embrace of it motivates them toward very different ends." The authors rightly expected in 2019 that Trump and his supporters would continue to tap into the power of Christian nationalism.[28]

Translating Religious Preferences into Law

All these religious, social, and political factors inevitably lead to the domain of law. Attempts to inject religion into broad policy issues and to institutionalize Christian cultural preferences required translating these demands into legal obligations or legal exemptions and, by extension, into Supreme Court decisions. Religious conservatives learned the hard way that precepts of law and court decisions could intrude into their way of life. In *Everson v. Board of Education* (1947), the Supreme Court wrote Jefferson's metaphor of a wall of separation between church and state into constitutional law. Soon a string of decisions followed, unsympathetic to the presence of religion in the public sphere, so by the end of the Warren Court era (1969), the wall of separation appeared firmly entrenched.[29] Decisions like *Engel*

---

26 Hacker, Jacob S./Pierson, Paul: *Let Them Eat Tweets. How the Right Rules in an Age of Extreme Inequality.* Liveright: New York 2020, p. 10.
27 FitzGerald, Frances: *op. cit.*, p. 626.
28 Whitehead, Andrew L./Perry, Samuel L.: *op. cit.*, pp. 153–156.
29 See: O'Brien, David. M.: *Constitutional Law and Politics. Volume Two. Civil Rights and Civil Liberties.* W.W. Norton: New York 2011, pp. 738–741.

v. Vitale in 1962 (school-led prayer in public schools violates the First Amendment) and *Abington v. Schempp* in 1963 (officially mandated Bible reading in public schools violates the First Amendment) frightened evangelicals and prompted Billy Graham, the prominent Christian leader, to declare in 1963 that secularism was the fastest-growing religion in America, and to warn against throwing God and the Bible out of national life.[30] Similarly, in the 1985 *Wallace v. Jaffree* decision, the Court thwarted an attempt to reintroduce in a less conspicuous way prayer into the public schools, declaring that an Alabama law authorizing a one-minute silence in public schools for meditation or voluntary prayer violated the Establishment Clause by expressing the state's endorsement of prayer activities. This decision "could easily be perceived, by both its supporters and its critics, as hostile to religious impulses in American public life" and contributed to "framing by conservative social forces of a counterstory, in which American religiosity was portrayed—sometimes accurately—as a victim of official discrimination."[31] This sentiment proved consequential in later years.

Religious conservatives suffered this series of painful defeats in the Court partially because they were unprepared to take up the legal fight over the role of religion in public life. Seasoned lawyers from groups like the American Civil Liberties Union and Americans United for Separation of Church and State most often faced— and almost always defeated in these early Establishment Clause battles—lawyers with little experience in First Amendment Law, recounted Peter Irons. It was only after the emergence and rapid growth of the Religious Right during the Reagan years that the legal arms of this movement were lavishly funded.[32]

The matter of abortion was another incentive to focus the attention of religious voters on federal courts. In 1973, the Supreme Court in *Roe v. Wade* invalidated most of the state-level restrictions on abortion. It has been exposed in recent years that the initial impact of *Roe v. Wade* was rather limited in evangelical circles. At first, the decision in *Roe* galvanized a right-to-life movement that gained cohesion by virtue of the 1973 landmark ruling and harnessed the power of single-issue politics.[33] It was not until the end of the 1970s that opposition to abortion gained traction among evangelical leaders. "Racism, not abortion, explains why evangelicals came together to pursue political action," forcefully argues Anthea Butler.[34] Historian Randall Balmer debunked the abortion myth in 2014, showing

---

30 Butler, Anthea: *White Evangelical Racism. The Politics of Morality in America*. University of North Carolina Press: Chapel Hill 2021, pp. 52–53.
31 Lupu, Ira C./Tuttle, Robert W.: *Secular Government, Religious People*. William B. Eerdmans Publishing Company: Grand Rapids, MI 2014, p. 127.
32 Irons, Peter: *God on Trial. Dispatches from America's Religious Battlefields*. Viking: New York 2007, pp. xvii–xviii.
33 Tribe, Laurence H.: *op. cit.*, p. 16.
34 Butler, Anthea: *op. cit.*, p. 65.

that it was not until 1979 that evangelical leaders, at the behest of conservative activist Paul Weyrich, seized on abortion as a rallying cry because the anti-abortion crusade was more palatable than the religious right's real motive: protecting segregated schools.[35] This origin myth of the Christian Right is important here, for if one accepts Sarah Posner's contention that the real story of the formation of this movement was not about protecting babies, families, or morality, but was instead "a story of racist backlash against school desegregation and other civil rights advances, all cloaked in the language of freedom and religion,"[36] then it exposes a significant strand of the long-fought anti-civil rights campaign.

Laurence Tribe points to a rather forgotten decision in *Planned Parenthood v. Danforth* of 1976 as the major setback suffered by those again trying to chip away at abortion rights through state legislative restrictions. A number of such restrictions (most notably the requirement of spousal and parental consent to obtain an abortion) were invalidated by the Supreme Court in this first post-*Roe* abortion ruling.[37] This was certainly yet another warning sign for the emerging Religious Right that save for a constitutional amendment any legal attempts to restrict abortion rights would have to be ratified by the Supreme Court. Hence, the Republican Party Platform of 1980 suggested that the appointment of federal judges be conditioned on opposition to abortion ("We will work for the appointment of judges at all levels of the judiciary who respect traditional family values and the sanctity of innocent human life."). Jerry Falwell, leader of the Moral Majority, attended the Republican National Convention and said that the platform "could easily be the constitution of a fundamentalist Baptist church."[38] The movement's engagement with the courts was strengthened after the disappointments of the Ronald Reagan and George H.W. Bush era. In the late 1990s, the leaders of the Christian Right learned that they were not championing the causes of the nation's majority, so their disillusionment with public, national politics made them turn their attention to the courts.[39] This strategy was pointedly described by Judith A. Garber in 2006:

> The current Christian Right is built upon its 1970s precursor, but it has moved well beyond it to become a more radical movement in both style and substance. A centrepiece

---

35 Balmer, Randall: "The Real Origins of the Religious Right." *Politico*, May 27, 2014, retrieved 07.01.2022, from https://www.politico.com/magazine/story/2014/05/religious-right-real-origins-107133/.
36 Posner, Sarah: *Unholy. How White Christian Nationalists Powered the Trump Presidency, and the Devastating Legacy They Left Behind.* Random House: New York 2021, p. 100.
37 Tribe, Laurence H.: *op. cit.*, p. 150.
38 FitzGerald, Frances: *op. cit.*, p. 313.
39 Hollis-Brusky, Amanda/Wilson, Joshua C.: *Separate but Faithful. The Christian Right's Radical Struggle to Transform Law and Legal Culture.* Oxford University Press: New York 2020, p. 29.

of this radicalism is a concerted, unabashed effort to make American courts—most obviously, but certainly not exclusively, the federal appellate courts—into conservative Christian adjuncts to the electoral, legislative, and administrative processes.[40]

Focusing attention on courts and judicial appointments was a safer course both for the Christian Right and for the Republican politicians, as Jacob S. Hacker and Paul Pierson unravel. Republican politicians understandably feared associating themselves too closely with a social agenda the majority of voters rejected. They were not willing to support forcefully conservative social legislation. On the other hand, judicial politics received less notice from voters, and, as James Dobson recognized, practically every issue evangelicals cared about was linked in one way or another to the courts.[41] As I argued, investing resources in litigation-based movements could be a win-win situation. Some victories may be achieved that would be hard to secure in elections. The length of the proceedings and the ability to produce case after case help to excite the attention of followers. Even defeats may be beneficial: they excite followers even further and encourage their sense of embattlement.[42]

It was then logical for the Christian Right to devote considerable resources to institution-building in the field of law. In a thorough analysis of these endeavors, Amanda Hollis-Brusky and Joshua C. Wilson observed that by creating law schools and legal training programs, the Christian Right has created institutions that in and of themselves stand as statements of defiance, and they also aim to equip the Christian Right with a new set of movement resources.[43] This stance has clearly followed the understanding that the complexity of the American legal system and the influence of legal culture require a wholesale approach to a transformation, especially against unfavorable cultural and demographic trends. Ultimately, however, it is the judges of federal courts and especially Justices of the Supreme Court who decide cases and shape the law, so securing the appointment of judges and Justices known for their conservative and religious commitments became for the religious voters and their leaders one of the most significant factors in determining the appeal of a presidential candidate. Accordingly, when Donald Trump sought the support of religious conservatives in 2016 he prepared a list of judicial candidates, "all pro-life," and promised that all his judges would be vetted by the conservative Federalist Society.[44] Later that year, exit polls showed that many more Trump voters than

---

40 Garber, Judith A.: "The Christian Right, the Federal Courts, and the Constitution in the United States." *Constitutional Forum Constitutionnel* 15 (1), 2006, p. 23.
41 Hacker, Jacob S./Pierson, Paul: *op. cit.*, pp. 86–87.
42 Kubas, Sebastian: "The Christian Right, Judicial Review, and the Exploitation of Religious Passions: Hidden Sources and Possible Jurisprudential Effects." A conference paper presented at GIRES International Conference: *Religion and Politics in the United States*, 17–18.07.2021.
43 Hollis-Brusky, Amanda/Wilson, Joshua C.: *op. cit.*, pp. 4–5.
44 Nelson, Anne: *op. cit.*, pp. 196–198.

Clinton voters viewed Supreme Court appointments as the most important factor in their decision.⁴⁵ They were not disappointed. During the 2018 Values Voter Summit conference, the assembled were pleased with the rapid pace of Trump's court appointments and particularly with Brett Kavanaugh's expected confirmation. According to Anne Nelson's account, one of them said, "Brett Kavanaugh will be Ruth Bader Ginsburg's age in 2050," while Mitch McConnell announced: "If we can hold on for two years, we're going to transform the federal judiciary."⁴⁶ Two years later, in September 2020, Lee Epstein and Eric A. Posner estimated that from 1953 to 2005, the Supreme Court ruled in favor of religious parties roughly 50% of the time. Under Chief Justice Roberts, that figure has soared—to almost 90%, but two Trump's appointees, Justice Brett Kavanaugh and Justice Neil Gorsuch, voted for the religious side 100% of the time.⁴⁷

In 2006, Mark Tushnet, writing the story of the Rehnquist Court, which ended in 2005, opined that cultural conservatives in the court lost on social issues like abortion, gay rights, and affirmative action. The reason was simple; the cultural conservatives were losing in the arena of politics as well.⁴⁸ Apparently, the Court decisions of recent years, favorable to the Christian Right, indicate a belated victory for the movement. This might be perceived as another paradox, for there is a visible decline in the percentage of the American population that identifies with a Christian tradition, and Christians no longer dominate the cultural and social context like they used to.⁴⁹ American women had a total of over 800,000 legal abortions in 2017, pornography is omnipresent on the internet, and homosexuality has been normalized to a great extent in American culture.⁵⁰ Yet this is where judicial review and the role of the Supreme Court in American politics come into play.

Divergent Understandings of the First Amendment's Religion Clauses

In the collective lore of American constitutionalism, the Supreme Court is the self-appointed guardian of the constitutional order and "the ultimate expositor of the constitutional text."⁵¹ Chief Justice Roberts insists that the Court is above

---

45 Whitehead, Andrew L./Perry, Samuel L.: *op. cit.*, p. 76.
46 Nelson, Anne: *op. cit.*, p. 238.
47 Epstein, Lee/Posner, Eric A.: "How the Religious Right Has Transformed the Supreme Court." *New York Times*, September 22, 2020, retrieved 07.01.2022, from https://www.nytimes.com/2020/09/22/opinion/supreme-court-religion.html.
48 Tushnet, Mark: A Court Divided. *The Rehnquist Court and the Future of Constitutional Law*. W.W. Norton: New York 2006, p. 10.
49 Whitehead, Andrew L./Perry, Samuel L.: *op. cit.*, pp. 44–45.
50 Klarman, Michael J.: *op. cit.*, p. 130.
51 *United States v. Morrison*, 529 U.S. 598 (2000).

politicking, and Justices do not work as Democrats or Republicans.[52] It would be much more realistic and factual to state that the rise and fall of political regimes shape partisan attitudes about the exercise of judicial review. As the dominant party gains control of the courts, it starts to recognize the advantages of judicial review in protecting and promoting the party's values and commitments.[53] Recent decades have shown that with a bit of luck and a significant amount of constitutional hardball,[54] which is a form of institutional combat aimed at permanently defeating one's partisan rival,[55] the Republican Party was able to take over the Supreme Court and exert an outsized influence over federal courts, despite losing the popular vote. Since 1992 the Republican regime has been unable to win national presidential majorities, with the single exception of George W. Bush's victory in 2004. The other two times Republican candidates gained the presidency only thanks to the Electoral College.[56] Yet, the last time the Supreme Court had a Chief Justice nominated by a Democratic president was in 1953, and the last time the Supreme Court had a majority of Justices nominated by Democratic presidents was May 1969.[57] In the fifty years between 1969 and 2019, there have been fourteen Republican Supreme Court appointments and only four Democratic appointments.[58] The appointment of Amy Coney Barrett in 2020 by President Trump only added to that tally. It is thus no surprise that slowly but surely the Supreme Court has proceeded toward the conservative vision of constitutional law. Each year, the late Justice William Brennan would ask his new law clerks whether they knew the most important rule of the Supreme Court. The correct response was invariably that it takes five votes to do anything in the Supreme Court.[59]

The ability of the Justices to shape and reorient the law according to the preferences of the Christian Right in the realm of the First Amendment is greatly enhanced by the open-ended text of the Amendment. The First Amendment includes two clauses dealing with religion, while the other provisions of the Amendment relate to freedom of expression. The first short sentence of the Amendment reads: "Congress shall make no law respecting an establishment of

---

52 Biskupic, Joan: *The Chief. The Life and Turbulent Times of Chief Justice*. Basic Books: New York 2019, p. 9.
53 Balkin, Jack M.: *op. cit.*, p. 69.
54 Tushnet, Mark: "Constitutional Hardball." *John Marshall Law Review* 37 (2), 2004, p. 523.
55 Levitsky, Steven/Ziblatt, Daniel: *How Democracies Die*. Crown: New York 2018, p. 109.
56 Balkin, Jack M.: *op. cit.*, p. 18.
57 Tushnet, Mark: *Taking Back the Constitution. Activist Judges and the Next Age of American Law*. Yale University Press: New Haven, CT 2020, p. vii.
58 Balkin, Jack M.: *op. cit.*, p. 77.
59 Savage, David G.: *Turning Right. The Making of the Rehnquist Supreme Court*. John Wiley & Sons: New York 1993, p. 12.

religion, or prohibiting the free exercise thereof." These phrases are commonly known as the Establishment Clause and the Free Exercise Clause, respectively. Although both of them are aimed at Congress (the federal government) and not at states, in the 1940s the Supreme Court "incorporated" them into the due-process clause of the Fourteenth Amendment, making them binding on the states as well as the federal government.[60] On the most general level, the Establishment Clause prohibits the government from establishing a religion, which means that there are some forms of government entanglement with religion that would be impermissible (an example would be an attempt to set up a national church akin to the Church of England). The Free Exercise Clause guarantees some degree of individual autonomy in religious matters. According to some scholars, both clauses are complementary, but there is also a tension between them.

> Government actions to facilitate free exercise might be challenged as impermissible establishments, and government efforts to refrain from establishing religion might be objected to as denying the free exercise of religion.[61]

It would be unwarranted, however, to think that these two provisions establish any internal equilibrium or offer a balanced approach in the sensitive area of religious freedom. First of all, the meaning of the First Amendment's religion clauses is far from clear. David M. O'Brien notes that neither the text nor the historical record of the First Amendment provides simple interpretative solutions for the continuing controversies over religious freedom. What is an "establishment of religion"? What is a "law respecting" the establishment of religion? What is "religion" and who defines it?[62] Both Religion Clauses are filled with essentially contested concepts that allow divergent constitutional interpretations. The Supreme Court's output in this area of law has been depressingly incoherent over the past 80 years. It would be hard to argue with Winnifred Fallers Sullivan that in the judicial interpretation of two Religion Clauses the meanings of the keywords—"establishment," "religion," and "free exercise"—"have been unstable, shifting from case to case, resulting in a highly unsatisfactory jurisprudence, one often mocked by commentators as lacking coherence and common sense."[63] A related problem is that "[t]here is little acknowledgment of or deference to the academic study of religion in American legislatures or courts."[64]

---

60 *Cantwell v. Connecticut*, 310 U.S. 296 (1940); *Everson v. Board of Education*, 330 U.S. 1 (1947).
61 Chemerinsky, Erwin: *Constitutional Law. Principles and Policies.* Aspen Publishers: New York 2006, pp. 1182–1183.
62 O'Brien, David M.: *op. cit.*, p. 729.
63 Sullivan, Winnifred Fallers: "Religion." In: Tushnet, Mark/Graber, Mark A./Levinson, Sanford (eds.): *The Oxford Handbook of the U.S. Constitution.* Oxford University Press: New York 2015, p. 608.
64 Sullivan, Winnifred Fallers: *op. cit.*, p. 609.

A useful basic approach to both Religion Clauses, lucidly presented by Howard Gillman and Erwin Chemerinsky, relies on two contrasting ideas of accommodation and separation. The "separation" view of the Establishment Clause is that there should be a wall that separates church and state, the government should be secular, and the place for religion is in the people's private realm. Conversely, the "accommodation" view holds there should be no wall of separation, and the government may support religion or cooperate with religion. In this view, what the Establishment Clause prohibits is the governmental coercion of religious beliefs or discriminating among religions. In a similar vein, the separation view of the Free Exercise Clause is that the government should stay out of the business of worship and the internal operations of religious institutions. It also means that religious people should not be offered special accommodations when the government is passing neutral laws of general applicability. On this point, the disparity is most acute, for an accommodation view of the Free Exercise Clause requires the government to impose the least restrictions on religious liberty, which essentially means exempting religious practitioners from general laws. Gillman and Chemerinsky, who offer a more complete explanation of Religion Clauses, point out that both of them are continuums, although competing approaches in this regard may be identified as four possible positions, from the strictest one [Separation Establishment Clause/Separation Free Exercise Clause], through two mixed ones [Accommodation Establishment Clause/Separation Free Exercise Clause] and [Separation Establishment Clause/Accommodation Free Exercise Clause], to the one most sympathetic toward religion [Accommodation Establishment Clause/Accommodation Free Exercise Clause].[65] It needs to be emphasized that the constitutional text of the First Amendment does not offer any compelling guidance as to which position is the correct one, although the full separationist approach envisages a political system very different from that based on the idea of accommodation. As a matter of fact, these technical legal terms reflect completely opposite assessments of the value of religion in public life. Accommodationists tend to believe that religion has beneficial consequences for the social order and regard religion as a source of social cohesion, whereas separationists argue in favor of depoliticization or domestication of religious belief through its confinement to a private sphere of activity, seeing religion as a "dangerous stranger" to democratic discourse and a fertile source of political instability since religious commitments tend to be absolute and inadaptable to compromise.[66]

---

65 Gillman, Howard/Chemerinsky, Erwin: *The Religion Clauses. The Case for Separating Church and State*. Oxford University Press: New York 2020, pp. 12–15.
66 Jelen, Ted G.: *To Serve God and Mammon. Church-State Relations in American Politics*. Georgetown University Press: Washington, DC 2010, pp. 11–12.

Toward the Legal Accommodation of Religion: The Evolution of the U.S. Supreme Court's Religious Freedom Jurisprudence

Against a background of these deeply contested constitutional provisions, there have been several important developments in recent decades relating to the legal sphere of state and church relations. After the series of separationist rulings, "the Court came over time to be seen by many as an agent of a secularizing and godless national elite."[67] Many of the heated disputes arose over the place of religion in public schools, most notably over school prayers.[68] Andrew Hartman notes that there was a paradox of American secularization which helps explain the culture wars and the stance conservative Christians took as cultural counterrevolutionaries—"the perplexing fact that religious authority dwindled even as the vast majority of Americans doggedly persisted in religious belief."[69] The almost immediate consequence was not only the growing political mobilization of religious conservatives but also a strong pattern of defiance against the Court's decisions on religious activities in public schools. Matthew E.K. Hall has shown that these decisions were extremely unpopular, and the Court's rulings had little causal effect in those areas where the decisions were least popular. For instance, in the South little more than one-fourth of teachers heeded the Court's instructions regarding the impermissibility of school prayers and Bible reading in public schools.[70]

As the relationship between the evangelicals and the Republican Party grew stronger in the 1990s, their demands became more persistent. The empowered religious conservatives no longer sought only to protect freedom of exercise, they also wanted the state to endorse "God designed institutions like the family and the church to run under certain authority structures."[71] This meant a push toward accommodation of religion by public authorities. The election of President Barack Obama in 2008 was another major event. The older evangelicals viewed him as an existential threat, so their grievances and ire increased, and they began to use the language of "religious freedom" as a way to exclude LGBTQ persons from civil rights and to lobby for special status of their group in the law.[72] These demands were skillfully translated into legal arguments that were deemed at least somewhat credible to the broader legal community due

---

67 Sullivan, Winnifred Fallers: *op. cit.*, p. 614.
68 See: Irons, Peter: *op. cit.*, pp. 21–43.
69 Hartman, Andrew: *op. cit.*, p. 79.
70 Hall, Matthew E.K.: *The Nature of Supreme Court Power*. Cambridge University Press: New York 2013, pp. 130–136.
71 Maxwell, Angie/Shields, Todd: *op. cit.*, pp. 288–289.
72 Butler, Anthea: *op. cit.*, p. 130.

to the efforts of legal scholars and activists engaged in the Christian conservative legal movement, efforts that are comprehensively discussed by Amanda Hollis-Brusky and Joshua C. Wilson. The frame of a persecuted minority proved to be particularly useful. It not only mobilized the evangelical community but also opened the door to the Christian Right engaging in the "politics of rights" which provided new rhetorical and legal resources.[73] In the famous "footnote four" to the Supreme Court's 1938 ruling in *United States v. Carolene Products Co.*, the Court heralded a new justification for judicial review of legislation stemming from the Court's role in protecting democracy by protecting democratic civil rights and "discrete and insular minorities." This justification became highly influential among legal scholars in the 1970s and 1980s; for many legal thinkers "footnote four" became symbolic of the general post-1937 approach to judicial review, and it spawned an enormous amount of scholarly literature.[74]

It may seem far-fetched to present American Christians as a discrete and insular minority but apparently, as Melissa Murray pointed out, the Court is ready to acknowledge that there is a broader climate of hostility and disdain directed toward people of faith, which means that conservative Christians are a beleaguered minority sect subject to invidious discrimination. In this way Christian evangelicals who were once trumpeted as a "moral majority" cloak themselves as a religious minority in need of state protection, thus inverting the traditional antidiscrimination narrative.[75] The result of this repositioning is that when an LGBT couple files an antidiscrimination complaint against a white evangelical Christian man, the latter assumes the role of the victim. Proponents of religious accommodation claim that LGBT people should go elsewhere to be served for the sake of allowing an embattled group to preserve its cultural and religious identity.[76]

This is but a part of a major shift in American constitutional jurisprudence, one which can be described as a "transition from the increasingly limited, if not repudiated, high separationism of the second half of the twentieth century."[77] It has been slow but steady progress toward the accommodation of religion in public life. In 1993, David G. Savage, commenting on the 1989 decision in *Allegheny County v. ACLU* (the Court in a five-to-four decision held that displaying a nativity scene in a county courthouse violated the Establishment Clause),

---

73 Hollis-Brusky, Amanda/Wilson, Joshua C.: *op. cit.*, pp. 29–30.
74 Brest, Paul et al.: *Processes of Constitutional Decision-Making. Cases and Materials.* Aspen Publishers: New York 2006, pp. 517–518.
75 Murray, Melissa: "Inverting Animus: Masterpiece Cakeshop and the New Minorities." *Supreme Court Review* 2018, 2018, p. 282.
76 Schragger, Richard/Schwartzman, Micah: "Religious Antiliberalism and the First Amendment." *Minnesota Law Review* 104 (3), 2020, pp. 1403–1404.
77 Sullivan, Winnifred Fallers: *op. cit.*, p. 608.

remarked that Justice Anthony Kennedy in his dissent had staked out a powerful new position on religion. With one more conservative vote, the wall of separation between church and state would be knocked down and replaced with government policies of accommodation, acknowledgment, and support for religion.[78] Ted G. Jelen, writing from the vantage point of 2010, noted that in recent years the Court had appeared to relax its separationist approach and the Court's rulings in cases such as *Zelman, Zobrest, Lamb's Chapel*, or *Pleasant Grove* indicated that the Rehnquist and perhaps the Roberts courts had moved in a more generally accommodationist direction with respect to issues involving religious establishment. For instance, in *Zobrest v. Catalina Foothills School District* (1993) the Court permitted state funding for a sign language interpreter for a deaf student enrolled in a parochial school. In *Zelman v. Simmons-Harris* (2002), the Court held that private school vouchers did not violate the Establishment Clause, even if the vouchers were used for religious schools.[79] Earlier conjectures regarding the accommodationist course the Supreme Court seemed to have been pursuing proved to be well grounded. Howard Gillman and Erwin Chemerinsky's 2020 book on the subject opens with a statement that the Supreme Court appeared to be on the verge of major shifts in interpreting the Religion Clauses. The five conservative Justices reject the idea of a wall separating church and state. Under their view, the government violates the Establishment Clause only if it coerces religious participation or discriminates among religions in the provision of benefits. These members of the Court also seem poised to interpret the Free Exercise Clause as requiring that the government accommodate religious beliefs by granting exceptions to general law. Moreover, the five conservative Justices seem ready to hold that the government is constitutionally required to provide benefits to religious institutions whenever it grants them to secular private institutions.[80] It appears that Justice Kennedy's views on the proper understanding of Religion Clauses have finally prevailed, and the simple reason is that there was an increase in conservative votes in the Court. To put it more specifically, the justices appointed by Republican presidents currently sitting on the Court support Chief Justice John Roberts's project to change the understanding of the Constitution Religion Clauses. Linda Greenhouse convincingly claims that this project

---

78 Savage, David G.: *op. cit.*, p. 297.
79 Jelen, Ted G.: *op. cit.*, p. 78.
80 Gillman, Howard/Chemerinsky, Erwin: *op. cit.*, pp. ix–x. It should be noted, referring to this complicated story, that the accommodationist interpretation of the Free Exercise Clause had prevailed much earlier, but it was usually applied to minority religious groups. Therefore, the recent jurisprudence may be presented as a return to the earlier tradition.

involved reinterpreting—one might say weaponizing—the Constitution's Free Exercise Clause, turning it from its historic role as a shield that protected believers from government interference into a sword that vaulted believers into a position of privilege.[81]

Several decisions of recent vintage exemplify this trend. In *Hosanna-Tabor Evangelical Lutheran Church & School v. EEOC* (2012), the Court held that ministers are not allowed to bring employment-related claims against their churches. The Court unanimously decided that the Free Exercise Clause forbids the government from holding a religious institution liable for the choices it makes as to who will be their ministers.[82] Although Chief Justice Roberts in his opinion for the Court stressed that this was a narrow holding and the "ministerial exception" does not cover other types of suits, the tendency to shield religious organizations from general law was furthered in later, more contentious free exercise cases.

A similar ostensible narrowing appeared in *Trinity Lutheran Church of Columbia v. Comer* (2017). In the state of Missouri, schools could apply for a grant to pay for resurfacing playgrounds. The state denied the grant to a religious school. The Supreme Court found this an odious violation of the principle that governments cannot discriminate between religion and nonreligion. Chief Justice Roberts wrote that the school operated by Trinity Lutheran Church had a right to participate in a government benefit program without having to disavow its religious character. As Mark Tushnet noted, this decision was a major development because it seemed to open the way for states to adopt programs whose effect is to send public money to church-related institutions.[83] However, Chief Justice Roberts writing for the majority once again attempted to underplay the importance of his ruling, adding a footnote: "This case involves express discrimination based on religious identity with respect to playground resurfacing. We do not address religious uses of funding or other forms of discrimination."[84] Linda Greenhouse speculates that the unusual footnote was included to mollify two liberal Justices, Kagan and Breyer, who did not object to the ruling.[85] Actually, *Trinity Lutheran* was far from being inconsequential. It meant that in a short time the Court "has moved from a regime that disallowed most kinds of direct funding to a regime that permitted

---

81 Greenhouse, Linda: *Justice on the Brink. The Death of Ruth Bader Ginsburg, the Rise of Amy Coney Barrett, and Twelve Months That Transformed the Supreme Court.* Random House: New York 2021, p. 14.
82 See: Lund, Christopher C.: "Free Exercise Reconceived: The Logic and Limits of Hosanna-Tabor." *Northwestern University Law Review* 108 (4), 2014; Gillman/Chemerinsky, pp. 198–199.
83 Tushnet, Mark: *Taking...*, *op. cit.*, pp. 93–94.
84 *Trinity Lutheran Church of Columbia, Inc. v. Comer*, 582 U.S. __ (2017).
85 Greenhouse, Linda: *op. cit.*, pp. 15–16.

indirect funding and now to a regime that requires direct funding [of religious enterprises]."[86]

These purportedly narrow decisions were later followed and expanded by the Roberts Court. In June 2014, the Court issued a decision in *Burwell v. Hobby Lobby*, which "sent shockwaves through the legal community."[87] The Court, in a five-to-four ruling, sided with employers objecting to a contraceptive mandate—the federal regulation established a minimum level of health coverage that employers must offer if they provide health benefits to their employees, and that requires employers to provide contraceptive coverage. The Court held that closely held, for-profit corporations can claim religious exemption and that their exercise of religion was substantially burdened by the contraceptive mandate. This holding means, for the first time in the Court's history, that a for-profit corporation can raise a successful religious objection to a federal law, which fundamentally changes the relationship between workers and employers with religious objections to the law because a for-profit employer may cite its owners' religious beliefs in order to diminish the rights of its employees.[88]

The 2018 *Masterpiece Cakeshop, Ltd. v. Colorado Civil Rights Commission* case featured a Colorado bakery whose owner refused to bake a cake for a same-sex wedding. These kinds of clashes with religious traditionalists became almost inevitable after states expanded their general nondiscrimination statutes to protect members of the LGBTQ community.[89] The Court managed to sidestep the central issue of the case, and instead found that the Colorado Civil Rights Commission, which had ruled in favor of the same-sex couple, had expressed impermissible hostility toward religion and thus violated the Free Exercise Clause.[90]

In 2020, the Supreme Court handed another three victories to the Christian Right. The case *Espinoza v. Montana Department of Revenue* was an extension of *Trinity Lutheran* (playground resurfacing). In 2017, Chief Justice Roberts declared that the Establishment Clause permitted indirect subsidies to religious schools. This time, Chief Justice, writing for a five-to-four majority, declared that the Free Exercise Clause requires such funding. A state need not subsidize private education, but once a state decides to do so, it cannot disqualify private schools solely because they are religious. A few days later, in the decision *Our Lady of Guadalupe School v. Morrissey-Berru*, the ministerial exception recognized in *Hosanna-Tabor* in

---

86 Schragger, Richard/Schwartzman, Micah: *op. cit.*, p. 1385.
87 D'Amato, Richard J.: "A "Very Specific" Holding: Analyzing the Effect of Hobby Lobby on Religious Liberty Challenges to Housing Discrimination Laws." *Columbia Law Review* 116 (4), 2016, p. 1063.
88 Millhiser, Ian: Injustices. *The Supreme Court's History of Comforting the Comfortable and Afflicting the Afflicted.* Nation Books: New York 2016, pp. 252–254.
89 Tushnet, Mark: *Taking...*, *op. cit.*, p. 89.
90 Gillman, Howard/Chemerinsky, Erwin: *op. cit.*, pp. 4–5, 150–155.

2012 was extended to ordinary elementary school teachers in a church-run school. The Court held that Religion Clauses foreclose the adjudication of employment-discrimination claims of these teachers because their schools saw them as playing a vital role in carrying out the church's mission.[91] On the same day, the Court in *Little Sisters of the Poor v. Pennsylvania* upheld the Trump administration's decision to grant an opt-out from the contraceptive mandate for any employer for religious or conscientious reasons. On the surface, it was a case of administrative law. Federal courts blocked the Trump administration's new rules, finding them invalid under basic principles of administrative law. When the case reached the Supreme Court, religious litigants, who found the *Hobby Lobby* accommodation inadequate, reframed it as an act of resistance against the government-sponsored contraception master plan.[92] For objectors, providing coverage for drugs that remove the potential for life is unacceptable, while providing coverage for drugs that have the potential to disrupt a life in being is tantamount to murder.[93] From another perspective, *Little Sisters* is a momentous decision because it portends a massive shift in how the Court treats religious accommodations. The Court implicitly undermined a doctrine of third-party harms that has long provided a limiting principle in cases where religious freedom and other rights clash. If the Court is no longer required to consider the harm done to third parties by religious exemptions, then numerous civil rights protections may be under threat, concluded "Harvard Law Review" authors.[94]

The winning streak for religious groups, which attracted widespread media attention, continued in 2021. In June 2021, in the case *Fulton v. City of Philadelphia*, the Court ruled in favor of Catholic Social Services, which was operating a foster care agency that was denied taxpayer-funding by the city of Philadelphia because the agency would not accept same-sex couples as foster parents. Once again, outwardly it may look like a local and limited issue. However, according to the American Civil Liberties Union's statement issued before the verdict, the case could allow private agencies that receive tax dollars to deny services to people who are LGBTQ, Jewish, Muslim, or Mormon.[95] Howard Gillman and Erwin Chemerinsky also expressed concern before the case was decided because it involved a question whether the Court should overturn the decision in *Employment Division v. Smith*

---

91 See: Greenhouse, Linda: *op. cit.*, pp. 218–220.
92 See: Greenhouse, Linda: *op. cit.*, pp. 22–26.
93 Bean, Tanner J/Wilson, Robin F.: "The Administrative State as a New Front in the Culture War: Little Sisters of the Poor v. Pennsylvania." *Cato Supreme Court Review* 2019–2020, 2019–2020, p. 231.
94 "Little Sisters of the Poor Saints Peter and Paul Home v. Pennsylvania." *Harvard Law Review* 134 (1), 2020, p. 565.
95 American Civil Liberties Union: "Fulton v. City of Philadelphia," retrieved 07.01.2022, from https://www.aclu.org/cases/fulton-v-city-philadelphia.

(1990) in which the Court rejected the claim that free exercise of religion required an exemption from an otherwise valid law. Four Justices already signaled that they would welcome an opportunity to reconsider the 1990 *Smith* decision.[96] It should be added that *Smith* is a case "that tops many religious freedom lawyers' list of most reviled court opinions."[97] By contrast, many civil rights advocates "now view religious liberty as a deeply contaminated, if not toxic, civil right."[98] In *Fulton v. City of Philadelphia*, the Court managed to avoid the expected showdown between gay people's right to be free from discrimination and religious people's right to discriminate. The decision was in favor of the Catholic agency but "without going the full distance to a true win for religion and against gay rights."[99] According to Chief Justice Roberts's opinion, there was no need to revisit the *Smith* decision because the City had burdened the religious exercise of Catholic Social Services through policies that did not meet the requirement of being neutral and generally applicable.

Regardless of this assurance and of the apparent narrowness of the Court's holding, the impact of the *Fulton* decision is substantial. Linda Greenhouse rightly claims that in *Fulton* Chief Justice Roberts deployed the subtle dexterity of a surgeon. The 1990 *Smith* decision formally remained on the books, but *Fulton* went far toward making the *Smith* decision irrelevant. The once exotic 1992 case, *Church of Lukumi Babalu Aye, Inc. v. City of Hialeah*, has been increasingly elevated to the status of controlling precedent. Under *Smith* the government defendant nearly always won, for a neutral, generally applicable law required no exemptions. Under *Church of Lukumi*'s much harsher framework, the government needs to demonstrate a compelling interest in targeting a religious practice.[100] Putting aside the intricacies of *stare decisis* doctrine (deferring to earlier cases), the *Fulton* case is yet another instance in which the Court has given license to discriminate against people whose relationship is legally valid. Bradley J. Lingo and Michael G. Schietzelt argue to the contrary, declaring that many of the disputes over religious liberty are not zero-sum conflicts, though framing them as such makes for compelling political theater. Two of the approximately thirty foster care agencies in Philadelphia held religious objections to placing foster children with same-sex couples. These couples had roughly twenty-eight other options from which to choose.[101]

---

96 Gillman, Howard/Chemerinsky, Erwin: *op. cit.*, p. 159.
97 Boden, Anastasia: "Looking Ahead: Déjà Vu at the Supreme Court." *Cato Supreme Court Review* 2019–2020, 2019–2020, p. 344.
98 Lingo, Bradley J./Schietzelt, Michael G.: "Fulton and the Future of Free Exercise." *Regent University Law Review* 33 (1), 2020, pp. 5–6.
99 Suk Gersen, Jeannie: "The Supreme Court's Surprising Term." *New Yorker*, July 5, 2021, p. 13.
100 See: Greenhouse, Linda: *op. cit.*, pp. 206–214.
101 Lingo, Bradley J./Schietzelt, Michael G.: *op. cit.*, p. 36.

Stephanie H. Barclay, who advances the idea that third-party harm theory fails to account for harms this approach would cause for religious minorities, in a similar fashion maintains that countless foster children and families are served by religious adoption agencies which can only operate because of specific religious exemptions under state law.[102]

The main question, however, still lingers. From a philosophical perspective, it was phrased by Brian Leiter in his seminal book: is there any special reason to tolerate beliefs whose distinctive character is defined by the categoricity of its demands conjoined with its insulation from ordinary standards of evidence and rational justification?[103] From the perspective of a legal professional who has litigated church-state cases, it is a matter of whether religious believers may be permitted to ignore the modern social norm of equality for all.[104] Cass R. Sunstein made a compelling argument that there is an anticaste principle which captures a commitment that has strong roots in legal understandings in constitutional democracies. The anticaste principle forbids social and legal practices from translating highly visible and morally irrelevant differences into a systemic source of social disadvantage unless there is a very good reason for a society to do so.[105] In the real world, the Supreme Court's decisions produce social disadvantages and are far from being political theater. Netta Barak-Corren attempted to deliver previously missing hard data on the effects of religious exemptions granted in Supreme Court decisions. Her findings show that after *Masterpiece Cakeshop* (a bakery's refusal to supply a cake supporting gay marriage) the odds that same-sex couples would experience discrimination from wedding vendors are estimated to be between 61% and 85%.[106] She also argues that the data unsettle the theory that religious objection is a result of permanent idiosyncratic features of the objectors' religious identity. It rather seems that religious objection is contingent on the seeming availability of an exemption. Moreover, writing before the *Fulton* decision, Netta Barak-Corren stated that the Justices should not mislead themselves into thinking that making a case-specific decision would avoid undesirable outcomes or that their decision would only expand the freedom of a negligible minority of extremely objecting individuals. Rather, exempting religious objectors would likely have a

---

102 Barclay, Stephanie H.: "First Amendment 'Harms.'" *Indiana Law Journal* 95 (2), 2020, p. 360.
103 See: Leiter, Brian: *Why Tolerate Religion?* Princeton University Press: Princeton 2014.
104 Luchenitser, Alex J.: "A New Era of Inequality? Hobby Lobby and Religious Exemptions from Anti-Discrimination Laws." *Harvard Law & Policy Review* 9 (1), 2015, p. 88.
105 Sunstein, Cass R.: *Designing Democracy. What Constitutions Do.* Oxford University Press: New York 2002, pp. 155–156.
106 Barak-Corren, Netta: "A License to Discriminate? The Market Response to Masterpiece Cakeshop." *Harvard Civil Rights–Civil Liberties Law Review* 56 (2), 2021, p. 320.

broad impact, including on decision-makers who were willing to provide services before the decision but would refuse to do so afterward.[107] It should also be reminded that these legal controversies do not involve religious freedom in itself. Most of the recent Supreme Court's rulings on religion deal with Christianity, so it is fair to conclude that

> conservative justices are interpreting the Constitution to further Christian religious beliefs, finding that the government does not violate the Establishment Clause if it acts to further Christianity and that it must, based on free exercise of religion, accommodate Christians who want exceptions from general laws.[108]

Free Exercise of Religion during the COVID-19 Pandemic

The Christian Right seeks exemptions from general law in various areas of life, but nowhere is the salience of these demands seen more clearly than in the area of public health in the context of the COVID-19 pandemic. Religious refusals to comply with compulsory vaccination laws reach back to those who treated the mode of smallpox vaccination pioneered in 1796 by Edward Jenner as contrary to God's will. Many early religious refusals were premised on a popular theory that diseases were mechanisms for controlling the balance between the blessed and the damned. Since then, religious refusals have evolved to include different justifications.[109] Interestingly, writing in 2017, Marie Killmond asserted that while vaccination is a hot political topic, it is largely settled as a matter of law. Since 1905, state governments have possessed the authority to enforce mandatory vaccination laws, and courts have long recognized that states are not required to provide religious exemptions to these vaccination mandates, though most do.[110] However, in 2016, Rebecca Bucchieri wrote that the increase in outbreaks of vaccine-preventable disease across the United States suggests that the state-by-state frameworks for controlling the spread of disease are inadequate. She argued that if religious and philosophical exemptions were unavailable across the country (forty-seven states offer religious exemptions), the measles outbreak in 2015 and similar outbreaks of disease likely would have faltered. Hence, she recommended adopting compulsory federal vaccination laws for schoolchildren that would permit only medical

---

107 Barak-Corren, Netta: *op. cit.*, pp. 364–365.
108 Gillman, Howard/Chemerinsky, Erwin: *op. cit.*, p. xiii.
109 Bucchieri, Rebecca: "Religious Freedom Versus Public Health: The Necessity of Compulsory Vaccination for Schoolchildren." *Boston University Public Interest Law Journal* 25 (2), 2016, pp. 271–277.
110 Killmond, Marie: "Why Is Vaccination Different? A Comparative Analysis of Religious Exemptions." *Columbia Law Review* 117 (4), 2017, p. 915.

exemptions, reasoning that the federal government holds a compelling interest in protecting the public health of its citizens.[111]

The risk that religious exemptions from vaccination rules and other health mandates pose to public health increased sharply in the wake of the COVID-19 pandemic, particularly at the time of the shift in First Amendment jurisprudence in the Supreme Court, which included the gradual abandonment of *Employment Division v. Smith*'s deferential standard of judicial review in free exercise cases. The doctrinal and political criticism of the *Smith* decision began shortly after the decision was issued. Actually, the outcome of this landmark case stupefied even the two lawyers who argued the decisive round of the case. "Was I there?" wondered Smith's lawyer.[112] James M. Oleske, Jr., who himself recommended a modestly heightened scrutiny in exemptions cases, stated that critiques of the *Smith* decision are legion, and as the first sin of *Smith* he considered "*Smith*'s shamelessly dishonest treatment of free exercise precedent."[113] In a recent critique, written in anticipation of the Court's ruling in *Fulton v. City of Philadelphia*, Holly M. Randall wrote unequivocally that restoring the Free Exercise Clause would require the Court to overrule *Employment Division v. Smith*: "This holding leaves religious citizens without a judicial avenue to seek an exemption or religious accommodation from a generally applicable law, forcing reliance on the legislative process."[114] Jurisprudential consistency and stability, so dear to legal scholars, is nonetheless a matter of far less importance than the real-world consequences of Supreme Court decisions. The Court itself quickly adapted to public health guidance, the Marble Palace was closed to the public in March 2020, and the Justices began hearing cases by telephone. A wide range of limitations on social and economic life was imposed by state and local authorities across the country. These restrictions and mandates also affected religious activities, disrupting gatherings of people of faith and worship, so they raised many religious liberty challenges.

Initially, the Court responded cautiously. In 2020, in two early cases, *South Bay United Pentecostal Church v. Newsom* and *Calvary Chapel Dayton Valley v. Sisolak*, the Court ruled against the religious organizations which argued that state lockdown orders (in California and Nevada, respectively) violated the Free Exercise Clause.[115] This approach was reversed in November 2020. As in the cases from

---

111 See: Bucchieri, Rebecca: *op. cit.*, pp. 282–297.
112 Rakove, Jack N.: *Beyond Belief, Beyond Conscience. The Radical Significance of the Free Exercise of Religion.* Oxford University Press: New York 2020, p. 166.
113 Oleske, James M. Jr.: "Free Exercise (Dis)honesty." *Wisconsin Law Review* 2019 (4), 2019, pp. 718–719.
114 Randall, Holly M.: "From Peyote to Parenthood: Why Employment Division v. Smith Must (and Might) Go." *Oklahoma City University Law Review* 45 (1), 2020, p. 67.
115 See: Epstein, Lee/Posner, Eric A.: "The Roberts Court and the Transformation of Constitutional Protections for Religion: A Statistical Portrait." *SSRN*, 2021, p. 4, retrieved 07.01.2022, from https://papers.ssrn.com/sol3/papers.cfm?abstract_id=3825759.

California and Nevada, the vote was 5 to 4, but in the New York case, it was a different 5 to 4.[116] This time, in *Roman Catholic Diocese of Brooklyn v. Cuomo*, the Court enjoined the Governor of New York from enforcing occupancy limits on religious services. This decision was quickly recognized as a watershed decision and it has been cited by the Supreme Court and other courts over one hundred times.[117] The reason behind this "different 5 to 4" vote was simple, and it was identified correctly beforehand by Holly M. Randall, who wrote: "I predict the Court will use the opportunity presented in *Fulton* to make a major change in the legal landscape, as prior musings by the Court have shown no shortage of desire, but merely a shortage of votes."[118] As it turned out, the *Fulton* decision left the deferential standard of *Employment Division v. Smith* nominally alive, but it was a major, if inconspicuous, jurisprudential revision. The shortage of votes was overcome in October 2020, when Amy Coney Barrett, the third appointee of President Donald Trump, took the seat of the late liberal Justice Ruth Bader Ginsburg. Delaine R. Swenson appropriately concluded that the Court's approach in these cases reflects the reality of the shifting majority in the Court as a result of new Justices appointed by President Trump:

> The Court has transitioned from a majority that opposed restrictions on governmental action during COVID to a majority that is more willing to stop governmental action that is deemed to be in violation of the Free Exercise of Religion Clause.[119]

This willingness was reflected in the *Tandon v. Newsom* case, decided by the Supreme Court in April 2021. The Court granted an injunction and prohibited enforcement of California's COVID-19 restrictions on private religious gatherings (California limited home gatherings of all kinds to three households). The five Justices in the majority found that California treated some comparable secular activities more favorably than at-home religious exercise, permitting hair salons, retail stores, etc. to bring together more than three households at a time. In a short dissent, Justice Kagan stated that at-home religious and secular gatherings are different from gatherings in commercial settings, and they do pose greater risk of virus transmission: interactions are longer, private houses are smaller and less ventilated, and social distancing and mask-wearing are less likely in private settings. These facts were presented in uncontested testimony by California's public health experts.

---

116 Greenhouse, Linda: *op. cit.*, p. 96.
117 McFadden, Trevor N./Kapoor, Vetan: "The Precedential Effects of the Supreme Court's Emergency Stays." *Harvard Journal of Law & Public Policy* 44 (3), 2021, p. 834.
118 Randall, Holly M.: *op. cit.*, p. 103.
119 Swenson, Delaine R.: "United States Supreme Court Approach to First Amendment Freedom of Religion in Response to the COVID Pandemic." *Review of European and Comparative Law* 66 (3), 2021, p. 237.

The winning streak for religion was interrupted in October 2021, when the Supreme Court, in a short order in *Does v. Mills*, rejected a religious exemption challenge to a COVID-19 vaccine mandate for health care workers in Maine. It remains to be seen whether this is a sign that there is some limit to the Court's willingness to grant exemptions for religious conservatives.[120] Justice Gorsuch, writing for the three dissenting Justices, cited *Tandon v. Newsom* to support the notion that a law is not neutral and generally applicable if it treats any comparable secular activity more favorably than religious exercise. The Maine vaccine mandate is not absolute: it provides a reasonable exemption for people with very rare medical conditions that would interfere with vaccinations. In Justice Gorsuch's view, this is a double standard that should trigger a strict scrutiny review.

Conclusion: Scopes Monkey Trial Revisited?

All the cases mentioned above could be described in much greater detail, but if we consider a broader picture of the Christian Right's legal revolt against modernity, some concluding remarks may be offered. On the whole, the conservative majority in the Supreme Court seems to have embarked on a time-travel mission back to the 1950s, attempting to reinstate the political and cultural dominance of white Christian Americans. As it is an impossible task in the current social, cultural, and demographic milieu, what the Court is doing amounts to laying the foundation for a Christian state within a state that may be insulated from general law requirements, yet also may be financed by taxpayer money. The COVID-19 pandemic brought into sharp relief the real-world consequences of granting religious exemptions from generally applicable laws to large swaths of the population. It is a problem of scale. Exempting relatively small groups like religious peyote users or even the Amish community is qualitatively different from enabling dozens of millions of Christians to disregard the law of the land. In the context of the COVID-19 pandemic, wide religious exemptions may delay or prevent reaching herd immunity. According to a recent study, "Christian nationalism's anti-science, anti-vaccine, anti-government intervention, pro-Trump ideology with a focus on protecting one's own freedom at the expense of protecting medically vulnerable people makes it the perfect storm for COVID-19 vaccine hesitancy."[121] The long-term social and political consequences of placing religious beliefs above the law

---

120 Millhiser, Ian: "The Supreme Court Finally Decides the Religious Right Asked for Too Much." *VOX*, October 29, 2021, retrieved 07.01.2022, from https://www.vox.com/2021/10/29/22753429/supreme-court-vaccine-mandate-maine-does-mills-religious-right-exemption-liberty-constitution.
121 Corcoran, Katie E./Scheitle, Christopher P./DiGregorio, Bernard D.: "Christian Nationalism and COVID-19 Vaccine Hesitancy and Uptake." *Vaccine* 39 (45), 2021, p. 6619.

will require thorough studies, but there is no reason to believe that this is going to contribute to better social cohesion, especially in a diversifying society.

The COVID-19 pandemic provides another useful vantage point for assessing the Supreme Court's record in the field of law and religion. I suggest that all in all, this is the Scopes Monkey Trial revisited. In 1925, a highly publicized trial took place in Tennessee. A high school teacher, John Scopes, was convicted of teaching evolution. This was only a short-lived victory for religious conservatives, for the national media depicted fundamentalists as backward buffoons outside the mainstream, and in the aftermath, many fundamentalists retreated from civic life.[122] Fundamentalists believed that Darwin's theory was an extremely dangerous challenge to the Biblical story of creation, so the preservation of Christianity required expunging Darwin's ideas. After the trial, they lost public support, and the fundamentalist movement became something of a religion of the rejected.[123]

The Supreme Court's recent record on religion bears similarities to the Scopes Trial in that on the one hand we have references to scientific data while on the other we have a mostly textual exegesis of a "sacred" text (the Constitution or the Bible). For instance, there is a striking contrast between the Court's reasoning in *Tandon v. Newsom* and arguments raised in *Opposition to Emergency Application for Writ of Injunction* filed in the Court by lawyers representing the state of California and defending California's pandemic response, which included restrictions on private gatherings. Apart from the honest lawyering, California's legal team used phrases and arguments like:

> These restrictions "have constantly evolved based on the scientific understanding of how COVID-19 spreads, the level of spread of COVID-19 in the State, and the extent to which the State's hospitals and ICUs lacked capacity."
>
> [T]he more people from different households a person interacts with at a gathering, the closer the physical interaction is, and the longer the interaction lasts, the higher the risk that a person with a COVID-19 infection, symptomatic or asymptomatic, may spread it to others.
>
> When individuals breathe, talk, sing, cough, or sneeze, they expel small respiratory droplets and aerosolized particles containing the virus that causes the disease.[124]

---

122 Domke, David/Coe, Kevin: *op. cit.*, p. 13.
123 Napierała, Paulina: *In God We Trust. Religia w sferze publicznej USA*. Księgarnia Akademicka: Kraków 2015, p. 202.
124 *Ritesh Tandon, et al., v. Gavin Newsom, et al. Opposition to Emergency Application for Writ of Injunction*, No. 20A151, retrieved 07.01.2022 from https://www.supremeco urt.gov/DocketPDF/20/20A151/175269/20210408143550366_Tandon%20v.%20New som%20-%20Opposition%20to%20Emergency%20Application%20-%204.8.21.pdf.

All this is supported by many references to documents produced by the California Department of Public Health and by Center for Disease Control and Prevention. What language did the Court use in rejecting California's arguments?

> Applicants are likely to succeed on the merits of their free exercise claim; they are irreparably harmed by the loss of free exercise rights "for even minimal periods of time"; and the State has not shown that "public health would be imperiled" by employing less restrictive measures.[125]

Obviously, it is a conclusion of a longer legal analysis, but this is the ultimate decision point. The Justices in Tandon had a concept of "free exercise," and they simply could not see that public health would be imperiled in a less restrictive setting. There was no need to analyze matters like respiratory droplets or interactions of a person with an asymptomatic infection.

The standard answer to this would be that Justices speak the language of law, and that they use it at the highest level, for it is a constitution they are expounding, so there was no need for them to engage in medical risk assessment. Yet, it should be troubling, or at least problematic, that governmental efforts to contain the COVID-19 pandemic, based on medical knowledge, could be thwarted by a handful of Supreme Court Justices who overtly do not rely on medical knowledge. The main objection, however, is that there is no law to speak of: there are no Religion Clauses of the First Amendment that Justices may assert that they are enforcing. Let us recall that there are four different major understandings of the Religion Clauses, from [Separation Establishment Clause/Separation Free Exercise] to [Accommodation Establishment Clause/Accommodation Free Exercise Clause], and that the meanings of keywords in these Clauses have been shifting from case to case. In fact, Justices use their own divergent versions of Religion Clauses which dictate the outcome of particular legal disputes, as could be clearly seen in the summary description of relevant cases presented above.

Many legal scholars rightly offer a strong critique of different aspects of Religion Clauses jurisprudence. For instance, James M. Oleske, Jr. harshly criticized the Court's achievements in this area of law:

> In addition to the foundational prevarications that marked the Court's major shifts from rejecting exemption rights to approving them and then back again, subsidiary inconsistencies and uncertainties have plagued the Court's free exercise jurisprudence for decades.[126]

Another scholar wrote that it is almost a necessary maxim for any article on the subject to begin with the phrase "hopelessly confused" when describing the

---

125 *Ritesh Tandon, et al. v. Gavin Newsom, Governor of California, et al.*, 593 U.S. ___ (2021).
126 Oleske, James M. Jr.: *op. cit.*, p. 691.

Supreme Court's Religion Clause cases.[127] Among the main causes of this failure on the part of the Court is the analogical approach to free exercise cases. According to *Harvard Law Review* authors, this approach is rooted in *Employment Division v. Smith*. If favored secular activities are sufficiently similar to the disfavored religious activity, the religious plaintiff will prevail. If they are markedly different, the court will defer to the state and reject the free exercise challenge. Ultimately, whether a free exercise challenge survives often turns on a single judge's view of what constitutes "similar" or "analogous" activity.[128] The COVID-19 cases decided by the Supreme Court and lower courts have demonstrated that similar facts can beget different outcomes, which means, for plaintiffs, that relief may depend not on the strength of a factual case but on the specific court that hears it.[129] Generally speaking, since the 1940s when the Supreme Court started its modern interpretation of Religion Clauses, the Court has proved unable to offer anything resembling reasoned analysis or robust reading of the First Amendment.

The American experience of judicial enforcement of Religion Clauses shows that attempts to legally regulate religious liberty require a balancing act. This is because the phenomenon of religion does not lend itself properly to legalization, while the idea of liberal constitutional democracy does not enjoy universal support among those living in Western liberal democracies. According to Karen Stenner and Jonathan Haidt, there is remarkably little evidence that living in a liberal democracy generally makes people more democratic and tolerant. This means that most societies "will *persistently* harbor a certain proportion of residents (by our calculations, roughly a third) who will always find diversity difficult to tolerate."[130] Therefore, the modern liberal constitutional state is not prone to engaging in a direct conflict with a competitive, religious system of power. The literal accommodation and recognition of religion in law would require accepting the notion that clergymen and people of faith fulfill the will of god, which would exclude, by and large, any possibility of infringing on religion by mere governmental regulations. Such an approach, which would be problematic, especially in religiously diverse countries, is not adopted in Western democracies. However, attempts to treat religious expression in its purely this-worldly dimension of life as a subtype of

---

127 Failinger, Marie A.: "Against Idols: The Court as a Symbol-Making or Rhetorical Institution." *University of Pennsylvania Journal of Constitutional Law* 8 (3), 2006, p. 372.
128 "Constitutional Constraints on Free Exercise Analogies." *Harvard Law Review* 134 (5), March 2021, pp. 1782–1784.
129 "Constitutional Constraints on Free Exercise Analogies," *op. cit.*, p. 1790.
130 Stenner, Karen/Haidt, Jonathan: "Authoritarianism Is Not a Momentary Madness, But an Eternal Dynamic Within Liberal Democracies." In: Sunstein, Cass R. (ed.): *Can It Happen Here? Authoritarianism in America*, HarperCollins: New York 2018, p. 210.

freedom of conscience are usually not consistent. There is a widespread belief that religion is special, which may lead in two opposite directions, either toward isolating the state from religion or to accommodation, being the basis of broad religious exemptions. What is also evident is a reluctance or inability of public authorities to appraise the public value of religious beliefs. The constitutional discourse performed in courts conceals a lack of readiness to confront directly religious attitudes incompatible with or even hostile to modern liberal democracy. Courts tend to evade this issue by inventing and inconsistently applying various tests or criteria, and by selective usage of prior judgments. This is feigned problem-solving, since we can observe how judges and justices who are educated, experienced in legal matters, and respected in their social circles reach opposite results.

Since the Supreme Court's Religion Clauses jurisprudence is rarely if ever lauded for its coherence and stability, there is a clear need for constantly and openly negotiating in parliamentary bodies the character of the polity which encompasses people of different faiths and nonreligious people. If we recall that the "Christian Right" project is mostly of a political nature, the need becomes more pressing because attempts to implement progressive reforms made by the Biden administration and Democrats in Congress may prompt plutocrats to tap into the reservoir of Christian nationalism and generate more outrage among people who experience their lives in this cultural framework.

References

American Civil Liberties Union: "Fulton v. City of Philadelphia," retrieved 07.01.2022, from https://www.aclu.org/cases/fulton-v-city-philadelphia.

Balkin, Jack M.: *The Cycles of Constitutional Time*. Oxford University Press: New York 2020.

Balmer, Randall: "The Real Origins of the Religious Right." *Politico*, May 27, 2014, retrieved 07.01.2022, from https://www.politico.com/magazine/story/2014/05/religious-right-real-origins-107133/.

Barak-Corren, Netta: "A License to Discriminate? The Market Response to Masterpiece Cakeshop." *Harvard Civil Rights: Civil Liberties Law Review* 56 (2), 2021.

Barclay, Stephanie H.: "First Amendment 'Harms.'" *Indiana Law Journal* 95 (2), 2020.

Bean, Tanner J./Wilson, Robin F.: "The Administrative State as a New Front in the Culture War: Little Sisters of the Poor v. Pennsylvania." *Cato Supreme Court Review* 2019–2020, 2019–2020.

Brest, Paul et al.: *Processes of Constitutional Decision-Making. Cases and Materials*. Aspen Publishers: New York 2006.

Biskupic, Joan: *The Chief. The Life and Turbulent Times of Chief Justice*. Basic Books: New York 2019.

Boden, Anastasia: "Looking Ahead: Déjà Vu at the Supreme Court." *Cato Supreme Court Review* 2019–2020, 2019–2020.

Boorstein, Michelle: "A Horn-Wearing 'Shaman.' A Cowboy Evangelist. For Some, the Capitol Attack Was a Kind of Christian Revolt." *The Washington Post*, June 7, 2021, retrieved 07.01.2022, from https://www.washingtonpost.com/religion/2021/07/06/capitol-insurrection-trump-christian-nationalism-shaman/.

Bucchieri, Rebecca: "Religious Freedom Versus Public Health: The Necessity of Compulsory Vaccination for Schoolchildren." *Boston University Public Interest Law Journal* 25 (2), 2016.

Butler, Anthea: *White Evangelical Racism. The Politics of Morality in America*. University of North Carolina Press: Chapel Hill 2021.

Chemerinsky, Erwin: *Constitutional Law. Principles and Policies*. Aspen Publishers: New York 2006.

"Constitutional Constraints on Free Exercise Analogies." *Harvard Law Review* 134 (5), March 2021.

Corcoran, Katie E./Scheitle, Christopher P./DiGregorio, Bernard D.: "Christian Nationalism and COVID-19 Vaccine Hesitancy and Uptake." *Vaccine* 39 (45), 2021.

D'Amato, Richard J.: "A "Very Specific" Holding: Analyzing the Effect of Hobby Lobby on Religious Liberty Challenges to Housing Discrimination Laws." *Columbia Law Review* 116 (4), 2016.

Domke, David/Coe, Kevin. *The God Strategy. How Religion Became a Political Weapon in America*. Oxford University Press: New York 2010.

Epstein, Lee/Posner, Eric A.: "The Roberts Court and the Transformation of Constitutional Protections for Religion: A Statistical Portrait." *SSRN*, 2021, p. 4, retrieved 07.01.2022, from https://papers.ssrn.com/sol3/papers.cfm?abstract_id=3825759.

Epstein, Lee/Posner, Eric A.: "How the Religious Right Has Transformed the Supreme Court." *New York Times*, September 22, 2020, retrieved 07.01.2022, from https://www.nytimes.com/2020/09/22/opinion/supreme-court-religion.html.

Failinger, Marie A.: "Against Idols: The Court as a Symbol-Making or Rhetorical Institution." *University of Pennsylvania Journal of Constitutional Law* 8 (3), 2006.

FitzGerald, Frances: *The Evangelicals. The Struggle to Shape America*. Simon & Schuster, Inc.: New York 2018.

Garber, Judith A.: "The Christian Right, the Federal Courts, and the Constitution in the United States." *Constitutional Forum Constitutionnel* 15 (1), 2006.

Gillman, Howard/Chemerinsky, Erwin: *The Religion Clauses. The Case for Separating Church and State*. Oxford University Press: New York 2020.

Greenhouse, Linda: *Justice on the Brink. The Death of Ruth Bader Ginsburg, the Rise of Amy Coney Barrett, and Twelve Months That Transformed the Supreme Court*. Random House: New York 2021.

Hacker, Jacob S./Pierson, Paul: *Let Them Eat Tweets. How the Right Rules in an Age of Extreme Inequality*. Liveright: New York 2020.

Hall, Matthew E.K.: *The Nature of Supreme Court Power*. Cambridge University Press: New York 2013.

Hartman, Andrew: *A War for the Soul of America. A History of the Culture Wars*. The University of Chicago Press: Chicago 2019.

Hirschl, Ran/Shachar, Ayelet: "'Religious Talk' in Narratives of Membership." In: Graber, Mark A./Levinson, Sanford/Tushnet, Mark (eds.): *Constitutional Democracy in Crisis?*. Oxford University Press: New York 2018.

Hollis-Brusky, Amanda/Wilson, Joshua C.: *Separate but Faithful. The Christian Right's Radical Struggle to Transform Law and Legal Culture*. Oxford University Press: New York 2020.

Irons, Peter: *God on Trial. Dispatches from America's Religious Battlefields*. Viking: New York 2007.

Jelen, Ted G.: *To Serve God and Mammon. Church-State Relations in American Politics*. Georgetown University Press: Washington, DC 2010.

Killmond, Marie: "Why Is Vaccination Different? A Comparative Analysis of Religious Exemptions." *Columbia Law Review* 117 (4), 2017.

Klarman, Michael J.: "Foreword: The Degradation of American Democracy—and the Court." *Harvard Law Review* 134 (1), 2020.

Kobes Du Mez, Kristin: *Jesus and John Wayne. How White Evangelicals Corrupted a Faith and Fractured a Nation*. W.W. Norton: New York 2021.

Kruse, Kevin M.: *One Nation Under God. How Corporate America Invented Christian America*. Basic Books: New York 2016.

Kubas, Sebastian: "The Christian Right, Judicial Review, and the Exploitation of Religious Passions: Hidden Sources and Possible Jurisprudential Effects." A conference paper presented at GIRES International Conference: *Religion and Politics in the United States*, 17–18.07.2021.

Leiter, Brian: *Why Tolerate Religion?* Princeton University Press: Princeton 2014.

Levitsky, Steven/Ziblatt, Daniel: *How Democracies Die*. Crown: New York 2018.

Lingo, Bradley J./Schietzelt, Michael G.: "Fulton and the Future of Free Exercise." *Regent University Law Review* 33 (1), 2020.

"Little Sisters of the Poor Saints Peter and Paul Home v. Pennsylvania." *Harvard Law Review* 134 (1), 2020.

Luchenitser, Alex J.: "A New Era of Inequality? Hobby Lobby and Religious Exemptions from Anti-Discrimination Laws." *Harvard Law & Policy Review* 9 (1), 2015.

Lund, Christopher C.: "Free Exercise Reconceived: The Logic and Limits of Hosanna-Tabor." *Northwestern University Law Review* 108 (4), 2014.

Lupu, Ira C./Tuttle, Robert W.: *Secular Government, Religious People*. William B. Eerdmans Publishing Company: Grand Rapids, MI 2014.

Maxwell, Angie/Shields, Todd: *The Long Southern Strategy. How Chasing White Voters in the South Changed American Politics.* Oxford University Press: New York 2019.

McFadden, Trevor N./Kapoor, Vetan: "The Precedential Effects of the Supreme Court's Emergency Stays." *Harvard Journal of Law & Public Policy* 44 (3), 2021.

Millhiser, Ian: "The Supreme Court Finally Decides the Religious Right Asked for Too Much." *VOX*, October 29, 2021, retrieved 07.01.2022, from https://www.vox.com/2021/10/29/22753429/supreme-court-vaccine-mandate-maine-does-mills-religious-right-exemption-liberty-constitution.

Millhiser, Ian: *Injustices. The Supreme Court's History of Comforting the Comfortable and Afflicting the Afflicted.* Nation Books: New York 2016.

Murray, Melissa: "Inverting Animus: Masterpiece Cakeshop and the New Minorities." *Supreme Court Review* 2018, 2018.

Napierała, Paulina: *In God We Trust. Religia w sferze publicznej USA.* Księgarnia Akademicka: Kraków 2015.

Nelson, Anne: *Shadow Network. Media, Money, and the Secret Hub of the Radical Right.* Bloomsbury Publishing: New York 2021.

Nichols, Tom: *Our Own Worst Enemy. The Assault from within on Modern Democracy.* Oxford University Press: New York 2021.

O'Brien, David. M.: *Constitutional Law and Politics. Volume Two. Civil Rights and Civil Liberties.* W.W. Norton: New York 2011.

Oleske, James M. Jr.: "Free Exercise (Dis)honesty." *Wisconsin Law Review* 2019 (4), 2019.

Posner, Sarah: *Unholy. How White Christian Nationalists Powered the Trump Presidency, and the Devastating Legacy They Left Behind.* Random House: New York 2021.

Rakove, Jack N.: *Beyond Belief, Beyond Conscience. The Radical Significance of the Free Exercise of Religion.* Oxford University Press: New York 2020.

Randall, Holly M.: "From Peyote to Parenthood: Why Employment Division v. Smith Must (and Might) Go." *Oklahoma City University Law Review* 45 (1), 2020.

Ritesh Tandon, et al. v. Gavin Newsom, Governor of California, et al., 593 U.S. ___ (2021).

Ritesh Tandon, et al., v. Gavin Newsom, et al. Opposition to Emergency Application for Writ of Injunction, No. 20A151, retrieved 07.01.2022, from https://www.supremecourt.gov/DocketPDF/20/20A151/175269/20210408143550366_Tandon%20v.%20Newsom%20-%20Opposition%20to%20Emergency%20Application%20-%204.8.21.pdf.

Rolsky, L. Benjamin: "Producing the Christian Right: Conservative Evangelicalism, Representation, and the Recent Religious Past." *Religions* 12 (3), 2021.

Savage, David G.: *Turning Right. The Making of the Rehnquist Supreme Court.* John Wiley & Sons: New York 1993.

Schragger, Richard/Schwartzman, Micah: "Religious Antiliberalism and the First Amendment." *Minnesota Law Review* 104 (3), 2020.

Stenner, Karen/Haidt, Jonathan: "Authoritarianism Is Not a Momentary Madness, But an Eternal Dynamic Within Liberal Democracies." In: Sunstein, Cass R. (ed.): *Can It Happen Here? Authoritarianism in America*, HarperCollins: New York 2018.

Suk Gersen, Jeannie: "The Supreme Court's Surprising Term." *New Yorker*, July 5, 2021.

Sullivan, Winnifred Fallers: "Religion." In: Tushnet, Mark/Graber, Mark A./Levinson, Sanford (eds.): *The Oxford Handbook of the U.S. Constitution.* Oxford University Press: New York 2015.

Sunstein, Cass R. (ed.): *Can It Happen Here? Authoritarianism in America.* HarperCollins: New York 2018.

Sunstein, Cass R.: *Designing Democracy. What Constitutions Do.* Oxford University Press: New York 2002.

Swenson, Delaine R.: "United States Supreme Court Approach to First Amendment Freedom of Religion in Response to the COVID Pandemic." *Review of European and Comparative Law* 66 (3), 2021.

Tribe, Laurence H.: *Abortion. The Clash of Absolutes.* W.W. Norton & Company: New York 1992.

Trinity Lutheran Church of Columbia, Inc. v. Comer, 582 U.S. __ (2017).

Tushnet, Mark: *Taking Back the Constitution. Activist Judges and the Next Age of American Law.* Yale University Press: New Haven, CT 2020.

Tushnet, Mark: *A Court Divided. The Rehnquist Court and the Future of Constitutional Law.* W.W. Norton: New York 2006.

Tushnet, Mark: "Constitutional Hardball." *John Marshall Law Review* 37 (2), 2004.

United States v. Morrison, 529 U.S. 598 (2000).

Wheeler, Lydia: "Religious Objections Stand in Path of Mask, Vaccine Mandates." *Bloomberg Law*, June 29, 2021, retrieved 07.01.2022, from https://news.bloomberglaw.com/health-law-and-business/religious-objections-stand-in-path-of-mask-vaccine-mandates.

West, Ellis: "The Case Against a Right to Religion-Based Exemptions." *Notre Dame Journal of Law, Ethics & Public Policy* 4 (3), 1990.

Whitehead, Andrew L./Perry, Samuel L.: *Taking America Back for God. Christian Nationalism in the United States.* Oxford University Press: New York 2020.

Williams, Daniel K.: *God's Own Party: The Making of the Christian Right.* Oxford University Press: New York 2012.

Jerold L. Waltman

The Legal and Political Context of Contemporary Free Exercise Jurisprudence

Abstract: The purpose of this chapter is to set the contemporary free exercise jurisprudence of the Supreme Court in legal and political contexts. An initial section will briefly lay out some background by discussing the evolution of how the Court handled free exercise cases up to the passage of the Religious Land Use and Institutionalized Persons Act (RLUIPA) of 2000. A second part will then turn to the social and political trends bearing on the politics of free exercise. Following that, I will examine three major cases from the last few terms of the Court. Finally, the threads will be drawn together to see if any new pathways are developing among the justices.

Keywords: Supreme Court, free exercise, religious liberty, religious diversity, LGBTQ rights

The Historical Background

The modern era of free exercise jurisprudence began in 1990. Before that, the Court had applied the "compelling interest" test when someone requested an exemption, on religious grounds, from an otherwise generally applicable law.[1] Even so, when the Court applied the test, governments won more often than they lost. For example, the test was not utilized at all in certain critical institutions, such as prisons and the military.[2] Occasionally, religious claimants prevailed, but they had to have an awfully strong case to do so.[3] In 1990, however, in the landmark case of *Employment Division of Oregon v. Smith*, the Court, with Justice Antonin Scalia writing for a 6–3 majority, jettisoned the compelling interest test and held that any future exemptions would have to be granted by the legislative branch.[4] Virtually

---

1 This test was developed in *Sherbert v. Verner*, 374 U.S. 398 (1963).
2 On prisons, see *O'Lone v. Estate of Shabazz*, 482 U.S. 342 (1987); on the military, see *Goldman v. Weinberger*, 475 U.S. 503 (1986).
3 See especially *Wisconsin v. Yoder*, 406 U.S. 205 (1972).
4 494 U.S. 872 (1990). For a thorough examination of the case, see Long, Carolyn: *Religious Freedom and Indian Rights: The Case of* Oregon v. Smith. University Press of Kansas: Lawrence 2000.

every civil rights group and religious organization in the country joined a coalition asking Congress to enact a law that would reinstate the compelling interest test. There was broad congressional support for doing so, but the problem was locating a constitutional basis for the statute. While Congress could presumably tie its own hands regarding federal legislation, there was more uncertainty when it came to their ordering the courts to apply the compelling interest test in state cases. After consulting a number of experts, the writers of the proposed law decided to rest it on section 5 of the Fourteenth Amendment. Recalling that the First Amendment, which contains the religion clauses, applies solely to the federal government,[5] the Court has repeatedly held that section 1 of the Fourteenth Amendment makes the First Amendment applicable to the states.[6] Section 5 of the Fourteenth Amendment then says: "The Congress shall have power to enforce, by appropriate legislation, the provisions of this article." Citing this authority, Congress passed the Religious Freedom Restoration Act (RFRA) in 1993, mandating that the courts adhere to the compelling interest test in all free exercise cases. However, in 1997, the Supreme Court held that RFRA exceeded Congress' power under section 5 and was therefore unconstitutional, at least as it applied to the states.[7]

Members of Congress sympathetic to the civil rights-religious coalition immediately drafted what they termed the Religious Liberty Protection Act (RLPA), which was almost identical to RFRA in substance but sought other constitutional grounds upon which to base it.[8] As this proposal was being debated, however, fissures began to appear in Congress among the groups which had earlier backed RFRA. The rub came from gay and lesbian groups. These organizations had begun to secure a handful of state and local ordinances that banned discrimination based on sexual orientation in housing and employment. They feared that religiously devout landlords and employers would use RLPA to claim exemptions from these measures, and any future ones they might obtain. Before long, civil rights groups

---

5 "Congress shall make no law respecting the establishment of religion, or prohibiting the free exercise thereof...."

6 The Court has repeatedly held that the due-process clause of the Fourteenth Amendment is the reason the First Amendment applies to the states. The pertinent part of section 1 of the Amendment reads as follows: "No State shall make or enforce any law which shall ... deprive any person of life, liberty, or property, without due process of law."

7 *City of Boerne v. Flores*, 521 U.S. 507 (1997). I analyzed this case in Waltman, Jerold: *Congress, the Supreme Court, and Religious Liberty: The Case of City of Boerne v. Flores*. Palgrave: New York 2013.

8 These were the commerce clause, the spending clause, and a more careful rendition of the evidentiary record for use of section 5. See Waltman, Jerold: *Religious Free Exercise and Contemporary American Politics: The Saga of the Religious Land Use and Institutionalized Persons Act of 2000*. Continuum: New York 2011, Chap. 3.

and other liberals began to withdraw their support for RLPA and, while it passed the House of Representatives, it stalled in the Senate. A scaled-back version, dealing only with land use planning and prisons (RLUIPA), passed later in 2000, but a new politics of religious free exercise had been born.

A Changing Social Reality

The social and political environment found in the country at any given moment affects the nature of Supreme Court jurisprudence in two important ways. First, it determines the types of conflicts that arise in society. These, in turn, generate the laws legislative bodies pass and then the cases the judiciary is called upon to decide. Second, ideas about the proper structure of social relations change with time. There are always unspoken assumptions and guiding ideas that are widely shared, especially among the educated strata of society, including judges. As Justice Benjamin Cardozo once famously said, "The great tides and currents which engulf the rest of men do not turn aside in their course and pass the judges by."[9] Today, there are four elements of the American social and religious landscape that seem to be driving free exercise jurisprudence.

First, the American social and religious environment has grown increasingly diverse. Protestants, of course, were the founding denominations—Puritans in New England and Anglicans in the southern colonies—during the colonial period. To be sure, there was a scattering of Catholics and Jews, but they were clear minorities. In the early nineteenth century, Catholic immigrants—chiefly from Ireland and Germany—came in greater numbers. By 1860, in fact, given the splits among Baptists, Methodists, and Presbyterians into Northern and Southern wings, Catholics became the largest single denomination. Nevertheless, in 1900, fully 80% of Americans still said that they were Protestants. And, while anti-Catholic feeling and anti-Semitism reared their heads periodically, by the late nineteenth century, such sentiments had largely subsided.

By the mid-twentieth century, Will Herberg and other analysts were celebrating the birth of an American "civil religion" which drew on all three religious traditions. This position, he argued, "has become one of the accepted aspects of the American Way of Life."[10] Still, as Joseph Bottum has pointed out, a broad ecumenical Protestantism remained the central pillar of the civil religion. "In truth, all the talk, from the eighteenth century on, of the United States as a religious nation was really just a make-nice way of saying it was a Christian nation—and even to call it a Christian nation was usually just a soft and ecumenical attempt to gloss over the obvious

---

9   Cardozo, Benjamin: *The Nature of the Judicial Process:* Yale University Press: New Haven, CT 1921, p. 168.
10 Herberg, Will: *Protestant, Catholic, Jew: An Essay in American Religious Sociology.* Doubleday: New York 1955, p. 260.

fact that the United States was, at its root, a *Protestant* nation. Catholics and Jews were tolerated, off and on, but 'the destiny of America,' as Alexis de Tocqueville observed in 1835, was 'embodied in the first Puritan who landed on these shores.'"[11]

All this changed, however, with the passage of the Immigration and Nationality Act of 1965.[12] Prior to this, immigrants from Europe, and even more narrowly Western Europe, were highly favored; this act, however, swept away the quota system, leading to an explosion of immigration from Asia and Latin America. In the 1950s, immigrants from Europe constituted 53% of the total, whereas those from Asia and Latin America made up 31%; in contrast, by the 1990s Europeans had fallen to 15%, and those hailing from Asia and Latin America had risen to 78%. While many of the Latin American immigrants replenished Catholic pews, Asians tended to bring adherents of non-Western religions. There were, for example, reportedly 962 mosques in the country in 1994 but by 2011, that number had grown to 2,106.[13] Concomitantly, the number of regular mosque participants has surged from 500,000 to 2,600,000. Parallel figures could be adduced for Buddhists and Hindus.

Christians, especially white Christians and Protestant Christians, have seen accompanying declines. Protestants of all types and ethnicities now make up only 45% of the population.[14] White Christians of all denominations have suffered the greatest declines, though. As recently as 1996, 65% of Americans counted themselves as white Christians; now the proportion is 44%.

Moreover, even a quick glance at the age distribution of Americans shows that the younger generations are even more diverse than older ones. For example, among those 18 to 29, only 28% are white Christians. Thus, as the population ages, these changes are likely to be magnified.

Alongside this growing diversity there has been a noticeable shift toward a more secular society. This can be seen, first, in the increasing number of Americans who claim to be religiously unaffiliated, or what are called the "nones" by social scientists, accounting now for 23% of the population. Looking at the age breakdown of those selecting this designation also points to a growth in this category. For example, in 1986, only 10% of those aged 18–29 said they were religiously unaffiliated; by 2020, 36% of those in this cohort did so.

---

11 Bottum, Joseph: "The Death of Protestant America: A Political Theory of the Protestant Mainline." *First Things*, August 2008.
12 Orchowski, Margaret Sands: *The Law that Changed the Face of America: The Immigration and Nationality Act of 1965*. Rowman and Littlefield: Lanham, MD 2015 provides a thorough analysis.
13 See Waltman, Jerold: *Church and State in the Roberts Court*. McFarland: Jefferson, NC 2019, Chap. 1.
14 Public Religion Research Institute, *The 2020 Census of American Religion*, July 8, 2021. Subsequent figures are also from this survey, unless otherwise indicated.

A second weather vane for this trend is how many people now openly say they are agnostics or atheists. At one time, hardly anyone told pollsters they took that position. In 2007, though, 25% of the "nones" said they were either agnostics or atheists; by 2014, this number had risen to 31%. Reflecting this fact, when President Obama issued the annual proclamation celebrating Religious Freedom Day in 2014, he, for the first time, explicitly included atheists and agnostics: "Today, America embraces people of all faiths, and of no faith. We are Christians and Jews, Muslims and Hindus, Buddhists and Sikhs, atheists and agnostics."

Another indicator of where we are has been the growth of well-organized militant anti-religious groups. One of the most prominent, and active, of these is the Freedom from Religion Foundation. They have pursued any number of lawsuits challenging religious liberty (and also fought Establishment Clause cases). Additionally, they have even sponsored ads on national television.[15]

A third noteworthy trend has been the remarkable shift in attitudes regarding homosexuality. In 1987, 75% of Americans said homosexual activity was always wrong, compared to only 12% who said it was not wrong at all.[16] By 2010, these figures were 44% and 41%, respectively. In 1988, a mere 11% thought homosexuals should have the right to marry, with 68% opposed. But in 2015, 55% supported the right of gays and lesbians to marry with only 39% opposed.[17] While significant differences among different demographic groups remain, there are interesting notes to be made even there. For example, among those born between 1928 and 1945, support for gay marriage rose from 21% in 2001 to 39% in 2015. And perhaps more surprisingly, it climbed from 13% to 24%, nearly doubling, among white evangelical Protestants.

This extraordinary shift has been accompanied, quite naturally, by a rise in organizations lobbying for more favorable public policies toward homosexuals. In the 1990s, they began achieving some successes at the state and local level, obtaining laws and ordinances outlawing discrimination in housing, employment, and service in public accommodations on the basis of sexual orientation. At the moment, there is also growing pressure in Congress to pass the wide-ranging Equality Act, which would ban discrimination against LGBTQ people throughout the country in a wide variety of areas.[18] We saw above how this changed milieu led to the undoing of the Religious Liberty Protection Act, and we will revisit it again below.

---

15 The ad, featuring former president Ronald Reagan's son, retrieved 15.08.2021, from https://ffrf.org/news/video.
16 National Opinion Research Center Poll, September 2011.
17 Pew Research Center, *Religion and Public Life Survey*, July 29, 2015.
18 Details on this proposed legislation, that at the moment has passed the House and is backed by the White House, can be found at Santos, Thee, Medina, Caroline, and Gruberg, Sharita: "What You Need to Know About the Equality Act." Center for American Progress, March 2021, retrieved 15.08.2021, from https://www.americanprogress.org/issues/lgbtqrights/reports.

Finally, these three trends have made traditional Christians, especially evangelical Protestants, but many conservative Catholics as well, uncomfortable. In fact, in many quarters of conservative Christianity, something close to a state of siege mentality has emerged. The world they inhabited is visibly slipping away, making them feel, rightly or wrongly, strangers in their own country.

To cite specific data, in one 2012 poll, for example, 56% of Americans indicated they did *not* believe religious liberty is under any threat; however, 61% of white evangelicals believed that it *is*.[19] Similarly, a 2015 survey found that 41% of the adult population but 77% of evangelical Protestants felt that "religious freedom in the U.S. has grown worse in the last 10 years."[20] In another survey, which asked whether they perceived that Christianity is under attack in the country, 68% of all Protestants, 54% of Catholics, but fully 81% of evangelical Protestants answered yes.[21]

In another poll, queried if they thought, "the gay and lesbian community is the most active group trying to remove Christian values from the country," only 30% of adults answered positively, but 49% of practicing Christians and fully 68% of evangelicals did so.[22]

In short, the American religious landscape has changed dramatically in the last few decades, and this has had enormous political ramifications. This has in turn had an important role in shaping the Supreme Court's jurisprudence regarding the Free Exercise Clause.

An Anatomy of Three Recent Cases

We can get a more concrete view of the direction of the contemporary Supreme Court by looking at three of its recent free exercise cases, involving the autonomy of religious organizations' personnel decisions, the wishes of religiously affiliated organizations to be exempt from antidiscrimination laws involving LGBTQ people, and claims by business firms to be exempt from those same laws.

The first of these is *Our Lady of Guadalupe School v. Morrisey-Berru*, which was decided along with a companion case, *St. James Catholic School v. Biel*, because the facts were so similar.[23] Both Morrisey-Berru and Biel were teachers at Catholic elementary schools. While most of their school day was spent on secular subjects, they also taught religion classes, regularly led their students in prayer, and prepared them to participate in the Mass. Both schools had clearly enunciated policies stipulating that Catholic tenets should inform all subjects, secular and religious.

---

19 Public Religion Research Institute Poll, March 15, 2012.
20 Barma Group Poll, October 1, 2015.
21 Fox News Poll, July 21, 2015.
22 Public Religion Research Institute Poll, June 11, 2014.
23 591 U.S. ___ (2020).

Both women were denied contract renewals: Morrisey-Berru claimed because of her age and Biel because she requested a leave of absence to obtain treatment for breast cancer. These rationales would be illegal under federal law, and the Equal Employment Opportunity Commission (EEOC), the federal agency charged with enforcing the relevant law, agreed. The schools maintained that the reason in both cases was poor performance. Nevertheless, the issue raised in the courts was whether their positions were covered by the "ministerial exception," a doctrine which shields religious bodies from antidiscrimination laws, and therefore the reasons for the terminations were irrelevant.

The ministerial exception grew out of the "church autonomy" doctrine, which courts had long used to announce that judges would not enter into disputes (most of which dealt with property issues) involving church doctrines and matters of internal organization. Although lower courts had developed and applied the ministerial exception to churches' decisions regarding whom to employ, the conditions of employment, and terminations for years, it was not until 2012 that the Supreme Court gave its imprimatur to the doctrine in the case of *Hosanna-Tabor Lutheran Church v. EEOC*.[24] A teacher at a Lutheran elementary school found herself in a dispute with the school's officials. After failing to resolve her rift with the school, she took her complaints to the EEOC. But this step violated the denomination's written policy that such matters had to be settled within the church's judicial system. Citing her taking of this step, her contract was terminated. Under federal law, initiating retribution for filing a complaint with the EEOC is itself illegal.

The case posed two critical issues: (1) Would the "ministerial exception" be explicitly ratified by the Supreme Court? (2) If so, did this teacher fall within it? The Court unanimously answered "yes" to both questions. For subsequent cases, though, how the justices answered the second question was crucial. Chief Justice John Roberts, writing for the Court, reviewed the teacher's duties and held that they were sufficiently infused with religious elements to place her within the category of a minister. What he did not do was establish any kind of clear framework that could be applied in the future, refusing to lay out which features of the teacher's job were the most significant.

In Morrisey-Berru and Biel's cases, several aspects of their jobs paralleled the one in *Hosanna-Tabor*, but there were also some important differences, chiefly that the teacher in the Lutheran school had been given the title "commissioned minister" and possessed academic credentials in religion, while both Morrisey-Berru and Biel, on the other hand, were clearly designated "lay teachers" by their schools and had no formal academic training in religion. Nevertheless, Justice Samuel Alito, writing for five of the seven justices in the majority, stressed that titles and academic preparation were important, but they were not determinative. "What matters, at bottom," he said, "is what an employee does." A court's task is "to take

---

24 565 U.S. ___ (2012).

all relevant circumstances into account and to determine whether each particular position implicated the fundamental purpose of the exception." He then took up a lengthy discussion of how important childhood education was to the development and maintenance of any religion's values. In addition, he quoted extensively from the faculty handbooks of the two schools that spelled out how vital it was for all staff to represent the Catholic position on all matters and to live a life consistent with those values. Consequently, he held that these teachers' positions were central to the role of the church, fitting them within the ministerial exception; therefore, their conditions of employment, including termination, were solely within the discretion of church officials and not subject to governmental oversight.

As a result of this holding, the ministerial exception enjoys a rather wide berth, and the autonomy of churches (and other religious bodies) has been thereby expanded. A concurring opinion by Justice Clarence Thomas, joined by Justice Neil Gorsuch, would have gone even further, reiterating a position taken by Thomas earlier in *Hosanna-Tabor*, that courts should merely defer to any religious institution's claim that someone is a minister without further inquiry. Justice Sonia Sotomayor, joined by Justice Ruth Ginsburg, dissented, arguing that the *Hosanna-Tabor* framework should be more narrowly applied and that the differences in the jobs at issue here put them outside the ministerial exception.

The next important case, *Fulton v. City of Philadelphia*, decided in 2021, lies at the intersection of LGBTQ rights and religious liberty.[25] It is an area that is controversial both politically and jurisprudentially and is still evolving. From one perspective, this case was a clear victory for religious liberty, especially inasmuch as it was unanimous. At the same time, the rationale the majority used to rule in favor of Catholic Social Services, and win the praise of advocates of religious liberty, puts the holding on tenuous grounds. Given this, as we shall see below, even the Human Rights Campaign, the major civil rights organization for LGBTQ rights, was not entirely dismayed.

Catholic Social Services of Philadelphia (CSS) had long worked to place children in foster homes. In this endeavor, along with several other agencies, both religious and secular, they operated under a contract with the city. Based on its religious tenets, CSS has a policy against placing foster children in the homes of gay (or unmarried) couples. No gay couple had ever applied to CSS to become foster parents; had they done so, CSS would simply have referred them to one of the other agencies in the city.

The city contract had a standard nondiscrimination provision. Moreover, Philadelphia had adopted a city ordinance banning discrimination in "public accommodations" on the basis of several traits, including sexual orientation (which had been added recently). Significantly, at least in the Court's reading, both the contract and the ordinance had a provision allowing public officials the power

---

25 593 U.S. ___ (2021).

to grant exemptions from these strictures. Notably, no exemptions had ever been granted.

When a local newspaper ran an article on CSS's restrictive policies, the city informed CSS that, based on the contract and the ordinance, they would be removed from the foster care program unless they agreed to accept gay couples.

Two previous cases are pertinent to understanding the Court's opinion in *Fulton*. The first is the *Smith* holding, noted above. The other, *Masterpiece Cakeshop v. Colorado Civil Rights Commission*,[26] was not a directly relevant legal precedent, but it too dealt with the collision between antidiscrimination laws involving LGBTQ people and religious liberty. A baker in Colorado had refused to bake a wedding cake for a gay couple because he had a strong religious objection to gay marriage. His action violated a state statute forbidding discrimination against LGBTQ people in commercial transactions, and the state Civil Rights Commission ordered him to provide the cake.

Following *Smith*, the Court has held that to escape strict scrutiny[27] a public policy must be both neutral and generally applicable. (To be neutral means that it cannot discriminate against religious people or institutions.)[28] Failing either of these criteria would subject the policy to strict scrutiny, requiring a compelling governmental interest in not allowing an exemption and the utilization of the least restrictive means of accomplishing the policy's objective. In the *Masterpiece Cakeshop* case, the Court found a way to waltz around the central issue by finding that members of the Colorado Human Rights Commission, the body charged with enforcing the law, had made statements hostile to religious freedom. This made their decision fail the neutrality test. The narrowness of the holding meant that the baker was bound to find himself back in court when another LGBTQ person sought his services, as has been the case.[29]

In the current case, Chief Justice John Roberts and the majority (Justices Stephen Breyer, Sonia Sotomayor, Elena Kagan, Brett Kavanaugh, and Amy Coney Barrett joined Roberts' opinion) turned to a similarly narrow ground, this time involving general applicability. They held that since both the contract and the ordinance allowed for exceptions, the policy was not truly generally applicable, as

---

26 584 U.S. ___ (2018).
27 "Compelling interest" test and "strict scrutiny" are often (and somewhat confusingly) used interchangeably. Strict scrutiny, technically, requires both a compelling interest and the use of the least restrictive means. The compelling interest test has an implication of least restrictive means. For our purposes here, they can be seen as identical.
28 The guiding case here is *Church of Lukumi Babalu Aye v. Hialeah*, 508 U.S. 520 (1993).
29 The current case is discussed in Verlee, Megan: "Denver Court Finds Masterpiece Cakeshop Baker Violated Anti-Discrimination Law in Refusing to Make Gender Transition Cake." *Colorado Public Radio*, June 17, 2021.

required by *Smith* to be immune from strict scrutiny. Then, applying strict scrutiny, they found the reasons the city offered for having a compelling interest wanting. The city, therefore, could not intrude on CSS's religious liberty.

Three concurring opinions were penned. Amy Coney Barrett honed in on the neutrality requirement; surely, she argued, the Free Exercise Clause must offer more protection than merely being free from direct discrimination. She pointed out that in other areas of first amendment jurisprudence, such as free speech, the Constitution's prohibitions are read more broadly. Thus, there is no reason a similar reading should not be given to free exercise. However, she, for the moment at least, was reluctant to overturn *Smith*, since careful consideration had not yet been given to what would replace it. Nevertheless, she was open to arguments that the decision should be overturned.

Justices Samuel Alito and Neil Gorsuch were much more direct and critical of the majority in concurring opinions joined by each other and Justice Thomas. Alito wrote the most comprehensive opinion, a thorough seventy-seven-page analysis of why *Smith* neither accorded with the original meaning of the Free Exercise Clause nor gave proper weight to the Court's previous precedents. Furthermore, he argued, it had proved largely unworkable in practice. This case presented a clear opportunity, he asserted, to overrule *Smith*, an opportunity the majority had unfortunately disregarded. By basing their holding on the technicality that exemptions could be granted, not only did the majority assure that would there now be a flood of other cases but also that this case itself was bound to continue. All the city had to do was alter the terms of the contract and the wording of the ordinance. "This decision might as well be written on the dissolving paper sold in magic shops," he said. Gorsuch endorsed Alito's thoughts in full, writing that "[h]ad we followed the path Justice Alito outlines—holding that the City's rules cannot avoid strict scrutiny even if they qualify as neutral and generally applicable—this case would end today. Instead, the majority's course guarantees that the litigation is only getting started."

The next case, *Arlene's Flowers v. State of Washington*, provides only a sliver of information since it was a denial of a petition to hear a case and did not result in extensive analysis of the issue.[30] However, since it seems to run contrary to *Fulton*, it poses some ambiguity. The proprietor of Arlene's Flowers in Richland, Washington, refused to create a floral arrangement for a gay wedding. Citing the state's antidiscrimination statute, Washington sued the florist. The state courts in Washington upheld the state. When the case first came to the Supreme Court in 2017, it was remanded to the state courts pending the decision in *Masterpiece Cakeshop*. Washington's courts, including the state Supreme Court, again upheld the state, triggering an appeal by the flower shop to the U.S. Supreme Court. In July of 2021,

---

30 See Liptak, Adam: "Supreme Court Turns Down Appeal in Clash Between Florist and Gay Couple." *New York Times*, July 2, 2021.

however, the high court declined to hear the case, even though three justices—Alito, Gorsuch, and Thomas—wished to do so.[31] Thus, the Washington Supreme Court's decision stands.

Conclusion

It seems that in the contest between the new American religious landscape—the growing diversity, the increasing numbers of atheists and agnostics, and the dramatic shift in ideas regarding LGBTQ people—and conservative Christians, when it comes to the Supreme Court, conservatives have scored solid victories. Overall, religious liberty is enjoying strong protection.

In *Morrisey-Berru*, the ministerial exception became deeply entrenched. Further, the reach of the exception was set broadly. The framework employed by the Court suggests that in future cases religious bodies and their associated institutions will have an almost free hand to select their employees and set the terms of their employment. Moreover, looking at the two dissenters (both of whom accepted the ministerial exception as the guiding doctrine, only quibbling over its application in this particular case), Justice Ginsburg has been replaced by Justice Barrett. From what we know of Barrett's stances before she came to the Court, she is likely to side with the majority. Thus, religious liberty has gained another defender.

In *Fulton* too, religious liberty again came out on top, a victory reinforced by the unanimity of the justices. At the same time, the rationale the majority used in this instance makes the precedential value of the case open to some questions. Had they done what Justices Alito, Thomas, and Gorsuch proposed and overruled *Smith*, reinstalling the compelling interest/strict scrutiny test in all free exercise cases, we could safely say religious liberty received a resounding endorsement. As it stands, though, religious liberty lacks robustness when it comes into conflict with LGBTQ rights. The reaction of Human Rights Campaign, the chief legal and lobbying organization of LGBTQ people, shows that they did not view the case as a complete loss, saying, "Though today's decision is not a complete victory, it does not negate the fact that every qualified family is valid and worthy."[32]

This shakiness is made clear in the *Arlene's Flowers* case, which at first glance seems to run counter to *Fulton*. While it is not possible, of course, to draw firm substantive conclusions from the denial of a hearing, the outcome here clearly was a victory for LGBTQ rights and a setback for religious liberty. This conclusion is reinforced by the vote: Alito, Thomas, and Gorsuch—the three wanting to use *Fulton* to overrule *Smith*—wanted to take the case. The reaction of the flower shop's attorneys and backers shows

---

31 According to Supreme Court rules, it takes four justices to agree to put a case on the docket.
32 Fields, Aryon: "The Human Rights Campaign Reacts to Supreme Court Decision in Fulton v. City of Philadelphia," retrieved 15.08.2021, from https://www.hrc.org/news.

how important they thought the case was. The press release of the Alliance Defending Freedom, the organization that represented the florist, said, "[T]he outcome of this case is tragic ... No one should be forced to express a message or celebrate an event they disagree with."[33]

Although the Court did not say, nor even hint, as much, perhaps there is a thread of consistency here. Religious liberty may enjoy an enhanced status when a religious organization is involved; when it comes to commercial enterprises, though, antidiscrimination legislation may trump. If so, this makes some sense. When someone embarks on a commercial endeavor, they should expect to be subject to all the normal regulatory policies of the government. Even if this is utilized as a guideline, however, there will still be some gray areas involving semi-commercial enterprises (publishing houses, broadcasters, bookstores, etc.) that serve religious purposes.

What seems certain is that, given the changing religious landscape in the United States, there will be a steady stream of cases landing on the Supreme Court's docket for some time to come.

References

Books and Articles

Bottum, Joseph: "The Death of Protestant America: A Political Theory of the Protestant Mainline." *First Things*, August 2008.

Cardozo, Benjamin: *The Nature of the Judicial Process*. Yale University Press: New Haven, CT 1921.

Fields, Aryon: "The Human Rights Campaign Reacts to Supreme Court Decision in Fulton v. City of Philadelphia." https://www.hrc.org/news.

Herberg, Will: *Protestant, Catholic, Jew: An Essay in American Religious Sociology*. Doubleday: New York 1955.

Liptak, Adam: "Supreme Court Turns Down Appeal in Clash Between Florist and Gay Couple." *New York Times*, July 2, 2021.

Long, Carolyn: *Religious Freedom and Indian Rights: The Case of Oregon v. Smith*. University Press of Kansas: Lawrence 2000.

Orchowski, Margaret Sands: *The Law that Changed the Face of America: The Immigration and Nationality Act of 1965*. Rowman and Littlefield: Lanham, MD 2015.

Santos, Thee/Medina, Caroline/Gruberg, Sharita: *What You Need to Know About the Equality Act*. Center for American Progress: Washington, DC 2021.

---

33 Alliance Defending Freedom press release, July 2, 2021. See also Waggoner, Kristen: "Supreme Court Leaves Americans Guessing About the Meaning of Tolerance." *Newsweek*, July 7, 2021. (Ms. Waggoner was the attorney who argued the case for the florist at the Supreme Court.)

Verlee, Megan: "Denver Court Finds Masterpiece Cakeshop Baker Violated Anti-Discrimination Law in Refusing to Make Gender Transition Cake." Colorado Public Radio, June 17, 2021.

Waggoner, Kristen: "Supreme Court Leaves Americans Guessing About the Meaning of Tolerance." Newsweek, July 7, 2021.

Waltman, Jerold: *Church and State in the Roberts Court*. McFarland: Jefferson, NC 2019.

Waltman, Jerold: *Congress, the Supreme Court and Religious Liberty: The Case of City of Boerne v. Flores*. Palgrave: New York 2013.

Waltman, Jerold: *Religious Free Exercise and Contemporary American Politics: The Saga of the Religious Land Use and Institutionalized Persons Act of 2000*. Continuum: New York 2011.

Court Cases

Church of Lukumi Babalu Aye v. Hialeah, 508 U.S. 520 (1993).
City of Boerne v. Flores, 521 U.S. 507 (1997).
Employment Division of Oregon v. Smith, 494 U.S. 872 (1990).
Fulton v. City of Philadelphia, 593 U.S. ____ (2021).
Goldman v. Weinberger, 475 U.S. 503 (1986).
Hosanna-Tabor Lutheran Church v. EEOC, 565 U.S. ____ (2012).
Masterpiece Cakeshop v. Colorado Civil Rights Commission, 584 U.S. ____ (2018).
O'Lone v. Estate of Shabazz, 482 U.S. 342 (1987).
Our Lady of Guadalope School v. Morrisey-Berru, 591 U.S. ____ (2020).
Sherbert v. Verner, 374 U.S. 398 (1963).
Wisconsin v. Yoder, 406 U.S. 205 (1972).

Public Opinion Polls

Barma Group Poll, October 1, 2015.
Fox News Poll, July 21, 2015.
National Opinion Research Center Poll, September 2011.
Pew Research Center, *Religion in Public Life Survey*, July 29, 2015.
Public Religion Research Institute Poll, March 15, 2012.
Public Religion Research Institute Poll, June 11, 2014.
Public Religion Research Institute, *The 2020 Census of American Religion*, July 8, 2021.

Emily R. Gill

Religion, Liberty, and Marriage Equality

Abstract: Conservative religionists subscribe to negative liberty or freedom from interference, whereas LGBT civil rights supporters argue for positive action to protect individuals and groups in the exercise of their own liberties. Both sides, however, advocate for policies that promote their own desired outcomes. This means that neither is satisfied with simple freedom from interference. Using *Obergefell v. Hodges* as a touchstone, this chapter describes four different positions concerning marriage equality and then addresses prior U.S. Supreme Court decisions to illustrate this tension. It then analyzes both majority and minority opinions in *Obergefell*, arguing in the end for attention to groups historically oppressed by a dominant consensus.

Keywords: *Obergefell*, marriage equality, negative liberty, positive liberty, rights

Introduction

Since the United States Supreme Court legitimized marriage equality for same-sex couples nationwide in *Obergefell v. Hodges* in 2015,[1] many conservative Christians have questioned its constitutional legitimacy. They have also opposed its impact upon what they view as their right to the free exercise of religion as guaranteed by the First Amendment to the Constitution. In fact, some powerful segments of the conservative religious community seek to promote a particular interpretation of Christianity rooted in a biblical worldview. Adherents of this Christian nationalism maintain that their own interpretation of Christianity is the only legitimate representation of American national identity. It is not simply a social or cultural movement but also a political one, holding that the Bible mandates adherence to right-wing positions in a broad range of policy areas. It therefore seeks to identify those who will vote on the basis of biblical values so that belonging to the movement is signified not by religious beliefs but by political ones.[2]

A hallmark of conservative religionists is the implication that religious believers should enjoy freedom from interference in instantiating their principles. Its subscribers rely upon a capacious interpretation of the Free Exercise Clause. Measures to protect

---

1 *Obergefell v. Hodges*, 135 S. Ct. 2584 (2015).
2 Stewart, Katherine: *The Power Worshipper: Inside the Dangerous Rise of Christian Nationalism*. Bloomsbury Publishing: New York 2019, pp. 3–11, 48–51, 90, 139.

the civil rights of dissenters from their aims, such as LGBT (lesbian, gay, bisexual, and transgender) individuals, are viewed as anathema. In philosophical terms, underlying this conflict is a tension between negative liberty or freedom from interference, on the one hand, and positive liberty, on the other. In this project, positive liberty means that individual freedom often requires not merely freedom from interference but also positive action to protect and enable individuals and groups in the exercise of their own rights and liberties. Christian conservatives want maximum freedom from interference (negative liberty) to live in accordance with their beliefs, but they also advocate for policies to promote their own programs (positive liberty) that impact both the negative and positive liberty of others. Although only some opponents of marriage equality could be classified as Christian nationalists, they share with the latter a broad interpretation of religious liberty.

Marriage in the United States, unlike in many other nations, can be celebrated by religious clergy who are deputized by the government, thereby combining the civil and religious aspects of the marriage contract. Clergy will never be forced to celebrate same-sex marriages. Historically, some clergy will not marry divorced people, and the Roman Catholic Church does not recognize civil divorce. Some individuals do hold sincere conscientious objections to participating in weddings or commitment ceremonies through the provision of food, photography, or floral arrangements. Although I do not address these details here, limited accommodations should be legitimate as long as these services can still be obtained by same-sex couples.[3]

First, I shall discuss four different positions concerning marriage equality in the lead-up to *Obergefell v. Hodges*. Next, I shall address several Supreme Court decisions prior to *Obergefell* as they illustrate the tension between negative and positive liberty. Third, I shall discuss the court's decision in *Obergefell* as positive support for what the majority viewed as a fundamental right to marry. Finally, I shall address the four dissenting opinions, summarizing each and commenting upon common themes. As we shall see, several maintain that liberty historically denotes freedom to live as one chooses without physical restraint or coercion. The concept of negative liberty alone, however, is too narrow to characterize liberty's full meaning. For the philosopher Charles Taylor, negative liberty is an opportunity concept. That is, an absence of hindrance or interference provides one with opportunities to do what one wishes. That is not always enough. Positive liberty, on this formulation, is an exercise concept. One may need positive action, in this context whether through civil rights laws or marriage equality, fully to exercise or to realize those opportunities.[4]

---

3   Gill, Emily R.: *Free Exercise of Religion in the Liberal Polity: Conflicting Interpretations*. Palgrave Macmillan: Cham, Switzerland 2019, pp. 168–191.
4   Taylor, Charles: "What's Wrong with Negative Liberty?" In: Stewart, Andrew M. (ed.): *Readings in Social and Political Philosophy*. 2nd ed. Oxford University Press: New York 1996, pp. 98–109.

Divergent Views of Marriage Equality

For traditionalist opponents of marriage equality, we tend to forget that marriage's "great universal anthropological imperative" is to create ties between parents and their biological offspring.[5] Similarly, "Marriage's main purpose is to make sure that any child born has two responsible parents, a mother and a father who are committed to the child and committed to each other."[6] Although adoption may ground caring families, adoptive families and stepfamilies are derivative institutions that result from a failure such as widowhood, divorce, remarriage, or the mistreatment or abandonment of children. Adoption or the use of reproductive technology "is not a stand-alone good"[7] but is simply an attempt to compensate for loss of the natural family. Advocates of what is termed the new natural law in fact argue that marriage is properly defined by sexual intercourse between two complementary bodies, those of a man and a woman. "Marriage is a two-in-one-flesh communion of persons that is consummated and actualized by acts that are procreative in type, whether or not they are procreative in effect."[8] Because any other form of sexual expression is not a marital act, marriage cannot be reinvented to suit individual choice and will.

Traditionalist proponents of same-sex marriage, on the other hand, maintain that same-sex marriage serves the same function as that served by traditional marriage: promotion of monogamy and stability. Rather than devaluing traditional marriage by admitting participants who are unsuited to it, marriage equality adds value to same-sex relationships by making them more like opposite-sex ones as models for commitment.[9] Rather than simply a lifestyle choice, marriage should be expected of all committed couples and privileged as "better than other ways of living. Not mandatory, not good where everything else is bad, but a general norm, rather than a personal taste."[10] Concerning child welfare, some appellate courts

---

5 Gallagher, Maggie: "Normal Marriage: Two Views." In: Lynn D. Wardle/Mark Strasser/William C. Duncan/David Orgon Coolidge (eds.): *Marriage and Same-Sex Unions: A Debate*. Praeger: Westport, CT 2003, p. 19; see pp. 17–19.
6 Blankenhorn, David: *The Future of Marriage*. Encounter Books: New York 2007, p. 153. See also pp. 15, 35, 49, 59-61, 83, 102, 155, 248–254.
7 *Ibid.*, p. 191; see pp. 189–194.
8 George, Robert: "Neutrality, Equality, and Same-Sex Marriage." In: Wardle et al. (eds.): *Marriage and Same-Sex Unions, op. cit.*, p. 120; see 120–121, 128.
9 Sullivan, Andrew: *Virtually Normal: An Argument about Homosexuality*. Vantage: New York 1996, pp. 107–116.
10 Rauch, Jonathan: *Gay Marriage: Why It Is Good for Gays, Good for Straights, and Good for America*. Owl Books: New York 2005, pp. 81–82; see also pp. 6, 42–43, 82, 89–94; Stephen Macedo: "Against the Old Sexual Morality of the New Natural Law." In: Robert P. George (ed.): *Natural Law, Liberalism, and Morality*. Oxford University Press: New York 2001, pp. 27–48.

ruled before marriage equality that because traditional couples can produce children quickly and unexpectedly, it is *they* who need the protections of marriage. Same-sex couples, they argued, who must incur deliberate effort and expense to reproduce, were already so stable that they did not need the protections of marriage. The ban on same-sex marriage, however, functioned "to prevent children *already being raised in same-sex households* from having the protections afforded by the benefits of marriage, a policy that has the irrational consequence of punishing children for the 'sins' of their parents."[11]

Skeptics about marriage as an institution have been wary about marriage as a desirable goal for anyone. Although marriage is grounded on consent, it is consent to a status, an arrangement whose terms are externally defined by the government rather than internally defined by its participants.[12] Although traditionalist advocates of marriage equality see institutionalized expectations as a benefit that militates in favor of expanding marriage to same-sex couples, skeptics view such expectations as a weakness of marriage in general and thus a burden upon all couples. As matters stand, contemporary family policy accords special rights to just one type of family form to the exclusion of all others, thereby privileging adults who marry—and their children—over those who cannot or will not marry. Benefits that typically accompany marriage, for example, might more justly be extended to any individual that a person chooses or perhaps to several individuals based upon their roles in the person's life, regardless of the type of relationship.[13] Many same-sex couples, however, would resist being told that their desire to marry is an instance of false consciousness that will succumb to rational reflection. Same-sex couples have arguably engaged in greater reflection on the advisability of marriage than many traditional couples who take marriage for granted.

---

11 Evan Gerstmann: *Same-Sex Marriage and the Constitution*. 2nd ed. Cambridge University Press: New York 2008, p. 39, emphasis original; see pp. 38–42.
12 Pateman, Carole: *The Sexual Contract*. Stanford University Press: Stanford, CA 1988, pp. 135–142; Okin, Susan Moller: *Justice, Gender, and the Family*. Basic Books: New York 1989, *passim*.
13 Lehr, Valerie: *Queer Family Values: Debunking the Myth of the Nuclear Family*. Temple University Press: Philadelphia 1999, pp. 33–34; Jakobsen, Janet R./Pellegrini, Ann: *Love the Sin: Sexual Regulation and the Limits of Religious Tolerance*. Beacon Press: Boston, MA 2004, pp. 140–147; Polikoff, Nancy D.: *Beyond (Straight and Gay) Marriage: Valuing All Families under the Law*. Beacon Press: Boston, MA 2008, *passim*; Metz, Tamara: *Untying the Knot: Marriage, the State, and the Case for Their Divorce*. Princeton University Press: Princeton 2010, *passim*; Brake, Elizabeth: *Minimizing Marriage: Marriage, Morality, and the Law*. Oxford University Press: New York 2012, *passim*; Chambers, Clare: *Against Marriage: An Egalitarian Defense of the Marriage-Free State*. Oxford University Press: New York 2017, pp. 212–215.

Finally, liberal rights advocates defend marriage equality as a right to conscience and to intimate life that should accrue to all individuals regardless of sexual orientation.[14] This right has been defended on various bases. First, the right to privacy functions as a beginning, but it does not comport easily with seeking legal recognition within a public status. Moreover, privacy can operate as a conservative value used by the dominant consensus to reinforce traditional relationships and to relegate others to the closet.[15] Most importantly, an emphasis on privacy valorizes the negative liberty of freedom from interference, as opposed to the positive and enabling freedom that can ground state action in recognizing same-sex relationships.[16] Second, arguments from equality highlight comparative disadvantage, but they depend upon some scale of value explaining why differential treatment is unjust.[17] Further, public policies can level down as well as level up.

A third basis for argument, that of autonomy, appears to be the strongest. Same-sex relationships can embody the same goods of interdependence and reciprocity that can characterize opposite-sex relationships and therefore carry the same intrinsic value. Human needs and capabilities for committed love and care merit not only noninterference but also the "creation of the necessary conditions that will promote and protect the ability of individuals to meet those additional needs and exercise those additional capabilities."[18] Privacy and equality are preconditions, but they are instrumental to intrinsic values that ground the justice of marriage equality. Although relationships based upon love and care can exist without public recognition and although not all couples, gay or straight, desire this recognition, for those who desire it, these relationships may be most fully realized when publicly protected through positive action.

---

14 Richards, David A.J.: *Identity and the Case for Gay Rights: Race, Gender, and Religion as Analogies.* University of Chicago Press: Chicago 1999, *passim*; Bamforth, Nicholas/Richards, David A.J.: *Patriarchal Religion, Sexuality, and Gender: A Critique of the New Natural Law.* Cambridge University Press: New York 2008, *passim.*
15 Boling, Patricia: *Privacy and the Politics of Intimate Life.* Cornell University Press: Ithaca, NY 1996, pp. 85–90, 101–103, 146–148.
16 Ball, Carlos: *The Morality of Gay Rights: An Exploration in Political Philosophy.* Routledge: New York 2003, pp. 103–112; Pierceson, Jason: *Courts, Liberalism, and Rights: Gay Law and Politics in the United States and Canada.* Temple University Press: Philadelphia 2005, pp. 32–38, 45–50, 125.
17 Bamforth and Richards: *Patriarchal Religion, Sexuality, and Gender, op. cit.*, pp. 200–211; Ball: *The Morality of Gay Rights, op. cit.*, 91–99; Ball, Carlos: "Against Neutrality in the Legal Recognition of Intimate Relationships." In: Gordon A. Babst/Emily R. Gill/Jason Pierceson (eds.): *Moral Argument, Religion, and Same-Sex Marriage: Advancing the Public Good.* Lexington Books: Lanham, MD 2009, pp. 76, 84–86.
18 Ball: *The Morality of Gay Rights, op. cit.*, p. 106; see pp. 105–115; 53.

The United States Supreme Court before *Obergefell*

In 2015 in *Obergefell v. Hodges*, the United States Supreme Court legitimized marriage equality for gays and lesbians nationwide.[19] It stated that the value of autonomy supported personal choice regarding marriage, that same-sex couples deserved the same fundamental right as traditional couples to the recognition of their relationships, that children deserved the stability of married parents, and that the exclusion of same-sex couples from civil marriage was demeaning in view of the central character of marriage in the nation's social order. This decision was the capstone of a trajectory of nearly thirty years that began in 1986 with the upholding of a Georgia state law that criminalized sodomy.[20] The majority in this case contended that sodomy was like none of the fundamental rights recognized in previous cases concerning family relationships, marriage, or procreation. In dissent, however, Justice Harry Blackmun argued that the rights already protected were recognized not because they were traditional, but because they were central to individual life and happiness. "Depriving individuals of the right to choose for themselves how to conduct their intimate relationships poses a far greater threat to our Nation's history than tolerance of nonconformity could ever do."[21] Blackmun was insightful to ground his dissent not upon communally shared values about the comparative goodness of various ways of life, but instead upon the intrinsic value of individual autonomy and choice. Otherwise, people were likely to rate individuals' choices on the basis of their similarity to conventional relationships such as traditional marriage, just as they often tolerate unusual religions in direct relation to their resemblance to conventional faiths.[22]

Although prosecutions under anti-sodomy laws were uncommon across the United States, the threat was always present where these statutes existed. A criminal record and sometimes sex offender registration could follow, and this specter haunted individuals who knew that they could be subject to conviction if apprehended and prosecuted. Moreover, individuals known to experience same-sex attraction were objects of contempt, subject to discrimination for no other reason than that they were breaking the law. These individuals did not even enjoy the negative liberty of freedom from interference, let alone any positive support for their relationships.

In 2003 in *Lawrence v. Texas*, however, the Supreme Court recognized the weakness in focusing on a narrow right to sodomy. Although the protection of sodomy was not deeply rooted in the nation's history and traditions, the protection of

---

19 *Obergefell v. Hodges*, 135 S. Ct. 2584 (2015).
20 *Bowers v. Hardwick*, 478 U.S. 186 (1986).
21 *Ibid.*, p. 214; see also pp. 204–206, 210–212.
22 Gill, Emily R.: *An Argument for Same-Sex Marriage: Religious Freedom, Sexual Freedom, and Public Expressions of Civic Equality*. Georgetown University Press: Washington, DC 2012, pp. 2–3, 170–175.

individual relationships and expressive associations has indeed been a core value. Intimate relationships are not necessarily just about sex any more than marriage is solely about sexual intercourse. As Justice Anthony Kennedy wrote, "When sexuality finds expression in intimate conduct with another person, the conduct can be but one element in a personal bond that is more enduring. The liberty protected by the Constitution allows homosexual persons the right to make this choice."[23] Disapproval based upon conventional convictions about religion and morality must be subordinate to the right to exercise autonomy in intimate relationships. Although they arrived at different conclusions, both *Bowers* and *Lawrence* focused on the appropriateness of affording individuals the freedom from interference or negative liberty necessary to conduct same-sex relationships.

Between the *Bowers* and *Lawrence* decisions, in 1996 in *Romer v. Evans* the Supreme Court struck down a state of Colorado constitutional amendment, Amendment 2, that had prohibited the enactment or enforcement of antidiscrimination legislation protecting any nonmajority sexual orientation. Justice Kennedy ruled that rights against discrimination were not special rights, as some argued, but protections already held by most people pertaining to countless aspects of ordinary civic life. The broad disability directed against one group by Amendment 2 seemed "inexplicable by anything but animus toward the class it affects," and therefore without any rational relationship to a legitimate state interest.[24] In dissent, however, Justice Antonin Scalia pointed out that five state constitutions in the nineteenth century had singled out a sexual practice by prohibiting polygamy with "the explicit approval of the United States Congress."[25] Striking down Amendment 2 was "an act, not of judicial judgment, but of political will."[26] In sum, the issue in *Romer* was whether those with conventional or majority views might use the power of the state to enforce those views, not as in *Bowers* or *Lawrence* by curtailing negative liberty through criminalizing specific conduct, but rather by prohibiting positive political action.

Although *Romer* focused upon the legitimate use of the political process, it is often unnoticed that opposition to a right to autonomy in intimate life, as well as to marriage equality, has often been based not upon the danger of harm to others, but instead on conventional notions about religion, morality, and family that are sectarian in nature. A compelling state interest might arguably justify banning certain forms of conduct, such as Mormon polygamy in the nineteenth-century United States, even if they are religious practices, but its advocates should not be penalized through deprivation of a basic right such as political advocacy. "The

---

23 *Lawrence v. Texas*, 539 U.S. 558 (2003), p. 567; see also p. 575.
24 *Romer v. Evans*, 575 U.S. 620 (1996), p. 632; see also pp. 630–631, 634–635.
25 *Ibid.*, p. 649; see pp. 647–651.
26 *Ibid.*, p. 653. See also *Lawrence v. Texas, op. cit.*, 603, for Scalia's view that these are legislative matters, not judicial.

expression through public law of one form of sectarian conscience against another form of conscience, without compelling justification in public arguments available to all, is constitutionally invidious, and therefore constitutionally suspect, religious intolerance."[27] Such intolerance both burdens the free exercise of some manifestations of conscience and establishes other, majoritarian manifestations. When Justice Kennedy stated that the disability imposed by Colorado's Amendment 2 seemed inexplicable by anything but hostility, he was suggesting an inability to make a rational case that would justify depriving those experiencing same-sex attraction of the ability to protect themselves through the passage of antidiscrimination laws. The civil rights of some were withheld because of the sectarian beliefs of others. Absent a rigorous case, reserving antidiscrimination laws—or the right to marry—for some groups while excluding others is a quintessential example of a "special right."

Matrimonial law in the United States is the province of the states, not of the national government. Between 2003 and 2015, a number of states instituted civil unions or domestic partnerships for same-sex couples, and many instituted marriage equality. Despite conservative arguments that civil unions were sufficient recognition, many state court opinions suggested in various ways that withholding the status of civil marriage amounted to relegating same-sex couples to second-class status. For example, the California Supreme Court ruled that the right to marry includes not only a negative right against undue governmental interference but also a positive right to affirmative state support for families. Accordingly, the court stated,

> We conclude that the distinction drawn [...] between the designation of the family relationships available to opposite-sex couples and the designation available to same-sex couples impinges upon the fundamental interest of same-sex couples in having their official family relationship accorded dignity and respect equal to that conferred upon the family relationships of opposite-sex couples.[28]

Reacting to the controversy over marriage equality, in 1996 Congress passed and President Bill Clinton signed the Defense of Marriage Act (DOMA). First, it defined

---

27 Richards, David A.J.: *The Case for Gay Rights: From Bowers to Lawrence and Beyond.* University Press of Kansas: Lawrence 2005, p. 117; see also p. 92; Babst, Gordon A.: *Liberal Constitutionalism, Marriage, and Sexual Orientation: A Contemporary Case for Dis-Establishment.* Peter Lang: New York 2002, *passim*; Gill: *An Argument for Same-Sex Marriage, op. cit.*, pp. 178–209.

28 *In re* Marriage Cases, 43 Cal. 4th 757 (2008), pp. 846–847; see also pp. 819, 855; *In re* Opinions of the Justices to the Senate, 440 Mass. 1201 (2004), pp. 1207, 1210; *Kerrigan v. Commissioner of Public Health*, 289 Conn. 135 (2008), p. 262; *Varnum v. Brien*, 763 N.W.2d 862 (2009), pp. 899–901; *Perry v. Schwarzenegger*, 704 F. Supp. 2d 921 (Cal. 2010), pp. 1002–1003.

marriage for federal purposes as comprising one man and one woman, thereby relieving the national government of according federal benefits that typically accompany marriage of any obligation to same-sex couples. Second, it relieved states of having to recognize same-sex marriages concluded in other states. A couple might be married in one state but considered unmarried by another state. The title of this law, however, spoke as loudly as its provisions. That is, supporters of traditional marriage positioned themselves as victims of the social movement for marriage equality. Expanding marriage rights to same-sex couples would deprive opponents of the right to hold a monopoly on their preferred definition of marriage. As put by Justice Scalia, for example, in his *Romer* dissent, "Amendment 2 is designed to prevent piecemeal deterioration of the sexual morality of a majority of Coloradans."[29]

On this characterization, those who would exclude sexual minorities from antidiscrimination protections, or later from the ability to marry, were portrayed as those who most merited legal protection. Those "whose rights are already recognized and enforced are the ones treated as if their rights are endangered."[30] As with Christian nationalists and many other conservative Christians today, only one interpretation of marriage was deemed the legitimate one. Negative liberty from interference with LGBT intimate relationships, especially as augmented by the availability of civil unions, was sufficient. Yet while criticizing same-sex couples' demands for the positive protections of marriage, opponents themselves sought positive protections for their right to exclude.

In 2013, however, the Supreme Court in *United States v. Windsor* declared unconstitutional the DOMA provision that allowed the national government to deny federal benefits to same-sex married couples. The state of New York had recognized marriage equality, including the marriage of two women who had been previously married in Canada. Upon the death of one spouse, however, the federal estate tax exemption for surviving spouses was denied to her survivor. Justice Kennedy stated that when a state exercises its traditional authority over marriage, the national government should not deviate from this tradition by imposing restrictions and disabilities upon it. "The avowed purpose and practical effect of the law here in question are to impose a disadvantage, a separate status, and so a stigma upon all who enter into same-sex marriages made lawful by the unquestioned authority of the States."[31] Therefore, DOMA deprived same-sex couples of the equal protection of the laws guaranteed by the Constitution's Fifth Amendment that was enjoyed in the state by opposite-sex couples. Among the three dissenting opinions, Justice Scalia asserted that the disputed provision of DOMA was simply a prudent assurance that federal law would operate uniformly in all states, whether or not they

---

29 *Romer v. Evans, op. cit.*, p. 653.
30 Jakobsen, Janet R., and Ann Pellegrini: *Love the Sin, op. cit.*, p. 43; see also pp. 42, 39.
31 *United States v. Windsor*, 570 U.S. 744 (2013), p. 770; see also pp. 766–775.

recognized marriage equality.[32] The dissenters overall argued that the question of marriage equality should be decided at the state level.

Obergefell v. Hodges

Obergefell was based upon the situations of three same-sex couples. James Obergefell and John Arthur resided in Ohio but had married in Maryland, where same-sex marriage was legal. When Arthur died, Ohio did not permit Obergefell to be listed as the surviving spouse on the death certificate. In Michigan, April DeBoer and Jayne Rowse were parenting three children, two of whom had special needs. Because the state, however, only permitted traditional married couples or single individuals to adopt, each child had only one legal parent. If something happened to the legal parent, the surviving parent would then have no legal right to parent that child. Another male couple had married in New York but resided in Tennessee, which did not recognize their marriage, which appeared and disappeared as they traveled across state lines.

Justice Kennedy stated for the Supreme Court that the value of autonomy supporting personal choice and the centrality of marriage as an expression of that choice militated against withholding marriage from same-sex couples. The insufficiency of mere freedom from interference emerged early in his opinion. "While *Lawrence* confirmed a dimension of freedom that allows individuals to engage in intimate association without criminal liability, it does not follow that freedom stops there. Outlaw to outcast may be a step forward, but it does not achieve the full promise of liberty."[33] Those seeking to marry view it as a setting like no other for the full development of their relationships. Positive action was therefore necessary if this promise was to be fulfilled. Moreover, many same-sex couples provide homes for children, either biological or adopted. These children needed the recognition and stability of married parents, rather than suffering from "the stigma of knowing their families are somehow lesser."[34] Finally, as with other fundamental rights, the right to marry cannot be defined simply by those who exercised it historically. "Decent and honorable religious or philosophical premises" certainly ground opposition to same-sex marriage. "But when sincere, personal opposition becomes enacted law and public policy, the necessary consequence is to put the imprimatur of the State itself on an exclusion that soon demeans or stigmatizes those whose own liberty is then denied."[35] Additionally, fundamental rights need not await assent by legislative action or the general public to be rightfully claimed. Rather than disrespecting the institution of marriage, those seeking to marry

---

32 *Ibid.*, p. 797; see pp. 795–799.
33 *Obergefell v. Hodges, op. cit.*, p. 2600; see pp. 2599–2600.
34 *Ibid.*, p. 2600; see pp. 2600–2601.
35 *Ibid.*, p. 2602; see also pp. 2603–2605, 2607–2608.

respected it so much that they desired to participate in it. Equal protection of the laws required marriage equality, including the recognition of existing same-sex marriages by all other states.

In this 5–4 decision, all four of the dissenting justice filed separate opinions, in each of which one or more of the other dissenters joined. Chief Justice John Roberts argued that the people acting through their representatives should take precedence over the opinions of five judges. Marriage equality's supporters had already enjoyed increasing success in the court of public opinion. The court foreclosed further debate and made this unnecessary change more difficult for its opponents to accept.[36] Even a right to marry should not force states to change their individual definitions of marriage. Although the Constitution forbids the deprivation of liberty without due process of law, unelected judges should not arbitrarily decide on the substance of those liberties. "Our cases have consistently refused to allow litigants to convert the shield provided by constitutional liberties into a sword to demand positive entitlements from the State." Although the right to privacy protects intimate conduct, "it provides no affirmative right to redefine marriage and no basis for striking down the laws at issue here."[37] The court could as easily justify plural marriage, for Roberts a shorter leap than the move to same-sex marriage. Finally, although the majority nodded toward decent religious beliefs, the First Amendment guarantee of the free *exercise* of these beliefs was not mentioned.[38] Overall, Roberts's opinion was in line with the view that the negative liberty of freedom from interference with couples' intimate relationships was sufficient. Granting anything further simply instantiated the majority's personal views. For practical purposes, this rendered the decision constitutionally illegitimate. This charge has inspired widespread resistance grounded on religious liberty claims.[39]

Like Roberts, Justice Scalia's dissent focused upon the highhandedness of the court's robbing the people of the United States of their right to govern themselves through their elected representatives. In "the hubris reflected in today's judicial Putsch," the majority implied that all states violated the Constitution between the ratification of the Fourteenth Amendment, which applied the due process and equal protection requirements to the states, and Massachusetts's allowing same-sex marriages in 2003.[40] However, the issue of marriage equality had not previously reached this decision point. Therefore, this imputation is irrelevant.

---

36 *Ibid.*, pp. 2612, 2624–2625.
37 *Ibid.*, p. 2620; see 2616–2622.
38 *Ibid.*, pp. 2625–2626.
39 Oleske, Jr., James M.: "A Regrettable Invitation to 'Constitutional Resistance,' Renewed Confusion Over Religious Exemptions, and the Future of Free Exercise." *Lewis & Clark Law Review* 20, 2017, pp. 1317–1371, especially pp. 1346–1355; Gill: *Free Exercise of Religion in the Liberal Polity, op. cit.*, pp. 168–193.
40 *Obergefell v. Hodges, op. cit.*, p. 2629.

Justice Clarence Thomas also expressed dismay at the idea that a small group of judges could hijack the marriage controversy from the normal democratic process. Starting with the Magna Carta of 1215 and the natural liberty expounded by John Locke, "it is hard to see how the 'liberty' protected by the [due process] Clause could be interpreted to include anything broader than freedom from physical restraint."[41] If the framers of the Constitution had recognized a natural right to marriage, they would have been alluding to activities analogous to those that no state hindered in 2015. These included intimacy by same-sex couples, public commitment ceremonies, religious marriage ceremonies, and the rearing of children by same-sex couples. When the court invalidated prohibitions on interracial marriage in *Loving v. Virginia*,[42] it did so simply by striking down the criminal convictions of a couple who had married in the District of Columbia but then resided in Virginia. The liberty to marry has meant the negative liberty of freedom from interference, not a right to governmental recognition and benefits.[43] Finally, like Roberts, Thomas expressed concern about the decision's implications for religious liberty as freedom of action, as marriage is a religious institution as well as a civil one.[44]

Justice Samuel Alito's dissent focused upon the contrast between the traditional understanding of marriage's purpose of providing a stable setting for the rearing of children, on the one hand, and the more recent idea that marriage is primarily to promote the well-being of the individuals who marry, on the other. Under the institution of federalism, it is the people of the several states through their representatives, not the court, that should be deciding whether to retain the original understanding or subscribe to the newer one.[45]

Commentary on Majority Opinion

Justice Kennedy initially focused upon the centrality of liberty to the personal autonomy and choice of same-sex couples desiring to marry. In the Fifth and Fourteenth Amendments to the Constitution, individuals may not be deprived of liberty without due process of law. Because marriage is a civil institution, freedom from interference was insufficient without state recognition and support like that accorded to traditional couples. Liberty claims often incur resistance as in *Bowers*, however, when they cannot display long-standing roots in traditional American values, as we also find in the *Obergefell* dissents. In *Lawrence*, however, the court recognized that some new liberties can merit positive protection even if they are not traditional. As the *Loving* court declared, "The freedom to marry has long been

---

41 *Ibid.*, p. 2633; see pp. 2632–2635.
42 *Loving v. Virginia*, 388 U.S. 1 (1967).
43 *Obergefell v. Hodges, op. cit.*, pp. 2635–2637.
44 *Ibid.*, pp. 2638–2639.
45 *Ibid.*, pp. 2640–2643.

recognized as one of the vital personal rights essential to the orderly pursuit of happiness by free men."[46] Limits must exist on many forms of liberty, however, a point made by Roberts in his *Obergefell* dissent when he criticized the majority for opening the possibility of plural marriage.[47]

In some situations, however, liberty requires more than a right to be left alone. "Due process protects the individual's ability to form and maintain relationships as well as to avoid them." For example, "due process decisions [can] go further and impose affirmative obligations on the state to *recognize* parent-child relationships—to respect bonds of caring developed outside marriage, even in relationships that the law historically deemed 'illegitimate.'"[48] What is true of parent–child relationships may also apply to couples' bonds of caring. As Kennedy observed, moreover, same-sex couples are rearing children, who merit the stability provided by parents who can marry. The importation of substantive rights into due-process protections often draws criticism, as will be evident in the discussion of the *Obergefell* dissents below. The legitimacy of this importation, however, depends upon the types of rights at issue. As put by Douglas NeJaime and Reva Siegel, when a century ago the court struck down wage-and-hour legislation protecting employees, "it invalidated legislation that sought to *empower* vulnerable parties and *unsettle* dominant power relations in the workplace. By contrast, in our modern substantive due process cases, the Court has struck down laws that *harmed* vulnerable individuals and *entrenched* dominant mores."[49] This point is well illustrated by *Romer*, which struck down Colorado's anti-antidiscrimination amendment, as well as by cases protecting reproductive freedom. It will be questioned, however, by those who do not want to unsettle a dominant consensus.

It is here that the Fifth and Fourteenth Amendment guarantees of equal protection of the law also play a valuable role. Liberty arguments speak to the intrinsic value of personal autonomy, while equality arguments contribute justifications for particular assertions of liberty rights as well as limits or stopping points. Although equality arguments do require some scale of value explaining why differential

---

46 *Loving v. Virginia, op. cit.*, p. 12.
47 *Obergefell v. Hodges, op. cit.*, pp. 2621–2622.
48 NeJaime, Douglas/Reva B. Siegel: "NeJaime and Siegel, JJ., Concurring." In: Jack M. Balkin (ed.): *What* Obergefell v. Hodges *Should Have Said: The Nation's Top Legal Experts Rewrite America's Same-Sex Marriage Decision*. Yale University Press: New Haven, CT 2020, p. 114, emphasis original; see pp. 112–116. See also Eskridge, William N., Jr.: "Eskridge, J., Concurring in the Judgment." In: Jack M. Balkin (ed.): *ibid.*, pp. 174–178; Smith, Catherine: "Smith, J., Concurring." In: Jack M. Balkin (ed.): *ibid.*, pp. 146–167.
49 NeJaime, Douglas/Reva B. Siegel: "NeJaime and Siegel, JJ., Concurring." In: Jack M. Balkin (ed.): *ibid.*, p. 119, emphasis original; see pp. 118–122, 125; *United States v. Carolene Products Co.*, 304 U.S. 144 (1938), p. 152 n. 4.

treatment is unjust, this issue can be addressed. First, the equal protection clause suggests that all citizens are equal citizens and that the law must not single out "groups for special burdens or benefits without adequate public reasons and justifications."[50] Classifications that prevent harm or promote the public interest may be justified, although not everyone will agree upon these definitions. The equal protection clause has come into play, however, "when legal classifications were deployed to entrench a social group as an underclass."[51] The Colorado amendment struck down in *Romer* again provides an example: it singled out sexual minorities as a group that could not protect itself through antidiscrimination legislation. Similarly, in *Windsor* the court ruled that the federal Defense of Marriage Act imposed a separate status and a stigma upon same-sex marriages legally contracted in the states.

Second, the classification at issue in the ban on marriage equality may be regarded more specifically as based upon sex, sexual orientation, and/or the traditional understanding of sex roles. Andrew Koppelman has suggested that marriage has traditionally been limited by the genders of the aspiring participants.[52] If Jane wanted to marry John, no problem existed. If James wanted to marry John, he was prohibited from doing so. Therefore, James was suffering from discrimination on the basis of his sex. The government did not attend to their sexual orientations but only to their gender. Sex-based classifications are subject to heightened scrutiny rather than simply justifiable because they have a rational basis. Moreover, some opposition to marriage equality has been grounded on sex-role stereotypes. That is, a married couple should comprise a man and a woman so that any children will have proper role models, whereas a same-sex couple will model gender nonconformity. But this also constitutes sex discrimination, as it suggests that each gender should hew to a particular type of performance. Others, such as Jack Balkin, argue that because both men desiring to marry men and women desiring to marry women were thwarted before marriage equality, neither sex was subordinated to the other. Therefore, sexual orientation rather than sex was a more accurate description of the faulty classification in the ban. He agrees with Koppelman, however, that the law subordinated sexual *orientation* minorities by enforcing state-sanctioned gender roles. These laws "enforce a particular conception of what it means to be masculine or feminine by regulating the form of sexual orientation that is permitted for persons of a particular gender."[53]

---

50 Balkin, Jack M.: "Jack M. Balkin (Judgment of the Court)." In: Jack M. Balkin (ed.): *op. cit.*, p. 96; see pp. 95–101.
51 Eskridge, William N., Jr.: "Eskridge, J., Concurring in the Judgment." In: Jack M. Balkin (ed.): *ibid.*, p. 171; see pp. 168–178.
52 Koppelman, Andrew: "Koppelman, J., Concurring." In: Jack M. Balkin (ed.): *ibid.*, pp. 129–145.
53 Balkin, Jack M.: "Jack M. Balkin (Judgment of the Court)." In: Jack M. Balkin (ed.): *ibid.*, p. 103; see pp. 98–104, 110.

Balkin concludes that although the right to marry is not itself a fundamental right, or one that the government may not abridge or abridge selectively, it is a fundamental *interest*. The government need not provide for a fundamental interest, but if it does so it must provide it equally to all. The right to marry is a particular type of interest. It is not a right to be free from state interference or regulation but "the right to have access to and to participate in a set of special legal rules, obligations, subsidies, and incentives created and administered by the state."[54] Because all states offer the status of marriage, it must be available to all on equal terms. Given the long history of discrimination against sexual orientation minorities, Balkin believes that laws discriminating against them should be subject to heightened scrutiny at least and that equal protection would dictate striking them down.

Third, the equal protection justification for striking down the marriage ban could go beyond the simple fact of a history of discrimination against sexual orientation minorities to the deeper meaning of these harmful classifications. First, just as anti-miscegenation laws were designed to uphold white supremacy, the same-sex marriage ban "is best understood as a measure designed to maintain heterosexual supremacy and to inflict a badge of inferiority on sexual minorities generally and lesbians and gay men particularly."[55] For this reason, Katherine Franke concurs with equal protection grounds for striking down this ban. Second, however, reflecting the marriage skeptics discussed above, she also argues that there is no constitutional duty for the government to support a civil marriage regime in the first place. Not all gays and lesbians desire to marry, and both same-sex and opposite-sex couples rear children outside of marriage. The remedy of marriage equality will "simultaneously dissolve one status hierarchy within the gay community while assembling another, privileging married gay people over unmarried gay people," while also reinforcing "the supremacy of married people as a class."[56] Franke would disestablish civil marriage altogether, letting the states replace this status hierarchy with arrangements that would protect the interests of all citizens.

Similarly, Melissa Murray contends that constitutional protection for the right to marry extends to the right not to marry and that marriage equality should not obviate the availability of a range of alternative statuses and visions of intimate life. She cites a number of cases in which the court under the equal protection clause has granted specific benefits to children born out of wedlock and legitimacy to households that included previously prohibited extended family members. Prior to

---

54 Balkin, Jack M.: *ibid.*, p. 108; see pp. 107–110; see also pp. 98–101.
55 Franke, Katherine: "Franke, J., Concurring in the Judgment." In: Jack M. Balkin (ed.): *What Obergefell v. Hodges Should Have Said*, *op. cit.*, p. 195; see pp. 190–196; Gill, Emily R.: *An Argument for Same-Sex Marriage*, *op. cit.*, pp. 19–25.
56 Franke, Katherine: "Franke, J., Concurring in the Judgment," *op. cit.*, p. 198; see pp. 196–200.

marriage equality, a number of states introduced a civil union status that endowed partners with the rights and responsibilities of traditional spouses. The state of Colorado even created a designated beneficiary status for unmarried individuals not in marriage-like relationships to confer benefits and protections upon a designated individual. Murray deplores the tendency of states to eliminate alternative statuses once same-sex marriages were legalized. Overall, "the Constitution, and our jurisprudence interpreting its text, underscores the individual's constitutionally protected interest in resisting the state's efforts to compel conformity in various aspects of life."[57] It may appear that Franke and Murray are reverting to an implicit preference for negative liberty, or freedom from interference, over the positive protections of civil marriage. They are instead suggesting, however, that civil marriage accords rights and responsibilities only to those who can or want to marry. The existence of specific benefits and alternative statuses creates frameworks within which a diversity of individuals and/or couples may flourish. Even skeptics about civil marriage such as those discussed above desire more than negative liberty.

Commentary on Dissenting Opinions

The *Obergefell* dissenters adhered to a much narrower view of what the constitutional guarantees of both liberty and equal protection required. This appears in Justice Thomas's opinion that the sort of liberty protected by the due-process clause extended only to freedom from physical restraint. Because the threat of criminal prosecution for same-sex intimacy was abrogated by *Lawrence v. Texas*, other protections were both superfluous and, in the dissenters' eyes, unconstitutional. All four dissenters agreed overwhelmingly that *Obergefell* robbed the people of the United States of their right to govern themselves through their elected representatives in their states. Therefore, I address this issue at the outset.

Matrimonial law in the United States is state law. For political philosopher Jeremy Waldron, however, this "law is the steward of an independently existing social reality." Thus "marriage, as an institution, belongs to the people whose social practice it is [...] not to the state or its judges,"[58] let alone to the federal judiciary. Marriage for same-sex couples implicitly affects straight marriage as well, just as the possibility of divorce casts a shadow over couples committed to a lifelong union. When *Obergefell* was decided, a number of states had adopted marriage

---

57 Murray, Melissa: "Murray, J., Concurring." In: Jack M. Balkin (ed.): *op. cit.*, p. 208; see pp. 202–220; Gill, Emily R.: *Free Exercise of Religion in the Liberal Polity*, *op. cit.*, pp. 199–256.

58 Waldron, Jeremy: "Waldron, J., Dissenting." In: Jack M. Balkin (ed.): *op. cit.*, p. 284; see pp. 281–299. See also Girgis, Sherif, and Robert P. George: "Girgis and George, JJ., Dissenting." In: Jack M. Balkin (ed.): *ibid.*, p. 221.

equality, and momentum was rapidly trending in that direction. Judges should be cautious about intervening in and overriding the democratic process, even when—as Waldron views *Obergefell*—the change *improves* the institution of marriage. He is wary of comparing *Obergefell* with *Loving*. This case did not change the definition of marriage, which was never understood as a commitment between a man and a woman of the same race. *Loving* only changed its application. The claim of same-sex couples to participate in marriage is best redeemed as the result of exhaustive public deliberation within the states. In sum, for Waldron the outcome of *Obergefell* was desirable but the process was inappropriate. As Roberts argued in his dissent, marriage equality proponents have lost "the opportunity to win the true acceptance that comes from persuading their fellow citizens of the justice of their cause."[59]

If the institution of civil marriage belongs to the people rather than the government, few would deny that the traditional vision of marriage emphasized responsible procreation and the importance of a stable setting for children, as Alito emphasized in his *Obergefell* dissent, rather than the happiness and well-being of the marrying couple. For Sherif Girgis and Robert George, for example, marriage cannot exist without the sexual complementarity provided by the union of a man and a woman. It carries social value precisely because it is not merely a social construct. This was a rational basis for states' reserving civil marriage for opposite-sex couples. Matrimonial law cannot be rooted in hostility or animus toward same-sex couples, as until recently marriage has been conceived of traditionally across both time and space.[60]

These arguments may be addressed both procedurally and substantively. First, the federal judiciary did not await the outcome of the political process in striking down laws concerning intimacy and marriage in *Loving, Romer, Lawrence, Windsor*, and various other cases. If legislative change is preferable to judicial pronouncements, the four states opposing marriage equality in *Obergefell* had already made a number of changes in their marriage laws, such as instituting no-fault divorce, repealing bars on unmarried cohabitation, and eliminating penalties applying to children born outside of wedlock. "These state policies are not channeling these couples toward 'responsible procreation' within marriage, but are instead liberating these couples to pursue their own choices for relational happiness."[61]

Second, although only Alito among the dissenters in *Obergefell* directly addressed the issue of children, the possible effect of marriage equality on children

---

59 *Obergefell v. Hodges, op. cit.*, p. 2625.
60 Girgis, Sherif/Robert P. George: "Girgis and George, JJ., Dissenting." In: Jack M. Balkin (ed.): *op. cit.*, pp. 221–235. See also *Obergefell v. Hodges, op. cit.*, pp. 2612–2615.
61 Eskridge, William N., Jr.: "Eskridge, J., Concurring in the Judgment." In: Jack M. Balkin (ed.): *op. cit.*, p. 186; see pp. 183–187.

was a major source of controversy on the part of its opponents. Defenders of traditional marriage championed the importance of kinship and blood ties for the well-being of dependent children, who are best protected from harm by living with their married biological parents. This decision removed "states' last tool for encouraging procreative adults to consider children's important need for a stable family structure," and thereby "transformed marriage into a privilege for adults."[62] With marriage equality, more children will live with same-sex partners as adoptive parents, as stepparents, or as the result of assisted birth technologies, while losing some or all ties with their biological kin. From this perspective, a rational basis grounded states' restricting marriage to opposite-sex couples.

Proponents of marriage equality, however, took a directly opposite view, arguing that this change would protect *existing* children who may have already experienced broken ties with their biological parents. Two of the petitioners, April DeBoer and Janet Rowse, adopted three children: one they had first fostered, the second born prematurely and abandoned by his biological mother, and the third with special needs.[63] As mentioned above, each child had a legal relationship with only one of their mothers, because Michigan permitted only single individuals or traditional married couples to adopt. The couple's only recourse was to be allowed to marry. What opponents of marriage equality appeared not to recognize was that excluding the parents of such children from marriage relegated the children to a lower caste status through no fault of their own. "The children also have no control over the most intractable cultural aspect of marriage bans, the state governments' moral judgments of adults—judgments that appear to be based in sexual and gender stereotypes."[64] Children are accordingly deprived of economic resources and benefits deriving from each of their parents individually and also from the marriage relationship. Stereotypes of LGBT individuals as selfish and antifamily have obscured the needs of existing same-sex couples and their children.[65]

Although these two views of the impact of marriage equality on children cannot be reconciled, the situation of children in existing settings, as with DeBoer and Rouse, is of paramount importance. "*All* children—nor simply those raised in opposite-sex marriages by their biological parents—deserve stable and nurturing environments in which to grow."[66] From this perspective, it does not

---

62 Alvaré, Helen: "Alvaré, J., Dissenting." In: Jack M. Balkin (ed.): *ibid.*, pp. 245–246, p. 244; see pp. 241–258.
63 *Obergefell v. Hodges, op. cit.*, p. 2595.
64 Smith, Catherine: "Smith, J., Concurring." In: Jack M. Balkin (ed.): *op. cit.*, p. 156; see pp. 146–163.
65 Eskridge, William N., Jr.: "Eskridge, J., Concurring in the Judgment." In: Jack M. Balkin (ed.): *ibid.*, pp. 181–187.
66 Balkin, Jack M.: "Jack M. Balkin (Judgment of the Court)." In: Jack M. Balkin (ed.): *ibid.*, p. 105, emphasis original; see 104–107.

matter whether the same-sex marriage ban was grounded upon sex, sexual orientation, and/or a traditional understanding of sex roles. What was crucial was the social understanding and impact of the law. This point was recognized by the *Obergefell* majority with reference to the burden on children "of knowing their families are somehow lesser."[67] It also emerged in *Windsor* when the court ruled that the effect of the DOMA denial of federal benefits to same-sex married couples imposed "a disadvantage, a separate status, and so a stigma" upon all same-sex married couples.[68] In sum, the effect of the marriage ban "was to target the family relationships of lesbian, gay, and bisexual individuals for unfavorable treatment and to single out those family relationships as inferior and not worthy of public respect."[69] A different remedy, of course, would be to disestablish the status of civil marriage altogether, as Franke and Murray suggest. This solution, however, would have been akin to communities in the American South after the passage of civil rights laws governing public accommodations, which closed and filled in their public pools rather than allowing interracial swimming.

One other issue bears addressing. As noted above, Roberts came down squarely in favor of negative liberty in his dissent, maintaining that the right to privacy "provides no affirmative right to redefine marriage."[70] A stronger argument, however, devolves from the point that because matrimonial law is the purview of the states, equal protection only requires that all persons within a state enjoy equal access to the status of marriage as the law of that state defines it. On John Harrison's interpretation, under the Fourteenth Amendment, "the Constitution leaves the content of legal rights to the states, while requiring that those rights be equally enjoyed."[71] Certain state offices, for example, may be filled by popular vote in one state but not in another, but all registered voters enjoy equal access to the ballot in the state in which they reside. The status of marriage is a positive right of state citizenship. However, if a state does not allow same-sex couples to marry, "in what sense can a state be said to abridge a right that is itself constituted by state law?"[72] This viewpoint directly contrasts with that of marriage equality proponents, who argued that because all states offer the status of marriage, it must be available to all on equal terms nationwide. For Harrison, however, marriage must be available on equal terms in accordance with a particular state's definition of marriage. At

---

67 *Obergefell v. Hodges, op. cit.*, p. 2600.
68 *United States v. Windsor, op. cit.*, p. 770.
69 NeJaime, Douglas/Reva B. Siegel: "NeJaime and Siegel, JJ., Concurring." In: Jack M. Balkin (ed.): *op. cit.*, p. 125; see pp. 123–126.
70 *Obergefell v. Hodges, op. cit.*, p. 2620.
71 Harrison, John C.: "Harrison, J., Dissenting." In: Jack M. Balkin (ed.): *op. cit.*, p. 266; see pp. 266–268.
72 *Ibid.*, p. 270; see pp. 268–275.

this time of global mobility and communication, however, the legal protections of marriage should not appear and disappear at the state line.

Conclusion

Traditional marriage laws were not created with the intent of discriminating against same-sex couples. Thus, it cannot be argued that animus or hostility is baked into them, so to speak. Hostility may emerge, however, when same-sex couples want to participate in this civil status for the same reasons that opposite-sex couples have long displayed, a public recognition of stability and commitment based on the freedom of autonomous choice. Although legal changes in time-honored social institutions should take place only after careful consideration, we should pay particular heed to vulnerable groups with a history of oppression by a dominant consensus.

It is sometimes assumed that groups that have achieved some success are no longer vulnerable and need only to be left alone and that the according of positive rights is unnecessary. Therefore, their interests need not be attended to. However, Patrick Neal suggests, "But what if this assumption is wrong? What if political actors and interests are thought of not as entities pre-existing the process of political activity, but as properties which emerge and constitute themselves through that process?"[73] Neal's example is in fact that of gay rights, which until the late twentieth century would not have been included on the public agenda. "Commentators and activists, however, have *made* themselves and their interests *recognizable.*"[74] If we are committed not only to opportunities to shape one's life as one chooses but also to the ability to exercise or realize those opportunities, we need to attend to these interests.

The social impact and understanding of law are crucial. During the long history of traditional marriage laws, until recently no one questioned the fact that it was open only to opposite-sex couples. Therefore, no hostility was involved. Once LGBT people had imagined that perhaps they too could aspire to the personal and social benefits of marriage, their exclusion relegated same-sex couples to a second-class status. Absent compelling reasons, a liberal democratic polity should avoid exclusions that create two classes of citizens, the favored and the disfavored. "Discriminatory exclusion is harmful when it *publicly expresses* the civic inequality of the excluded even in the absence of any other showing that it *causes* the civic inequality in question."[75]

---

73 Neal, Patrick: *Liberalism and Its Discontents.* New York University Press: New York 1997, p. 124.
74 *Ibid.*, p. 125, emphasis original.
75 Gutmann, Amy: *Identity in Democracy.* Princeton University Press: Princeton, NJ 2003, p. 97.

References

Alvaré, Helen: "Alvaré, J., Dissenting." In: Jack M. Balkin (ed.): *What Obergefell v. Hodges Should Have Said*. Yale University Press: New Haven, CT 2020, pp. 241–261.

Babst, Gordon A.: *Liberal Constitutionalism, Marriage, and Sexual Orientation: A Contemporary Case for Dis-establishment*. Peter Lang: New York 2002.

Balkin, Jack M.: "Jack M. Balkin (Judgment of the Court)." In: Jack M. Balkin (ed.): *What Obergefell v. Hodges Should Have Said*. Yale University Press: New Haven, CT 2020, pp. 93–111.

Ball, Carlos A.: "Against Neutrality in the Legal Recognition of Intimate Relationships." In: Gordon A. Babst/Emily R. Gill/Jason Pierceson (eds.): *Moral Argument, Religion, and Same-Sex Marriage: Advancing the Public Good*. Lexington Books: Lanham, MD 2009.

Ball, Carlos A.: *The Morality of Gay Rights: An Exploration in Political Philosophy*. Routledge: New York 2003.

Bamforth, Nicholas/Richards, David A.J.: *Patriarchal Religion, Sexuality, and Gender: A Critique of the New Natural Law*. Cambridge University Press: New York 2008.

Blankenhorn, David: *The Future of Marriage*. Encounter Books: New York 2007.

Boling, Patricia: *Privacy and the Politics of Intimate Life*. Cornell University Press: Ithaca, NY 1996.

Bowers v. Hardwick, 478 U.S. 186 (1986).

Brake, Elizabeth: *Minimizing Marriage: Marriage, Morality, and the Law*. Oxford University Press: New York 2012.

Chambers, Clare: *Against Marriage: An Egalitarian Defense of the Marriage-Free State*. Oxford University Press: New York 2017.

Eskridge, William N., Jr.: "Eskridge, J., Concurring in the Judgment." In: Jack M. Balkin (ed.): *What Obergefell v. Hodges Should Have Said*. Yale University Press: New Haven, CT 2020, pp. 168–188.

Franke, Katherine: "Franke, J., concurring in the judgment." In: Jack M. Balkin (ed.): *What Obergefell v. Hodges Should Have Said*. Yale University Press: New Haven, CT 2020, pp. 189–201.

Gallagher, Maggie: "Normal Marriage: Two Views." In: Lynn D. Wardle/Mark Strasser/William C. Duncan/David Orgon Coolidge (eds.): *Marriage and Same-Sex Unions: A Debate*. Praeger: Westport, CT 2003, pp. 13–24.

George, Robert: "Neutrality, Equality, and Same-Sex Marriage." In: Lynn D. Wardle/Mark Strasser/William C. Duncan/David Orgon Coolidge (eds.): *Marriage and Same-Sex Unions: A Debate*. Praeger: Westport, CT 2003, pp. 119–132.

Gerstmann, Evan: *Same-Sex Marriage and the Constitution.* 2nd ed. Cambridge University Press: New York 2008.

Gill, Emily R.: *An Argument for Same-Sex Marriage: Religious Freedom, Sexual Freedom, and Public Expressions of Civic Equality.* Georgetown University Press: Washington, DC 2012.

Gill, Emily R.: *Free Exercise of Religion in the Liberal Polity: Conflicting Interpretations.* Palgrave Macmillan: Cham, Switzerland 2019.

Girgis, Sherif/George, Robert P.: "Girgis and George, JJ., Dissenting." In: Jack M. Balkin, *What* Obergefell v. Hodges *Should Have Said.* Yale University Press: New Haven, CT 2020, pp. 221–240.

Gutmann, Amy: *Identity in Democracy.* Princeton University Press: Princeton 2003.

Harrison, John C.: "Harrison, J., Dissenting." In: Jack M. Balkin (ed.): *What* Obergefell v. Hodges *Should Have Said.* Yale University Press: New Haven, CT 2020, pp. 262–280.

In re Marriage Cases, 43 Cal. 4th 757 (2008).

In re Opinions of the Justices to the Senate, 440 Mass. 1201 (2004).

Jakobsen, Janet R./Pellegrini, Ann: *Love the Sin: Sexual Regulation and the Limits of Religious Tolerance.* Beacon Press: Boston, MA 2004.

Kerrigan v. Commissioner of Public Health, 289 Conn. 135 (2008).

Koppelman, Andrew: "Koppelman, J., concurring." In: Jack M. Balkin (ed.): *What* Obergefell v. Hodges *Should Have Said.* Yale University Press: New Haven, CT 2020, pp. 129–145.

Lawrence v. Texas, 539 U.S. 558 (2003).

Lehr, Valerie: *Queer Family Values: Debunking the Myth of the Nuclear Family.* Temple University Press: Philadelphia 1999.

Loving v. Virginia, 388 U.S. 1 (1967).

Macedo, Stephen: "Against the Old Sexual Morality of the New Natural Law." In: Robert P. George (ed.): *Natural Law, Liberalism, and Morality.* Oxford University Press: New York 2001, pp. 27–48.

Metz, Tamara: *Untying the Knot: Marriage, the State, and the Case for Their Divorce.* Princeton University Press: Princeton 2010.

Murray, Melissa: "Murray, J., concurring." In: Jack M. Balkin, ed.: *What* Obergefell v. Hodges *Should Have Said.* Yale University Press: New Haven, CT 2020, pp. 202–220.

Neal, Patrick: *Liberalism and Its Discontents.* New York University Press: New York 1997.

NeJaime, Douglas/Siegel, Reva B.: "NeJaime and Siegel, JJ., Concurring." In: Jack M. Balkin (ed.): *What* Obergefell v. Hodges *Should Have Said.* Yale University Press: New Haven, CT 2020, pp. 112–128.

Obergefell v. Hodges, 135 S. Ct. 2584 (2015).

Okin, Susan Moller: *Justice, Gender, and the Family*. Basic Books: New York 1989.

Oleske, Jr., James M.: "A Regrettable Invitation to 'Constitutional Resistance,' Renewed Confusion Over Religious Exemption, and the Future of Free Exercise." *Lewis & Clark Law Review* 20, 2017, pp. 1317–1371.

Pateman, Carole: *The Sexual Contract*. Stanford University Press: Stanford, CA 1988.

Perry v. Schwartzenegger, 704 F. Supp. 2d 921 (Cal. 2010).

Pierceson, Jason: *Courts, Liberalism, and Rights: Gay Law and Politics in the United States and Canada*. Temple University Press: Philadelphia 2005.

Polikoff, Nancy D.: *Beyond (Straight and Gay) Marriage: Valuing All Families Under the Law*. Beacon Press: Boston, MA 2008.

Rauch, Jonathan: *Gay Marriage: Why It Is Good for Gays, Good for Straights, and Good for America*. Owl Books: New York 2005.

Richards, David A.J.: *Identity and the Case for Gay Rights: Race, Gender, and Religion as Analogies*. University of Chicago Press: Chicago 1999.

Richards, David A.J.: *The Case for Gay Rights: From* Bowers *to* Lawrence *and Beyond*. University Press of Kansas: Lawrence 2005.

Romer v. Evans, 575 U.S. 620 (1996).

Smith, Catherine: "Smith, J., concurring." In: Jack M. Balkin (ed.): *What Obergefell v. Hodges Should Have Said*. Yale University Press: New Haven, CT 2020, pp. 146–167.

Stewart, Katherine: *The Power Worshippers: Inside the Dangerous Rise of Christian Nationalism*. Bloomsbury Publishing: New York 2019.

Sullivan, Andrew: *Virtually Normal: An Argument about Homosexuality*. Vantage: New York 1996.

Taylor, Charles: "What's Wrong with Negative Liberty?" In: Stewart, Andrew M. (ed.): *Readings in Social and Political Philosophy*. 2nd ed. Oxford University Press: New York 1996, pp. 98–109.

United States v. Carolene Products Co., 304 U.S. 144 (1938).

United States v. Windsor, 570 U.S. 744 (2013).

Varnum v. Brien, 763 N.W.2d 862 (2009).

Waldron, Jeremy. "Waldron, J., dissenting." In: Jack M. Balkin (ed.): *What Obergefell v. Hodges Should Have Said*. Yale University Press: New Haven, CT 2020, pp. 281–301.

Elad Ben David

Religious Clauses of the First Amendment in the Concept of "American Islam" of Post-9/11 Era: The Case of Yasir Qadhi

Abstract: The Establishment Clause and the Free Exercise Clause have been a basis for crucial debates and contemporary controversies throughout history, especially regarding Christianity aspects in its historical prohibition on state-sponsored churches. Nevertheless, the September-11 attacks that caused the rise of Islamophobia highlighted new controversies that have been challenging the Muslim community in America. Those anti-Islam and anti-Muslim incidents have stimulated the boundaries of those clauses in light of the post-9/11 era. Sheikh Dr. Yasir Qadhi, a prominent American cleric, who held hardcore Islamic views in the past, was affected by the dramatic consequences of 9/11 and tried to navigate those clauses as an incentive to reconcile the fragile American Muslim identity within the American social fabric. In this chapter, I argue that the post-September-11 era, along with the First Amendment to the U.S. Constitution, served as a fundamental basis to Qadhi in carving out the balance between religious clauses, preserving Islam within the Muslim community, and bolstering its American identity in light of contemporary challenges.[1]

Keywords: Religious clauses of the First Amendment, September-11 attacks, Islamophobia, Yasir Qadhi, Islam in America

Introduction

The religious clauses of the First Amendment form an essential part of the Bill of Rights and protect religious freedom in the United States. Being a part of the United States Constitution, the First Amendment includes two religious clauses—the Establishment Clause and the Free Exercise Clause—which were ratified as part of the Bill of Rights in 1791 and initially applied to the federal government only. In the twentieth century, however, the Supreme Court made them binding to the states too, by incorporating them into the due-process clause of the Fourteenth

---

1 This chapter is based on my Ph.D. dissertation which was written at the Department of Middle Eastern Studies at Bar-Ilan University.

Amendment.[2] These two clauses promote individual freedom of religion as well as separation of church and state,[3] stating: "Congress shall make no law respecting an establishment of religion, or prohibiting the free exercise thereof."[4]

While there are several interpretations of the religious clauses (including separationist and accommodationist one), it is generally understood that the Establishment Clause prohibits the government from establishing an official state religion or giving preferential treatment to any particular religion, and regulates the relationship between state and religion in the United States. The Free Exercise Clause, on the other hand, guarantees the right of individuals to freely practice their religion without any government interference and protects individuals from government actions that would encumber or limit their religious beliefs and practice. The breadth of these clauses has allowed debates over their proper scope since ratification, and it has also led to some internal inconsistency in the Supreme Court's judgments interpreting these clauses and interpretations that have shifted over time.[5]

While together, these two clauses that aim to ensure religious freedom and prevent government involvement in religious matters are considered an essential part of the constitutional protection of individual liberties in the United States, there have been many legal cases concerning their scope and boundaries. These cases have grappled with the balance between religious freedom and the need to uphold the principle of the separation of church and state. For example, in the case of *Engel v. Vitale* in 1962, which involved the mandatory daily recitation by public school officials of a prayer written by the New York Board of Regents, the practice was deemed unconstitutional by the Supreme Court and violated the Establishment Clause.[6] An example of the Free Exercise Clause was reflected in the famous case of the *Church of Lukumi Babalu Aye v. City of Hialeah* in Florida. The Supreme Court ruled unconstitutional a local Florida ban on Santería ritual animal sacrifice because it violated Freedom of religion.[7]

---

2   The Free Exercise Clause war incorporated in 1940 in *Cantwell v. Connecticut*, the Establishment Clause was incorporated in 1947 in *Everson v. Board of Education*.
3   Cornell Law School, Overview of the Religion Clauses, retrieved 09.10.2023, from https://www.law.cornell.edu/constitution-conan/amendment-1/overview-of-the-religion-clauses.
4   "The Constitution of the United States of America: Analysis and Interpretation," retrieved 09.10.2023, from https://constitution.congress.gov/browse/essay/amdt1-2-1/ALDE_00013267/.
5   *Ibid.*
6   "Facts and Case Summary—Engel v. Vitale," retrieved 27.12.2021, from https://www.uscourts.gov/educational-resources/educational-activities/facts-and-case-summary-engel-v-vitale.
7   For more information about this case, see: https://www.law.cornell.edu/supct/html/91-948.ZO.html, retrieved 10.09.2023.

During most of U.S. history, many of these legal verdicts have focused more on debates and controversies regarding the Judeo-Christian faith practices. The post-9/11 era has, however, sparked new debates regarding the religious clauses within the American Muslim community, especially in regard to religious freedom, discrimination, and the balance between national security concerns, and the right to practice Islam. For example, the Grand Zero Mosque case was a famous incident that served as a classic reflection to the boundaries of the freedom of worship, which illustrated the ideological battlefield over the place of Islam in America.[8] In this paper, I will examine the doctrine of Sheikh Yasir Qadhi, a prominent American cleric, who tried to carve out a balance between these religious clauses, by emphasizing the crucial advantages of the First Amendment, in preserving Islam and bolstering the Muslims' American identity, in light of contemporary challenges of post-9/11 era.

Islam in America of the Post-9/11 Era

By and large, Muslims in the United States have lived quite peacefully for many decades, despite a few tolerable incidents that occurred from time to time.[9] However, the rise of Islamophobia in the post-9/11 era challenged the Muslim community, with actions that increased the tension within the Freedom of Religion, such as the Grand Zero Mosque controversy in 2010.[10] Generally, Islam in America has been part of the country for the last few centuries but started to coalesce by regaining more presence and collective strength since the sixties in the last century.[11] By and large, the status of Muslims in America during that time was widened in part due to the Hart-Celler Act of President Lyndon Johnson, which opened the door to mass immigration.[12] Also, the foundation of prominent Muslim organizations at that period, such as the MSA[13] (Muslim Student Association) and ICNA[14] (Islamic Circle of North America), set a goal to spread Islam to Muslims and non-Muslims (da'wa) in North America, which bolstered the concept of

---

8   Takim, Liyakat, "The Ground Zero Mosque Controversy: Implications for American Islam." *Religions*, 2011, p. 132.
9   Ba-Yunus, Ilyas/Kone, Kassim: *Muslims in the United States*. Greenwood Press: Westport, CT 2006, p. 70.
10 Rohrer, Finlo: "The Battle over the 'Ground Zero Mosque.'" *BBC News*, August 3, 2010, retrieved 20.01.2022, from https://www.bbc.com/news/world-us-canada-10846716.
11 Ukeles, Raquel: *The Evolving Muslim Community in America: The Impact of 9/11*. Mosaica: Research Center for Religion State and Society, 2003, p. 7.
12 Ghazali, Abdus Sattar: *Islam & Muslims in the Post-9/11 America*. No press edition, 2012, p. 223.
13 The official site of the MSA, retrieved 22.12.2021, from https://www.msanational.org/.
14 The official site of ICNA, retrieved 22.12.2021, from https://www.icna.org/.

Islam in America.[15] Other significant Muslim organizations, founded later, included ISNA[16] (Islamic Society of North America) in 1981 and CAIR[17] (Council on American-Islamic Relations) in 1994. ISNA, which has traced its origin from the MSA, continued with the focus on the spread of Islam and the unity of the Muslim community, while CAIR functioned as a legal platform to promote a positive image of Muslims through media communication, lobbying, education, and legal protection. Consequently, the conception beginning of the "melting pot" ideal ended with a "multiculturalism" that made Muslims, in general, feel more accepted in American society.[18] By and large, the negative perception of Islam has a long historical record in America, though shorter than other ethnic or racial minority groups, such as the Afro-American community and the Jewish community. Islam's negative perception was related in part to significant events in the Middle East, such as the Islamic revolution in Iran in 1979, the bombings of the Marine headquarters in Beirut in 1982, and the continuous Israeli-Arab war. Those global activities were motives that helped to perpetuate Islam's negative image in America.[19]

However, the September-11 attacks symbolized a new era of Islam in America that, according to Larry Poston, "marked a watershed moment for Islam in the Western Hemisphere."[20] The waves of Islamophobia, that took place as a result, have exacerbated the rage and the anti-Islamic hatred and boosted the rise of Islamophobia,[21] which included, for example, issuing the Patriot Act in 2001[22] or spying on mosques and Islamic charity institutions such as Zakat, that were frozen or shut down.[23]

This hardship placed many American Muslims in the frontline of new controversies, with challenges that forced them to realize that to protect their reputation and religion, they must enhance their integration with their fellow

---

15 Poston, Larry: "Da'wa in the West." In: Yvonne Yazbeck Haddad (ed.): *The Muslims of America*. Oxford University Press: Oxford 1991, pp. 131–132.
16 The official site of ISNA, retrieved 22.12.2021, from https://isna.net/.
17 The official site of CAIR, retrieved 22.12.2021, from https://www.cair.com/.
18 Poston, Larry/Guzik, Elysia: "Da'wa in North America: The Past, the Present, and the Future." In: Itzchak Weismann and Jamal Malik (eds.): *Culture of Da'wa: Islamic Preaching in the Modern World*. The University of Utah Press: Salt Lake City 2020, p. 161.
19 Haddad, Yvonne Yazbeck/T. Lummis, Adair: *Islamic Values in the United States: A Comparative Study*. Oxford University Press: New York, p. 158.
20 Poston, Larry/Guzik, Elysia: *op. cit.*, p. 166.
21 Ba-Yunus, Ilyas/Kone, Kassim: *op. cit.*, pp. 158, 164.
22 The Patriot Act was a landmark Act of the United States Congress, after the 9/11 attacks to tight national security against acts of terrorism. Ghazali, Abdus Sattar: *op. cit.*, pp. 2–3.
23 *Ibid.*, pp. 69–89.

American non-Muslims by performing more vital social involvement and civic responsibility roles.[24] Those activities included cooperation and consolidating the ties between Muslim communities, creating a broad interfaith encounter with Christians and Jews, and enhancing Muslim involvement in the political arena.[25] So ironically, those attacks against Islam and Muslims caused Islam in America to rise and spread. Poston argued that the September-11 attacks "functioned as a grandiose advertisement for the religion of Islam," where leading Muslim voices tried to mitigate the religion peacefully, while refuting the concept that Islam is a "religion of the sword."[26]

Another essential part that helped facilitate the increase of Islam was the rise of new media platforms that emerged a few years after the attacks and were subsequently used by Muslim preachers and activists to present Islam and Muslims positively.[27] Consequently, the combination of contending with Islamophobia and spreading the religion through social media was one of the reasons that the 9/11 catastrophe served as a window of opportunity for the Muslim community to become more noticeable in the public sphere.

One of the main results of 9/11 and its egregious consequences was also reflected in bolstering the American identity of many Muslims, especially within the immigrant community of second and third generations born in America. While the concept of the "Americanization of Muslims" is not new and had been shaped back in the last century,[28] after 9/11, this conception was solidified and intensified. For example, Yvonne Yazbeck Haddad and Nader Harb claimed that 9/11 caused many American Muslims to embrace the American identity and integrate more into American society, creating a form of "American Islam" that constituted Islamic value practices.[29]

Today Islam in America is considered the third largest religion, after Christianity and Judaism, and is estimated to become the second largest religion in the future.[30] The American Muslim community is very diverse and consists of three main

---

24 Ukeles, Raquel: *op. cit.*, pp. 8–9.
25 Curiel, Jonathan: *Islam in America*. I.B. Tauris: London and New York 2015, pp. 51–53. The first Muslim Congress was elected following this activity, Keith Ellison in 2006. *Ibid.*, p. 52.
26 Poston, Larry/Guzik, Elysia: *op. cit.*, pp. 166–167.
27 Ben David, Elad: "Marketing Daʿwa in America Through Social Media." *Beehive: Middle East Social Media* 8 (6), 2020, pp. 8–13.
28 Esposito, John: "Muslims in America or American Muslims." In: Haddad, Yvonne Yazbeck/Esposito, John (eds.): *Muslims on the Americanization Path?* Oxford University Press: New York 2000, p. 3.
29 Haddad, Yvonne Yazbeck/Harb, Nasir Nader: "Post-9/11: Making Islam an American Religion." *Religions* 5, 2014, p. 491.
30 Willingham, A.J.: "By 2040, Islam Could Be the Second-Largest Religion in the US." *CNN Politics*, January 11, 2018, retrieved 02.12.2021, from https://edition.cnn.

groups: Afro-Americans, immigrants from South Asia, and Arabs from the Middle East. The precise number of Muslims is unknown but is estimated at about three and a half to six and even nine million.[31] According to a study by the Association of Religion Data Archives from 2010, the Muslim population increased by 67% in the decade following the September-11 attacks.[32] The study above is also manifested in the rising number of mosques: In the year 2000, for example, there were only 1209 mosques, and in the year 2011, the number had jumped to 2106.[33]

The Figure of Yasir Qadhi

Sheikh Dr. Yasir Qadhi is considered one of America's most famous and prominent scholars and was described by the *New York Times* Magazine as "one of the most influential conservative clerics in American Islam."[34] Qadhi is a resident scholar in "Epic Masjid" in Plano, Texas,[35] and the dean of The Islamic Seminary of America,[36] after serving as the dean of academic affairs at Al-Maghrib Institute[37] in Texas from 2002 until 2019. Qadhi is essentially part of the generation of young American-born preachers who burst into the public's awareness after the September-11 attacks, by defending Islam and spreading its message in fluent English to an audience of millions, with the help of new media platforms like YouTube and Facebook.[38]

Born in 1975 in Houston, Texas, to immigrant parents from Pakistan, Qadhi spent his early years in Jeddah, Saudi Arabia, due to his father's job location. When he returned to America as a teenager, he studied and graduated with a B.Sc. in Chemical Engineering from the University of Houston. During this time, Qadhi was eager to delve more into the Islamic profession, and after he graduated from Houston University, he started his studies at the Islamic University of Madinah

---

com/2018/01/10/politics/muslim-population-growth-second-religious-group-trnd/index.html.
31 Curiel, Jonathan: *op. cit.*, pp. 65–66.
32 Neal, Meghan: "Number of Muslims in the U.S. Doubles since 9/11." *New York Daily News*, March 3, 2012, retrieved 22.12.2021, from https://www.nydailynews.com/news/national/number-muslims-u-s-doubles-9-11-article-1.1071895.
33 Curiel, Jonathan: *op. cit.*, pp. 68–69.
34 Elliott, Andrea: "Why Yasir Qadhi Wants to Talk About Jihad." *The New York Times Magazine*, March 17, 2011, p. 1.
35 The official site of Epic Masjid, retrieved 22.12.2021, from https://epicmasjid.org/.
36 The official site of The Islamic Seminary of America, retrieved 22.12.2021, from https://www.islamicseminary.us/.
37 The official site of Al-Maghrib, retrieved 22.12.2021, from https://www.almaghrib.org/.
38 Ben David, Elad: *op. cit.*, pp. 8–13.

(IUM). There, he completed a second Bachelor degree specializing in Hadith studies and continued to complete an M.A. in Islamic Theology from the College of Dawah. When he returned to the United States during the early 2000s, he started his Ph.D. in Religious Studies at Yale University from 2005 to 2013.[39]

During his Madinah phase, Qadhi was considered a hardcore Salafist[40] Muslim, but the combination of the 9/11 attacks and his studies at Yale softened much of his ultra-conservative and rigid doctrine. The consequences of 9/11 caused him to see the need to build bridges between Muslims and non-Muslims,[41] and his studies at Yale exposed him in depth to Islam from a Western liberal perspective.[42] Gradually, Qadhi has also started to disconnect himself as part of the Salafism movement, claiming that it fails to confront modern challenges successfully and cannot be fitted into the context of a Western Islam, especially in the post-9/11 era in the United States.[43] Since the last decade, Qadhi has been depicted as a pragmatic scholar who combines unique elements, assisting him in bridging the gap between the East and the West, due to his profound involvement in the Islamic theological and the Western intellectual paradigms. Therefore, ISNA described him as "one of the few people who has combined a traditional Eastern Islamic seminary education with a Western academic training of the study of Islam."[44]

---

39 Razavian, Christopher Pooya: "Yasir Qadhi and the Development of Reasonable Salafism." In: Bano, Masooda (ed.): *Modern Islamic Authority and Social Change*. Edinburgh University Press: Edinburgh 2018, pp. 155–156, 175.

40 Salafism is considered a harsh interpretation of Islam, and its followers see themselves as the original successors of the Muslims who lived in the first three centuries of Islam. The Salafist ideology is characterized by a rigid understanding of the Islamic concept, and therefore it sees in liberal or Sufi (mystic) Muslims to be mistaken Islamic sects. See: Wiedl-Menashe, Nina: *Contemporary Calls to Islam—Salafi Da'wa in Germany 2002–2011*. Ph.D. Dissertation, Ben-Gurion University, 2015, pp. 31–34.

41 Hannini, Daniyah M.: "The "Spiritualization" of Islam in America: A Study of Highly Individualistic Forms of Islamic Practice in the U.S." MA Thesis, The State University of New Jersey, 2016, p. 57.

42 Qadhi has addressed that issue many times. See, for example: Yasir Qadhi, "Muslims Studying Islamic Sciences in Western Universities." *YouTube*, January 28, 2015, retrieved 22.12.2021, from https://www.youtube.com/watch?v=LhtCEUw5MKQ&t=90s.

43 See, for example: Yasir, Qadhi, "Have You Left the Way of the Salaf?" *YouTube*, April 9, 2014, retrieved 22.12.2021, from https://www.youtube.com/watch?v=8GYkedPkxlI.

44 Hannini, Daniyah, M.: *op. cit.*, p. 56.

Qadhi's Use of the Freedom of Religion to Bolster the Concept of "American Islam"

The post-9/11 consequences, combined with the model of the American Constitution, enhanced Qadhi to empower American Muslims to be more connected to their American-Western identity, out of the goal to practice Islam as an American Muslim minority. In this chapter, I include three main elements, in which he aims to intensify the attachment of American Muslims toward their state, using the unique benefits of the Religious Clauses of the First Amendment.

The Pros of Religious Freedom in America, in Comparison to France

One of the primary arguments of Qadhi that aims to bolster the American identity is his distinction drawn between the United States of America and France, as a representative of the "anti-Islamic West." Highlighting this comparison helps him argue that the United States is still considered a "safe" place for Muslims to express their religion in public despite all its flaws. Qadhi points out that the attitude toward religion in France's public religious sphere was influenced by secular philosophers, such as Jean-Jacques Rousseau "that could not imagine a religion flourishing in public if it was competing with power" and claimed that it should be outlawed. Using Rousseau's harsh approach to religion, Qadhi argues that the France of our time has adopted his attitude, demonstrating its modern Islamophobic actions, such as the Niqab (full-face veil) and the Burqa[45] banning,[46] which were legislated in 2011.[47]

But unlike France, which has become an "anti-Islamic" country, Qadhi stresses the different and the favorable situation in America, that was influenced by intellectuals such as Thomas Hobbes, Thomas Jefferson, and especially John Locke. Qadhi points out that Locke's moderate attitude to religion in the public sphere still has an influence on America today, despite the fact that the United States is considered a secular country. Locke argued that religious ritual is a private matter of the believer with God, and therefore even if that ritual takes place in public, the

---

45 Burqa is a loose enveloping garment that covers the face and body, especially common in countries such as Afghanistan.
46 "European Court of Human Rights judgment on French laws banning the niqab and burqa." *Islamic Human Rights Commission*, August 23, 2014, retrieved 22.12.2021, from https://www.ihrc.org.uk/publications/briefings/11159-european-court-of-human-rights-judgement-on-french-laws-banning-the-niqab-and-burqa/.
47 Yasir, Qadhi: "Relationship between Church & State Comparison with Islamic Caliphate." Hartford, CT, *YouTube*, May 26, 2012, retrieved 22.12.2021, from https://www.youtube.com/watch?v=prrtGF4LAfQ.

State should preserve and keep that right.[48] In Qadhi's emphasis on the Founding Fathers and those philosophers, he aims to present them as figures who had vision and tolerance, which positively impacted religion (Islam) in America. For example, Qadhi addresses George Washington, who wrote in one of his letters that he would have no problem welcoming Mohammedans (Muslims) to his place of residence at Mount Vernon, if they were good workmen (loyal citizens). In a reference to John Adams,[49] Qadhi addresses the "Moors Sundry Act" of 1790, which dealt with a Moroccan group who arrived in the United States and petitioned to be tried as citizens rather than being subject to the Negro Act of 1740.[50] The resolution offered the opinion that free citizens of Morocco were not subject to laws governing Blacks and slaves, which was reflected in Adams' declaration, "that the US has no enmity against the laws, religion, or tranquility of Musulman" (Muslims). In another example, Qadhi also mentions the "patriotic" attitude of Thomas Jefferson, while he was a senator, that in his Bill of Religious Liberty, he had written the state of Virginia, he called for religious worship protection to all people from all religions.[51] Jefferson's own famous copy of the Qur'an, also serves as an outstanding case to demonstrate its impact more than 200 hundred years later, when it was used at the swearing-in ceremony by the first Muslim Congress, Keith Ellison, in 2006.[52]

By using the religious model of America in comparison to France, Qadhi wishes to distinguish France's aversion to the connection between religion and State, which has been ingrained since the French Revolution and embodied in the *laïcité l*aw. Therefore, although most of the Founding Fathers were deists, they still appreciated the ethical dimension of religion in society, and their decisions have had lasting effects until today. From this perspective, Qadhi emphasizes the superiority of the United States concerning religious freedom and *Sharia* (Islamic law) practice contrary to other Western countries such as France. He admits, however,

---

48 Schaap, Andrew: *Political Reconciliation*. Routledge: New York 2005, p. 5.
49 Adams was the second President of the United States (1735–1826).
50 The Negro Act of 1740 was a South Carolina law that harshly restricted the rights and freedoms of enslaved Africans and their descendants, by imposing harsh regulations on their behavior, movement, and activities.
51 Yasir Qadhi, "History of Islam in America: Whither and Where," *YouTube*, May 5, 2008, retrieved 08.10.2023, from https://www.youtube.com/watch?v=rdxSWwWDwT8. The full quotation of Jefferson was as follows: "An attempt to provide religious freedom to the Jew, the Gentile, the Christian, the Mahometan (Muslim), the Hindoo, and [the] infidel of every denomination.": "A Bill for Establishing Religious Freedom," retrieved 10.10.2023, from http://constitutioncenter.org/the-constitution/historic-document-library/detail/thomas-jefferson-a-bill-for-establishing-religious-freedom.
52 Douglas, Hicks: *With God on All Sides: Leadership in a Devout and Diverse America*. Oxford University Press: New York 2009, p. xvii.

that *Sharia* practice in a Western secular country remains a complex challenge, but the pros of the First Amendment, which protects religious freedom, is considered a privilege to the status of American Muslims, allowing them to remain faithful to Islam while being law-abiding citizens. Therefore, he calls on American Muslims to appreciate that freedom in their country, which allows them to live by their faith without any external fear.

In order to illustrate the religious freedom in America that enables Muslims to express their religious opinions freely, Qadhi addresses public religious controversies in American history, such as the *Roe v. Wade* case.[53] Qadhi uses this example as an incentive to encourage American Muslims to use that right given to them by the Constitution, to protest against "immoral issues, that contradict the religion of Islam, such as abortion." Concerning this case, he emphasizes that although many Americans (non-Muslims) opposed the abortion law in *Roe v. Wade* case, it did not challenge their loyalty to their country, nor did it harm their solid American identity. Therefore, Qadhi justifies the battle of fundamentalist Christians who use the American law system to oppose what they call public "injustice," such as in the abortion case, that contradicts their religious faith. Thus, from Qadhi's perspective, American Muslims should not be an exception in this regard, and he calls them to join the benefits of the constitutional system as Americans, without any fear from mainstream society. From this example, we can see how Qadhi sees Islam in America as part and parcel of the country, just like Christianity or Judaism, by encouraging Muslims to express their faith, even when this attitude is against the mainstream public's opinion.[54]

The Importance of the Islamic Practice in the Private Sphere

In addition, one of the primary arguments of Qadhi is that Muslims who live in America are compelled to abolish any goal or dream to establish an Islamic State in the country, and their only religious practice is in the domain of their private life. In this regard, he rejects the doctrine of famous Muslim thinkers such as Khurram Murad, whose doctrine claimed that the only justification for Muslims to live permanently in the West is out of the ultimate vision to make "American society Islamic and Muslim."[55] Qadhi views this approach as problematic—first and foremost

---

53 The *Roe v. Wade* case was a precedent-setting ruling by the Supreme Court that any law prohibiting an abortion violates the Constitution for violating the right to a fair trial. The *Roe v. Wade* case has recently sparked another controversy, see: Camosy, Charles: "Supreme Court's Hearing of Mississippi Abortion Law Is a Gut Check for Pro-Lifers." *Religion News Service*, May 28, 2021, retrieved 09.10.2023, from https://religionnews.com/2021/05/28/supreme-courts-review-of-roes-abortion-limits-is-a-gut-check-for-pro-lifers/.
54 Yasir, Qadhi: "Relationship...," *op. cit.*
55 Poston, Larry: *Islamic Da'wa in the West: Muslim Missionary Activity and the Dynamics of Conversion to Islam*. Oxford University Press: New York 1992, p. 83.

due to a social standpoint that justifies the conception that the Muslim agenda in America is opposed to the State by wishing to "misuse and abuse the constitution" instead of contributing to the country where they live.[56]

To back his argument, he refers to the migration of Muslims to Abyssinia, known as the first Hijra (migration) of Muslims in the early days of Islam. During this era, Muslims fled Mecca due to torture and killings that did not allow them to worship Allah. This hardship brought the Prophet Muhammad to permit one hundred people to immigrate to Abyssinia, which was controlled by King Ashama ibn Abjar, known as Al-Najashi, that enabled them to perform their Islamic worship without fear.[57]

Qadhi points out that the Muslims in Abyssinia remained there for an extended period, studied different social elements such as language and culture, and even tried to expose Islam to others. Nevertheless, it never occurred to them "to plot and plan against Abyssinia to establish a Khalifa (Islamic) State." This was because they understood that this behavior would be unfair and unjustified toward King Al-Najashi himself, who permitted them freedom of worship in his land.[58] In these words, Qadhi parallels the situation of the Muslims in Abyssinia to the situation of Muslims in America today:

> We as American Muslims, it is not our responsibility to establish a *khalifa* in America. It is not our responsibility to see a full and running Sharia here in America. Our responsibility is to make sure that we can worship Allah as Muslims in our private lives, this is our responsibility because we are Americans, because we have been allowed residence here. We are like the Muslims of Abyssinia, and our job and our duty cannot be to betray Abyssinia, it cannot be to plot and plan against Abyssinia. Nobody who resides here legally is permitted to do that, that would go against the very contract that has been given to you. You have been given a contract of citizenship, a contract, a visa, and a part of that contract means you will uphold our laws, and the Muslim is not a liar, a Muslim is not to cheat, a Muslim does not break his word.[59]

From this case, we see that Qadhi uses the Establishment Clause by alienating Muslims in America from the "Sharia State" concept, which opposed the American Constitution, and instead urges them to become more connected to their civil society responsibilities which arise from their residence in the United States. This methodology helps him pave the way to stay away from hardcore fundamentalist views which see America and any other Western country, as an opportunity to establish an Islamic rule.

---

56 Yasir, Qadhi: "Ummah vs. Nation State." *YouTube*, retrieved 22.12.2021, from https://www.youtube.com/watch?v=bdP-f9SvWd4&t=2468s.
57 *Ibid.*
58 *Ibid.*
59 *Ibid.*

The Distinction Between "Morality and Legality"

This important methodology of Yasir Qadhi was described by Christopher Pooya Razavian as an "understanding of reasonable citizens," in which Qadhi "denies the implementations of any coercive practices by Muslims in the West and defends the freedom of others based on the notion of reciprocity."[60] Although this methodology also needs to confront gray areas because it may contradict Islamic values, it consequently grants a prominent advantage to the Muslim community, because it preserves their religious freedom to practice Islam without any fear of outside interference to ban it. The following examples aim to explore three critical case studies that would reflect Qadhi's distinction between morality and legality in contemporary events, related to the Muslim community in America.

"Proposition 8" Case

Proposition 8 was a California ballot proposition and a state constitutional amendment created by opponents of same-sex marriage and intended to ban same-sex marriage, which was passed in the November 2008 California State elections and was later overturned in court.[61] In comparison to the *Roe v. Wade* case, Qadhi distinguishes between practice and theory and argues that sometimes the Constitutional right to battle "immoral injustice" should be tested individually and not taken as a rule of thumb. Qadhi expressed this attitude at a conference at Harvard University in 2014, titled "Religious Freedom and its Implications." Concerning the case, Qadhi exposed his "unpopular" refusal to support it, clarifying that Muslims would have gained nothing by publicly supporting the Proposition, which would have created negative consequences on their image.[62] His position to the "Proposition 8" case argued that despite the Muslims' right to participate in "moral battles," it is not the government nor the court's job to impose "morality" on others:

> I might believe something is immoral even if it is legal in America. I think it's immoral to drink, I'm not calling for the banning of drinking. I think it's immoral—premarital extramarital sex, intercourse and homosexuality. I believe it is immoral but I'm not calling for it to be made illegal, and the fact that I believe it is immoral is also a

---

60 Razavian, Christopher Pooya: *op. cit.*, p. 175.
61 Sheffrin, Alexander J.: "Pro-Family Group Says Effort to Ban Calif. Gay 'Marriage' Looks 'Strong.'" *The Christian Post Reporter*, April 5, 2008, retrieved 22.12.2021, from https://www.christianpost.com/news/pro-family-group-says-effort-to-ban-calif-gay-marriage-looks-strong-31814.
62 Yasir, Qadhi: "Religious Freedom and Its Implications." Harvard University, *YouTube*, May 1, 2014, retrieved 22.12.2021, from https://www.youtube.com/watch?v=LCNsONdSo44.

guaranteed right under this country—you cannot dictate to me what is my morality nor can you force me to act in a way that is contrary to my belief.[63]

In other words, when Muslims do not try to force their morality on others, others would not have the "excuse" to force their morality on Muslims, which would assist Islamic rituals to be preserved. Additionally, Qadhi also claims that forcing any religious "morality" on Muslims in America is also prohibited, and there is no Islamic authority that can force anything on them:

> Even within our own community, if a Muslim chooses not to practice the sharia, well, I know plenty of Muslims like that, what are you going to do about it that's their business [...] if they come to me as a scholar, as a cleric, I will tell them this is the law of God, you should try to apply it, you should try to practice in your personal life [...] but if they refuse to do so, that's their business and it's not my business to force it on them.[64]

Using the concept of the distinction between morality and legality, Qadhi also tries to bolster the inter-religious partnership between Orthodox Jews, Fundamental Christians, and practicing Muslims. This methodology assists him in weaving the "unique" challenges of the Muslim community and presenting the Islamic faith as part of mainstream religious American groups, that sometimes their faith contradicts the law of the State. Therefore, despite liberal Western values, Qadhi optimistically believes that this distinction between morality and legality would enable Muslims in America to stay faithful to their religion and their State:

> Our vision in North America is to be moral in our personal lives and not to force that morality on other people, then *Insha-Allah* we can very easily [...] carve out a coexistence, carve out an area where we can be faithful to our religion, we can be faithful to our religious texts, we can be sincere Muslims, and we can also be law-abiding and loyal citizens of this country [...] where there's a will there's a way, those who wish to cause problems will find it, those who wish to solve problems will also be able to do so.[65]

As we see from these examples, Qadhi argues that Islam is a religious obligation that should focus on the private sphere and cannot be compelled on any American Muslim. Also, he claims that although American Muslims should use their constitutional right to protest "immoral issues," there are nonetheless situations when there is a need to see the pros and cons that would come out of this action. In the

---

63 Yasir, Qadhi: "Relationship...," *op. cit.*
64 Yasir Qadhi: "Should Americans Be Scared of a Sharia Law?" *YouTube*, February 11, 2012, retrieved 10.08.2023, from https://www.youtube.com/watch?v=MxkhrCWXnM.
65 Yasir, Qadhi: "Relationship Between Church & State Comparison with Islamic Caliphate."

"Proposition 8" case, he feared that the consequences of supporting the law would not be beneficial for the Muslim community.

The Reaction to the Blasphemy of the Prophet Muhammad: The Movie "Innocence of Muslims"

Blasphemy in Islam is considered to be actions that are an expression of mocking or vilifying the attributes of Islam, such as God (Allah) himself, fundamental beliefs of the faith, and denying the Qur'an revelation or the Prophet Muhammad.[66] One of the famous examples of blasphemy—drawing the Prophet in a vulgar manner—occurred in the Charlie-Hebdo cases of 2015 and 2020.[67] A similar example of such blasphemy in the United States was the anti-Islamic short film, "Innocence of Muslims," written and produced by Nakoula Basseley Nakoula, an Egyptian Coptic priest who lives in America. The movie was uploaded to YouTube in July 2012 and was perceived as defamation to the Prophet Muhammad. As a result, demonstrations and violent protests started in Egypt and spread to other Arab, Muslim, and Western countries.

This case can demonstrate how Qadhi uses it to bolster the American Muslim identity, by connecting the response to the blasphemy to fit the life in a Western country such as America. First, Qadhi finds any violent reaction to blasphemy or other Islamophobic actions to be explicitly prohibited, especially in a Western state that is not governed by the law of Islam. To prove it, he uses the figure of the Prophet Muhammad himself, who did not react in violence in Mecca, although he was mocked and ridiculed on many occasions during this time, such as in Surat Al-Ḥijr, when he was told by Allah: "We certainly know that your heart is truly distressed by what they say."[68] Like the Abyssinian example, here Qadhi parallels the Meccan case of the Prophet, to the American Muslim minority, that should avoid any physical response to those blasphemies and instead react in a restrained activity, such as writing, speaking, and protesting legally.[69]

Using the pro-active response to blasphemy, Qadhi navigates it to cause American Muslims to cherish the religious clauses of the First Amendment that allow them religious freedom, although it enables others to mock Islam. In this regard,

---

66 McAuliffe, Jane: *The Qur'an: What Everyone Needs to Know*. Oxford University Press 2020, pp. 194–196.
67 For more information about these terror attacks, see for example: "Charlie Hebdo attack: Three days of terror," *BBC News*, 14 January, 2015, retrieved 26.11.23, from https://www.bbc.com/news/world-europe-30708237.
68 Quran 15:97.
69 Yasir, Qadhi: "Response to the Insults towards the Prophet Muhammad (PBUH)." Memphis, TN, *YouTube*, January 21, 2012, retrieved 22.12.2021, from https://www.youtube.com/watch?v=vJ00DxfzgKM&t=877s.

as in the "Proposition 8" case, Qadhi ironically warns against any type of trying to "ban" Islamophobia in America because of the fear that it would open a door for the far-right groups who wish to find an excuse to ban the practice of Sharia or the Qur'an itself. Therefore, although he thinks that situations such as blasphemy put Muslims in America "between a rock and a hard stone," it still guarantees their Islamic religious freedom to be preserved in the country and protects them from fundamentalist, conservative right-wing groups, who wish to ban the practice of Islam in America.[70]

The LGBTQ and the Supreme Court Decision in 2015

The LGBTQ community in America and the West is a phenomenon that has been increasing in recent decades leaving the Western Muslim community with a conundrum due to the prominent Islamic prohibition on this kind of lifestyle. Qadhi remains true to the theological prohibition of those acts and argues that it is impossible to "bend the Sharia," since the Qur'an is explicit on this prohibition, for example, in the case of sodomy.[71] Nevertheless, he rejects other Muslim preachers' offensive rhetoric and vulgarity against the LGBTQ community, and calls to "set them in a different language."[72]

The upholding of the U.S. Supreme Court to Same-Sex Marriage in 2015, that same-sex marriage is part of the constitutional right of the Fourteenth Amendment,[73] exposed another critical aspect of Qadhi's morality and legality doctrine. Qadhi understands that the rise of LGBTQ in America is considered a "lost battle," where Muslims as a minority cannot halt it. However, he extrapolated a critical advantage from the Supreme Court decision that serves his morality and legality doctrine in favor of the Muslim community. Qadhi argues that every aspect of liberty given to other groups or minorities is also translated as freedom to the Muslim community. Therefore, the right of LGBTQ for same-sex marriage allows the right of American Muslims to act upon their theological moral compass.[74] In comparison to the blasphemy case, Qadhi points out that if the right of the LGBTQ community to same-sex marriage was banned, the religious freedom of Muslims, theoretically, could have also been limited, and he stresses the advantages of the church and state separation:

---

70 *Ibid.*
71 As it is written in the Qu'ran: 7:80–81.
72 Yasir, Qadhi: "LGBT Issues in Modern Islam: Questions in Singapore." Islamic Religious Council of Singapore, *YouTube*, May 15, 2015, retrieved 22.12.2021, from https://www.youtube.com/watch?v=9Tsf29m9_O4&t=1399s.
73 "US: Supreme Court Upholds Same-Sex Marriage." *Human Rights Watch*, June 26, 2015, retrieved 22.12.2021, from https://www.hrw.org/news/2015/06/26/us-supreme-court-upholds-same-sex-marriage.
74 Yasir, Qadhi: "LGBT Issues in Modern Islam: Questions in Singapore."

> We should not jump on the bandwagon of supporting legal gay marriage, nor should we jump [...] trying to prohibit it. Rather our position should be, and it's a controversial one—the American government should not have any right to decide what is or is not a marriage. It's not the role of our government [...] from an American perspective, morality is not in the domain of the government, but the government cannot impose on churches and synagogues and mosques its definition of marriage, because that's not the domain of the Constitution to tell us what is moral or immoral. So let the churches and synagogues and mosques preach their version of morality and marriage, and let the US Constitution and the government and the courts decide whatever they want.[75]

As we can see, Qadhi addresses Jews and Christians, aiming to connect Islam to other religious groups so that non-consent on homosexuality's "immorality" would combine Islam with other American religions and will stress the concept that Islam is part and parcel of the American mainstream religious fabric. Also, another essential aspect of Qadhi's distinction in that regard is that in light of the continuous rise of the LGBTQ in America, the Muslim community as a minority should try to collaborate with their community, as it has gained significant political and social power. Perhaps to soften the theological disagreement, Qadhi points out that LGBTQ has naturally more awareness of the fragile situation of Muslims in America and is considered one of the biggest supporters of the battle against Islamophobia. Therefore, despite the theological differences, he argues that collaboration on political and social issues is wise, although he admits that this cooperation has to face deep theological gaps that are considered a complex challenge.

Summary and Conclusions

This chapter dealt with the combination of the religious clauses of the First Amendment challenges of the American Muslim community, using the doctrine of Yasir Qadhi. As a prominent American Muslim preacher, Qadhi has been active in America since the post-9/11 era and used some of the recent cases of religious clauses to bolster American Muslim identity. Qadhi's doctrine in this regard represents the new wave of clerics and imams after the catastrophe and severe consequences of 9/11 that tried to "Americanize" Islam in order to improve the religion's status in the United States, which will positively impact the Muslim community.

Qadhi's central argument is that Muslims in America should cherish American freedom, allowing them to continue to practice Islam in the country and openly be proud of their religion, just as other religious groups are. Nevertheless, he is aware of the fine line of those clauses and understands that trying to force Islamic morality on others could lead to a "dangerous" path which can put the practice of

---

75 *Ibid.*

Islam itself in a vague future. Therefore, according to his view, implying the separation of morality and legality, just as the separation from church and state, assists Muslims to abide by the law and continue to practice their religion according to the Western American context. In that manner, Qadhi hopes that the American constitutional system will fortify Islam and assist it in flourishing in the United States in the future. Although American Muslims still battle with flaws and vices, compared to other Western Muslim minorities, it is considered a unique demographic thanks to the Constitutional protection of the First Amendment, which almost guarantees that Islam would continue to be preserved in the care of future generations.

References

Ba-Yunus, Ilyas/Kone, Kassim: *Muslims in the United States*. Greenwood Press: Westport, CT 2006.

BBC News, "Charlie Hebdo attack: Three days of terror," 14 January, 2015, retrieved 26.11.23, from https://www.bbc.com/news/world-europe-30708237

Ben David, Elad: "Marketing Daʿwa in America Through Social Media." *Beehive: Middle East Social Media* 8 (6), 2020.

Borrud, Gabriel: "Germany Expels Openly Homophobic Imam." *DW*, April 21, 2011, retrieved 12.22.2021, from https://www.dw.com/en/germany-expels-openly-homophobic-imam/a-6510494-1.

Camosy, Charles: "Supreme Court's Hearing of Mississippi Abortion Law Is a Gut Check for Pro-lifers." *Religion News Service*, May 28, 2021, retrieved 09.10.2023, from https://religionnews.com/2021/05/28/supreme-courts-review-of-roes-abortion-limits-is-a-gut-check-for-pro-lifers/.

Curiel, Jonathan: *Islam in America*. I.B. Tauris: London and New York 2015.

Curry, Brett: "Lee v. Weisman (1992)." *The Free Speech Center*, retrieved 27.12.2021, from https://www.mtsu.edu/first-amendment/article/670/lee-v-weisman.

Douglas, Hicks: *With God on All Sides: Leadership in a Devout and Diverse America*. Oxford University Press: New York 2009.

Elliott, Andrea: "Why Yasir Qadhi Wants to Talk About Jihad." *The New York Times Magazine*, March 17, 2011.

Esposito, John: "Muslims in America or American Muslims." In: Haddad, Yvonne Yazbeck/Esposito, John (eds.): *Muslims on the Americanization Path?* Oxford University Press: New York 2000.

"European Court of Human Rights Judgment on French Laws Banning the Niqab and Burqa." *Islamic Human Rights Commission*, August 23, 2014, retrieved 22.12.2021, from https://www.ihrc.org.uk/publications/briefings/11159-european-court-of-human-rights-judgement-on-french-laws-banning-the-niqab-and-burqa.

Ghazali, Abdus Sattar: *Islam & Muslims in the Post-9/11 America*, no press edition 2012.

Haddad, Yvonne Yazbek/T. Lummis, Adair: *Islamic Values in the United States: A Comparative Study.* Oxford University Press: New York 1987.

Haddad/Harb, Nasir Nader: "Post-9/11: Making Islam an American Religion." *Religions* 5, 2014.

Hannini, Daniyah M.: "The 'Spiritualization' of Islam in America: A Study of Highly Individualistic Forms of Islamic Practice in the U.S." MA Thesis, The State University of New Jersey 2016.

Keany, Francis: "Malcolm Turnbull Regrets Hosting Homophobic Islamic Cleric Sheikh Shady Alsuleiman at Kirribilli." *ABC News*, January 17, 2016, retrieved 22.12.2021, from https://www.abc.net.au/news/2016-06-17/pm-criticises-islamic-clerics-homophobic-comments/7520884.

Legal Information Institute, retrieved 27.12.2021 from https://www.law.cornell.edu/wex/first_amendment.

McAuliffe, Jane: *The Qur'an: What Everyone Needs to Know.* Oxford University Press: New York 2020.

Neal, Meghan: "Number of Muslims in the U.S. Doubles since 9/11." *New York Daily News*, March 3, 2012, retrieved 22.12.2021, from https://www.nydailynews.com/news/national/number-muslims-u-s-doubles-9-11-article-1.1071895.

Poston, Larry: "Da'wa in the West." In: Yvonne Yazbeck Haddad (ed.): *The Muslims of America.* Oxford University Press: Oxford 1991.

Poston, Larry: *Islamic Da'wa in the West: Muslim Missionary Activity and the Dynamics of Conversion to Islam.* Oxford University Press: New York 1992.

Poston, Larry/Guzik, Elysia: "Da'wa in North America: The Past, the Present, and the Future." In: Itzchak Weismann/Jamal Malik (eds.): *Culture of Da'wa: Islamic Preaching in the Modern World.* The University of Utah Press: Salt Lake City 2020.

Qadhi, Yasir: "Have You Left the Way of the Salaf?" *YouTube*, April 4, 2014, retrieved 22.12.2021, from https://www.youtube.com/watch?v=8GYkedPkxII.

Qadhi, Yasir: "History of Islam in America: Whither and Where." *YouTube*, May 5, 2008, retrieved 10.08.2023, from https://www.youtube.com/watch?v=rdxSWwWDwT8.

Qadhi, Yasir: "LGBT Issues in Modern Islam: Questions in Singapore." Islamic Religious Council of Singapore, *YouTube*, May 15, 2015, retrieved 22.12.2021, from https://www.youtube.com/watch?v=9Tsf29m9_O4&t=1399s.

Qadhi, Yasir: "Relationship between Church & State comparison with Islamic Caliphate." Hartford, CT, *YouTube*, May 26, 2012, retrieved 22.12.2021, from https://www.youtube.com/watch?v=prrtGF4LAfQ.

Qadhi, Yasir: "Religious Freedom and Its Implications." Harvard University, *YouTube*, May 1, 2014, retrieved 22.12.2021, from https://www.youtube.com/watch?v=LCNsONdSo44.

Qadhi, Yasir: "Response to the Insults towards the Prophet Muhammad (PBUH)." Memphis, TN, *YouTube*, January 21, 2012, retrieved 22.12.2021, from https://www.youtube.com/watch?v=vJ00DxfzgKM&t=877s.

Qadhi, Yasir: "Should Americans Be Scared of a Sharia Law?" *YouTube*, February 11, 2012, retrieved 10.08.2023, from https://www.youtube.com/watch?v=MxkhrCWXnM.

Qadhi, Yasir: "Ummah vs. Nation State." *YouTube*, retrieved 22.12.2021, from https://www.youtube.com/watch?v=bdP-f9SvWd4&t=2468s.

Razavian, Christopher Pooya: "Yasir Qadhi and the Development of Reasonable Salafism." In: Bano, Masooda (ed.): *Modern Islamic Authority and Social Change*. Edinburgh University Press: Edinburgh 2018.

Rohrer, Finlo: "The Battle over the 'Ground Zero Mosque,'" *BBC News*, August 3, 2010, retrieved from 20.01.2022, https://www.bbc.com/news/world-us-canada-10846716.

Schaap, Andrew: *Political Reconciliation*. Routledge: New York 2005.

Sheffrin, Alexander J.: "Pro-Family Group Says Effort to Ban Calif. Gay 'Marriage' Looks 'Strong,'" *The Christian Post Reporter*, April 5, 2008, retrieved 22.12.2021, from https://www.christianpost.com/news/pro-family-group-says-effort-to-ban-calif-gay-marriage-looks-strong-31814.

Takim, Liyakat, "The Ground Zero Mosque Controversy: Implications for American Islam." *Religions* 2011.

Ukeles, Raquel: *The Evolving Muslim Community in America: The Impact of 9/11*. Mosaica: Research Center for Religion State and Society 2003.

Wiedl-Menashe, Nina: *Contemporary Calls to Islam—Salafi Da'wa in Germany 2002–2011*: Ph.D. Dissertation, Ben-Gurion University, Be'er Sheva 2015.

Willingham, AJ: "By 2040, Islam Could Be the Second-Largest Religion in the US." *CNN Politics*, January 11, 2018, retrieved 02.12.2021, from https://edition.cnn.com/2018/01/10/politics/muslim-population-growth-second-religious-group-trnd/index.html.

Religion, Race, and Politics: The Political Role of the Black Church

Paulina Napierała

The Ebenezer Baptist Church in Atlanta and the Activist Tradition of the Black Church

Abstract: In this chapter, I analyze how the Ebenezer Baptist Church in Atlanta has continued the activist tradition of the Black Church since its very inception in the nineteenth century. I focus on different forms of Ebenezer's socio-political involvement throughout history, especially on the role of its pastors and how they justified and encouraged congregation-based activism. I also examine what internal and external factors might have influenced their decisions. My analysis has been placed in both historical and theoretical perspectives.

Keywords: The Ebenezer Baptist Church in Atlanta, The Black Church, Martin Luther King Sr., Martin Luther King Jr., Raphael G. Warnock, social gospel

Introduction

The Black Church has played a unique role in Black[1] American history, and it has been long seen as the most dominant institution in Black society. It has provided shelter and spiritual uplift for the downtrodden, while additionally serving as a cultural repository and often as a forum for socio-political mobilization for the disenfranchised.[2] And although not all Black congregations have been equally active in social and political matters, some of them have even been called "freedom

---

1   There is a debate among scholars whether to capitalize the term *Black/black*. For example, the authors of *Black Church Studies. An Introduction*, capitalize it as "a means of moving beyond skin color towards a notion of shared history, cultural heritage, and group identity." In this text I follow their decision - as do other contributors to this volume. In: Floyd-Thomas, Stacey/Floyd-Thomas, Juan M./Duncan, Carol B., et al.: *Black Church Studies. An Introduction*. Abington Press: Westfield N.L. 2007, p. xxvi).
2   Gains, Robert W., II: "Looking Back, Moving Forward: How the Civil Rights Era Church Can Guide the Modern Black Church in Improving Black Student Achievement." *The Journal of Negro Education* 79 (3), 2010, pp. 366–379.

churches"—due to their role in the African American struggle against slavery, segregation, and discrimination.

This chapter analyzes the continued public engagement of one of such churches—the Ebenezer Baptist Church in Atlanta—which rose to fame during the civil rights era. It became globally known when Martin Luther King Jr. accepted his father's call to serve as a co-pastor and delivered some of his most famous sermons there. It had been known for its social activism, however, long before King Jr.'s tenure. It had never turned to, what some Black Church scholars call "quietism," and soon became a symbol of an activist church. Today, its current senior pastor, Rev. Raphael G. Warnock, who is not only a charismatic minister but also the first Black Senator from Georgia (elected in 2020), continues the Ebenezer's activist tradition. Just like his predecessors, he has used his congregation as a base for social and political mobilization[3] and brought it back into the public spotlight.

As history reveals, however, not all Black churches have been as active as the Atlanta church. According to Black Church scholars, there have been many factors influencing churches' stances on political engagement, including the role of charismatic pastors.[4] Therefore, not only will I focus on how the Ebenezer Baptist Church in Atlanta has continued the activist tradition of the Black Church by analyzing different forms of its socio-political engagement throughout history but also on how its pastors have justified and encouraged the congregation's socio-political activism. I will further examine various factors that might have influenced their decisions.[5] My analysis will be placed in both historical and theoretical contexts.

The Historical Context

In order to analyze the activist tradition of the Ebenezer Baptist Church in Atlanta, it is useful to briefly consider a history of Black churches, as the tradition of their social engagement started early on. The formation of the first Black congregations in America began soon after the First Great Awakening.[6] The revivalist message of evangelical preachers brought not only new hope of more equality but also some affinity to the spiritual style of the enslaved.[7] Following the revivals, they

---

3   Abstaining, however, from promoting his own political campaign in the church—respecting the provisions of the Johnson Amendment.
4   Several theoretical approaches stress different factors. I will discuss them below.
5   Using elements of McDaniel's model (2008). McDaniel, Eric C.: *Politics in the Pews. The Political Mobilization of Black Churches.* University of Michigan Press: Ann Arbor 2008.
6   I have written more about this in my previous articles. Here I present only a short overview, using previous analyses.
7   Marsden, George M.: *Religion and American Culture.* Hartcourt Brace College Publishers: Orlando 1990, p. 67.

created a kind of Christianity that somewhat reflected their African past and the situation in which they found themselves—instead of simply accepting the teachings of obedience used by the white masters to control them.[8] They first developed what is called the "invisible institution,"[9] then they created early small Black congregations, and with time (initially in the North) separate and fully independent Black denominations.[10] The early Black churches often focused on the story of Exodus and liberation, which was understood in both otherworldly and this-worldly contexts.[11] Thanks to these new (and initially sole) Black institutions, Black Christians could practice their religion without being discriminated against by white church members. Christianity became important not only for "[...] introducing a new sense of communal identity"[12] but also for preventing total dehumanization of the enslaved and providing them with feelings of self-worth.[13]

The Black Church, founded during the period of slavery, "in the constant reality of racial discrimination, human bondage," soon started to serve "as an agent for social change."[14] Many African American pastors and lay church leaders were involved in the Underground Railroad and other abolitionist initiatives. The first independent Black denominations: the African Methodist Episcopal Church (AME) and the AME Zion Church, became known as "the freedom churches" because they hid escaped slaves and created a safe space for legendary figures of the African

---

8   Raboteau, Albert J.: *Canaan Land. A Religious History of African Americans.* Oxford University Press: New York 2001, pp. 17–18.
9   Idem.: *Slave Religion. "The Invisible Institution" in the Antebellum South.* Oxford University Press: New York 2004.
10 The African Methodist Episcopal Church, AME (1816); The African Methodist Episcopal Church Zion, AME Zion (1821); The Colored Methodist Episcopal Church, CME (1870, it was later renamed: The Christian Methodist Episcopal Church); The National Baptist Convention, USA, Inc., NBC USA (1895); The National Baptist Convention of America International, Inc., NBC America (1915); The Progressive National Baptist Convention, PNBC (1961); The Church of God in Christ, COGIC (1907).
11 It is believed that even *spirituals* had a double meaning. More in: Cone, James H.: *The Spirituals and the Blues: An Interpretation.* Orbis Books: Maryknoll, NY 1992. This-worldly interpretation can also be found in the so-called "liberation tradition" that called for radical revolutionary activity. In fact, three slave revolts were led by slave preachers who used their status as religious leaders to mobilize the enslaved into action: Nat Turner's (1831), Gabriel Prosser's (1800) and Denmark Vesey's (1822). James, Vaughn E.: "The African-American Church, Political Activity, and Tax Exemption." *Seton Hall Law Review* 37, 2007, pp. 374–376.
12 Marsden, George: *op. cit.,* p. 68.
13 Corbett, Michael, Mitchell-Corbett, Julia: *Politics and Religion in the USA.* Graland Publishing: New York 1999, p. 304.
14 James, Vaughn E.: *op. cit.,* p. 390.

American abolitionist movement (e.g., Frederick Douglass, Harriet Tubman, and Sojourner Truth). Therefore, scholars have often stressed that the Black Church has been, since its very inception, not only a religious organization but a social and political institution as well.[15]

During the Civil War and soon after, many Black congregations became even more publicly engaged. During the Reconstruction they could do it more formally, adding some aspects of strictly political activity.[16] In fact, between 1865 and 1877, some Black pastors emerged as Black political leaders. They were empowered by their literacy and roles in building their churches, which served as the first forums for collective political organizing.[17] Several ministers were even elected to public office.

The political activities of Black preachers could, however, create problems for their congregations, including seeing their churches burned down by whites who felt they upset the status quo. And while Black churches remained cornerstones of the Black community, they were not homogenous in their reactions to such violence. Some Black ministers preached messages of liberation, while others preached messages of compromise and accommodation,[18] often concentrating on otherworldly themes.

This division was also true during the Great Migration, both in the South and in the North. Some preachers, especially those who were poorly educated and had little resources, retreated to revivalist Christianity and "defensive accommodationism,"[19] while others stressed the social gospel,[20] seeking to apply the biblical principles of

---

15 *Ibid.*
16 Within the limits of the American model of the separation of church and state.
17 Savage, Barbara D.: *Your Spirits Walk Beside Us. The Politics of Black Religion.* The Belknap Press: Cambridge MA 2008, p. 4.
18 Barber, Kendra, "Whither Shall We Go? The Past and Present of Black Churches and the Public Sphere." *Religions* 6 (1), 2015, p. 252.
19 Lincoln, Eric C./Mamiya Lawrence H.: *The Black Church in the African American Experience.* Duke University Press: Durham, NC 1990, p. 121. Some scholars, however, stress that accommodation as a survival strategy can still be subversive, for example, Barber, Kendra: *op. cit.* Some also state that "pietistic proclamation" in a racist context could represent resistance. More in: Warnock, Raphael G.: *The Divided Mind of the Black Church. Theology, Piety, and Public Witness.* New York University Press: New York 2014, p. 14.
20 The social gospel movement as a religious movement within Protestantism that began in the late nineteenth century and gained prominence especially in the early twentieth century. It was a Christian ethical response to social problems such as urban poverty, child labor, low wages, economic inequality, crime, and racial tensions. Developed by Washington Gladden and Walter Rauschenbusch, it was inspired by New Testament passages that present Christ as a challenger of the status quo. It was a response to conservative theological ideas that stressed individual sin over

love and justice in their efforts to transform society.[21] The needs of the new Black urban community, however, most often exceeded the capacity of churches to serve them.[22] During the Great Depression, many Black churches faced difficulties due to increased financial dependency on whites. Thus, it is often argued that the "quietist" period for the Black Church, as it was called by Lincoln and Mamiya,[23] lasted practically until the 1950s when Rev. Martin Luther King Jr. became the leader of the civil rights struggle.

Nevertheless, there were exceptions to this rule, for example, Adam Clayton Powell, Sr. of the Abyssinian Baptist Church in Harlem and later his son Adam Clayton Powell, Jr. never gave up on the idea of an activist Black church. The same held true for the Ebenezer Baptist Church in Atlanta, which being based in the South operated in even more difficult circumstances.

The 1950s and early 1960s seemed to have marked the end of the "quietist" period, however. During the civil rights era, a considerably higher number of Black churches became involved in social issues and social protests. Nonetheless, contemporary scholars argue that these churches were never in the majority, and that often they were late supporters of the movement rather than frontrunners.[24] Moreover, although after this period, many Black congregations remained socially

---

socioeconomic justice. More in: Marsden, George: *op. cit.*, pp. 55–56. Importantly, although it soon became characteristic of liberal and mainline Protestantism, in the beginning it was also accepted by pre-fundamentalist, postmillennial evangelicals (including Black evangelicals).

21 Baldwin, Lewis: "Revisiting the 'All-Comprehending Institution': Historical Reflections on the Public Roles of Black Churches." In: Smith Drew R. (ed.): *New Day Begun. African American Churches and Civic Culture in Post-Civil Rights America.* Duke University Press: Durham, NC 2003, p. 30.
22 Savage, Barbara D.: *op. cit.*, p. 6.
23 Lincoln, Eric C./Mamiya Lawrence H.: *op. cit.*, pp. 120–121.
24 E.g., Payne, Charles: *I've Got the Light of Freedom: The Organizing Tradition and the Mississippi Freedom Struggle.* University of California Press: Berkeley 1995. More about it in: Raboteau, Albert, *Canaan...*, *op. cit.*; Savage, Barbara D.: *op. cit.*; Harvey, Paul: *Freedom's Coming: Religious Culture and the Shaping of the South from the Civil War Through the Civil Rights Era.* University of North Carolina Press: Chapel Hill 2005; Best, Wallace D.: "The Right Achieved and the Wrong Way Conquered: J.H. Jackson, Martin Luther King, Jr., and the Conflict over Civil Rights." *Religion and American Culture* 16 (2), 2006, pp. 195–226; Marable, Manning: "The Role of the African American Church in the Civil Rights Movement." *NBC Learn. NBC Universal Media* 2015, retrieved 02.07.2019, from https://archives.nbclearn.com/portal/site/k-12/browse/?cuecard=5041; Martin, Lerone: "Bureau Clergyman: How the FBI Colluded with an African American Televangelist to Destroy Dr. Martin Luther King, Jr." *Religion and American Culture: A Journal of Interpretation* 28 (1), 2018, pp. 1–51.

involved, the majority of them concentrated on partnering with the government in providing social services rather than advocating broader social reforms or engaging in protest politics. As Anthony Pinn argues, in the 1970s many Black churches withdrew from direct political organizing, focusing more on individual salvation.[25] Additionally, the Prosperity Gospel[26] was gaining popularity among some Black churches, making them, as scholars note, less focused on structural reforms and more on individual spiritual and financial growth.[27] Then again, some churches remained committed to social activism, such as the Ebenezer Baptist Church in Atlanta.

Before analyzing its activity and possible explanations for its constant engagement, it will be useful to clarify the terms used in the further analysis, discuss differences among definitions of the Black Church (including those concerning its social activism), and present a brief overview of the debate on the role of the Black Church and of the theoretical models explaining the varied levels of its sociopolitical engagement.

"The Black Church": Definitions, Debates, Theoretical Perspectives, and Frameworks

While a number of scholars have analyzed the historical and social importance of the Black Church, there has been an ongoing debate on what the term "Black Church" actually denotes. Historically speaking, the term "Black Church" evolved from the phrase "the Negro Church," which comes from a pioneering sociological study by W.E.B. Du Bois (1903). According to Lincoln and Mamiya, it is "a kind of sociological and theological shorthand reference to the pluralism of black Christian churches in the United States."[28] Originally, the phrase was just an academic category, as most African Americans described themselves according to

---

25 Pinn, Anthony B.: *The Black Church in the Post-Civil Rights Era*. Orbis Books: Maryknoll, NY 2002, p. 18.
26 It is a variation of the evangelical thought rooted in the Pentecostal and charismatic tradition that adds a certain this-worldly dimension to the predominantly otherworldly theology by stressing that people of faith will be rewarded not only in heaven but also on earth (with prosperity, wealth and health). It generally tends to see poverty and illness as results of poor faith. More in: McDaniel, Eric L./Dwidar, Maraam A./Calderon, Hadill: "The Faith of Black Politics: The Relationship Between Black Religious and Political Beliefs." *Journal of Black Studies* 49 (3), 2018, pp. 256–283.
27 Pinn, Anthony: *op. cit.*; McDaniel, Eric L. et al.: *op. cit.*; Glaude, Eddie S.: "The Black Church Is Dead." *Huffington Post*, 2010, retrieved 02.10.2019, from https://www.huffpost.com/entry/the-black-church-is-dead_b_473815.
28 Lincoln, Eric C./Mamiya Lawrence H.: *op. cit.*, p. 1.

denominational affiliations. Although they were never religiously monolithic, during the twentieth century the concept of the Black Church achieved popular resonance and became an "euphemistic generalization for the collective identity of African American Christians [...]."[29]

It is worth noting that, according to a narrow definition promoted by Lincoln and Mamiya, the term "Black Church" refers only to seven historically Black Protestant denominations.[30] Other authors, however, use broader definitions that include all the Christian churches that currently or historically have ministered to predominantly Black congregations (some of them belonging to historically Black denominations and some to predominantly white denominations). For Raphael Warnock, for example, Lincoln and Mamiya's "designation is too narrow, given the current reality of black Christianity and given the development of independent black Christian reflection (black theology) among black people and black caucuses in predominantly white denominations." As he explains, "[w]hile this historical phenomenon has its deep roots in the independent black church movement, the tragedy and depth of racism ensures the relevance of such a designation for black congregations and caucuses of various configurations who, consciously and unconsciously, live within the conflicting intersectionality of being black and Christian in America."[31]

Some authors find not only the experience of racism crucial to the definition of the Black Church but social activism as well. Robert W. Gaines II writes, for example, "[t]herefore, the phrase 'the Black Church,' as used from this point forward, will refer to the collective, largely denominational body of churches comprised primarily of African American people who, through communal worship, race consciousness, and *civic engagement*, operate as a locus of spiritual empowerment and *social agency*."[32] Other scholars add: "The Black Church represents that tradition of African American Christian religion that has been on the side of freedom, justice and equality." At the same time, they acknowledge, however, that "ideological and pastoral differences can undermine a collective memory and political activism."[33]

Some scholars additionally stress that "despite common usage, there is no such thing as the 'Black church' [...]. The term is a political, intellectual, and theological construction that symbolizes unity and homogeneity while masking the enormous diversity and independence among African American religious institutions and

---

29 Floyd-Thomas, Stacey et al.: *op. cit.*, p. xxiv.
30 Although the authors do recognize the existence of predominantly Black local churches in white denominations.
31 Warnock, Raphael G.: *op. cit.*, p. 9.
32 Gaines, Rober W., II.: *op. cit.*, p. 368, my italics.
33 In: Barnes, Sandra L./Nwosu, Oluchi: "Black Church Electoral and Protest Politics from 2002 to 2012: A Social Media Analysis of the Resistance Versus Accommodation Dialectic." *Journal of African American Studies* 18 (2), 2014, p. 226.

believers."[34] This diversity also concerns Black churches' attitudes toward sociopolitical involvement.

Therefore, to acknowledge this complexity some researchers additionally distinguish the terms "Black Church" and "Black churches." Anthony Pinn, for example, uses the term "Black Church" to denote "the collective reality of black Christianity across denomination lines" and the term "Black churches" to describe local Protestant churches within a particular denomination.[35] Acknowledging the multiplicity of Black churches and their various responses to social protest, I will use the terms "Black Church" and "Black churches" according to his distinction and depending on the context.

There is no doubt that Ebenezer embraces an activist spirit of the Black Church that has been included in many definitions. It is a local Southern urban Black congregation belonging to a larger historically Black denomination (currently to the most famous activist one—the Progressive National Baptist Convention—and previously to the National Baptist Convention, USA), and it has been promoting race consciousness, freedom, and justice almost since its very beginnings in the late nineteenth century. Due to the fact, however, that not all Black churches have embraced such an activist spirit as Ebenezer,[36] it is worth looking at the debate concerning the role of the Black Church and at some of the most common explanations of the varied levels of its social activism.

Interestingly, early studies on the Black Church indicated that it fell silent during some critical times in Black political history and did not live up to its potential. Some scholars even claimed that historically the majority of Black churches were politically passive and promoted quietism among its members. This perspective dominated especially in the early twentieth century and was represented by such scholars as W.E.B. Du Bois, Carter G. Woodson, Benjamin E. Mays, Joseph W. Nicholson, Gunnar Myrdal, St. Clair Drake, and Horace Clayton.[37] There were also scholars (e.g., E. Franklin Frazier, Gary Marx, and Adolph Reed)[38] who promoted

---

34 Savage, Barbara D.: *op. cit.*, p. 9.
35 Pinn, Anthony: *op. cit.*, p. ix.
36 Although most of them have supported Black consciousness and Black empowerment in various—not necessarily politically activ—ways.
37 Du Bois, Burghardt, W. E.: *The Souls of Black Folk: Essays and Sketches*. A.C. McClurg & Co.: Chicago 1903; Woodson, Carter G.: *The History of the Negro Church*. Associated Publishers: Washington, DC 1921; Mays, Benjamin E./Nicholson, Joseph W.: *The Negro's Church*. ISRR: New York 1933; Myrdal, Gunnar: *An American Dilemma: The Negro Problem and Modern Democracy*. Harper and Brothers: New York 1944; Drake, St. Clair/Clayton, Horace: *Black Metropolis a Study of Negro Life in a Northern City*. University Of Chicago Press: Chicago 1993 (1945).
38 Frazier, Franklin E.: *The Negro Church in America*. Schocken Books: New York 1963; Marx, Gary: *Protest and Prejudice. A Study of Belief in Black Community*. Harper and

this approach even later, despite the fact that after the civil rights era an increasing number of researchers were paying much more attention to the inspirational and active role of Black churches (e.g., Hart M. Nelsen and Anne Kusener-Nelsen, Dough McAdam, Aldon Morris, Lincoln and Mamiya, David Chappell, Albert Raboteau, and Frederick Harris).[39]

Researchers who focused on the passivity of the Black Church as a dominating trend often represented the so-called "opiate view", which is based on the belief that the otherworldly focus of religion defers happiness and rewards to the afterlife and teaches resigned acceptance of the existing conditions of this life. Those who preferred the "inspiration view," on the other hand, believed that religion might be a radical force in society—a force for change. They concentrated on a thisworldly focus of religion and argued that the Black Church most often embraced a reformist-activist ethic aimed at the transformation of earthly society.[40]

The proponents of the "opiate view" usually connected higher levels of religiosity to the otherworldly orientation. Some of them acknowledged, however, that both thisworldly and otherworldly orientations were present within the Black Church.[41] Gary Marx, for example, who generally argued that high level of religiosity in the Black Church reduced the activism of African Americans, also stressed that otherworldliness was usually expressed by more fundamentalist branches of Christianity while the thisworldly focus was characteristic of the traditional mainline churches which embraced the social gospel and more social action.[42] The division as outlined in Marx's research was, to some extent, confirmed by studies conducted by Ronald L. Johnstone and later by Stephen D. Johnson, who strongly stressed that high levels of civil activism were

---

Row: New York 1967; Reed, Adolph Jr.: *The Jessie Jackson Phenomenon: The Crisis of Purpose in Afro-American Politics*. Yale University Press: New Haven, CT 1986.

39 Nelsen, Hart M./Kusener-Nelsen, Anne: *Black Church in the Sixties*. The University Press of Kentucky: Lexington 1975; McAdam, Doug: *Political process and the development of Black insurgency, 1930–1970*. University of Chicago Press: Chicago 1982; Morris, Aldon D.: *The Origins of the Civil Rights Movement: Black Communities Organizing for Change*. Free Press New York: 1984; Lincoln, Eric C./Mamiya Lawrence H.: *op. cit.*; Chappell, David L.: *A Stone of Hope: Prophetic Religion and the Death of Jim Crow*. The University of North Carolina Press: Chapel Hill 2004; Raboteau, Albert: *op. cit.*; Harris, Frederick C.: *Something Within: Religion in African American Political Activism*. Oxford University Press: New York 1999.

40 Baldwin, Lewis: *op. cit.*, p. 15. I wrote more about both perspectives in: Napierała, Paulina: "Black Churches and African American Social Activism. The 'Opiate View' and the 'Inspiration View' of Black Religion in the Selected Literature." *B.A.S./British and American Studies* 27, 2021, pp. 95–111; I present only the most important points here.

41 Marx, Gary: *op. cit.*

42 *Ibid.*; Barnes, Sandra L.: *op. cit.*

found among members of mainline Black churches that had a social gospel orientation.[43] Gary Marx was, however, criticized by a number of scholars, such as by Nelsen and Nelsen, Lincoln and Mamiya, and Hunt and Hunt—mostly for not paying enough attention to sectarianism and for overestimating the links between high religiosity and otherworldliness, which, in their view, gave readers the impression that higher religiosity was generally inversely related to militancy.[44]

With time, Black Church scholars came to put more emphasis on the complicated nature of the Black Church and the duality inherent in most religious traditions.[45] Lincoln and Mamiya, for example, framed Black churches as institutions involved in a constant series of dialectical tensions between otherworldly/this-worldly, priestly/prophetic, and other polar opposites[46] influencing their levels of activism. But although they acknowledged the tension between this-worldly and otherworldly orientations in the Black Church, they did not accept Gary Marx's explanation that it was exactly the otherworldliness preventing some churches and their members from engaging in activism. They argued that practical reasons, such as alienation rooted in the distrust of a racially unjust system, prevented them from participating in protests to a much higher degree than the otherworldliness of their churches.[47]

In 2008 Eric C. McDaniel, who also disagreed with the "opiate view" and explanations focused on otherworldly/this-worldly divisions stressed that while many earlier models saw church-based political activism as a constant, static state, it is in fact "better understood as a process than a condition."[48] In his view, "the process by which churches become politically active is quite dynamic." Therefore, "not

---

43 Johnstone, Ronald L.: "Negro Preachers Take Sides." *Review of Religious Research* 11 (1), 1969, pp. 81–89; Johnson, Stephen D.: "The Role of the Black Church in Black Civil Rights Movement." In: Johnson Stephen D./Tamney Joseph B. (eds.): *The Political Role of Religion in the United States.* Westview: Boulder 1986, pp. 307–324.

44 Hunt and Hunt thought that G. Marx did not properly delineate between otherworldly and this-worldly orientations. They found that only sectarian beliefs were inversely related with civil rights militancy, while church orthodoxy was positively associated with militancy. Hunt, Larry L./Hunt, Janet G.: "Black Religion as Both Opiate and Inspiration of Civil Rights Militance: Putting Marx's Data to Test." *Social Forces* 86, 1977, p. 2.

45 E.g., Lincoln, Eric C./Mamiya Lawrence H.: *op. cit.*; Harris, Frederick C.: *op. cit.*; Baer, Hans A./Singer Merrill: *African-American Religion: Varieties of Protest and Accommodation.* University of Tennessee Press: Knoxville 2002.

46 Such as: universalism and particularism, communal and "privatistic," charismatic and bureaucratic; resistance and accommodation. In: Lincoln, Eric C./Mamiya Lawrence H.: *op. cit.*, pp. 11–15.

47 *Ibid.*, p. 213.

48 McDaniel, Eric L.: *op. cit.*, p. 3.

only does the number of churches that engage in politics vary, but so too does the level of political activity within a single church over time."⁴⁹ He stressed the role of the so-called political churches⁵⁰ in mobilizing its members and attempted to examine multiple factors that influenced their decisions to become politically active.

The explanatory models and different perspectives mentioned above make the question of Ebenezer's continuous engagement even more interesting. Therefore, in order to analyze the reasons behind its socio-political activism, I will refer to the assumptions concerning theological orientations present in the earlier models as well as to the elements of a multifactor model proposed by E. McDaniel.

His theoretical framework was an attempt to create a comprehensive model that explains why some churches decide to become politically involved while others do not.⁵¹ In his opinion, the "opiate or inspiration" debate existed because scholars were focusing only on one or two factors while neglecting the fact that church-based political activism depends on many determinants.⁵² According to his model, for a church to choose to become political: the pastor must be interested in involving his or her church in politics, the members must be receptive to the idea of having a politically active church, the church itself cannot be restricted from having a presence in political matters, and the current political climate has to both necessitate and allow political action.⁵³

Nevertheless, McDaniel admits that although all these factors play a role in determining whether a church becomes politically engaged, pastors still have considerable power in directing their congregations. As he points out, "much of the variation in church activism stems from pastors' interests."⁵⁴ And while pastors are usually influenced by other factors, McDaniel agrees that in the case of charismatic pastors (researched, e.g., by DuBois), their rhetorical skills and personality are crucial in persuading a congregation into activism, especially in churches whose pastors have long tenures: "[w]ith lengthy tenures came higher levels of influence in churches."⁵⁵

Since most of the pastors of Ebenezer could be classified as long-term and charismatic, I will pay special attention to their motivations, attitudes, and actions. Other factors from McDaniel's model will be considered when they directly influence pastors' decisions to convey the importance of a political identity of a church.

---

49 *Ibid.*, p. 5.
50 For him "a political church is a church that holds political awareness and activity as salient pieces of its identity." *Ibid.*, p. 21.
51 In his view, previous research had focused more on the behavior of the members than on the organization itself. *Ibid.*, p. 10.
52 *Ibid.*, p. 3.
53 *Ibid.*, p. 5, near *verbatim*.
54 *Ibid.*, p. 48.
55 *Ibid.*

McDaniel enumerates three kinds of such determinants: internal, organizational, and environmental.[56]

Among the internal factors are demographics (e.g., education, sex/gender, age, political interest, theology, and socialization). As the author explains, education should have a positive relationship with a pastor's willingness to stress the importance of political participation.[57] Higher levels of pastors' political interest also promote political conveyance, while the theology of a pastor determines how he interprets religious doctrine and "guides the decision to become active individually or to utilize the church as a vessel for social action."[58] Socialization also plays an important role. According to previous research, "clergy who have experienced church-based political action in the past should be more likely to support church involvement in political matters."[59]

The organizational determinants influencing pastors' decisions include institutional constraints on certain types of activities in which the organization can participate, which might be a result of denominational or congregational differences.[60] Other organizational determinants include the resources that are available to the church, pastor-members relations, and members' attitudes (as well as their demographics, political interests, theology, etc.).[61] Environmental determinants, on the other hand, include the region where the church is located, the community, its affluence, and agitation as well as the levels of comfort, safety, tensions, and historical circumstances.[62] All of these factors will be taken into consideration while analyzing the Ebenezer pastors' activism.

Although McDaniel is skeptical about the "opiate/inspiration debate," which had dominated earlier, especially of the "opiate view" (also in its modified version which stresses the differences among churches with otherworldly or this-worldly

---

56 Ibid., p. 99.
57 Ibid., pp. 99–100. Gender and age also matter, but in Ebenezer all the pastors were men who started to serve at a similar age.
58 Ibid., p. 100; More in: Guth, James/Green John C./Smidt, Corwin E., et al.: *The Bully Pulpit: The Politics of Protestant Clergy*. University of Kansas Press: Lawrence 1997.
59 McDaniel, Eric L.: *op. cit.*, pp. 99–100.
60 McDaniel does not concentrate on theological differences among different Black denominations, however. He stresses that according to research each church develops a particular culture regardless of denomination or location. Ibid., p. 83.
61 He generally thinks that members' influence was neglected in previous research, although he admits that Du Bois, Myrdal, and Payne mention it, as does Dennis Chong in his book *Collective Action and the Civil Rights Movement*. University of Chicago Press: Chicago 1991.
62 Ibid., pp. 100–101. He refers to research that indicates that clergy serving churches in poor neighborhoods are more likely to address social needs than are clergy serving churches in more affluent neighborhoods.

theological orientations), he does include theology in his model. While not a major consideration, it is treated as a sub-factor influencing both the pastor and the members (not necessarily being connected to organizational or denominational influences). He also admits that in order to justify their stance on politics and social engagement, pastors often give theological reasons, and that "pastors who have religious justifications for engaging the political process are more likely to convey the importance of political activity by their churches."[63] I will thus pay special attention to their theological reasoning.

The Ebenezer Baptist Church in Atlanta and Its Pastors
The Beginnings: Rev. John Andrew Parker

The church was founded in 1886 by John Andrew Parker—a pastor and a freedman who had studied at Atlanta Baptist Seminary and worked as a drayman.[64] Initially, the church had between 13 and 44 members and no house of worship.[65] Nevertheless, the choice of the church's name (Ebenezer comes from the Bible and means "stone of help") would, as some scholars stress, be "profoundly prophetic"—as it fit "the role the church would later play in the Black struggle for civil rights and social justice."[66] Although the church's mission was symbolically defined early on, financial problems prevented it from fulfilling it on a large scale in the first years. Reverend Parker served as the pastor of Ebenezer until 1894 without providing the church with its own building.[67] This changed when Alfred Daniel Williams (known as A.D. Williams) succeeded Parker after his death in 1894.

---

63 *Ibid.*
64 The MLK, Jr. Papers Project, The Martin Luther King, Jr. Research and Education Institute, Stanford University: Stanford, CA, retrieved 04.11.2021, from https://kinginstitute.stanford.edu/sites/mlk/files/publications/vol1intro.pdf, pp. 2, 26; Ridgeway, Benjamin C.: *Atlanta's Ebenezer Baptist Church*. Arcadia Publishing: Mount Pleasant, SC 2009, pp. 6, 9.
65 Ridgeway, Benjamin C.: *op. cit.*, p. 7.
66 Evans, Jason O.: "How the Ebenezer Baptist Church Has Been a Seat of Black Power for Generations in Atlanta." *The Conversation*, 2021, retrieved 20.12.2021, from https://theconversation.com/how-the-ebenezer-baptist-church-has-been-a-seat-of-black-power-for-generations-in-atlanta-152804.
67 Dennis, Carol A.: "Ebenezer Baptist Church, Atlanta, Georgia 1885." *Black Past*, 2014, retrieved 12.10.2021, from https://www.blackpast.org/african-american-history/ebenezer-baptist-church-atlanta-georgia-1885/.

Rev. Alfred Daniel Williams: 1894–1931

Williams came from a religious family. His father, Willis Williams, had joined the Shiloh Baptist Church in rural Georgia during the Great Awakening, before the Civil War, and was known as "an old slavery time preacher" and an "exhorter."[68] The church was initially white, but it recruited the enslaved who, while subordinate to whites in church governance, did actively participate in church affairs and on committees—as did Alfred's father.[69] By the end of the Civil War, Black members had become the majority in Shiloh, but as newly freed people, they soon left and organized their own congregation. Willis and his wife were among them. Alfred D. Williams was born in 1863, and while observing his father preach in the Black church, he imagined himself doing the same.[70]

After Willis' death in 1874, Alfred's family moved and joined Bethabara Baptist Church. There young Williams underwent a conversion (the evangelical "born-again" experience), was baptized in 1884, and earned his license to preach in 1888.[71] In the 1980s and early 1890s, he worked as an itinerant preacher in rural Georgia, but in 1893 he left for Atlanta, where he preached in two Baptist churches while working in a machine store.[72] When he was called to lead the Ebenezer Baptist Church in 1894, it was one of many small congregations in Atlanta. It was also deeply in debt, and its membership had shrunk to between 7 and 13.[73]

Having a church with so few congregants and no church building was challenging, but A.D. Williams quickly proved his leadership skills, adding around sixty-five members to the church in the first year.[74] Ebenezer grew in popularity over the next few years as Williams kept preaching in other churches as well. He came to concentrate exclusively on Ebenezer and enrolled at Atlanta Baptist College[75] to study elementary English and ministry—although formal education was not necessary for evangelical pastors at that time. As Raphael Warnock stresses, Williams became a preacher with little formal education, just like his father, but

---

68 The MLK, Jr. Papers: *op. cit.*, p. 1.
69 *Ibid.*
70 *Ibid.*, p. 2.
71 Ridgeway, Benjamin C.: *op. cit.*, p. 12.
72 The MLK Jr. Papers: *op. cit.*, p. 2.
73 Ridgeway, Benjamin C.: *op. cit.*, p. 12.
74 The MLK Jr. Papers: *op. cit.*, p. 2.
75 *Ibid.* It is worth mentioning that this is the same school that Andrew Parker had attended. In 1879, after moving from Augusta to Atlanta, the Augusta Institute (established in 1867) changed its name to the Atlanta Baptist Seminary, in 1897 to Atlanta Baptist College, and in 1913 to Morehouse College. More in: Morehouse College: *Our History*, retrieved 13.12.2021, from https://morehouse.edu/about/our-history_/.

after becoming pastor of Ebenezer he earned a certificate from a ministry training program at a school that would later become Morehouse College.[76]

Apart from serving his own congregation, Williams also actively participated in the establishment of new regional and national Baptist institutions. In 1895, he joined other Baptist ministers to organize the National Baptist Convention, the first historically Black Baptist denomination in the United States. By 1904 he was chosen as president of the Atlanta Baptist Ministers' Union, chairman of the executive board, and to serve on the finance committee of the General State Baptist Convention and numerous Baptist boards.[77] At the same time, under his lead, Ebenezer grew into one of Atlanta's most prominent congregations. It moved to different locations, eventually settling in the newly thriving Black community of Sweet Auburn in 1913. With Williams's efforts, by then, the church membership had grown to nearly 750 members.[78]

According to historical records, between 1894 and 1931 Williams was leading a socially aware religious community that was also ready to fight the segregationist policies in Georgia.[79] The circumstances in which this community was formed cannot be overlooked. The beginning of the twentieth century was a time of a "rapid economic growth and intensified racial restrictions." Black migrants (who by 1900 constituted 40% of the city's population) made attempts to participate in Atlanta's economic growth but were blocked by segregation and electoral policies.[80] Increasing numbers of Atlanta's Black citizens were departing from Booker T. Washington's accommodationist strategy.[81] At the same time, like other Black ministers from similar backgrounds, Williams, apart from addressing strictly religious matters, was building his congregation through dynamic preaching that addressed the problems of poor and working-class residents.[82] He is thus considered a pioneer of what became to be known as the Black social gospel.[83]

Although the social gospel, was initially popular among postmillennial evangelicals, it was eventually rejected by conservative evangelicals, especially

---

76 Warnock, Raphael G.: *A Way Out of No Way. A Memoir of Truth, Transformation, and the New American Story.* Penguin Press: New York 2022, p. 121. He completed it in 1898. Morehouse would later become famous for educating many leaders of the civil rights movement. In 1914 Williams became chairman of the finance committee of the Morehouse College Alumni Association and later was honored with the title of a Doctor of Divinity degree. The MLK Jr. Papers: *op. cit.*, p. 4.
77 *Ibid.*, p. 3.
78 Evans, Jason O.: *op. cit.*
79 *Ibid.*
80 The MLK Jr. Papers: *op. cit.*, p. 3.
81 In 1900 some of them launched an unsuccessful streetcar boycott. *Ibid.*
82 *Ibid.*
83 See also: Warnock, Raphael G.: *A Way...*, *op. cit.*, p. 121.

white premillennialists and Christian fundamentalists. Nonetheless, a number of Black evangelicals seemed to have adhered to it—despite conservative shifts in theology.[84] With time, they created their own Black social gospel.[85] As the authors of the MLK Jr. Papers emphasize, the distinctive African American version of the social gospel developed by Williams and other Black religious leaders promoted "a strategy that combined elements of Washington's emphasis on black business development and W.E.B. Du Bois's call for civil rights activism."[86]

Remaining committed to conservative evangelical principles, Williams preached individual salvation and personal relation with Jesus alongside issues like home ownership and human rights.[87] His stress on the social gospel was connected with different forms of activism. He soon decided to join or lead several local initiatives opposing racism. They included boycotts against local Atlanta newspaper, *The Georgian*, known for its racist language, and the 1906 campaign to end the white primary system which prohibited African Americans from voting in the Georgia primaries.[88] In February 1906 he joined other Black Georgians (including the famous AME Bishop Henry McNeal Turner and CME Bishop R.S. Williams) in organizing the Georgia Equal Rights League to protest the system and promote racial pride. He also signed—together with Turner and sixteen other leaders (including W.E.B. DuBois)—an address to the public which "protested lynching, peonage, the convict lease system, inequitable treatment in the courts, inferior segregated public transportation, unequal distribution of funds for public education, and exclusion of black men from the electorate, juries, and the state militia."[89]

In September 1906, however, their efforts were hindered by a large-scale race riot in Atlanta. After the riot, the Black community turned inward, supporting its own institutions while the trend toward residential segregation in the Auburn Avenue neighborhood increased. It was due to the "white flight" from the Auburn Avenue area, though, that within several years Williams was able to buy both a big house and a lot for his church on Auburn Avenue.[90] The Ebenezer's building was finally completed in 1922 and became known for both frequent evangelical

---

84 Fundamentalism was created in white evangelical churches but it found its way in various forms into some Black churches, too.
85 More about Black social gospel in: Dorrien, Gary J.: *Breaking White Supremacy: Martin Luther King Jr. and the Black Social Gospel*. Yale University Press: New Haven, CT 2018.
86 The MLK Jr. Papers: *op. cit.*, p. 3.
87 More in: Warnock, Raphael G.: *A Way ...*, *op. cit.*, p. 121.
88 Evans, Jason O.: *op. cit.*
89 The MLK Jr. Papers: *op. cit.*, p. 3.
90 *Ibid.*, pp. 3–4.

revivals and socially oriented sermons.⁹¹ Although Auburn Avenue businesses were growing, Black Atlanta residents faced new racial barriers, which Williams continued to oppose.

In the meantime, he continued his engagement in denominational matters. In 1913, he was elected moderator of the Atlanta Missionary Baptist Association and took part in internal leadership disputes which in 1915 eventually led to a split into two Black Baptist conventions: the National Baptist Convention USA, Inc. and the National Baptist Convention of America.⁹² Williams remained with the former, and despite internal debates on the limits and forms of social engagement, he stayed committed to social issues.

In 1917, he helped establish the Atlanta chapter of the National Association for the Advancement of Colored People, the NAACP, and he was soon elected as branch president.⁹³ Together with local groups, he initiated several campaigns, including one to improve conditions in Black schools.⁹⁴ As Warnock stresses, Williams was active in the NAACP, advancing the efforts to register Black voters at the very time of brutal racism in the South—when the KKK were burning crosses and the memory of the race riot eleven years ago was still fresh.⁹⁵

While doing so, "[...] Williams used the [Ebenezer] church as a power base and rallying point for such activities, an approach that would also be used by [Martin Luther] King, Sr. and King, Jr."⁹⁶ Therefore, while he was considered one of the leading activists in the city, his church was seen as a powerful social mobilization base. In his socio-political activism, Williams continued in his efforts to increase membership of the NAACP, register Black voters, advocate passage of bond issues for more and better schools, support boycotts of office buildings where Black people were not allowed to enter elevators, improve parks and recreational facilities for the Black community, and gain additional funding for Atlanta's Black public schools.⁹⁷

---

91 *Ibid.*, p. 4. Until 1922 the congregation worshiped in a hall above a storefront on Edgewood Avenue as the completion of the sanctuary was delayed by a lack of funds and a fire in 1917. More in: Ridgeway, Benjamin C.: *op. cit.*, p. 15.
92 The dispute mainly concerned the ownership of the National Baptist Publishing House in Nashville, Tennessee.
93 Evans, Jason O.: *op. cit.* By May 1920, Williams was forced to step away from this position due to disputes over a press boycott. In 1924 he was reelected as president.
94 He cooperated with the Neighborhood Union or Black women's group. More in: The MLK Jr. Papers: *op. cit.*, p. 5.
95 Warnock, Raphael G.: *A Way ...*, *op. cit.*, p. 121.
96 Evans, Jason O.: *op. cit.*
97 Including Booker T. Washington High School in 1924. More in: The MLK Jr. Papers: *op. cit.*, pp. 6–7; Ridgeway, Benjamin C.: *op. cit.*, p. 17.

After almost forty years as the pastor of Ebenezer—which became a socially engaged congregation—Williams decided to retire. Before stepping down in 1931, he appointed Michael King, his son-in-law, not only to act as the new senior pastor but also to continue the social engagement of the congregation.

The Ebenezer Baptist Church Between 1931 and 1975: Rev. Martin Luther King Sr. and His Co-Pastors

Michael King, who later changed his name to Martin Luther King,[98] also had family roots in rural Georgia. He was born in 1899, and his socialization in the church followed a different path than that of Williams. His father was not religious and had serious problems, including alcoholism and violence. Michael joined the church, thanks to his mother, and while he first felt he had found a refuge from reality, he soon also developed great respect for "the few black preachers who were willing to speak out against racial injustices, despite the risk of violent white retaliation."[99] At the same time, he admired preachers "who could recite Scripture largely from memory, preach in rich cadences," and adhered to conservative evangelicalism.[100]

When he decided to become a minister, he chose the Baptist church due to its nonhierarchical structure, which offered more opportunities for a person with little education. He began preaching in a small rural church between Jonesboro and Atlanta and was eventually ordained. He arrived in Atlanta in 1918 as a barely literate rural preacher.[101] In 1919 he met Alberta, the daughter of pastor A.D. Williams, and remained committed to her while she departed to attend school. Meanwhile, he was encouraged by her parents to improve his education. While preaching in several churches in College Park and Atlanta, he finished Bryant Preparatory School.[102] In 1926 he was finally admitted to the Morehouse School of Religion (despite poor test grades), which he found difficult, but he continued his studies and graduated after having completed a three-year minister's program.[103] He married Alberta the same year he was admitted to Morehouse. Before he became a senior pastor of Ebenezer in 1931, he had served as an assistant pastor to his father-in-law.[104]

---

98 Two years after becoming senior pastor. Warnock, Raphael G.: *A Way ..., op. cit.*, p. 123.
99 The MLK Jr. Papers: *op. cit.*, p. 8.
100 *Ibid.*
101 *Ibid.* Lack of education was not unusual for rural preachers. King could read but not write and his religious training was based on his pastor's instruction. *Ibid.*
102 Ridgeway, Benjamin C.: *op. cit.*, p. 19.
103 The MLK Jr. Papers: *op. cit.*, p. 9.
104 Warnock, Raphael G.: *A Way ..., op. cit.*, p. 126.

As he later recollected, he had been inspired by the preaching style of A.D. Williams.[105] Therefore, he "led Ebenezer with a mixture of evangelical faith and progressive social action,"[106] preaching "a social-gospel Christianity that combined a belief in personal salvation with the need to apply the teachings of Jesus to the daily problems of their black congregations."[107] Although, like Williams, King Sr.,[108] tried to avoid "an overreliance on emotional oratory," which "sometimes was meant to disguise lack of content,"[109] Martin Luther King Jr. would later stress that they had both adhered to an evangelical style that "appealed to emotions rather than to the intellect,"[110] especially during frequent revivals. King Jr., on the other hand, would later come to reject such religious practices as well as his father's doctrinal conservatism and fundamentalism.[111]

Still, King Jr. knew that his father and grandfather's conservative evangelical faith did not prevent them from engaging in this-worldly issues, having both priestly and prophetic overtones. It is worth stressing that King Sr. not only found warrant for social action in the Christian scriptures, but he also challenged other Black churches to embrace the social gospel.[112] In one speech, he expressed his views on "the true mission of the Church" by telling his fellow clergymen that "the church must touch every phase of the community life." He explicitly opposed the vision of a solely otherworldly church, referring directly to the principles of social gospel:

> Quite often we say the church has no place in politics, forgetting the words of the Lord, "The spirit of the Lord is upon me, because he hath anointed me to preach the Gospel to the poor; he hath sent me to heal the broken-hearted, to preach deliverance to the captives, and the recovering of sight to the blind, to set at liberty them that are bruised."[113]

Moreover, King Sr., just like A.D. Williams, was for a long time committed to the National Baptist Convention USA Inc., which despite being a theologically conservative body, at that point in history, included a number of members known for

---

105 The MLK Jr. Papers: *op. cit.*, p. 10.
106 Evans, Jason O.: *op. cit.*
107 The MLK Jr. Papers: *op. cit.*, p. 10.
108 After naming his son Martin Luther King Jr., he became known as Martin Luther King Sr., and later in life as Daddy King. I will refer to him as King Sr.
109 The MLK Jr. Papers: *op. cit.*, p. 10.
110 The MLK Jr. Papers: *op. cit.*, pp. 17–18.
111 In the sense of adhering to Biblical literalism. More in: Rathbun, John W.: "Martin Luther King: The Theology of Social Action," *American Quarterly* 20 (1), 1968, pp. 38–53, p. 38.
112 Evans, Jason O.: *op. cit.*
113 Qtd. in: The MLK Jr. Papers: *op. cit.*, p. 13.

their engagement in many NAACP initiatives. Within the Convention, along with Black pastors who supported a progressive approach, King Sr. stressed the need for an educated, politically active ministry.[114]

Being a civic and civil rights leader, especially through serving on executive committees of Atlanta's NAACP and the Atlanta Civic and Political League,[115] he frequently used the Ebenezer Church as a mobilization center. For example, in 1935 he led several hundred members of his congregation to a courthouse where they registered to vote.[116] In 1939, he pushed for a march on Atlanta City Hall as part of a massive voter registration drive, defying the more conservative clergy who opposed such a protest action.[117] At an Ebenezer rally, he spoke to a group of around one thousand people, encouraging them to greater militancy: "[...] I am going to move forward toward freedom, and I'm hoping everybody here today is going right along with me!"[118]

Ebenezer grew under King Sr.'s leadership skills. Although it had gone through financial difficulties after A.D. Williams's death, King managed to reinvigorate the church, pay off its debts, and attract many new members.[119] During his first fifteen years as senior pastor, church membership grew to 3,700.[120] At the same time, he continued his social engagement. He led marches and rallies to protest discriminatory policies in Atlanta, including those for the desegregation of the Atlanta Police Department and the Atlanta Board of Education.[121] He opposed policies that approved of paying white teachers more than Black teachers with the same credentials. In 1942, he also urged other more progressive Baptist preachers at the National Baptist Convention to pressure President Franklin D. Roosevelt into ending racially discriminatory practices on trains.[122] Additionally, he frequently engaged in individual acts of dissent, like riding the "whites only" City Hall elevator to reach the voter registrar's office. He also left a shop which he was visiting with his son Martin Jr. after the clerk had told him to wait to be served in the back of the store.[123]

---

114 *Ibid.*
115 Warnock, Raphael G.: *A Way* ..., *op. cit.*, p. 124.
116 James, Vaughn E.: *op. cit.*, p. 393.
117 Warnock, Raphael G.: *A Way* ..., *op. cit.*, p. 124.
118 *Ibid.*
119 The MLK Jr. Papers: *op. cit.*, p. 12.
120 Evans, Jason O.: *op. cit.*
121 *Ibid.*
122 Warnock, Raphael G.: *A Way* ..., *op. cit.*, p. 124. King also became chair of the Committee on the Equalization of Teachers' Salaries, despite racist threats. More in: The MLK Jr. Papers: *op. cit.*, p. 13.
123 This experience supposedly strongly influenced MLK Jr.'s. More in: The MLK Jr. Papers: *op. cit.*, pp. 12–13; Warnock, Raphael G.: *A Way* ..., *op. cit.*, p. 124.

Under King Sr.'s tenure, Ebenezer became one of the city's most influential and active congregations led by a charismatic leader, "known for his bold, blunt personality, which he used at will with considerable political influence."[124] King Sr. was also one of the best-paid Black pastors in Atlanta and his family's financial situation significantly improved (along with that of the church). Nonetheless, he never joined the migration to more prestigious neighborhoods popular among the Black middle-class, and he discouraged his children from elitist attitudes and feelings of class superiority.[125] And although he had always wanted his sons to become ministers and ideally to also serve as pastors for Ebenezer, he agreed with them making their own career choices.[126]

Rev. Dr. Martin Luther King Jr. as Co-Pastor

Martin Luther King, Jr., born in 1929, grew up aware of his father's vocal opposition to segregation. As he admitted later, his father's activism largely shaped his understanding of the ministry.[127] When King Jr. entered Morehouse College, however, he was planning to become a lawyer or a physician, not a pastor.[128] Eventually, he changed his mind, became a pastor, and in 1960 (already after having served from 1954 to 1959 at Dexter Avenue Baptist Church in Montgomery, Alabama) accepted the call to join his father as co-pastor. With this decision, Ebenezer came into the global spotlight, known not only as a symbol of socio-political engagement but also as a harbor for the civil rights movement (CRM).[129]

And while the civil rights campaigns and sermons delivered by Martin Luther King Jr. in Ebenezer are widely known (and do not need to be extensively analyzed anew here), it is worth taking a closer look at the internal and external factors that shaped his attitude toward social engagement (as in the case of his predecessors). One of the very important determinants was his socialization in a politically active church, observing his father and grandfather, both as preachers and as community leaders, and learning from them but also critically analyzing their beliefs and style. Other important internal factors include his education and theological development, while the external determinants that played a significant role in his case, include organizational (especially denominational) constraints and environmental (historical, economic, national, and regional) influences of the era. It is useful to begin the discussion with his spiritual and intellectual development and focus especially on his education, which strongly influenced his theological evolution (and led him to depart from some of his father's and grandfather's views).

---

124 Warnock, Raphael G.: *A Way* ..., *op. cit.*, p. 125.
125 The MLK Jr. Papers: *op. cit.*, p. 12.
126 *Ibid.*, p. 17.
127 *Ibid.*, p. 12.
128 *Ibid.*, p. 17.
129 Evans, Jason O.: *op. cit.*

In fact, King Jr.'s initial reluctance to become a minister emerged from his discomfort with the intense emotionalism on display, especially at the revivals of guest evangelists in his father's church.[130] During his studies at Morehouse, he analyzed and questioned literal interpretations of the Bible, and this made him even more critical of traditional Baptist teachings. Years later, he wrote about his time at Morehouse: "[t]he shackles of fundamentalism were removed from my body."[131] Instead of departing from religion, however, his newly acquired education had led him to understand that he could become a minister without adhering to fundamentalist interpretations and an excessively emotional religious style of evangelical worship. In 1944, he delivered a trial sermon at Ebenezer and was licensed to preach, which he would occasionally do at Ebenezer during his final year at Morehouse before being ordained in 1948.[132]

At Morehouse, he was strongly influenced by Benjamin E. Mays' teachings that promoted a prophetic social gospel and the philosophy of Mahatma Gandhi. However, King's theological views were also shaped by professor George D. Kelsey, who not only stressed the implications of the Christian gospel for social and racial reform but also accentuated the sinful nature of man.[133] In general, the experience at Morehouse opened him to liberalism as a potentially acceptable religious orientation.[134] Interestingly though, while King Jr. remained in opposition to fundamentalist Christianity, with time and years of study he would come to acknowledge the limitations of liberal theology.[135]

Before that happened, he had decided to continue his studies in a northern, theologically liberal school, Crozer Theological Seminary,[136] which strengthened his commitment to social engagement. In his papers written there, King Jr. consistently argued that Christians should never "become sponsors and supporters

---

130 He later explained that he also felt discomfort with emotional "conversion" or "being born-again" experiences. For him conversion was not "abrupt," but rather "unconscious" and a "gradual intaking of the noble ideals." He did, however, go through a conversion at one revival, but as he later disclosed, that was mostly because he was following his sister. More in: The MLK Jr. Papers: *op. cit.*, p. 14. His "kitchen table experience" in 1956, often described by his biographers, was of a different kind.
131 *Ibid.*, p. 17.
132 *Ibid.*, p. 18.
133 Kelsey also gave King his only A at Morehouse. *Ibid.*, p. 17.
134 *Ibid.* He later explained that he had rejected literal interpretations of Christian beliefs that contradicted "the laws of modern science," including the divinity of Jesus, the virgin birth, the second coming, and the bodily resurrection, which in his view should be understood metaphorically. He believed, however, in "a society in which all men and women will be controlled by the eternal love of God." *Ibid.*, p. 21.
135 *Ibid.*, p. 21. More in: Rathbun, John W.: *op. cit.*
136 The MLK Jr. Papers: *op. cit.*, pp. 18–19.

of the status quo."¹³⁷ His understanding of both modern Christian liberalism and the social gospel was further expanded by the writings of Walter Rauschenbusch.

Being strongly committed to the social gospel, King Jr. was initially skeptical toward the views of Karl Barth and other neo-orthodox theologians "who argued that man, corrupted by original sin, could never come to know God through reason."¹³⁸ As some scholars argue, before his introduction to the ideas of Reinhold Niebuhr at Crozer, King "was absolutely convinced of the natural goodness of man and the natural power of human reason."¹³⁹ With time, however, he started paying more attention to neo-orthodox ideas—due to his southern experiences with "a vicious race problem."¹⁴⁰ Therefore, while continuing to stress main convictions tied to liberalism, especially social gospel, he gradually came to appreciate a "mild neo-orthodoxy" in support of his own conclusion that reason might be sometimes "darkened by sin."¹⁴¹ For King Jr., segregation became "[...] an expression of [man's] awful estrangement, his terrible sinfulness."¹⁴² Thus, he eventually acknowledged Reinhold Niebuhr's "less hopeful philosophy of Christian realism."¹⁴³ While still at Crozer, he wrote, however, of his attempts to "synthesize the best in liberal theology with the best in neo-orthodox theology."¹⁴⁴

Although he continued to appreciate Niebuhr's philosophy during his Ph.D. studies at Boston University and also later—as he rose to fame¹⁴⁵—he eventually identified himself more with the views of the Boston University personalist theologian Edgar S. Brightman.¹⁴⁶ Personalism, "the belief that all human life is created in

---

137 Qtd. in: *ibid.*, p. 20.
138 *Ibid.*, p. 21. He gradually modified his approach, however. More in: *Niebuhr Reinhold. Biography*. The Martin Luther King, Jr. Research and Education Institute, Stanford University: Stanford, CA, retrieved 18.12.2021, from https://kinginstitute.stanford.edu/encyclopedia/niebuhr-reinhold.
139 *Niebuhr, op. cit.* Other scholars notice the earlier exposure to Kelsey's balanced teachings on sin. Niebuhr's thought went further, however. In his book *Moral Man and Immoral Society* (1932), he "challenged the usefulness of moral idealism in struggles for social justice." About U.S. racial problems he declared, "However large the number of individual white men who do and who will identify themselves completely with the Negro cause, the white race in America will not admit the Negro to equal rights if he is not forced to do so." *Ibid.*
140 The MLK Jr. Papers: *op. cit.*, p. 21. More in: Rathbun, John W.: *op. cit.*, p. 39.
141 Rathbun, John W.: *op. cit.*, pp. 39–40.
142 *Ibid.* However, to counter this harsh deadlock, King stresses man's freedom. *Ibid.*
143 *Niebuhr, op. cit.*
144 Qtd. in: The MLK Jr. Papers: *op. cit.*, p. 22.
145 *Niebuhr, op. cit.*
146 The MLK Jr. Papers: *op. cit.*, p. 21.

God's image and, therefore, has dignity, value, and a fraternal linkage,"[147] gave King a "metaphysical and philosophical grounding for the idea of a personal God" and for "the dignity and worth of all human personality."[148] For him, social gospel and personalism conveyed the most important message that the highest "law" for man is love, which he later connected with the "Gandhian method of non-violence."[149]

Among the other thinkers and role models who influenced Martin Luther King Jr.'s theology and philosophy were Howard Thurman with his mystic nondenominational and nonviolent Gandhian approach,[150] Mordecai Johnson, William Stuart Nelson, and Melvin Watson, who used Rauschenbusch's and Niebuhr's theoretical concepts to develop a practical theology applicable to the African American struggle for civil rights.[151] Rathbun summarizes King's views as being influenced by the social gospel of Rauschenbusch,[152] mild neo-orthodoxy, personalism, and "the nonviolent philosophy of love fashioned by Gandhi,"[153] which, as other scholars stress, he took "from the academy to the streets."[154] These theological influences together with his socialization in an activist church—and in the socio-economic context of the (turbulent) era—made King an opponent to the "quietism" of churches.[155]

Therefore, soon after he was called to be a minister at The Dexter Avenue Baptist Church in Montgomery (1954), he agreed to cooperate with the Black activists responsible for the bus boycott (1955–1956). He became their spokesman and the president of the Montgomery Improvement Association, supporting their protests.[156] In 1957 King, along with Ralph Abernathy and other civil rights

---

147 As Rivers explains, "what laypersons might call the 'soul,' Boston personalists call 'personality': self-conscious experience capable of rational thought and moral judgment. These scholars consider personality to be the most useful clue toward understanding reality." More in: Rivers, Larry O.: "The Morehouse College Scholar-Activist Pedagogy and Boston Personalism." *The Journal of African American History* 101 (4), 2016, p. 536.

148 Qtd. in: Rathbun, John W.: *op. cit.*, p. 45.

149 *Ibid.*, pp. 47–48.

150 Thurman, Howard: *Jesus and the Disinherited*. Beacon Press: Boston, MA 1996 (1949).

151 Rivers, Larry O.: *op. cit.*, p. 540. King also studied other theologians, including Paul Tillich, whose teachings he analyzed in his Ph.D. dissertation.

152 He extended the social gospel tradition of his father's church with Walter Rauschenbusch's liberal theology perspective.

153 Rathbun, John W.: *op. cit.*, p. 38.

154 Rivers, Larry O.: *op. cit.*, p. 540.

155 Rathbun, John W.: *op. cit.*, p. 50.

156 His agreement to accept this role connected directly Black churches to the CRM. The strategy of "direct action," including boycotts and marches was, however, first organized by many local grassroots organizations, including women's organizations. More in: Payne, Charles: *op. cit.*

activists, founded the Southern Christian Leadership Conference (SCLC) known as "the political arm of the Black Church."[157]

He returned to Ebenezer after his famous arrest in 1960. With its stable finances, large activist congregation, and renowned leaders, the church almost immediately started to play an even more profound political role. Not only was it engaged in the CRM, but it also played a role in electoral politics, especially in the 1960 presidential election.[158] King Jr.'s sermons at Ebenezer encouraged people to even more social activism as he also continued to coordinate the SCLC's efforts. It was during his tenure at Ebenezer that he organized famous campaigns, including the Birmingham campaign, the March on Washington (where he delivered his famous "I have a Dream" sermon) in 1963, the Selma to Montgomery marches of 1965, and many other widely publicized protests.

King Jr. was also hoping to make the denomination Ebenezer belonged to, the National Baptist Convention (NBC USA), the "institutional basis" for the CRM.[159] Neither the extent to which Ebenezer, its pastors, and congregants became engaged in the civil rights struggle in the 1950s and 1960s nor their methods were, however, approved by the NBC USA. Although its doctrinal and institutional conservatism had not previously prevented it from supporting anti-racist activism, at the time of the CRM its leaders were often preaching spiritual salvation and a gradual approach to civil rights.[160] The NBC's president, Rev. Dr. Joseph Harrison Jackson, was one of the strongest opponents of the civil disobedience strategy. Some scholars argue that it was the institutional conservatism of the Convention that prevented its leaders from supporting the CRM.[161] Others stress that "the conflict was essentially religious in nature and was predicated on questions regarding what constituted church work among black Baptists."[162] While King drew heavily from the social gospel and other philosophical ideas that justified challenging the status quo, Jackson was committed to "correcting" the social ills of society through national and religious unity.[163]

Much more committed to social justice than to the denomination's orthodoxy, King Jr. departed from the NBC, creating a new Black Baptist denomination, the Progressive National Baptist Convention (PNBC) with other progressive pastors

---

157 Lincoln, Eric C./Mamiya Lawrence H.: *op. cit.*, p. 211.
158 It is argued that after John F. Kennedy's intervention concerning King Jr.'s arrest and an unofficial call to his wife, Coretta Scott King, King Sr.'s political support for JFK mattered significantly to African American voters. More in: Warnock, Raphael G.: *A Way...*, *op. cit.*, p. 125.
159 Best, Wallace D.: *op. cit.*, 195.
160 Lincoln, Eric C./Mamiya Lawrence H.: *op. cit.*, p. 31.
161 *Ibid.*
162 Best, Wallace D.: *op. cit.*, 195.
163 *Ibid.*

(including Gardner C. Taylor). Established in 1961, it strongly supported the CRM. This move resulted not only from practical reasons, but it was also a consequence of the deep theological transformation King Jr. experienced over his years of study. And although the PNBC tended to accept liberal theology since the very beginning, King Sr. agreed for the Ebenezer Church to leave the denomination it had belonged to since its very creation to join the new progressive formation. At that time the PNBC was considerably more dedicated to the social gospel than his previous denomination—a denomination created through the efforts of his own family. It was thus a difficult choice between his family traditions (including theological conservatism) and his dedication to social gospel and social activism. He chose the latter, gradually moving toward a more liberal approach.

Following these changes, Ebenezer provided Martin Luther King Jr. with an even firmer base to serve in the ministry, lead the SCLC, and coordinate the CRM's actions in the 1960s.[164] His ministry at the Ebenezer, however, lasted only eight years—until his assassination at the Lorraine Motel in Memphis in April 1968.

Rev. Alfred Daniel King as Co-Pastor of Ebenezer

On the death of Martin Luther King Jr., his fahter nominated his youngest son, Alfred Daniel (known as A.D. King), as co-pastor. Although not as famous as his brother, A.D. was also active in the CRM, attending famous civil rights initiatives in Atlanta and Birmingham.[165] Initially, just like his brother, A.D. was not convinced whether the pastoral path was for him. Socialized and educated in the same environment as King Jr., and after also studying at Morehouse College, he eventually decided to become a minister. In 1959, he began work as a pastor in Newnan, Georgia, and joined the CRM.[166] A.D. King not only believed in an active church bringing about social changes and in the role of Black clergy in civil rights actions, but also in the importance of maintaining nonviolence in direct action campaigns.[167] Unlike his brother, however, he was able to remain mostly outside of the media spotlight. And yet, he was quite successful in his attempts to continue the advancement of civil rights in the South, including in Louisville, Kentucky, where from 1965 he pastored a church.[168] He also continued to travel with Martin Luther King Jr. and was with him in the Lorraine Motel.[169]

---

164 Warnock, Raphael G.: *A Way...*, *op. cit.*, p. 127.
165 More in: *Ibid.*
166 *King, Alfred Daniel Williams. Biography.* The Martin Luther King, Jr. Research and Education Institute, Stanford University: Stanford, CA, retrieved 18.12.2021, from https://kinginstitute.stanford.edu/encyclopedia/king-alfred-daniel-williams.
167 He is known for saying "[...] Stand up for your rights, but with nonviolence" even after the bombing of his brother's house in 1963. *Ibid.*
168 *Ibid.*
169 Warnock, Raphael G.: *A Way...*, *op. cit.*, pp. 127–128.

After his brother's death, he made no effort to assume King Jr.'s role as president of the SCLC, but he continued to work for the SCLC and remained active in the Poor People's Campaign.[170] He returned to Ebenezer in September 1968 to join his father in their long-term religiously and socially active mission. He did not have a chance to serve long as his father's co-pastor, however. He was found dead on July 21, 1969.[171]

Rev. Otis Moss as Co-Pastor of Ebenezer

After the passing of his two sons, King Sr. continued his work at Ebenezer for another six years. Between 1971 and 1975, he was helped by the Reverend Otis Moss, regional director of SCLC in Ohio, known for his friendship with Martin Luther King Jr. and involvement in the CRM. He strongly believed in an active "revolutionary" church and, just like previous pastors of Ebenezer, he was educated at Morehouse College. In fact, Moss and King Jr. were both mentored by Benjamin Mays,[172] who shaped their understanding of the social gospel and the philosophy of Mahatma Gandhi. Moss became socially active already while at Morehouse, helping lead sit-ins and other activities to protest segregation at that time. Later he studied at the Interdenominational Theological Center and participated in the Selma, Alabama civil rights march with King Jr.[173]

As the third co-pastor of Ebenezer, he contributed to its activist tradition, spending almost all of 1971 away from his church in Ohio, helping King Sr. in Atlanta with both religious and social activities and remaining active in the civil rights campaigns in both Georgia and Ohio.[174] After leaving Ebenezer, he continued his work as an influential figure in social justice movements. Interestingly, in 1990 he earned his Ph.D. at the highly progressive Union Theological Seminary,

---

170 *King, Alfred, op. cit.*
171 Warnock, Raphael G.: *A Way ..., op. cit.*, p. 128. Although his death was formally attributed to accidental drowning, there have been doubts and suspicions about it. A possible assassination has never been officially confirmed, however. Another factor contributing to his death, as reported in the media, might have been the trauma after his brother's assassination and its influence on his heart condition.
172 Metro News: *Otis Moss Jr., Senior Pastor of Historic Olivet Church, Retires*, retrieved 12.12.2021, from https://www.cleveland.com/metro/2008/04/otis_moss_jr_senior_pastor_of.html.
173 *Ibid.*
174 After 1975 he pastored the largest Black church in the state of Ohio. Later he even became an advisor to President Jimmy Carter and to President Barack Obama. More in: Buchholz, Brad: "'Every Time it's Tried, It Wins'." *The Statesman*, retrieved, from https://archive.ph/20120915065238/http://www.statesman.com/life/faith/every-time-its-tried-it-wins-181554.html.

where he met Samuel DeWitt Proctor and scholars who helped give rise to Black liberation theology.[175]

While Moss was still helping at Ebenezer, King Sr.'s wife, Alberta Williams King was killed during a Sunday service in 1974.[176] After the loss of three close family members, King Sr. started to think about retirement. The members of Ebenezer called Rev. Dr. Joseph L. Roberts—a Presbyterian minister who worked as Director of the Corporate and Social Mission for the Presbyterian Church in Atlanta and had sometimes preached at Ebenezer—to ask him to work as King's co-pastor. Roberts declined, explaining that he was not used to co-pastoring.[177] Nevertheless, in November 1974 he was offered the position of a senior pastor by King Sr. himself, who had definitely decided to retire.[178]

The offer was unexpected—as a Presbyterian, Roberts was welcome as a co-pastor, but not all church members were warm to the idea of having a Presbyterian senior pastor in a Baptist church. At this time, however, denominational affiliations were less important for King Sr. than Roberts' long history of social engagement and his education.[179] In 1975, after forty-four years, King Sr. nominated Roberts and formally retired, although he remained active as pastor emeritus until his death in 1984.

Rev. Dr. Joseph L. Roberts Jr.: 1975–2005

Joseph Lawrence Robert, Jr., the fourth senior pastor of Ebenezer, was born into an educated family in Chicago in 1935. An important aspect of Roberts' socialization took place in the Coppin Memorial African Methodist Episcopal Church, where his father was a pastor. The family lived in all-Black neighborhood on Chicago's

---

175 It is a Christian theology developed systematically from a Black perspective. Its controlling theme is the idea that Jesus is the liberator of the poor and the oppressed and that God is either metaphorically or literally Black. For Black Liberation theologians, it generally means that God is on the side of the oppressed (who most often happen to be Black). It was an attempt to reconcile Black Power with the social message of the Bible. More in: Cone, James H.: *Black Theology & Black Power*. Orbis Books: Maryknoll, NY 1969.

176 By Marcus W. Chenault Jr., who wanted to shoot King Sr. and claimed that "black ministers were a menace to black people." More in: African American Registry: *Marcus W. Chenault Jr., Murderer Born*, retrieved 13.11.2021, from https://aaregistry.org/story/marcus-w-chenault-jr-murderer-born/.

177 Warnock, Raphael G.: *A Way ...*, op. cit., p. 129.

178 *Ibid.*, p. 130.

179 *Ibid.*, p. 132.

South Side.[180] After attending public schools, Roberts, unlike previous pastors of Ebenezer, studied at Knoxville College, not at Morehouse.

He later changed his denomination from AME to Presbyterian for several reasons. He felt that "in the Presbyterian church the general assembly spoke to contemporary issues." As he put it, "It just wasn't the Bible, the blood, and the blessed hope," but also CRM, "community organization and economic development."[181] Roberts also accepted the fact that "Presbyterians are colder, more analytical, more intellectual."[182] He admitted that another factor in his decision was the Presbyterian church's offer of scholarships to pursue theological studies. Thanks to these scholarships, he earned his first master's degree from one of the most progressive and liberal schools, where Black liberation theology would be soon developed—Union Theological Seminary—and his second master's degree from Princeton Theological Seminary.[183] He absorbed the same theologically liberal ideas as King Jr. did in his studies, taking even more progressive approaches to some issues. As a Presbyterian, he also departed from evangelicalism with its conservatism and emotionalism, accepting mainline Protestant intellectualism (which had also attracted King Jr.).

During the civil rights era, Roberts was a pastor in a Presbyterian church in New Jersey, where he became engaged in the struggle for employing Black administrators in the school system. He did not march in Selma for family reasons, and while his involvement was most often from behind the pulpit, for example, by promoting the Voting Rights Act of 1965 and the Civil Rights Act of 1964, he had participated in the March on Washington in 1963.[184] While serving in two churches in New Jersey, he gained experience as an administrator and a social work organizer,[185] which turned out helpful in continuing Ebenezer's mission. Roberts joined a church that not only had a long tradition and financial resources, but was also a national symbol. According to his colleagues, however, "[h]e didn't

---

180 The History Makers: *Oral History with Reverend Dr. Joseph L. Roberts*, retrieved 20.12.2021, from https://www.thehistorymakers.org/sites/default/files/A2007_263_EAD.pdf.
181 The History Makers Digital Archive. Interview with Dr. Joseph L. Roberts, 2007. Session 1, tape 3, story 3, retrieved 20.12.2021, from https://da.thehistorymakers.org/story/633411.
182 *Ibid.*
183 The History Makers Digital Archive. Interview with Dr. Joseph L. Roberts, 2007. Session 1, tape 3, story 10, retrieved 20.12.2021, from https://da.thehistorymakers.org/story/633418. He later received five honorary doctorates.
184 *Ibid.*
185 The Presbyterian Outlook: *Joseph Lawrence Roberts Jr., Pastor and Preacher Dies*, retrieved 15.12.2021, from https://pres-outlook.org/2015/03/joseph-lawrence-roberts-jr-pastor-and-preacher-dies/.

want Ebenezer Baptist Church to be just a shrine to Dr. King, but a living, breathing church serving those in need."[186] He demonstrated his commitment to the legacy of Dr. King, Jr.,[187] working for the church to be an "intergenerational, intercultural, and inter-educational" space.[188]

Over his thirty-year tenure, he created many outreach programs for the community and oversaw the construction of a new larger church across the street from the Heritage Sanctuary (as the former building of Ebenezer was called).[189] The new building was intended to create the experience of an African meeting house, focused on community and drawing the metropolitan Atlanta community, including urban professionals.[190] Roberts also saw to it that the Educational Community Services Resource Center (named after Martin Luther King, Sr.) would relocate and continue its mission there. It was designed to provide for the needs of the community, especially the urgent inner-city needs of "homeless, hungry people desperate for health care or adequate day care or clothes or a shower or just old and poor."[191] He stressed that the Kings never moved out of the heart of the poor community, setting an example for pastors of Black churches. The outreach programs introduced by Roberts at Ebenezer also included the Teenage Mother's Ministry, a tutoring program, counseling, a food co-op, and an adult day care center.[192]

Commenting on the continued mission of the CRM, he stressed that "[w]hen movement solidifies into orthodoxy, it must be challenged. Again and again and again." He also emphasized that "[i]f 'diversity' is ever to be taken seriously, empowerment must accompany it."[193] Roberts was concerned about social issues like domestic violence, low wages, unequal wages for men and women, discrimination against women, gang warfare, and children with incarcerated fathers[194]—which reflected the historical context and new problems faced by African American communities. He stressed the distance America had to go to accomplish the Kings' aims. He was also aware of different approaches to accomplishing significant societal change. And although he remained focused on social work (largely done

---

186 *Ibid.* The Paula Gordon Show: *Authentic Faith-Based Initiative*, 2002, retrieved 16.12.2021, from https://www.paulagordon.com/shows/roberts/.
187 The Presbyterian ..., *op. cit.*
188 The History Makers: *op. cit.*
189 The new church building for 2,400 people, the Horizon Sanctuary, was opened in 1999. More in: Warnock, Raphael G.: *A Way* ..., *op. cit.*, pp. 132–133.
190 The Paula ..., *op. cit.*
191 The Paula ..., *op. cit.*
192 The Presbyterian ..., *op. cit.*
193 The Paula ..., *op. cit.*
194 The History Makers Digital Archive. Interview with Dr. Joseph L. Roberts, 2007. Session 1, tape 6, story 8, retrieved 20.12.2021, from https://da.thehistorymakers.org/story/633446.

through Ebenezer's facilities) rather than political protests, he did state that "[i]t's 'dangerous' for the faith community not to grapple with hard social and political issues."[195]

Before his retirement, to select a new pastor in cooperation with church members, he organized a committee which out of more than thirty applicants selected Rev. Raphael Warnock.

2005: Rev. Dr. Raphael Warnock at the Ebenezer Baptist Church in Atlanta

Raphael Warnock was born in 1969, in Savannah, Georgia to a religious household of two Pentecostal pastors. In high school he participated in the Upward Bound program for outstanding students.[196] After high school, like most Ebenezer pastors, Warnock attended Morehouse College, where he earned his B.A. in psychology (1991).[197] At the end of his junior year, he did an internship at the Sixth Avenue Baptist Church in Birmingham. He was mentored there by one of the CRM leaders, Rev. John Thomas Porter, who shared stories about Dr. King. This experience influenced his future theological and social views.[198]

After finishing his senior year at Morehouse, Warnock returned to the Sixth Avenue Baptist Church and made a decision which had been influenced by his studies at Morehouse and by his work at Porter's church. As he recalls, "[...] having connected so strongly with the social gospel vision of the progressive Baptists surrounding the movement, I decided to be baptized in the Baptist tradition and was ordained therein to Christian ministry."[199] As much as he appreciated the Pentecostal tradition he had grown in, he did acknowledge its limited social engagement and focus on emotional and personal religiosity. The social justice issues and social gospel tradition that appealed to him were, as he pointed out, seldom mentioned at Pentecostal churches.[200] Apart from joining a more socially oriented and theologically progressive tradition, Warnock also enrolled at the progressive Union Theological Seminary in New York, where he earned his master's (1994) and doctoral degrees (2006).[201]

---

195 The Paula ..., *op. cit.*
196 More in: Brack, Naomii: "Raphael G. Warnock." *Black Past*, 2020, retrieved 12.10.2021, from https://www.blackpast.org/african-american-history/raphael-g-warnock-1969/.
197 *Ibid.*
198 Warnock, Raphael G.: *A Way ..., op. cit.*, pp. 66–69.
199 *Ibid.*, pp. 71–72.
200 *Ibid.*, p. 33, 43. Warnock, Raphael G.: *The Divided ..., op. cit.*, pp. 7–8.
201 Brack, Naomii: *op. cit.*

While at Union, he visited a nearby Riverside Church, "which had been considered the citadel of Protestant liberalism and was the place in April 1967 where Dr. King delivered his powerful speech condemning the Vietnam War."[202] It was important for him that at that time the church was led by Dr. James A. Forbes Jr., its first African American pastor. Warnock found affinities with Forbes, who also had Pentecostal roots but studied at progressive Union and eventually became a leader of "one of the most prominent multicultural and interdenominational congregations in the country."[203]

During his studies in New York, Warnock visited churches (such as Bethany Baptist Church and Concord Baptist Church) led by other progressive ministers from the PNBC.[204] He also got a job at the historic activist Abyssinian Baptist Church in Harlem.[205] There, he witnessed close up the activist ministry of Dr. Calvin O. Butts III, another Union graduate and a former Morehouse student. Butts was known for his civil activism, responding to the challenges of affordable housing, police brutality in New York, and Rudy Giuliani's workfare programs in the 1990s.[206]

In the meantime, Warnock studied progressive theology at Union, including newly created womanist theology taught by Delores S. Williams.[207] Most importantly, however, he was tutored by James H. Cone, known as the father of modern Black liberation theology—understood as an expression of Black consciousness and a protest against the role of "white theology" in justifying racial division in the United States.[208] Strongly influenced by James. H. Cone's thought and the liberationist tradition of African American Christianity, Warnock wrote his doctoral dissertation on the role of Black liberation theology and womanist theology in contemporary Black churches.[209]

---

202 Warnock, Raphael G.: *A Way ..., op. cit.*, p. 74.
203 *Ibid.*
204 *Ibid.*
205 He served there for six years as youth pastor and four years as assistant pastor.
206 *Ibid.*, p. 120; Greenhouse, Steven: "2 Well-Known Churches Say No to Workfare Jobs." *New York Times*, 1997, retrieved 14.10.2021, from https://www.nytimes.com/1997/08/04/nyregion/2-well-known-churches-say-no-to-workfare-jobs.html; In 1995 the church even hosted Fidel Castro. More in: Hollis, Henri: "Campaign check: Loeffler tries to link Warnock to Cuban dictator." *The Atlanta Journal-Constitution*, 2020, retrieved 05.06.2021, from https://www.ajc.com/politics/senate-watch/campaign-check-loeffler-tries-to-link-warnock-to-cuban-dictator/4B6IBR72CVB47MV2KNTPLZVPUY/.
207 Warnock, Raphael G.: *A Way ..., op. cit.*, p. 76.
208 More in: Cone, James H.: *Black ..., op. cit.*
209 It was published in 2014 under the title *The Divided Mind of the Black Church. Theology, Piety and Public Witness.*

He confessed in his memoirs that although his mind "had begun to open at Morehouse," his time at Union was crucial in shaping his social views. Progressive Protestantism, liberal theology, social gospel, the spirituality of Howard Thurman, Black liberation theology and womanist theology shaped not only his approach to politics and his active stance on racial issues but also to issues like homosexuality (which was considered a sin in his own Pentecostal church).[210] He added, however, "[w]hile Union expanded my mind, Abyssinian showed me how to put my faith into action in the world around me."[211]

In 2001 Warnock became senior pastor at Douglas Memorial Community Church in Baltimore, Maryland (whose previous pastors had also been known for social activism).[212] There he focused on actions concerning HIV/AIDS awareness. As he explains, he chose to preach about the "unholy trinity of silence, shame, and stigma"[213] in order to make the religious community confront their fears and see that "HIV/AIDS is a sickness, not a sin."[214]

In 2005 he applied for the position at Ebenezer and was selected. Rev. Roberts soon came to appreciate the new energy Warnock brought to the church. He stressed that the new pastor was responding to the contemporary needs and desires of the younger generation and acknowledged that Warnock had a more informal style than that Roberts had brought from the Presbyterian Church. He attributed it to Warnock's Pentecostal background and felt it added more vitality to Ebenezer. As he put it: "[...] in a church you go through periods of form and then you have vitality and every now and then you've got to break out of your form so that vitality can express itself. [...] I see him bringing vitality to the form that I left, and, and forming new forms."[215]

Generally, Warnock brought to Ebenezer leadership skills[216] and liberal theology (as did several previous pastors), adding to it Black liberation theology, but also emotional elements of Black Christianity. In fact, he employed several auxiliary pastors, including Chelsea D. Waite and Darien A. Waite, a married couple of ministers, who would provide a more emotional prayer style, while he would deliver his sermons and services in an informal but more reserved style. This way he

---

210 Warnock, Raphael G.: *A Way ...*, *op. cit.*, pp. 83–103.
211 *Ibid.*, p. 87.
212 *Ibid.*, pp. 108–109.
213 *Ibid.*, p. 114.
214 *Ibid.*, pp. 112–113.
215 The History Makers: *op. cit.*, retrieved 20.12.2020, from https://da.thehistorymakers.org/story/633440.
216 Polished at the Leadership Program sponsored by the Greater Baltimore Committee, the Summer Leadership Institute of Harvard University, and Leadership Atlanta. More in: Brack, Naomii: *op. cit.*

seemed to have returned to some otherworldly aspects of Black religiosity while connecting it with liberal theology.[217]

His dedication to social justice issues was also manifested soon after his arrival in Atlanta. Not only was he an initiator of church events that blended with social justice issues,[218] but he was also active as a member of 100 Black Men of Atlanta and the NAACP.[219] At the same time, he worked to expand the Martin Luther King, Sr. Community Resources Complex, partnering with various nonprofit agencies.[220] Not long after assuming his post at Ebenezer, he also got involved in helping New Orleans citizens after Hurricane Katrina. He organized protests against mayoral elections taking place there in the absence of many Black evacuees, cooperating with such activist clergy like Jesse Jackson and Al Sharpton.[221]

Apart from fighting for Black citizens' rights, he soon expressed his dedication to women's rights.[222] Moreover, he became strongly engaged in promoting reforms of criminal justice system.[223] In 2007, he was involved in the case of Genarlow Wilson[224] and in 2008 that of death row inmate Troy Davis.[225] Warnock argued that Davis' trial demonstrated "the race and class contradictions that are characteristic

---

[217] Examples in: The Ebenezer Baptist Church Livestream, retrieved 30.04.2021, from https://livestream.com/historicebenezerbaptistchurch.

[218] Andrews, Becca: "'We Shall Overcome': Raphael Warnock's (Not-So-Long-Shot) Bid to Be Georgia's First Black Senator." *Mother Jones*, 2020, retrieved 05.03.2021, from https://www.motherjones.com/politics/2020/10/georgia-first-black-senator-reverend-raphael-warnock-loeffler-collins/.

[219] Brack, Naomii: *op. cit.*

[220] Which were helping raise credit scores among residents, moving them from renting to home ownership, and helping entrepreneurs develop their small businesses. He also involved Ebenezer in the B.E.S.T. Academy for a middle and high schools in one of the poorest neighborhoods of Atlanta. *Ibid.*, pp. 168–171.

[221] Warnock, Raphael G.: *A Way ..., op. cit.*, pp. 144–149.

[222] *Ibid.*, p. 50.

[223] This issue has been particularly important to Warnock, whose older brother spent twenty-two years in prison for a nonviolent drug-related offense. More in: Andrews, Becca: *op. cit.*

[224] A teenager sentenced to ten years in prison for having sex with a 15-year-old girl in 2005. When in 2006 the law was modified and consensual sex between teenagers 4 or less years apart started to be considered as misdemeanor, Wilson was not released (the law was not retroactive). Finally, in 2007 the Georgia Supreme Court overturned his sentence. More in: Warnock, Raphael G.: *A Way ..., op. cit.*, pp. 156–157.

[225] Davis had been sentenced to death for the 1989 killing of an off-duty Savannah police officer. There were, however, controversies as seven of the nine witnesses testifying in the trial had recanted or changed their stories. More in: *ibid.*, pp. 158–159.

of death penalty cases in general."[226] For him, incarceration had long been among the most serious problems in the United States, disproportionately affecting people of color.[227] He agrees with Michelle Alexander, who calls the mass incarceration of many Black men for nonviolent drug-related offenses "the new Jim Crow."[228] Warnock considers the opposition to it "a new kind of Poor People's Campaign," and thus encouraged his congregation to take part in a Multi-faith Initiative to End Mass Incarceration.[229]

His political involvement was also evident in 2008, when he invited then presidential candidate Barack Obama to Ebenezer. In Obama's presence, he preached a sermon, entitled "Unfinished Business," referring to Martin Luther King Jr.'s call to deal with "the triple evils of racism, poverty, and war." After the service, Obama asked the congregation for help in healing the nation.[230] As part of this effort, in 2014 Warnock engaged himself and Ebenezer in campaigns to expand Medicaid, something Georgia was refusing to do.[231] Feeling that it was a way of punishing the working poor, he referred in his sermons to King Jr.'s calls to increase social protections.[232] He also helped lead a rally inside the state Capitol, urging lawmakers to stop opposing Medicaid expansion. The protesters were blocking the entrance to the governor's office and singing spirituals.[233]

---

226 Dreyfuss, Joel: "Noted Reverend on Troy Davis: 'Moral Disaster.'" *The Root*, 2011, retrieved 12.12.2021, from https://www.theroot.com/noted-reverend-on-troy-davis-moral-disaster-1790865952. Other public figures were also involve in trying to halt the execution, including Pope Benedict XVI, Jimmy Carter, Desmond Tutu, and representatives of the NAACP and Amnesty International. Despite their efforts, Davis was executed in 2011.
227 Warnock, Raphael G.: *A Way ...*, op. cit., p. 163.
228 Because, as Alexander argues, ex-prisoners are unable to vote in many states, participate in democratic processes, and access upward mobility. More in Alexander, Michelle, *The New Jim Crow: Mass Incarceration in the Age of Colorblindness*. The New Press: New York 2010.
229 Warnock, Raphael G.: *A Way ...*, op. cit., pp. 164–165.
230 *Ibid.*, pp. 166–167.
231 Bunn, Curtis: "'My Ideals Are Driven by My Faith': Raphael Warnock on His Senate Runoff Race." *NBC News*, retrieved 13.12.2021, from https://web.archive.org/web/20210106141521/https://www.nbcnews.com/news/nbcblk/my-ideals-are-driven-my-faith-raphael-warnock-his-senate-n1246879.
232 Warnock, Raphael G.: *A Way ...*, op. cit., p. 179.
233 In total, thirty-nine of them, including Warnock, were arrested, and the action was unsuccessful. More in: Buchsbaum, Herbert: "Budding Liberal Protest Movements Begin to Take Root in South." *The New York Times*, 2014, retrieved 10.11.2021, from https://web.archive.org/web/20221203013229/https://www.nytimes.com/2014/03/19/us/protest-disrupts-georgia-senate-session-on-bill-to-block-medicaid-expansion.html.

Not long after that, he supported Stacey Abrams' New Georgia Project—a nonprofit nonpartisan civic engagement organization working to register "low-propensity voters."[234] He saw it as a legacy of many Black churches, including Ebenezer, that had been long involved in voter registration drives. In 2018 Warnock became the project's chairman (while Abrams announced her run in the 2018 gubernatorial elections), engaging himself and his church in its campaigns.[235]

Two years after Abrams' unsuccessful campaign and four years after Donald Trump's presidential victory, Warnock decided to run in the 2020 special election for the United States Senate seat held by Kelly Loeffler. He explained his decision, saying: "I've always thought that my impact doesn't stop at the church door. That's actually where it starts."[236] He officially announced his candidacy on January 30, 2020, promising to protect voting rights and to fight for access to affordable health care, fair treatment for all, and against mass incarceration.[237]

In the midst of the Covid-19 pandemic and his campaign, in May 2020 George Floyd was killed by a white policeman. The event triggered Black Lives Matter movement protests. Although the movement was condemned by those on the far right, and initially criticized by some Black churches (for being too militant), Warnock supported the protesters and their calls for police reform, making it clear that Ebenezer was on their side.[238] Despite Loeffler calling him "radical liberal Raphael Warnock,"[239] on January 5, 2021 he became the first African American to represent Georgia in the U.S. Senate and the first Black Democratic U.S. Senator elected in the South. In 2022 he repeated his victory in the regular U.S. Senate elections, and he still serves in the Senate.

---

234 Abrams was the minority leader of the state house at that time.
235 Warnock, Raphael G.: *A Way ...*, *op. cit.*, p. 184.
236 Bluestein, Greg: "Raphael Warnock, pastor of famed church, enters Georgia Senate race." *The Atlanta Journal-Constitution*, retrieved 11.10.2021, from https://www.ajc.com/news/state--regional-govt--politics/raphael-warnock-pastor-famed-church-enters-georgia-senate-race/sDPRVuKbd2w1QPZtrQrjMK/.
237 Warnock, Raphael G.: *A Way ...*, *op. cit.*, p. 189. He was also "pro-choice," which later attracted criticism from other Black pastors. More in: Ziegler, Mary: "How Raphael Warnock Came to Be an Abortion-Rights Outlier." *The Atlantic*, 2020, retrieved 13.10.2021, from https://www.theatlantic.com/ideas/archive/2020/12/liberal-religion-abortion/617491/.
238 More in: Napierała, Paulina: "The Black Lives Matter Movement and the Politics of the Black Church. Theological Divisions and Socio-political Engagement." In: Miroljub, Jevtić/Vekovic Marko (eds.): *Politology of Religion III Bi-Annual Conference 2021: Conference Proceedings*, pp. 147–183, retrieved 12.12.2021, from https://drive.google.com/file/d/19bTGWRy_0IfbwtVQ4Q25H9wU-XD9i8FO/view.
239 Warnock, Raphael G.: *A Way ...*, *op. cit.*, pp. 200–201.

Commenting on his mission, he said, "In my workaday life I have moved from agitator to legislator, but in my heart I am still an activist and pastor [...]."[240] He also added, "I see politics as ... one tool in the toolkit for the creation of a more blessed and beloved community that embraces everybody ... for me, that is the work of the gospel, and a mandate that comes clearly from my faith."[241] This religious reasoning not only brought him to politics, but it also increased Ebenezer's role in continuing the activist tradition of the Black Church.[242]

Conclusions

In this chapter, the continuous activism of the Ebenezer Baptist Church in Atlanta has been analyzed. The text has presented the different forms of social engagement of the Ebenezer's pastors, through which they have continued the activist tradition of the Black Church. Because Ebenezer has been led—through most of its history— by long-term charismatic senior pastors (and several charismatic co-pastors), whose dedication to social issues as well as rhetoric abilities were crucial in influencing congregation's stance on activism, the text generally concentrates on their role. Acknowledging the value of McDaniel's model in analyzing social and political activism of Black churches, however, a number of factors distinguished in his framework were taken into consideration. The focus has mostly been on these determinants that directly influence the pastors' decisions to convey the importance of a political identity of a church. Both internal and external factors affecting pastors' attitudes (as distinguished by McDaniel) have been considered. Among the internal factors, the attention has been mostly paid to education (as other demographic factors, like gender and age of the pastors, did not present much variation) as well as to the socio-political interest, theologies, and socialization of the pastors. The organizational determinants, including denominational constraints and resources (especially, financial, but also social and cultural ones, including church culture) have been considered, along with environmental determinants of historical circumstances, church's location, the economic standing of the community, and agitation.[243] At the same time, taking into account early theories and

---

240 Warnock, Raphael G.: *A Way ...*, *op. cit.*, pp. 221–222.
241 Andrews, Becca: *op. cit.*
242 Although he had been addressing political problems in his church, which continues to be an activist base, he was careful not to break Johnson's Amendment by promoting his own political campaign during services. He mentioned it only after he had already won. In order to verify it, Warnock's Sunday sermons between December 2019 and January 2021 have been analyzed. Available at: The Ebenezer Baptist Church Livestream, retrieved 04.03.2021, from https://livestream.com/historicebenezerbaptistchurch.
243 Other elements of McDaniel's model have not been analyzed separately due to the stress on the role of charismatic leaders at Ebenezer.

previous explanations concerning the activism of Black churches, special attention has been paid to the pastors' theology—which in McDaniel's model is also addressed—as one of the sub-determinants influencing the pastor and the congregation, but not a major one.

The analysis, based on historical and biographical sources, leads to several important conclusions. First, all Ebenezer pastors were highly educated, including the early leaders who were building the congregation at a time when it was not a strict requirement to have a formal education, and it was still quite rare (especially in rural areas). Moreover, most pastors of the Atlanta congregation were educated at Morehouse College (or schools and seminaries that evolved into it), including Rev. Parker, Rev. Williams, Rev. King Sr. (despite initial problems with studying), Rev. King Jr., Rev. A.D. King, Rev. Moss, and Rev. Warnock. This historically Black men's school and later liberal arts college in Atlanta has been long known for its high standards, and later for the three-decade tenure of Benjamin Mays (since 1940), as well as for its role in the development of the civil rights movement.[244] The only pastor of Ebenezer who did not attend Morehouse was Rev. Roberts. He attended, however, another famous academic institution, which over time came to be considered even more socially engaged and more progressive than Morehouse—The Union Theological Seminary. He was not the only one to attend Union, as at some point of their education Rev. Moss and Rev. Warnock studied there, and both were deeply influenced by the Black liberation theology taught at Union. Rev. King Jr., on the other hand, attended the liberal Crozer Theological Seminary and Boston University (after studying at Morehouse). It has been suggested by previous research that education has a positive relationship with pastors' social activism and willingness to stress the importance of churches' political participation—and this seems to be confirmed by the example of Ebenezer. The education of its pastors has always been above average (at particular periods). Over time the level of the Ebenezer pastors' education has also become more advanced. Apart from the several honorary doctorates that Ebenezer pastors have been awarded (Williams, King Sr., Roberts), the most active pastors (Rev. King Jr. and Rev. Warnock) earned regular Ph.D. diplomas from prestigious academic institutions.[245] The fact that the universities they attended were increasingly progressive is also not without consequence.

Second, most of the Ebenezer pastors were socialized in the environment of the Black Church, and most of them had fathers or both parents who were preachers or

---

244 It is also important to mention that since the tenure of its first African American president, John Hope, it has been focusing more on academic rigor than teaching practical skills (in agriculture and trade) while the latter was promoted by Booker T. Washington.

245 As well as Rev. Moss, who however earned his Ph.D. from Union after his tenure at Ebenezer.

ministers (including Williams, King Jr., A.D. King, Roberts, and Warnock).[246] Many of the churches they grew up in were activist, and if not, at a certain point the future pastors were exposed to the work of activist congregations. Williams observed his father's efforts to establish a separate Black church; King Sr. was impressed by the socially oriented preachers of rural Georgia, and he later followed the social activities of his father-in-law. King Jr. and A.D. King grew up in a household where both their father-pastor and their grandfather-pastor led a highly activist church. Roberts joined a more activist church than the one he attended as a child, and so did Warnock—who was exposed to Black church activism at Morehouse and the historic Birmingham congregation. Therefore, previous research indicating that clergy who experienced church-based activism in the past are more likely to support church involvement in political matters[247] also seems to find confirmation at Ebenezer.

All the pastors of Ebenezer[248] were also personally deeply interested in socio-political issues and either belonged to, cooperated with, or supported such organizations as the NAACP, the Atlanta Civic and Political League, the Montgomery Improvement Association, the SCLC, and 100 Black Men of Atlanta. Their personal engagement in socio-political issues sometimes took place outside of the church environment but was often a driving force for engaging the church, which frequently served a role of a mobilization center.

The fact that Ebenezer could serve this role was a result of organizational and environmental factors, as well. In the beginning, however, these factors had a negative influence over Ebenezer's activities. Historical records point not only to financial problems in the church's early years but also to sparse membership— which most likely influenced Parker's activity. Moreover, the situation in the South (not long after the end of the Reconstruction era) was particularly difficult. Later, during Rev. Williams' tenure, the membership grew along with its economic resources and political interests. The church moved to a better location in a more affluent area, as the Black population of Atlanta was advancing economically. At the same time, African Americans were facing political and social restrictions, so many of them were departing from the accommodationist strategy. The growth in membership and an increased activity of the church at that time was thus most likely a result of political interests of the congregation, whose pastor spoke to their needs and who had the resources to act. Charismatic leadership skills were, however, also not without significance, especially when Williams continued his

---

246 There are no data concerning Rev. Parker's socialization. King Sr. did not have a father-pastor, but learned from his father-in-law.
247 McDaniel, Eric L., *op. cit.*, pp. 99–100.
248 There are no available historical sources on Rev. Parker's activism, which in his case and at that time might have been difficult.

mission despite the threats of the KKK (which generally made the activism of Southern Black churches more difficult).

When King Sr. became senior pastor, the church already had, despite financial problems, a good location and potential resources which increased with the growth in membership. And although some middle-class members were moving out of the area to more affluent neighborhoods, it did not mean they were abandoning the church. The pastor and the church achieved financial security. The historical environment also influenced King Sr.'s stance on social issues: the continued discrimination against the Black population in the 1930s and after World War II (despite their military service), inequalities in wealth distribution (as economy boomed in the 1950s), and the increased activity of Black secular civil rights organizations mobilizing against these problems. Apart from the external environment, what has to be also taken into account during King Sr.'s term, as well as during the consecutive pastoral tenures at Ebenezer, is church culture (as a cultural and organizational resource). According to previous research, "churches with histories of political involvement are more likely to continue this involvement."[249] Therefore, while financial resources and the environment certainly influenced the engagement of King Sr. and Ebenezer, so did the activist church culture left by Williams. It is worth stressing again, however, that the level of this (inherited) activism still depended on charismatic leadership.

All of the above-considered organizational and environmental factors influenced the successive pastors of Ebenezer. And although some of these ministers (especially King Jr. and Warnock) are recognized mostly for their charismatic leadership skills, it is important to remember that other factors like church culture and specific historical circumstances also played a significant role in the decisions they made concerning the church's socio-political activities. Even Rev. King Jr. experienced immense historical pressure, as he joined the committees and initiatives that had been established by local women and Black civic organizations before he arrived in Alabama. In the midst of the civil rights struggle, he used his charismatic leadership skills to head and advance the CRM with the help of his churches, but the process itself had been started earlier. At the same time, his belief in the social gospel and the emphasis he placed on the Black churches' duty to act and play a role in nonviolent civil disobedience protests cannot be underestimated. Rev. Roberts, while also influenced by historical circumstances, experienced these in a slightly different way. He took his post at Ebenezer at the hopeful time of the advancements achieved by the CRM, and he used his leadership abilities and progressive convictions to expand social work and local political negotiations rather than to engage in political protests. In taking notice of new challenges, however, he admitted that for a church not to confront difficult social and political issues would

---

249 Eric, McDaniel: *op. cit.*, p. 18. As McDaniel stresses, this history of political involvement can also work to socialize both members and the pastor (p. 56).

be a mistake. Thus, Ebenezer remained socially active, albeit with slight changes to the forms of activism it took. When Rev. Warnock took his post, on the other hand, history had made it clear that the achievements of the CRM had not advanced as expected, and new problems had arisen and multiplied. Under these circumstances, his protest activity and direct political engagement increased. This was enabled by several internal and organizational factors, including Warnock's theological approach and leadership skills, the Ebenezer's church culture, and resources.

There were also such organizational determinants that—at a certain point in history—were actually hindering the church's activity. This refers especially to the denominational constraints put upon Ebenezer in the 1950s and 1960s. Although many members of the NBC USA (a denomination established also through the efforts of the Williams-King family), had been active in NAACP, in the 1950s its leadership withdrew their support for the civil disobedience as promoted by Rev. King Jr. This led to the departure of Ebenezer from the NBC and to the establishment of the PNBC—a much more progressive and activist denomination. And while the conflict was multilayered, it also partly concerned theology (as that of the PNBC was more liberal). Interestingly, denominational constraints, apart from playing a role in the Ebenezer Church's activity during King Jr.'s tenure, also mattered in the case of two other pastors, who left their denominations in order to join those which, in their view, supported activism at a more adequate level: Rev. Roberts and Rev. Warnock. And while the reasons behind the lesser political activity of their previous churches might be complex and dependent on many factors (as suggested by McDaniel), they also seem to include theology—as the move in both cases was toward denominations endorsing a more liberal approach.

Importantly, besides being a part of denomination's identity, theology is also one of the internal factors shaping pastors' attitudes. And while according to McDaniel's model it is not considered a major factor in the former, it might play a partial role in the latter. Therefore, this chapter paid special attention to theology understood as a sub-factor shaping the attitudes of pastors. When taken into consideration as such, the analysis indicates certain liberal shifts in the Ebenezer pastors' theology throughout the church's history. While Rev. Williams and King Sr. were both deeply rooted in the American evangelical movement and adhered to doctrinal conservatism, fundamentalism—in their literal approach to the Bible—as well as to revivalist emotionalism, Rev. King Jr. was the first pastor of Ebenezer to depart from it in the direction of intellectualism, liberal theology, personalism, and to reach for elements of other philosophical and theological traditions. In consequence, he brought a more progressive approach to Ebenezer.[250] It was gradually accepted by his senior pastor-father as well as his brother and Rev. Moss, who were also influenced by some of these ideas through their education at Morehouse. Rev.

---

250 Although he also added some elements of neo-orthodoxy to his theology, personalism, social gospel and progressive theology dominated.

Roberts, who had studied at even more progressive schools, and was a member of a mainline Protestant liberal denomination, not only helped keep Ebenezer on this track but also brought a great deal of intellectualism (appreciated by King Jr.), liberal theology, and a more reserved style of worship to the church. Eventually, Rev. Warnock went even further. Not only has he adhered to liberal theology but has also been promoting elements of Black liberation theology and womanist theology, becoming Ebenezer's most theologically progressive pastor.[251]

Shifts in theology can be observed not only at the church level (with consecutive pastors being increasingly liberal) but also at a personal level of each pastor. All of them became more progressive and this-worldly oriented over their lifetimes. Williams was the first to add social gospel to the evangelical theology that dominated in the churches he knew growing up. King Sr., who initially found refuge from the hardships of life in rural evangelical churches, not only followed in Williams' footsteps, developing a Black version of social gospel, but with time and under the influence of his son, he came to accept the more liberal orientation of the PNBC. Moreover, by nominating a Presbyterian as his successor, apart from showing his appreciation for Robert's social work and education, he also acknowledged the liberal theology characteristic of his successor's mainline Protestant denomination. Dr. King Jr., who grew up in the evangelical tradition, departed from its doctrinal conservatism early on, appreciating a broader approach to liberal theology, which in fact helped him in his decision to become a pastor. Rev. Moss was on the same track but later in his life went even further, pursuing Black liberation theology. Roberts left a more conservative denomination[252] for a more liberal one. So did Warnock, who left the conservative Pentecostal church for the PNBC, feeling that quite strongly otherworldly-oriented Pentecostals were not addressing this-worldly issues at the same level as the social gospel, Black liberation, and womanist theologies. Interestingly, however, while taking the most progressive approach to theology among the Ebenezer pastors (and coming the longest way on an individual theological path), he appreciated some elements of a more emotional style of prayer (characteristic of the early Black Church). As Warnock stressed, both aspects of Black religion—the otherworldly and the this-worldly—were close to him. With this attitude, he was coming closer to what Rev. King Sr. and Williams were representing—although in his case in style rather than theology.

This is not to suggest, however, that conservative theology prevented the Ebenezer pastors from engaging in social activism. The faith of those who adhered to it (especially Williams and King Sr.) had both priestly and prophetic overtones. Moreover, they found warrant for both these approaches in the Bible. Like many

---

251 Not rejecting, however, certain aspects of evangelical emotional prayer style and reintroducing them at Ebenezer.
252 Despite the fact that AME was a historically Black denomination known for certain forms of activism while retaining elements of conservative theology.

Black pastors, they did not see evangelical theology (even after conservative shifts influenced by the fundamentalist movement) as preventing them from applying elements of the social gospel approach.[253] Both Williams and King Sr. not only adhered to a mixture of evangelical faith and progressive social action, but they also helped develop a specific version of the Black social gospel. In fact, it seems that the social gospel approach was crucial to both their acceptance of social activism and finding its theological justification.

For Rev. King Jr., the social gospel was also essential. He stressed it at every level of his theological development and never departed from it. And although he appreciated his father's version of the social gospel, he expanded it using Rauschenbusch's liberal theology approach. The social gospel version developed by liberal theologians seemed more appropriate to King Jr. (especially in this particular period in history) than the mix of social gospel and conservative theology of his predecessors. Especially since it seemed that the previous version—also accepted by many members of the NBC USA—was not enough to convince all Black pastors to support the CRM.[254]

When looking at the consecutive pastors' attitudes toward the social gospel, it is easy to observe that Rev. A.D. King and Rev. Moss were (to differing extents) shaped by an approach similar to that of King; Jr. Rev. Roberts also adhered to the broad liberal approach to the social gospel, as did Rev. Warnock, who even stressed that he wanted to follow the social gospel version of the progressive Baptists (instead of the limited one of his previous church). Fascinated by this version, which is connected to liberal theology and its later variants found in Black liberation theology and womanist theology, he extended its scope even further than King Jr. So while for all Ebenezer's pastors social gospel has been crucial in shaping and justifying their approach to socio-political activism, its versions sometimes varied.

Apart from different interpretations, the levels of emphasis placed on the social gospel also seem to differ in various Black churches (as also noticed by the Ebenezer pastors). And although it is true that there does not have to be a contradiction between conservative theology and social gospel (unlike in white evangelical churches), the extent to which the latter is stressed seems to influence their stance on socio-political activity and its forms. Roberts and Warnock both experienced this. To the former, the stress on social justice in his AME church seemed lower than at his Presbyterian church. Pentecostals, on the other hand, have been known to put more emphasis on conservative theology, adherence to Biblical literalism and, as Warnock put it himself, personal piety, than on the social gospel. As

---

253 Unlike most white conservative evangelicals who soon departed from the social gospel, stressing the otherworldly orientation or keeping socio-political interest only in issues related to morality, and not social justice.

254 While certainly there were also other reasons that prevented some of them from joining it.

he writes, "few of them saw social justice issues as central to their Christian identity or the church's mission."[255] Although McDaniel argues that this attitude might be more influenced by factors other than theology or tradition (e.g., church income or pastors' education levels),[256] the Pentecostal stress on the social gospel does seem less frequent. Moreover, although some studies suggest that in Pentecostal churches some theological elements may limit engagement in social activism but others can be used to facilitate it, the same research also indicates that when Pentecostal pastors get involved in social issues they seem to prefer church-based efforts designed to propagate Christian moral standards.[257] Therefore, while they might be involved in social issues, the involvement might take different forms than the involvement of socially and theologically progressive churches.[258] The fact that Warnock (and, for example, Rev. Forbes of the Riverside Church) felt that the social gospel, social justice, and social action have been stressed more in more progressive and more liberal churches might actually be an indicator of a certain trend.

Interestingly, although McDaniel is an opponent of the "opium/inspiration" debate and the otherworldliness thesis, some of his studies also suggest that orthodoxy significantly decreases political interest, especially in comparison with liberation theology. As he stresses, however, "to conclude that orthodoxy is an opiate, as past scholars have, would ignore the complexity of the concept. Orthodoxy may not promote activism, but it does not necessarily completely stop activism."[259]

This analysis of the theology of Ebenezer pastors confirms this claim while also demonstrating the importance of the social gospel as a kind of mediating factor.[260] In general, it seems that the more social gospel is accepted by both theologically conservative and theologically liberal pastors, the more politically active they (and their churches) might become. It is worth stressing, however, that not all Black churches and pastors accept and/or emphasize the social gospel (certainly not at the same level). But although conservative churches seem to have put less stress

---

255 Warnock, Raphael G.: *A Way ..., op. cit.*, p. 43.
256 McDaniel, Eric: *op. cit.*, p. 94. While creating his model in 2008 McDaniel saw theology more as a cultural resource that believers can use to justify both activism and retreatism and he meant both liberal and conservative theology.
257 McRoberts, Omar M.: "Understanding the 'New' Black Pentecostal Activism: Lessons from Ecumenical Urban Ministries in Boston." *Sociology of Religion* 60 (1), 1999, pp. 47–70.
258 Although Pentecostalism need not be detrimental to political activity. *Ibid.*
259 McDaniel, Eric: *op. cit.*, p. 122.
260 Interestingly, when McDaniel researched what makes congregants more receptive to political messages, he also found out that it seemed that orthodoxy, if connected with social gospel or liberation theology, might encourage political involvement. More in: McDaniel, Eric: *op. cit.*, p. 143.

on the social gospel than liberal ones, if their conservative theology is joined by (elements of) it, their support for activism might grow.[261]

This conclusion might also suggest that the earlier Black Church scholars were not entirely wrong when they discussed the role of the social gospel, this-worldliness and otherworldliness in social and political activism. But while the social gospel does seem crucial to social and especially political activism, it is not, however, connected exclusively to liberal mainline churches, as previous research has suggested. Many conservative Black churches including these with overwhelmingly otherworldly approaches might also accept it. At the same time, the levels and variants of the social gospel chosen by liberal and conservative churches still seem to vary (as the cases of Warnock and Roberts show), which might also translate into different levels and forms of activism. This choice is an outcome not only of a pastor's individual theological decision but also of the previous theological choices taken by a particular organization/denomination.

Therefore, while agreeing with McDaniel's multifactor approach, this case study suggests that theology might play a role at even more levels than indicated in his model. Focusing on many factors and resources, the model is seated in social movement theories, but placing more stress on theology (although not exclusively) might bring in more elements of the cultural approach.[262] It could also allow to consider the potential applicability of certain elements of the restructuring model in analyzing the levels and forms of political behavior of Black churches.[263]

---

261 While other factors might also be important for their decisions. McDaniel in his later research put more stress on theology and found that certain theological orientations do matter in the level of Black activism and ideology. He suggested, however, that in the past most Black churches adhered to the social gospel, which motivated them to social action, while nowadays a new form of theology, the Prosperity Gospel, prevents it (2018).

262 Which, according to Potz, is useful in analyzing "individual motivations and social mechanisms behind the religiously inspired political behavior of individuals and religious organizations." Potz, Maciej: *Political Science of Religion. Theorising the Political Role of Religion*. Palgrave Macmillan: Cham, Switzerland 2020, p. 48.

263 While the ethnoreligious model has been traditionally applied to African American voting behavior (and partisan political choices), the restructuring model could be useful in analyzing the forms and levels of activism promoted by Black churches (depending on theologies and the accepted levels of the social gospel). More about the two perspectives in chapter one, and in: Smidt, Corwin/Kellstedt, Lyman/Guth, James (eds.): *The Oxford Handbook of Religion and American Politics*. Oxford University Press: New York 2009.

Although the "opiate/inspiration" and otherworldliness debate might resemble the restructuring debate, the divisions there are too simplistic.

While theology has not been the only factor, it has played a significant role in the activist history of the Ebenezer Church.

It should be concluded that this well-known church in Atlanta remained committed to the activist tradition associated with the Black Church (often included in its definitions), retaining a similar level of engagement throughout the years (although its forms might have changed over time). And while many factors influenced its stance on activism, one of the most important ones was the choice of its pastors to place the social gospel at the center of their theology.

References

African American Registry: *Marcus W. Chenault Jr., Murderer Born*, retrieved 13.11.2021, from https://aaregistry.org/story/marcus-w-chenault-jr-murderer-born/.

Alexander, Michelle: *The New Jim Crow: Mass Incarceration in the Age of Colorblindness.* The New Press: New York 2010.

Andrews, Becca: "'We Shall Overcome': Raphael Warnock's (Not-So-Long-Shot) Bid to Be Georgia's First Black Senator." *Mother Jones*, 2020, retrieved 05.03.2021, from https://www.motherjones.com/politics/2020/10/georgia-first-black-senator-reverend-raphael-warnock-loeffler-collins/.

Baldwin, Lewis: "Revisiting the 'All-Comprehending Institution:' Historical Reflections on the Public Roles of Black Churches." In: Smith Drew R. (ed.), *New Day Begun. African American Churches and Civic Culture in Post-Civil Rights America.* Duke University Press: Durham, NC 2003.

Barber, Kendra, "Whiter Shall We Go? The Past and Present of Black Churches and the Public Sphere." *Religions* 6 (1), 2015.

Barnes, Sandra L./Nwosu, Oluchi: "Black Church Electoral and Protest Politics from 2002 to 2012: A Social Media Analysis of the Resistance Versus Accommodation Dialectic." *Journal of African American Studies* 18 (2), 2014, pp. 209–235.

Best, Wallace D.: "The Right Achieved and the Wrong Way Conquered: J.H. Jackson, Martin Luther King, Jr., and the Conflict over Civil Rights." *Religion and American Culture* 16 (2), 2006, pp. 195–226.

Bluestein, Greg: "Raphael Warnock, Pastor of Famed Church, Enters Georgia Senate Race." *The Atlanta Journal-Constitution*, retrieved 11.10.2021, from https://www.ajc.com/news/state--regional-govt--politics/raphael-warnock-pastor-famed-church-enters-georgia-senate-race/sDPRVuKbd2w1QPZtrQrjMK/.

Brack, Naomii: "Raphael G. Warnock." *Black Past*, 2020, retrieved 12.10.2021, from https://www.blackpast.org/african-american-history/raphael-g-warnock-1969/.

Buchholz, Brad: "'Every Time It's Tried, It Wins'." *The Statesman*, retrieved from https://archive.ph/20120915065238/http://www.statesman.com/life/faith/every-time-its-tried-it-wins-181554.html.

Buchsbaum, Herbert: "Budding Liberal Protest Movements Begin to Take Root in South." *The New York Times*, 2014, retrieved 10.11.2021, from https://web.archive.org/web/20221203013229/https://www.nytimes.com/2014/03/19/us/protest-disrupts-georgia-senate-session-on-bill-to-block-medicaid-expansion.html.

Bunn, Curtis: "My Ideals Are Driven by My Faith': Raphael Warnock on His Senate Runoff Race." *NBC News*, retrieved 13.12.2021, from https://web.archive.org/web/20210106141521/https://www.nbcnews.com/news/nbcblk/my-ideals-are-driven-my-faith-raphael-warnock-his-senate-n1246879.

Chappell, David L.: *A Stone of Hope: Prophetic Religion and the Death of Jim Crow.* The University of North Carolina Press: Chapel Hill 2004.

Chong, Dennis: *Collective Action and the Civil Rights Movement.* University of Chicago Press: Chicago 1991.

Cone, James H.: *Black Theology & Black Power.* Orbis Books: Maryknoll, NY 1969.

Cone, James H.: *The Spirituals and the Blues: An Interpretation.* Orbis Books: Maryknoll, NY 1992.

Corbett, Michael, Mitchell-Corbett, Julia: *Politics and Religion in the USA.* Graland Publishing: New York 1999.

Dennis, Carol A.: "Ebenezer Baptist Church, Atlanta, Georgia 1885." *Black Past*, 2014, retrieved 12.10.2021, from https://www.blackpast.org/african-american-history/ebenezer-baptist-church-atlanta-georgia-1885/.

Dorrien, Gary J.: *Breaking White Supremacy: Martin Luther King Jr. and the Black Social Gospel.* Yale University Press: New Haven, CT 2018.

Drake, St. Clair/Clayton, Horace: *Black Metropolis a Study of Negro Life in a Northern City.* University Of Chicago Press: Chicago 1993 (1945).

Dreyfuss, Joel: "Noted Reverend on Troy Davis: 'Moral Disaster.'" *The Root*, 2011, retrieved 12.12.2021, from https://www.theroot.com/noted-reverend-on-troy-davis-moral-disaster-1790865952.

Du Bois, Burghardt, W.E.: *The Souls of Black Folk: Essays and Sketches.* A.C. McClurg & Co.: Chicago 1903.

The Ebenezer Baptist Church Livestream, retrieved 04.03.2021, from https://livestream.com/historicebenezerbaptistchurch.

Evans, Jason O.: "How the Ebenezer Baptist Church Has Been a Seat of Black Power for Generations in Atlanta." *The Conversation*, 2021, retrieved 20.12.2021, from https://theconversation.com/how-the-ebenezer-baptist-church-has-been-a-seat-of-black-power-for-generations-in-atlanta-152804.

Floyd-Thomas, Stacey/Floyd-Thomas, Juan M./Duncan, Carol B., et al.: *Black Church Studies. An Introduction.* Abington Press: Westfield NL 2007.

Frazier, Franklin E.: *The Negro Church in America.* Schocken Books: New York 1963.

Gains, Robert W., II: "Looking Back, Moving Forward: How the Civil Rights Era Church Can Guide the Modern Black Church in Improving Black Student Achievement." *The Journal of Negro Education* 79 (3), 2010, pp. 366–379.

Glaude, Eddie S.: "The Black Church is Dead." *Huffington Post*, 2010, retrieved 02.10.2019, from https://www.huffpost.com/entry/the-black-church-is-dead_b_473815.

Greenhouse, Steven: "2 Well-Known Churches Say no to Workfare Jobs." *New York Times* 1997, retrieved 14.10.2021, from https://www.nytimes.com/1997/08/04/nyregion/2-well-known-churches-say-no-to-workfare-jobs.html.

Guth, James/Green John C./Smidt, Corwin E., et al.: *The Bully Pulpit: The Politics of Protestant Clergy*. University of Kansas Press: Lawrence 1997.

Harris, Frederick C.: *Something Within: Religion in African American Political Activism*. Oxford University Press: New York 1999.

Harvey, Paul: *Freedom's Coming: Religious Culture and the Shaping of the South from the Civil War Through the Civil Rights Era*. University of North Carolina Press: Chapel Hill 2005.

The History Makers: *Oral History with Reverend Dr. Joseph L. Roberts*, interviewed by Denise Gines, retrieved 20.12.2021, from https://www.thehistorymakers.org/sites/default/files/A2007_263_EAD.pdf.

The History Makers Digital Archive. Interview with Dr. Joseph L. Roberts, 2007. Session 1, tape 3, story 3, retrieved 20.12.2021, from https://da.thehistorymakers.org/story/633411.

The History Makers Digital Archive. Interview with Dr. Joseph L. Roberts, 2007. Session 1, tape 6, story 8, retrieved 20.12.2021, from https://da.thehistorymakers.org/story/633446.

The History Makers Digital Archive. Interview with Dr. Joseph L. Roberts, 2007. Session 1, tape 3, story 10, retrieved 20.12.2021, from https://da.thehistorymakers.org/story/633418.

Hollis, Henri: "Campaign Check: Loeffler Tries to Link Warnock to Cuban Dictator." *The Atlanta Journal-Constitution*, 2020, retrieved 05.06.2021, from https://www.ajc.com/politics/senate-watch/campaign-check-loeffler-tries-to-link-warnock-to-cuban-dictator/4B6IBR72CVB47MV2KNTPLZVPUY/.

Hunt, Larry L./Hunt, Janet G.: "Black Religion as Both Opiate and Inspiration of Civil Rights Militance: Putting Marx's Data to Test." *Social Forces* 86, 1977, pp. 1–14.

James, Vaughn. E.: "The African-American Church, Political Activity, and Tax Exemption." *Seton Hall Law Review*, 37, 2007, pp. 371–412.

Johnson, Stephen D.: "The Role of the Black Church in Black Civil Rights Movement." In: Johnson Stephen D./Tamney Joseph B. (eds.): *The Political Role of Religion in the United States*. Westview: Boulder 1986, pp. 307–324.

Johnstone, Ronald L.: "Negro Preachers Take Sides." *Review of Religious Research* 11 (1), 1969, pp. 81–89.

King, Alfred Daniel Williams. Biography. The Martin Luther King, Jr. Research and Education Institute, Stanford University: Stanford, CA, retrieved 18.12.2021, from https://kinginstitute.stanford.edu/encyclopedia/king-alfred-daniel-williams.

Lincoln, Eric C./Mamiya Lawrence H.: *The Black Church in the African American Experience*. Duke University Press: Durham, NC 1990.

Marable, Manning: "The Role of the African American Church in the Civil Rights Movement." *NBC Learn*. NBC Universal Media, 2015, retrieved 02.07.2019, from https://archives.nbclearn.com/portal/site/k-12/browse/?cuecard=5041.

Marsden, George M.: *Religion and American Culture*. Hartcourt Brace College Publishers: Orlando 1990.

Martin, Lerone: "Bureau Clergyman: How the FBI Colluded with an African American Televangelist to Destroy Dr. Martin Luther King, Jr." *Religion and American Culture: A Journal of Interpretation* 28 (1), 2018, pp. 1–51.

Marx, Gary: *Protest and Prejudice. A Study of Belief in Black Community*. Harper and Row: New York 1967.

Mays, Benjamin E./Nicholson, Joseph W.: *The Negro's Church*. ISRR: New York 1933.

McAdam, Doug: *Political Process and the Development of Black Insurgency, 1930–1970*. University of Chicago Press: Chicago 1982.

McDaniel, Eric C.: *Politics in the Pews. The Political Mobilization of Black Churches*. University of Michigan Press: Ann Arbor 2008.

McDaniel, Eric L./Dwidar, Maraam A./Calderon, Hadill: "The Faith of Black Politics: The Relationship Between Black Religious and Political Beliefs." *Journal of Black Studies* 49 (3), 2018, pp. 256–283.

McRoberts, Omar M.: "Understanding the 'New' Black Pentecostal Activism: Lessons from Ecumenical Urban Ministries in Boston." *Sociology of Religion* 60 (1), 1999, pp. 47–70.

Metro News: *Otis Moss Jr., Senior Pastor of Historic Olivet Church, Retires*, retrieved 12.12.2021, from https://www.cleveland.com/metro/2008/04/otis_moss_jr_senior_pastor_of.html.

The MLK, Jr. Papers Project, The Martin Luther King, Jr. Research and Education Institute, Stanford University: Stanford, CA, retrieved 04.11.2021, from https://kinginstitute.stanford.edu/sites/mlk/files/publications/vol1intro.pdf.

Morehouse College: *Our History*, retrieved 13.12.2021, from https://morehouse.edu/about/our-history_/.

Morris, Aldon D.: *The Origins of the Civil Rights Movement: Black Communities Organizing for Change*. Free Press: New York 1984.

Myrdal, Gunnar: *An American Dilemma: The Negro Problem and Modern Democracy*. Harper and Brothers: New York 1944.

Napierała, Paulina: "Black Churches and African American Social Activism. The 'Opiate View' and the 'Inspiration View' of Black Religion in the Selected Literature." *B.A.S./British and American Studies* 27, 2021, pp. 95–111.

Napierała, Paulina: "The Black Lives Matter Movement and the Politics of the Black Church. Theological Divisions and Socio-political Engagement." In: Miroljub, Jevtić/Vekovic Marko (eds.): *Politology of Religion III Bi-Annual Conference 2021: Conference Proceedings*, pp. 147–183, retrieved 12.12.2021, from https://drive.google.com/file/d/19bTGWRy_0IfbwtVQ4Q25H9wU-XD9i8FO/view.

Nelsen, Hart M./Kusener-Nelsen, Anne: *Black Church in the Sixties*. The University Press of Kentucky: Lexington 1975.

Niebuhr Reinhold. Biography, The Martin Luther King, Jr. Research and Education Institute, Stanford University: Stanford, CA, retrieved 18.12.2021, from https://kinginstitute.stanford.edu/encyclopedia/niebuhr-reinhold.

Payne, Charles: *I've Got the Light of Freedom: The Organizing Tradition and the Mississippi Freedom Struggle*. University of California Press: Berkeley 1995.

The Paula Gordon Show: *Authentic Faith-Based Initiative*, 2002, retrieved 16.12.2021, from https://www.paulagordon.com/shows/roberts/.

Pinn, Anthony B.: *The Black Church in the Post-Civil Rights Era*. Orbis Books: Maryknoll, NY 2002.

Potz, Maciej: *Political Science of Religion. Theorising the Political Role of Religion*. Palgrave Macmillan: Cham, Switzerland 2020.

The Presbyterian Outlook: *Joseph Lawrence Roberts Jr., Pastor and Preacher Dies*, retrieved 15.12.2021, from https://pres-outlook.org/2015/03/joseph-lawrence-roberts-jr-pastor-and-preacher-dies/.

Raboteau, Albert J.: *Canaan Land. A Religious History of African Americans*. Oxford University Press: New York 2001.

Raboteau, Albert J.: *Slave Religion. "The Invisible Institution" in the Antebellum South*. Oxford University Press: New York 2004.

Rathbun, John W.: "Martin Luther King: The Theology of Social Action." *American Quarterly* 20 (1), 1968, pp. 38–53.

Reed, Adolph Jr.: *The Jessie Jackson Phenomenon: The Crisis of Purpose in Afro-American Politics*. Yale University Press: New Haven, CT 1986.

Ridgeway, Benjamin C.: *Atlanta's Ebenezer Baptist Church*. Arcadia Publishing: Mount Pleasant, SC 2009.

Rivers, Larry O.: "The Morehouse College Scholar-Activist Pedagogy and Boston Personalism." *The Journal of African American History* 101 (4), 2016, pp. 535–546.

Savage, Barbara D.: *Your Spirits Walk Beside Us. The Politics of Black Religion.* The Belknap Press: Cambridge MA 2008.

Smidt, Corwin/Kellstedt, Lyman/Guth, James (eds.): *The Oxford Handbook of Religion and American Politics.* Oxford University Press: New York 2009.

Thurman, Howard: *Jesus and the Disinherited.* Beacon Press: Boston, MA 1996 (1949).

Warnock, Raphael G.: *A Way Out of No Way. A Memoir of Truth, Transformation, and the New American Story.* Penguin Press: New York 2022.

Warnock, Raphael: *The Divided Mind of the Black Church. Theology, Piety, and Public Witness.* New York University Press: New York 2014.

Woodson, Carter G.: *The History of the Negro Church.* Associated Publishers: Washington, DC 1921.

Ziegler, Mary: "How Raphael Warnock Came to Be an Abortion-Rights Outlier." *The Atlantic*, 2020, retrieved 13.10.2021, from https://www.theatlantic.com/ideas/archive/2020/12/liberal-religion-abortion/617491/.

Cristóbal Serrán-Pagán y Fuentes

Martin Luther King, Jr. on the Three Social Evils in the United States: Racism, Poverty, and Militarism

Abstract: This chapter will examine the life and the writings of Dr. Martin Luther King, Jr. in light of his prophetic standing against the "triplet social evils" in the United States: racism, poverty, and militarism. The purpose of this chapter is to explore how King's religious messages of hope, love, and nonviolence contributed to building the "beloved community" that he dreamed of. I will divide this chapter into three parts. First, I will briefly introduce the life of Dr. Martin Luther King, Jr. and place him in the historical context of African American Baptist tradition, the civil rights movement, and the war in Vietnam. Second, I will analyze the political impact of King's prophetic mysticism in addressing the three social evils in the 1960s. And third, I will conclude with how King impregnated the civil rights movement with a vital philosophy in which spirituality and social justice are both seen as having been well integrated through his deeds and words. King never created his prophetic social writings in isolation from his religious and cultural environments. Rather, King needs to be seen in the light of a continuous line of prophetic mystics who are primarily rooted in the Judeo-Christian biblical tradition (following Moses and Jesus), and yet not completely deprived of other possible influences coming from Asia, namely King's method of nonviolence which owed its influence to the Indian sage Mohandas Karamchand Gandhi, also known as the *Mahatma* (or "great soul").

Keywords: Martin Luther King, Jr., poverty, racism, militarism, the beloved community, prophetic mysticism, Mohandas K. Gandhi

The Life of Dr. Martin Luther King, Jr.: Its Historical Context

Martin Luther King, Jr. was born on January 15, 1929, in Atlanta, Georgia. King came from a lineage of African American Southern Baptist preachers and ministers. All of them were pastors at Ebenezer Baptist Church in Atlanta, and the King family lived in this prosperous middle-class neighborhood on Auburn Avenue, steps away from the church. King received a very good education, although he started attending segregated schools where he learned early on in his life what it is like to be an African American in a white country. Before going to college,

King spent a summer working on a tobacco farm in Connecticut where he learned about race relations outside his Southern segregated region. In 1944, at the age of 15, King entered Morehouse College in Atlanta where he studied for the ministry under the tutelage of Benjamin Mays, the college president and a social gospel activist. Mays was highly critical of the Black Church in those days for not being so proactive in terms of working toward their own political and spiritual liberation and for overstressing the afterlife religious motif of escapism, instead of putting more emphasis on the liberation "here and now." King graduated from Morehouse College in 1948. Then he earned a Bachelor of Divinity degree at Crozer Theological Seminary in Chester, Pennsylvania, in 1951, where he first learned about Gandhi's method of nonviolence and continued to gain knowledge of social gospel Protestant theologians. At Crozer, King was elected President of the student body in an academic institution in which most students were white. Next, he went to the graduate school at Boston University where he studied theology and ethics under the influence of the philosophy school of personalism. His doctoral dissertation was titled "A Comparison of the Conceptions of God in the Thinking of Paul Tillich and Henry Nelson Wieman." In 1955, King received his doctoral degree. In Boston, King met Coretta Scott with whom he later had four children. Before King became the political and spiritual leader of the civil rights movement (1955–1968), he was named pastor of Dexter Avenue Baptist Church in Montgomery, Alabama. There, he learned how to put his prophetic faith and ministry into action.

The African American modern prophet (as seen by many) led the Montgomery bus boycott (1955) in his ongoing social struggles in the United States until his death. King received ill-treatment by whites and some African Americans, including receiving an almost fatal wound with a knife from a Black woman, Izola Ware Curry, who was mentally disturbed. She attempted to kill King on September 20, 1958, and was later diagnosed as a paranoid schizophrenic and ended up in a hospital for the criminally insane people. Also, the preacher-turned-activist had to spend many weeks under arrest in custody. His home was bombed several times with his wife and children inside. King's full commitment to the civil rights movement is a testament of his faith and hope, and his belief in God. For the next few years, he sacrificed his family time and traveled extensively at home and abroad. He worked hard to create the right conditions for building his dream of the "beloved community." As a leader of the civil rights movement, he became President of the Southern Christian Leadership Conference (SCLP) and led the movement in the South. In 1960, King took his family back to live in Atlanta following his father's advice. There he was soon arrested after protesting against segregation at a lunch counter.

The Atlanta pastor became one of the most iconic leaders in the 1960s. He organized the historic March on Washington, gathering thousands of marchers. It was August 28, 1963, when he delivered his famous speech, "I Have a Dream," at the Lincoln Memorial. More than 250,000 people gathered to demand civil rights for all U.S. citizens. In December of that year, Dr. King was awarded the Nobel

Peace Prize in Oslo, Norway, for his contributions as a major leader in the civil rights movement.

In his later years, King urged leaders and lay people to take a real stance against racism, poverty, and unnecessary wars like Vietnam. Dr. King and others like Rabbi Heschel joined demonstrators in Selma, Alabama, to demand the need for a federal voting-rights law. They marched together from Selma to Montgomery with more than a thousand marchers, which resulted in the passage of the Voting Rights Act of 1965. Just like King, Heschel gained numerous enemies, even among his Jewish contemporaries, because he "became closely involved in the issues of his time—Vietnam, civil rights, racism, poverty, Soviet Jewry and Israel."[1] Furthermore, some Jews attacked Heschel directly because of his social protests against the war in Vietnam, reflecting the inner divisions and splits found within the Jewish tradition in the twentieth century. Similarly, King's prophetic stance made him a target among his own people. On April 4, 1967, just a year before his assassination while at Riverside Church in New York City, Dr. King delivered one of the most prophetic speeches ever given against the U.S. foreign policies and their involvement in the war in Vietnam. After talking to Heschel and Nhat Hanh, King took direct action and prophetically raised his voice "to speak truth to power." King was clearly convinced that the three social evils in the United States were interrelated. The people who were killed were people of color on both sides of the spectrum. He stressed that the people fighting this war were people of color and white poor people who were misled into participating in one more war for corporate profit.

King knew his death was coming. It was a matter of choosing his "Golgotha time." He traveled to Memphis, but first he had to wait at the airport because the police were alerted of a bomb threat in his plane. Once in Memphis, King landed in his room at the Lorraine Motel and planned to rest; his advisers told him that he had to attend the evening meeting at the Mason Temple Church because there was a big crowd waiting for him. On April 3, King delivered one of his most profound sermons without reading any note from a paper. His famous sermon, "I've Seen the Promised Land," remained a testament to his courage and faith in God despite all the opposition he was facing. He was received by the audience as the "Black Moses," the liberator of his people. Before King, the four top names of "Black Moses" in the African American community were given to Harriet Tubman for helping her people escape slavery, Frederick Douglass who worked as an abolitionist leader, Marcus Garvey who helped organize their communities and gain more economic independence, and finally W.E.B. DuBois who promoted the idea of Pan-Africanism. That night in Memphis King told his audience he might not get to the promised land with them, but he "had seen the glory of the Lord with his

---

1   Shire, Michael J.: *The Jewish Prophet: Visionary Words from Moses and Miriam to Henrietta Szold and A.J. Heschel.* Jewish Lights Publishing: Woodstock, VT 2001, p. 121.

own eyes." The metaphorical references to Moses during King's last famous speech did not go unnoticed by the crowd in Memphis who were attending this public event. On April 4, 1968, King was shot and killed at the Lorraine Motel where he was standing on the second-story balcony. There were riots in many cities around the United States, with the exception of Minneapolis where Robert F. Kennedy was informed during a political campaign speech that Dr. King had been shot and killed. James Earl Ray was charged with the murder of King and pleaded guilty, although later he said he had been forced by the police to confess he was the shooter. The killing of Martin Luther King, Jr. remains unsolved, and the controversy surrounding his death still brings painful memories to many who believed King was the only hope for the United States to tackle the three social evils.

King's Prophetic Mysticism in Addressing the Three Social Evils in the 1960s

On August 31, 1967, Dr. King delivered his most radical prophetic message to an audience of thousands at the National Conference for New Politics in Chicago, calling the main social evils the giant triplets of racism, economic exploitation, and militarism. From the theological perspective, modern prophets and mystics do not turn their backs on the suffering of millions of people at home and around the world. King often spoke that all life is interrelated. He understood the need to address these problems globally, not in total isolation from the rest of the world. As James H. Cone put it,

> Martin King's foremost contribution as a moral thinker was his penetrating insight into the meaning of justice during his time. No one understood justice with more depth or communicated it with greater clarity in the area of race relations in the United States and the world than Martin Luther King, Jr. Because of King, the world is not only more aware of the problem of racial injustice but equally aware of its interrelatedness with poverty and war. "Injustice anywhere is a threat to justice everywhere."[2]

Prophetic mystics do not withdraw completely from society in search of solitude. Instead, their engaged spirituality is based on the ideal of building a compassionate world where "peace, justice and love would reign." King's prophetic response to social injustices was, according to his own account, ultimately rooted in his innermost experience of the divine. As King himself reported during his famous "dark night of the soul," also known as his kitchen prayer after receiving a death threat by phone:

---

2   Cone, James H.: *Risks of Faith: The Emergence of a Black Theology of Liberation, 1968–1998*. Beacon Press: Boston, MA 1999, p. 94.

> At that moment I experienced the presence of the Divine as I had never before experienced him. It seemed as though I could hear the quiet assurance of an inner voice, saying, "Stand up for righteousness, stand up for truth, God will be at your side forever." Almost at once my fears began to pass from me. My uncertainty disappeared. I was ready to face anything. The outer situation remained the same, but God had given me inner calm.
> Three nights later, our home was bombed. Strangely enough, I accepted the word of the bombing calmly. My experience with God had given me a new strength and trust. I knew now that God is able to give us the interior resources to face the storms and problems of life.[3]

Therefore, King can be seen as a mystic if we define the mystical experience as the direct, personal, and intimate experience of God.[4] Despite some controversies around such a definition, it is worth stressing that King was nurtured and inspired by his Quaker friends and meetings with the proponents of mystical approach to religious experience, like John R. Yungblut (author of the book *Discovering God Within*), Bayard Rustin, and Howard Thurman. King was not a total stranger to the beloved community of great mystics in his own time. In Boston, he had the spiritual friendship of Howard Thurman who became his mentor during his graduate years at Boston University. Thurman told King to read books by Rufus Jones.[5] As a matter of fact, it was through the Yungbluts (John and his wife June) that the Catholic mystic Thomas Merton attempted to bring King to the Abbey of Gethsemani for a spiritual retreat organized around the idea to address the needs of religious leaders and peace activists like the Berrigans et al. Unfortunately, the meeting never took place. King was assassinated that same year on April 4, 1968.

Theologically speaking, the mystic returns to the world enriched and transformed by the loving knowledge of God. At this point, the mystic feels the presence of God everywhere, even in the midst of terrible pain and suffering. Yet prophetic mystics

---

3   King, Martin L., Jr.: *Strength to Love*. Fortress Press: Philadelphia 1988, pp. 113–114.
4   In 2007, I treated this subject of King being a mystic at two different conferences, one in March at the Mid-Atlantic American Academy of Religion Meeting in Baltimore and the other one in June at the Tenth Conference of the International Thomas Merton Society's Christian Brothers University in Memphis. Surprisingly, a few members of the AAR in Baltimore were shocked after hearing during my presentation that King was a mystic. They saw him more as an activist but not as a real mystic. As a result, I sent my revised paper to the Merton Seasonal and it was published by the end of that same year. See more in: Serrán-Pagán, Cristóbal: "Builders of the Kingdom of Heaven on Earth: The Transforming Power of Agape Love in King and Merton." *The Merton Seasonal* 32 (4), Winter 2007, pp. 3–11.
5   Macy, Howard R.: "Intersections Between Martin Luther King Jr. and the Quakers." *Quaker Religious Thought* 103 (2), 2004, pp. 7–14, retrieved 01.10.2023, from https://digitalcommons.georgefox.edu/qrt/vol103/iss1/2.

acknowledge that God is not ultimately responsible for the source of that suffering, as King did. And it is because of their mystical experiences that modern prophets would be called to bear witness to the social injustices of their time. The prophetic mystic is one who takes part—in a responsible manner—in building the kingdom of heaven on earth. As prophets, they are responsible for sharing God's revelations not only among the oppressed but also with the oppressors. Genuine mystics in action are those who are able to integrate a contemplative love for the glory and honor of God and an apostolic and social commitment to the neighbor and all creation. As William Johnston said,

> I believe that the great prophets were mystics in action—their inner eye was awakened so that they saw not only the glory of God but also the suffering, the injustice, the inequality, the sin of the world. This drove them into action and often led to their death. And just as the great prophets were mystics, so the great mystics had a prophetic role.[6]

The biblical sources play an essential role in understanding the Christian message of Martin Luther King, Jr. One of the major problems in the Christian mystical tradition, however, is to solve the apparent contradiction between the active life, symbolized by the busy Martha, and the contemplative life, represented by the quiet Mary Magdalene. There is a tendency in some theological circles and among some religious people to negate one aspect in favor of the other, especially when they interpret this biblical passage from the Gospel of Luke in a literal context. The exegetical problem that this biblical text poses to the Christian tradition is whether or not active apostolic work, by itself, promotes union with God and leads practitioners to salvation. The paradigmatic models for this active type of Christian mysticism are St. Ignatius of Loyola and St. Teresa of Avila. In modern times Dorothy Day, Martin Luther King, Jr., and Thomas Merton might be considered as such. These Christians found God in all things. They were mystics in action. They thought of apostolic service as a peculiar way of prayer and as a way of worshiping the Lord, which resulted from mystical graces from God. But King also learned from the great Hindu sage, Mahatma Gandhi, about the mystical path of action (*karma yoga*) by detaching himself even from the fruits of his own action. King identified the Gandhian principle of spiritual detachment with the Christian idea of *agape* love, or unrestricted and unconditional love.

Clearly, King was influenced by both the Christic message of the Sermon of the Mountain in the Gospels and the Gandhian interpretation of *ahimsa* or nonviolence. He understood that he could not completely withdraw from the world just for the sake of his personal salvation, since God's calling demanded a human response to partake in building the "beloved community." As Susannah Heschel revealed in her approach to King's definition of the "beloved community,"

---

6 Johnston, William: *The Inner Eye of Love: Mysticism and Religion*. Harper & Row: San Francisco 1982, p. 11.

[...] King's "beloved community" is a moral community, recognizing that its bond of justice is prior to the state. This may be an alternative citizenship, a beloved community of nonviolence seeking to overcome what King identified as the state's three evils of poverty, racism, and militarism.[7]

This is why King's "beloved community" must be all inclusive and holistic in addressing the major social evils in the United States and abroad. King was a firm believer in the need for international cooperation among the nations. In his political view, the United Nations must be true to its global mission and must work passionately and unrelentingly to address these three social evils in the United States and in underdeveloped countries. King prayed for racial justice, economic justice, and peace to bring his unfulfilled dreams to fruition. As King beautifully put it in his prayers:

We must pray earnestly for peace, but we must also work vigorously for disarmament and the suspension of weapon testing. We must use our minds as rigorously to plan for peace as we have used them to plan for war. We must pray with unceasing passion for racial justice, but we must also use our minds to develop a programme, organize ourselves into mass nonviolent action, and employ every resource of our bodies and souls to bring an end to racial injustice. We must pray unrelentingly to bring into being those social changes that make for a better distribution of wealth within our nation and in the undeveloped countries of the world.[8]

King's Prophetic Mysticism Stance Against Racism in the United States

The prophetic mystic King was ahead of his time when he rightly saw the urgent necessity to courageously confront the racial problems that were affecting the fragile thread of the American family. For King, racism was a disease. As he defined it, "Racism is a philosophy based on a contempt for life. [...] Racism is total estrangement" [...].[9] Even worse, King acknowledged that this segregated mindset is heavily promoted in many Christian churches. As King famously said in his sermons, "We must face the sad fact that at eleven o'clock on Sunday morning [...] we stand in the most segregated hour of America."[10] King advocated for a

---

7   Heschel, Susannah: "A Friendship in the Prophetic Tradition: Abraham Joshua Heschel and Martin Luther King, Jr." *Telos* 182, 2018, p. 79.
8   King, Martin Luther Jr.: *Strength to Love*. Fortress Press: Philadelphia 1988, p. 132.
9   King, Martin Luther Jr.: *Where Do We Go from Here: Chaos or Community?* Harper & Row: New York 1967, p. 70.
10 King, Martin Luther, Jr.: "Remaining Awake Through a Great Revolution." In: Carson, Clayborne/Peter Holloran (eds.): *A Knock at Midnight: Inspiration from the Great Sermons of Reverend Martin Luther King, Jr.* Warner Books: New York 2000, p. 209.

nonviolent way to solve the problem of racism following the Gandhian principles of *ahimsa* and *satyagraha* (truth-force or love-force). King wrote the following in his "Letter from Birmingham Jail," dated April 16, 1963:

> [...] I must confess that over the past few years I have been gravely disappointed with the white moderate. I have almost reached the regrettable conclusion that the Negro's great stumbling block in his stride toward freedom is not the White Citizen's Councilor or the Ku Klux Klanner, but the white moderate, who is more devoted to "order" than to justice; who prefers a negative peace which is the absence of tension to a positive peace which is the presence of justice; who constantly says: I agree with you in the goal you seek, but I cannot agree with your methods of direct action; who paternalistically believes he can set the timetable for another man's freedom; who lives by a mythical concept of time and who constantly advises the Negro to wait for a more convenient season.[11]

King, after all, was able to create in the midst of a harsh environment of hatred and resentment a nonviolent movement rooted in the Christian social ethics of the Gospels. King summarized his philosophy of nonviolence in his essay "The Negro Revolution—Why 1963?" by stating:

> Nonviolence is a powerful and just weapon. It is a weapon unique in history, which cuts without wounding and ennobles the man who wields it. It is a sword that heals. Both a practical and a moral answer to the Negro's cry for justice, nonviolent direct action proved that it could win victories without losing wars, and so became the triumphant tactic of the Negro Revolution of 1963.[12]

King publicly exposed the systematic expressions of evil actions against the human race that were part of the social and religious establishment of their time. The Baptist pastor, although he wrote numerous essays and sermons, directed all his energies to the realm of action through marches and other exterior means. He followed his family's Christian ministry as a preacher. He was licensed to preach in 1947 when he was 18 years old. He was ordained a Christian minister in 1948. But he knew from his earlier years that he would commit his life to a fight against all sorts of social evils and injustice. And yet, he was also convinced that the African American response comes from the center of the soul which has its deep source in a Christian spiritual vision of the world. As King put it in "The Sword that Heals":

> [...] perhaps even more vital in the Negro's resistance to violence was the force of his deeply rooted spiritual beliefs. In Montgomery, after a courageous woman, Rosa Parks, had refused to move to the back of the bus, and so began the revolt that led to the boycott of 1955–56, the Negro's developing campaign against that city's racial injustice was based in the churches of the community.[13]

11　King, Martin Luther, Jr.: *Why We Can't Wait*. Harper & Row: New York 1964, p. 87.
12　*Ibid.*, p. 14.
13　*Ibid.*, p. 24.

Ultimately, King believed that love would overcome evil from an eschatological point of view. The main reason why he unconditionally accepted this theological assumption rests in his belief in the existence of God, not from a mere abstraction point of view but from a very personal relationship with God, which he described in the following way:

> [...] In the midst of outer dangers I have felt an inner calm and known resources of strength that only God could give. In many instances I have felt the power of God transforming the fatigue of despair into the buoyancy of hope. I am convinced that the universe is under the control of a loving purpose and that in the struggle for righteousness man has cosmic companionship. Behind the harsh appearances of the world there is a benign power. To say God is personal is not to make him an object among other objects or attribute to him the finiteness and limitations of human personality [...]. So in the truest sense of the word, God is a living God. In him there is feeling and will, responsive to the deepest yearnings of the human heart: this God both evokes and answers prayers.[14]

In 1963, King witnessed the turmoil of American society trying to pass the civil rights bill, yet the sense of hope diminished after hearing the news about the Birmingham Baptist church bombing that killed four Black girls on a Sunday morning. King wrote the eulogy for the martyred children, trying to keep the flame of the movement alive by saying that these children did not die in vain. The Birmingham criminal event galvanized the civil rights movement and was perhaps the prelude for advancing the civil rights bill in 1964. He learned from his own personal experience that all life is interrelated. His passion for peace and justice did not stop in one place or with one race. As King said in his famous "Letter from Birmingham Jail":

> Moreover, I am cognizant of the interrelatedness of all communities and states. I cannot sit idly by in Atlanta and not be concerned about what happens in Birmingham. Injustice anywhere is a threat to justice everywhere. We are caught in an inescapable network of mutuality, tied in a single garment of destiny. Whatever affects one directly, affects all indirectly [...].[15]

In 1965, King marched in Selma, Alabama, advancing a new day for North Americans by demanding the right to vote for African Americans. King was arrested together with hundreds of demonstrators. A few months later he called for a march from Selma to Montgomery. This produced one of the most brutal racist actions ever captured on film. The televised images roused the consciousness of the

---

14 King, Martin Luther Jr.: "Pilgrimage to Nonviolence." In: James Melvin Washington (ed.): *A Testament of Hope: The Essential Writings and Speeches of Martin Luther King, Jr.* HarperSanFrancisco: San Francisco 1991, p. 40.
15 King, Martin Luther, Jr.: *Why We Can't Wait*. Harper & Row: New York 1964, pp. 78–79.

American people. Thanks to the brave and courageous nonviolent demonstrators, the civil rights movement marched on and won the hearts and minds of many white citizens in the United States. Many African Americans learned that real change was possible, but as King warned many times, it does not come quickly or easily. He was certain that one must do whatever one can to accelerate the process toward peace and reconciliation—by getting fully engaged in the racial and social struggles of the time. This is why King stood up not only as a prophetic leader for African American people but also denounced the racial injustices directed against Native Americans, Hispanics, Jews, Asians, and other targeted minority groups and people of color.

King's Prophetic Mysticism Stance Against Poverty

King's propositions as a civil rights activist did not become more effective and more threatening to the status quo until he and the rest of the activist leaders within the civil rights movement developed an economic strategy to deliberately hurt business in North America. There were plenty of people on both sides (Blacks and whites) who chose to preserve the status quo by living in an unjust and segregated society. His last days were full of anxiety and sadness, which probably caused the loss of his health. On top of receiving personal death threats, King had to confront the social unrest coming from Black Power militants, including Malcolm X, who denounced him for being too passive at the time when their people were suffering physical and mental deprivation, from as far as the slums of the North to the segregated towns in the South. They demanded more effective actions from the leader of the nonviolent civil rights movement. As a result, King moved to Chicago and rented a place in a troubled neighborhood to learn the social conditions of his people. The main goal was to solve the problem of housing, but King experienced the unexpected racism in the North and received great opposition from the mayor of Chicago, Richard J. Daley. King's nonviolent method worked well in the context of segregation laws in the South, but now he saw that his presence had little effect in a wider situation. After all these social and political upheavals and failures, King decided to adopt a more radical position in his approach. As a personal testimony to his radical prophetic voice in Memphis, King declared:

> And I come by here to say that America to is going to hell if she doesn't use her wealth. If America does not use her vast resources of wealth to end poverty and make it possible for all God's children to have the basic necessities of life, she too will go to hell [...]. And so you cannot enter the kingdom of greatness. This may well be the indictment on America. [...][16]

---

16 King, Martin Luther Jr.: "The Poor People's Campaign." In: Carson, Clayborne (ed.): *The Autobiography of Martin Luther King, Jr.* Grand Central Publishing: New York 1998, p. 354.

King was no longer concerned about fighting nonviolently against racism and poverty in the ghettos of the United States, but he got more actively involved in the international problems that all U.S. citizens were facing in the war in Vietnam. As James Colaiaco observed:

> During the final year and a half of his life, King challenged the nation to undertake radical reforms. Stiffening white resistance to black equality, in addition to the spreading ghetto riots and the escalating Vietnam conflict, had created the greatest crisis in America since the Civil war. King saw these developments as symptoms of a moral sickness afflicting the nation that could be remedied only by radical changes in its political, social and economic structure. [...][17]

In 1968, King was exhausted both physically and mentally. He was confronting too many social and moral issues at once, and this alone took a big toll on him. During his final months of life, King confessed he was very tired of marching, being arrested, and receiving death threats, but he kept going because he was convinced he was following God's will. As a modern prophet, he led his ultimate campaign on earth for a Poor People's March to Washington forming an eclectic amalgam of people in their collaborative effort to demand solutions from their leaders in Washington, D.C. Their intention was to tackle, once and for all, the poor social conditions of the disinherited people (or in biblical words known as the *anawim*) who suffered extreme poverty for decades in the richest country in history. As King said in one of his sermons:

> [...] We are coming to Washington in a Poor People's Campaign. Yes, we are going to bring the tired, the poor, the huddled masses. We are going to bring those who have known long years of hurt and neglect. [...] Why do we do it this way? We do it this way because it is our experience that the nation doesn't move around questions of genuine equality for the poor and for black people until it is confronted massively, dramatically in terms of direct action.[18]

For King, this situation of economic deprivation was morally and spiritually unacceptable. He understood that poverty has been an integral part of human history but he was convinced that in his times there were the economic and technological resources to eliminate it or at least to minimize the impact of economic starvation at home and abroad. As part of King's social measures needed to bring his revolution of values, Marshall Frady announced:

---

17 Colaiaco, James A.: *Martin Luther King, Jr.: Apostle of Militant Nonviolence*. MacMillan: London 1993, p. 178.
18 King, Martin Luther, Jr.: "Remaining Awake Through a Great Revolution." In: Carson, Clayborne/Peter Holloran (eds.): *A Knock at Midnight: Inspiration from the Great Sermons of Reverend Martin Luther King, Jr*. Warner Books: New York 2000, p. 217.

> [...] social peace must spring from economic justice and [...] a massive assault upon slums, inferior education, inadequate medical care [...] the entire culture of poverty [...] to redress at last the past systemic economic depredations of both blacks and whites.[19]

In the final analysis, King saw that what was missing was a moral and spiritual deficit in human will. There was a moral indifference held by the powerful nations to preserve their economic status quo with disregard for those least among us. As King prophetically declared:

> The time has come for an all-out word war against poverty. The rich nations must use their vast resources of wealth to develop the underdeveloped, school the unschooled and feed the unfed. The well-off and the secure have too often become indifferent and oblivious to the poverty and deprivation in their midst. [...] Ultimately a great nation is a compassionate nation. No individual or nation can be great if it does not have a concern for "the least of these."[20]

King knew the United States, as the richest nation in the world, has not met its moral and economic obligations and its responsibilities to the poor. Neither the Christian churches in the United States nor those abroad, have done enough to address this moral and spiritual crisis. As King stated:

> As long as there is poverty in the world I can never be rich, even if I have a million dollars. [...] I can never be what I ought to be until you are what you ought to be. This is the way our world is made. No individual or nation can stand out boasting of being independent. We are interdependent. [...][21]

However, in March 1968, King was sent to Memphis, Tennessee, to support the sanitation workers who were receiving low salaries and were demanding more fair wages so they could raise their families well. After the mayor of the city had declined their proposals, King went to Memphis giving his full support for the garbage collectors in Tennessee. He advocated for a true revolution of spiritual and economic values to tackle the moral issue of poverty. In his view, all American workers should be paid adequate wages if we want to make the United States a great compassionate nation. According to King, all work and labor have dignity in the eyes of God. He further said:

> There is nothing except shortsightedness to prevent us from guaranteeing an annual minimum—and livable—income for every American family. [...] This kind of positive

---

19　Frady, Marshall: *Martin Luther King, Jr.; A Life*. Penguin Book: New York 2006, p. 168.
20　King, Martin Luther Jr.: *Where Do We Go from Here: Chaos or Community?* Harper & Row: New York 1967, p. 178.
21　King, Martin Luther Jr.: *The Measure of Man*. Fortress Press: Minneapolis, MN 2001, pp. 45–46.

revolution of values is our best defense against Communism. [...] We must with affirmative action seek to remove those conditions of poverty, insecurity and injustice which are the fertile soil in which the seed of Communism grows and develops.[22]

Unfortunately, King was assassinated in Memphis while he was bearing witness to the racial and economic injustices. These were caused by the bad policies promulgated by those white racists working against hundreds of sanitation workers, who were exercising their right to go on strike by demanding better and fair salaries. African Americans were tired of being treated as second-class citizens. They stood up with signs demanding to be treated with more respect—respect resulting from the simple fact that they were human beings, created in the image and likeness of God. It was stressed that human dignity was an integral part of the biblical teachings found in the Gospels. Moreover, this concept could also be found in the spirit of the Declaration of Emancipation and in the Jeffersonian proclamation of liberty, justice, and the pursuit of happiness for all American citizens.

King's Prophetic Mysticism Stance Against Militarism and the War in Vietnam

Before his speech at Riverside, King had planned to denounce the war in Vietnam, and eventually, in order to satisfy his morals and hold true to his integrity, he began openly criticizing it, despite the ire that came. Notably:

> Martin Luther King's public opposition to the Vietnam War was more continuous with his early internationalism and more radical [...]. The conventional story runs that King suddenly called for unconditional negotiations with the DRV and NLF in August 1965 but backed down under a storm of criticism. He struggled with his conscience until the winter of 1967, when he could "remain silent" no longer. Then in a famous address to Riverside Church in New York in April, he boldly denounced U.S. "aggression" in Southeast Asia. These are the milestones of the story, but King's critiques of militarism and imperialism and his identification with anticolonial movements were longstanding, and King was hardly "silent" in 1966. Over the course of 1965, King increasingly had argued that U.S. intervention unacceptably risked nuclear war. He also argued that the United States was not exploiting diplomatic avenues for nonviolent resolution. War crippled civil liberties at home when dissenters were smeared with the red paint of disloyalty, he said. King had long maintained that it was hypocritical to ask black Americans to fight for freedom abroad when they were forced into second-class citizenship at home.[23]

---

22 King, Martin Luther Jr.: *Where Do We Go from Here: Chaos or Community?* Harper & Row: New York 1967, p. 189.
23 Jackson, Thomas F.: *From Civil Rights to Human Rights: Martin Luther King, Jr., and the Struggle for Economic Justice*. University of Pennsylvania Press: Philadelphia 2013, p. 309.

At first, King chose not to begin arguing against the war, on account of the criticism, and the advice of those close to him who insisted that he would stop before he begins. If he had chosen to start defying it in 1965, it is possible that he may have backed down and never fully committed later, but by waiting until 1967, King gained the moral courage he needed to thoroughly commit to the anti-war effort. This meant that he was able to stay true to his spiritual principles and political ideals. Additionally, "[h]e spoke of how the War was draining resources away from antipoverty programs while at the same time sending droves of poor Americans to their death, of how segregation and war were both poisoning America's soul."[24] As the war began heating up toward the later end of the 1960s, King began to see how it was affecting the United States domestically. In particular, King realized how the war was ruining the social programs that were intended to help those in need, and also detracting attention from the civil rights movement, meaning that continued segregation was given more time to solidify and strengthen. Because of the international issues that he was beginning to recognize, I think that King came to realize that if the problems of racism, poverty, and war were not seen as interrelated problems, then they could not solve domestic issues. Moreover, King's remarks betrayed at times a sense of bitterness by holding a radical vision rooted in a revolution of values that had not been present in the first ten years of his public career. Certain occasions clearly reflected King's mature realization that what he understood as his God-given mission required him to speak the Truth no matter what the personal costs and suffering.[25] Part of the motivation that helped compel King through the civil rights movement hails from his experiential faith and his belief that he must speak out against immoral acts: not just as a man attempting to end racism and bring unity, but as a preacher, whose very occupation deals with serving God as well as possible. Because of his prophetic faith, I argue that King felt compelled to speak against the Vietnam War, alongside his other reasons, and by actually denouncing the immorality of this war, King proved that he was willing to stay committed to his faith, even with the dangers that come from speaking out against a war, especially one that was still happening at the time. His prophetic denunciations against the U.S. involvement in the war in Vietnam are spelled out in the following passage:

> [...] This business of burning human beings with napalm, of filling our nation's homes with orphans and widows, of injecting poisonous drugs of hate into the veins of peoples normally humane, of sending men home from dark and bloody battlefields physically handicapped and psychologically deranged, cannot be reconciled with wisdom,

---

24 Patel, Eboo: "Martin Luther King Jr. and the Light of Other Faiths." *CrossCurrents* 63 (3), 2013, pp. 270–275, retrieved 10.10.2022, from https://doi.org/10.1111/cros.12032.
25 Garrow, David J.: "Martin Luther King, Jr. and the Cross of Leadership." *Peace & Change* 12 (1/2), 1987, retrieved 01.10.2022, from https://doi.org/10.1111/j.1468-0130.1987.tb00089.x.

justice and love. A nation that continues year after year to spend more money on military defense than on programs of social uplift is approaching spiritual death.[26]

King did not enjoy criticizing his government. He loved the United States deeply, particularly its democratic and religious traditions of equality and justice. But he could not overlook the great contradictions of racism, poverty, and militarism. For King there was no greater inconsistency between creed and deed than North America's military adventures in Vietnam.[27] Despite how much King treasured the United States of America, he still chose to stay committed, proving his integrity in his ideals. Rather than simply choosing to focus only on civil rights in the United States and forgetting the fighters on both sides who were suffering, King chose to acknowledge them and argued for why they should be considered—especially African American soldiers— and why the war effort should cease.

In spite of all of the arguments that were leveled against him by his allies, friends, enemies, and more, King spoke prophetically against the U.S. war in Vietnam. In order to prove his commitment to his ideals, King went forward with his defiance and I believe this is one major reason why he may have been killed. He directly addressed the problem of the military-industrial complex during the U.S. conflict in Vietnam, and with other witnesses in 1968 ("the year of the beast"), they seem to have posed a major threat to the status quo by raising their prophetic voices. We know many of them were either assassinated, arrested, or in the case of Thomas Merton censored and banned from publishing books on war and peace. As noted, King championed ideas such as nonviolence, and because of the success of his nonviolent protests, he earned the Nobel Peace Prize award. If King had chosen not to openly denounce the Vietnam War, I believe that he would have been remembered as a man who had only focused on African Americans and the United States and that his words about peace, love, and unity for all of humanity would not have had as strong an impact on society as they do now. Since King chose to denounce the Vietnam War, he proved that he would stay true to the ideals that brought him so far on his journey, including his own martyrdom.

Before explaining how exactly the fissure blew up, I will first examine how it started. Initially, King chose to begin defying the war in 1965, but by that point, "[o]n the strong advice of his colleagues, however, who presumed such a position would damage the civil rights movement, King subdued his public opposition to

---

26 King, Martin Luther Jr.: *Where Do We Go from Here: Chaos or Community?* Harper & Row: New York 1967, p. 188.
27 Cone, James H.: "Martin Luther King, Jr., and the Third World." *The Journal of American History* 74 (2), 1987, pp. 455–467, retrieved 20.09.2022, from www.jstor.org/stable/1900033.

the war until the early months of 1967 [...]."²⁸ Here, through King's decision to not tackle the debate of Vietnam openly until 1967, it is revealed that there were a substantial number of individuals and groups within the civil rights movement who did not wish him to begin openly opposing the war, such as the SCLC:

> [...] when King met with the SCLC board, he found its normally compliant members unsettled by the plan. Although the board recognised [sic] King's right to speak out against the war as an individual, the SCLC reaffirmed that its primary goal was the pursuit of "full citizenship rights for Negro citizens', and maintained that "resources are not sufficient to assume the burden of two major issues'. Nevertheless, King remained determined to pursue his letter-writing initiative, regardless of the board's reservations.²⁹

Likewise:

> Well-known civil rights leaders and other prominent blacks such as James Farmer, Director of the Congress of Racial Equality; Roy Wilkins of the National Association for the Advancement of Colored People; Whitney Young of the National Urban League; Ralph Bunche, former United Nations Undersecretary, Edward Brooke, Senator from Massachusetts; Carl T. Rowan, newspaper columnist; Jackie Robinson, then Special Assistant on Community Affairs to Governor Rockefeller of New York; and some members of SCLC were fearful that King's opposition would result in a loss of support for the civil rights movement.³⁰

Here, a common sentiment among supporters of the civil rights movement, but not the anti-war movement, appears, with the idea being that a significant number of activists did not wish to begin campaigning against the Vietnam War, because it would weaken the movement as a whole. Specifically, the movement would weaken, because, by overextending itself, the movement would not be able to make any significant progress as a whole, meaning that things such as segregation would continue to exist in the country. Individuals who supported the given sentiment wanted a unified front from the movement so that real change could occur in the United States. As a result, while his denunciation of the Vietnam War thrilled the Student Nonviolent Coordinating Committee (SNCC) and the Congress of Racial Equality (CORE)—which had come out against the war in 1966—it provoked a torrent of criticism from the liberal establishment. This included the "moderate" wing of the civil rights movement, consisting of the National Association for the

---

28 Sturm, Douglas: "Martin Luther King, Jr., as Democratic Socialist." *The Journal of Religious Ethics* 18 (2), 1990, pp. 79–105, retrieved 20.09.2022, from www.jstor.org/stable/40015109.
29 Kirk, John A.: *Martin Luther King Jr*. Routledge: New York 2013, p. 163.
30 Darby, Henry E./Rowley N., Margaret: "King on Vietnam and Beyond." *Phylon* 47 (1), 1986, pp. 43–50, retrieved 09.09.2022, from www.jstor.org/stable/274693.

Advancement of Colored People (NAACP), the National Urban League, and other pillars of the establishment. The NAACP distanced itself from King's speech and viewed the anti-war movement through a red communist prism. A few days after the Riverside speech, Gloster Current, NAACP Director of Branches urged the association to take measures to ensure that it is not perceived as a "tool of the international communist conspiracy."[31]

Due to King choosing to be fully engaged in the anti-war movement, he caused the widening fissure to gape significantly, causing factions to suddenly begin sprinting in different directions. Known groups with significant influence for the civil rights movement, such as the SNCC, CORE, and NAACP, were breaking away from each other, which, if it had become permanent, could have completely splintered the movement, and completely ruined it. I believe that if the movement had been destroyed as a result of King's choice, it would have had extremely negative consequences in the United States, leading to a period that would be defined by even more racial conflict and poverty. King's decision to campaign against the war had important ramifications for the movement. These ramifications are worth considering for the future—in the event that a new civil rights group finds itself in a similar situation. But ultimately, a modern prophet like King does not play with numbers or calculate the benefits or losses of his followers. As King himself stated, "[...] Ultimately a genuine leader is not a searcher for consensus but a molder of consensus."[32] King's moral courage prevailed, and it is in my humble opinion a testimony of his great faith in God being the ultimate companion in his pilgrimage to nonviolence.

King was assassinated while he was bearing witness to the social injustices caused by the city against hundreds of sanitation workers. One of King's mentors, Howard Thurman, thought that the roots of war and unnecessary violence was fear of the other. As Thurman said in his eulogy on Dr. King, "[...] it was this fear that pulled the trigger of the assassin's gun that took his life."[33] The tragic death of this great North American modern prophet brings us closer to a better understanding of King's spiritual and political legacy."

---

31 Lucks, Daniel S.: "Martin Luther King, Jr.'s Riverside Speech and Cold War Civil Rights." *Peace & Change* 40 (3), 2015, pp. 395–422, retrieved 15.09.2022, from https://doi.org/10.1111/pech.12136.
32 King, Martin Luther, Jr.: "Remaining Awake Through a Great Revolution." In: Carson, Clayborne/Peter Holloran (eds.): *A Knock at Midnight: Inspiration from the Great Sermons of Reverend Martin Luther King, Jr.* Warner Books: New York 2000, p. 221.
33 Thurman, Howard: *With Head and Heart.* Harcourt Brace Jovanovich, Publishers: New York 1979, p. 223.

Dr. Martin Luther King, Jr.'s Legacy

After King's death, he rose to the status of the greatest moral and spiritual leader of the civil rights movement. Before his assassination, King himself reminded his audience that all his life was an attempt to love and to serve humanity by following God's will. As a Christian, he felt his moral and spiritual duty was to serve God and to bring healing and reconciliation to all His children around the world. King could die at peace because he recognized that all the years dedicated to his passion for justice, peace, righteousness, and love were not in vain if he stayed true to his Christian faith message. As a historical figure, Martin Luther King Jr. holds a significant impact on the civil rights movement due to his choice on whether or not to openly criticize the war while at the same time continuing the social struggles against racism and poverty. Ultimately, King chose to denounce the war proving that he was fully committed to his ideals of nonviolence, truth, love, compassion, and unity.

Martin Luther King's method of nonviolent resistance which he learned from Gandhi, was built on love, understanding, and reconciliation. The Kingian method helped white Americans and other citizens to awaken their societal conscience against the oppression of African Americans by purposefully provoking outrageous violence against nonviolent demonstrations in the United States. The normative nature of King's nonviolent appeal enabled him to reach a broader white society, and he drew many of them to his side, especially after pointing their attention to the high level of oppression and brutality employed by the North American government against its own people. First, they saw it at home, and then they observed the tragedy of other people of color abroad (the war in Vietnam).

The popular discourse surrounding this period in history tends to frame King as a noble hero. This is a highly simplistic view of history, of course, and leaves almost no room to consider the humanness and complexity of this religious thinker and political activist. King was a flawed person with infamous lapses in character in his personal life. Also, he was considerably more radical compared to how he is often portrayed. King was not only deeply concerned with the economic and social inequities he found in the United States. He also spent the last year of his life working extremely hard toward ending the brutal and controversial war in Vietnam. He had thousands of activists working behind the scenes, including Rosa Parks and so many others. But King's major vision as a leader of the Movement provided a roadmap for all of them. He inspired millions of people at home and abroad to a revolution of values, hoping that his freedom struggles would bring massive relief to the racial and economic problems—problems that both people of color and poor whites would face on their daily basis. He was a firm believer in democracy or what he called "democratic socialism" because he saw it as a middle way of avoiding the extremes caught between a wild, ruthless capitalism and a totalitarian communist regime. After all, King's eschatological vision was deeply rooted in his Christian faith: God is able to bring a brighter future and hope to humanity if we as human beings cooperate and make God's dream a real possibility on earth by serving others and by putting this great cosmic Love into action as co-partners in the building of the "beloved community." As Luther D. Ivory remarkably put it:

> King acknowledged the presence of sin and evil in interpersonal relationships and corporate structures [...]. King identified those barriers as racism, poverty, and war. King consistently leveled radical, prophetic criticism against racially based, de jure and de facto segregation, poverty, militarism, and materialism. [...] King's communitarian ethic emphasized courageous action designed to remedy the impact of alienating oppressive policies and practices that worked to diminish freedom and deface the image of God in human personhood. Therefore, nothing less than a revolution of values and a radical restructuring of American society was required.[34]

On November 3, 1983, Congress voted to commemorate King's birthday on the third Monday in January as a national holiday and President Reagan finally signed the bill after his initial doubts. The King holiday bill was sponsored by Senator Ted Kennedy. However, it was not until June 7, 1999, that the Governor of New Hampshire, Jean Shaheen, signed the King holiday legislation into law, completing enactment of this national holiday in all states. New Hampshire was the last state to follow this official holiday in North America. Just two decades ago in South Carolina, the state House amended the King holiday bill to strip his name from it although on January 15, 2001, South Carolina officially joined the rest of the nation to commemorate Dr. King's Day. The King National Memorial near the mall was approved and finally opened to the public on August 22, 2011. This Memorial in D.C. includes the Stone of Hope craved by sculptor Lei Yixin. This fact, among others, proves to me that there are great signs of hope and progress based on race relations in America, and yet there are still huge differences based on social discrimination and economic gaps. There are also many unnecessary and unjust wars that have been fought in the last decades. For that very reason, the spiritual legacy of King seems to still be relevant in our own times. The three social evils in the United States are still present and affect not only North Americans but millions of people around the globe, as we have recently seen in the wars in Afghanistan and Iraq. The struggles against these three social evils continue today. I contend that today, Dr. King would have added to this list, the struggles against climate change and sexism as ecofeminist scholars such as Sallie McFague and Rosemary Ruether have done in their respective fields of knowledge. As Richard Deats has reported in his critique on King's short list of social evils:

> As prophetic and significant as King's call for a revolution of values was, he did not include among the interrelated evils that of sexism. Despite outstanding women in the movement—such as Rosa Parks, Coretta Scott King, Dorothy Cotton, Septima Clark,

---

34 Ivory, Luther D.: *Toward a Theology of Radical Involvement: The Theological Legacy of Martin Luther King, Jr.* Abingdon Press: Nashville 1997, pp. 142–143.

Ella Baker—on this issue King was a man of his time, who failed to evince a willingness to battle sexism as he did racism, classism and militarism [...]. Not only sexism but homophobia and environmental degradation would doubtless in time have come to be seen as evils intrinsic to what the New Testament scholar Walter Wink calls "the domination system."[35]

Nevertheless, King can be seen as a modern prophet who has planted the seeds of love and nonviolence all over the world. He was able to articulate in refreshing ways the intimate relationship that exists between spirituality and social justice through his deeds and words. His prophetic voice is even more urgent for us today because we are in the midst of great social, political, ecological, spiritual, and religious turmoil. It is my personal hope that this chapter will serve as a reminder of how much can be accomplished when one is truly committed to building the "beloved community" and how much work still needs to be done.

References

Colaiaco, James A.: *Martin Luther King, Jr.: Apostle of Militant Nonviolence*. MacMillan: London 1993.

Cone, James H.: "Martin Luther King, Jr., and the Third World." *The Journal of American History* 74 (2), 1987, pp. 455–467, retrieved 20.09.2021, from www.jstor.org/stable/1900033.

Darby, Henry E./Rowley N., Margaret: "King on Vietnam and Beyond." *Phylon* 47 (1), 1986, pp. 43–50, retrieved 09.09.2022, from www.jstor.org/stable/274693.

Deats, Richard: *Martin Luther King, Jr. Spirit-Led Prophet: A Biography*. New City Press: Hyde Park, NY 2003.

Frady, Marshall: *Martin Luther King, Jr.; A Life*. Penguin Book: New York 2006.

Garrow, David J.: "Martin Luther King, Jr. and the Cross of Leadership." *Peace & Change* 12 (1/2), 1987, retrieved 01.10.2022, from https://doi.org/10.1111/j.1468-0130.1987.tb00089.x.

Heschel, Susannah: "A Friendship in the Prophetic Tradition: Abraham Joshua Heschel and Martin Luther King, Jr." *Telos* 182, 2018.

Ivory, Luther D.: *Toward a Theology of Radical Involvement: The Theological Legacy of Martin Luther King, Jr.* Abingdon Press: Nashville 1997.

Jackson, Thomas F.: *From Civil Rights to Human Rights: Martin Luther King, Jr., and the Struggle for Economic Justice*. University of Pennsylvania Press: Philadelphia 2013.

---

35 Deats, Richard: *Martin Luther King, Jr. Spirit-Led Prophet: A Biography*. New City Press: Hyde Park, NY 2003, pp. 121–122.

Johnston, William: *The Inner Eye of Love: Mysticism and Religion*. Harper & Row: San Francisco 1982.

King, Martin Luther Jr.: *The Measure of Man*. Fortress Press: Minneapolis, MN 2001.

King, Martin Luther Jr.: "Pilgrimage to Nonviolence." In: James Melvin Washington (ed.): *A Testament of Hope: The Essential Writings and Speeches of Martin Luther King, Jr.* HarperSanFrancisco: San Francisco 1991.

King, Martin Luther Jr.: "The Poor People's Campaign." In: Carson, Clayborne (ed.): *The Autobiography of Martin Luther King, Jr.* Grand Central Publishing: New York 1998.

King, Martin Luther, Jr.: "Remaining Awake Through a Great Revolution." In: Carson, Clayborne Peter Holloran (eds.): *A Knock at Midnight: Inspiration from the Great Sermons of Reverend Martin Luther King, Jr.* Warner Books: New York 2000.

King, Martin Luther Jr.: *Strength to Love*. Fortress Press: Philadelphia 1988.

King, Martin Luther Jr.: *Where Do We Go from Here: Chaos or Community?* Harper & Row: New York 1967.

King, Martin Luther, Jr.: *Why We Can't Wait*. Harper & Row: New York 1964.

Kirk, John A.: *Martin Luther King Jr.* Routledge: Oxfordshire 2013.

Lucks, Daniel S.: "Martin Luther King, Jr.'s Riverside Speech and Cold War Civil Rights." *Peace & Change* 40 (3), 2015, pp. 395–422, retrieved 15.09.2022, from https://doi.org/10.1111/pech.12136.

Macy, Howard R.: "Intersections Between Martin Luther King Jr. and the Quakers." *Quaker Religious Thought* 103 (2), 2004, pp. 7–14, retrieved 01.10.2023, from https://digitalcommons.georgefox.edu/qrt/vol103/iss1/2.

Patel, Eboo: "Martin Luther King Jr. and the Light of Other Faiths." *CrossCurrents* 63 (3), 2013, pp. 270–275, retrieved 10.10.2022, from https://doi.org/10.1111/cros.12032.

Shire, Michael J.: *The Jewish Prophet: Visionary Words from Moses and Miriam to Henrietta Szold and A.J. Heschel*. Jewish Lights Publishing: Woodstock, VT 2001.

Sturm, Douglas: "Martin Luther King, Jr., as Democratic Socialist." *The Journal of Religious Ethics* 18 (2), 1990, pp. 79–105, retrieved 20.09.2022, from www.jstor.org/stable/40015109.

Thurman, Howard: *With Head and Heart*. Harcourt Brace Jovanovich: New York 1979.

Michael McLaughlin

Cooking Up the Revolution: The Black Panthers, Church Kitchens, and the Place of Religion in the Black Power Movement

Abstract: This chapter uses historical newspapers to present a lived history of the Oakland, California-based Black Panther Party. Placing in conversation religious studies and Black Power studies, and centering the Black Panther's Free Breakfast for Schoolchildren Program, this chapter considers the interactions between Black Panther Party members and the various church communities who proved vital to the Breakfast Program. This chapter argues that the Black Panthers influenced church communities, and that, by offering space and support to the Black Panthers, churches themselves played a crucial role in the survival and expansion of the Black Panther Party. Within church buildings, the Black Panthers and their Christian supporters constructed worlds that challenged the presumed dichotomies of religion and politics, Christianity and Marxism, and Civil Rights and Black Power. The sanctuary provided by churches was always incomplete, yet, despite harassment by law enforcement agents, the Black Panthers' revolutionary legacy survived in the children fed and lives transformed by the Breakfast Program.

Keywords: Black Panther Party, Black Power, Civil Rights, religion, history

Introduction

On April 3, 1968, members of the Black Panther Party were holding their regular Wednesday evening meeting when they heard several police cars pulling up outside the building where they were gathered, St. Augustine's Episcopal Church in Oakland, California. Black Panther Chief of Staff, David Hilliard, who was conducting the meeting, grabbed the pastor of the church, Rev. Earl A. Neil, on his way to the church doors. Outside, Hilliard and Neil encountered twenty Oakland police officers seeking entry to the building, claiming a drunken man with a gun was inside. Rev. Neil later recounted the experience this way,

> David [Hilliard] and I went to the door of the church and were greeted with the sight of approximately ten police cruisers, two officers to a car, with shotguns held at the ready, and a sergeant and another officer demanding to enter the church. We told them that a private meeting was in progress, that police were not welcome, and that guns were not allowed in the meeting. However, if they would provide a description

we would search for the man and hand him over to them. After a period of verbal stand off, a captain arrived and following a firm discussion with him, the police left.[1]

The Panthers planned a press conference to address this instance of police harassment; however, this never took place as Martin Luther King Jr. was assassinated the following day, and two days after that, Oakland police officers shot and killed Black Panther Bobby Hutton and wounded Eldridge Cleaver. While the story of the Oakland police department's attempted raid on St. Augustine's has been largely overlooked in the historical record, this chapter centers such moments to offer a history of how churches served as spaces where the Black Panthers survived and thrived.

The story of the attempted police raid on St. Augustine's brings up three themes explored within this chapter. First is the fact that the Black Panthers built partnerships with churches in the cities where they operated. These collaborations emerged from the Panthers' search for functional spaces for their free breakfast program, yet grew into strategic partnerships. Second, the fact that Rev. Neil, as a priest, stood between the Panthers and the police seems to have prevented a significant instance of police violence toward the Panthers. This chapter explores the limits of churches as sanctuaries from state-sanctioned violence and repression. Finally, this chapter considers how churches served as spaces where the Panthers worked with their community to both recognize the awesome disjoint between how society treated them as Black people and what they knew themselves to be as agentive humans, and to orient their lives in response to that realization.[2] Here I draw on Charles H. Long's understanding of religion as "orientation in the ultimate sense, that is, how one comes to terms with the ultimate significance of one's place in the world."[3] With Long as a guide, I consider how church kitchens, as spaces where the Panthers brought together Party members, community volunteers, and religious supporters to serve free breakfasts, became places where the Black Panthers re-oriented the lives of many in their community toward a radical critique of racial capitalism enacted through a commitment to building infrastructure that supports the basic needs of oppressed people.

Moving Breakfast to the Center of Panther Historiography

Two young Black men Huey Newton and Bobby Seale founded the Black Panther Party for Self-Defense in October 1966, in Oakland, California. Newton and Seale

---

1 Dale, Adrianne: "Earl A. Neil, African American Civil Rights Reformer: A Profile." *Anglican and Episcopal History* 75 (1), 2006, p. 84.
2 Long, Charles H.: *Significations: Signs, Symbols, and Images in the Interpretation of Religion*. Fortress Press: Minneapolis, MN 1986, p. 170.
3 Long, Charles: *op. cit.*, p. 7.

worked with the "brothers off the block" to organize their community against the brutal harassment of the Oakland Police Department by conducting armed patrols in which Panthers would sousveil the police.[4] With a gun in one hand and a law book in the other, the Panthers confronted police officers as they harassed and infringed upon the rights of Black Oakland residents. Despite the legality of the Panther's armed patrols, white California voters and their elected officials saw the Panthers' armed community patrols as a threat, and in May 1967, Governor Ronald Reagan signed a bill banning the open carrying of firearms within city limits. Thirty Panthers drove to Sacramento to protest this bill and their armed, yet legal, protest at the State Capitol drew the attention of the national public as well as the Federal Bureau of Investigation (FBI).[5]

Over the next few years, as Party chapters sprang up across the United States and membership grew rapidly, peaking at about 5,000 in 1969, the Black Panthers faced increasing repression from the FBI, which would ultimately dismember the Party.[6] In 1969, under the leadership of Party Chairman Bobby Seale and Chief of Staff David Hilliard, the Black Panthers began implementing a series of programs, including the Free Breakfast for Schoolchildren program, that came to be known as "survival programs." Through these programs, the Panthers turned their energy from instigating revolution to what Huey Newton called "survival pending revolution." By 1971 the FBI had generated a split within the Party between chapters who agreed with Newton's embrace of social democracy and those who aligned with Cleaver's insistence on revolutionary violence.[7] The following year Newton consolidated what was left of the Party to Oakland, where the Panthers remained focused on service work and electoral politics for its final decade. Two themes run throughout this history: the Panthers' fight for liberation, and their care for their

---

4   Murch, Donna Jean: *Living for the City. Migration, Education, and the Rise of the Black Panther Party in Oakland, California.* University of North Carolina Press: Chapel Hill 2010, pp. 126–127; Simone Browne builds on Steve Mann's definition of the term *sousveillance*: "observing and recording by an entity not in a position of power or authority over the subject of the veillance." Browne, Simone: *Dark Matters. On the Surveillance of Blackness.* Duke University Press: Durham, NC 2015, p. 19.

5   Bloom, Joshua/Waldo E. Martin: *Black Against Empire. The History and Politics of the Black Panther Party.* University of California Press: Berkeley 2016, pp. 58–61.

6   In their extensive history of the Black Panther Party, Bloom and Martin argue that FBI repression actually helped increase membership in the Black Panther Party. Navid Farnia argues that Bloom and Martin do not simply deviate from the standard historiography which centers the harm caused by the FBI, but also are historically incorrect. Farnia, Navid: "State Repression and the Black Panther Party: Analyzing Joshua Bloom and Waldo E. Martin's *Black Against Empire*." *Journal of African American Studies* 21, 2017, pp. 172–179.

7   Murch, Donna Jean: *op. cit.*, pp. 186–188; Farnia, Navid: *op. cit.*, p. 177.

own survival. This chapter traces the development of the breakfast program which fused these two threads.⁸

The history of the Panthers is often told as a declension narrative with the Party sliding from its early peak of public displays of armed self-defense and rhetoric supporting guerrilla warfare to mainstream, reform-minded electoral politics as Party members are killed, imprisoned, exiled, or expelled. Rather than understanding the history of the Black Panther Party in terms of chapters opened or closed and members gained or lost, this chapter positions the Black Panthers as emerging from, and remaining in relationship with, their broader social networks. In particular, this chapter builds on historian Akinyele Omowale Umoja's call to expand historical analysis of the Panthers beyond the official Party structure to trace the impact of the Party on others who were shaped by their work.⁹ Consequently, this chapter approaches the Black Panthers as an ever-evolving assemblage of people, ideas, firearms, houses, pamphlets, alliances, hungry schoolchildren, supportive Christian ministers, dedicated neighborhood mothers, newspapers, money, hope, and survival. By centering churches and the breakfast program, this chapter decenters the violence that did occur between the Panthers and law enforcement and instead considers the world created and envisioned by the Black Panthers. This is not to ignore the horrors and trauma of police violence against the Panthers, which, as Charles Austin shows, played a critical role in the Panthers' history.¹⁰ Rather, I build on the social historical work of scholars like Donna Jean Murch to center what Katherine McKittrick calls "iterations of black life that cannot be contained by black death."¹¹ By positioning the Panthers as an open movement of people, objects, organizations, and ideas evolving within a complex sea of Black, and non-Black, radical movements, that drew to it Black women and others in

---

8   Gayraud S. Wilmore argued that the survival, elevation, and liberation "strands of black religion and culture ... coalesced in the black power movement." While the Black Power movement included groups more concerned with racial uplift than the Black Panthers were, the Panthers nevertheless synthesized the survival and liberation traditions. Wilmore, Gayraud S.: *Black Religion and Black Radicalism. An Interpretation of the Religious History of African Americans*. 3rd ed. Orbis Books: Maryknoll, NY 1998, pp. 253–281.

9   Umoja, Akinyele Omowale: "Repression Breeds Resistance: The Black Liberation Army and the Radical Legacy of the Black Panther Party." In: Kathleen Cleaver/ George Katsiaficas (eds.): *Liberation, Imagination, and the Black Panther Party: A New Look at the Panthers and Their Legacy*. Routledge: New York 2001, pp. 3–4.

10 Austin, Curtis J.: *Up Against the Wall: Violence in the Making and Unmaking of the Black Panther Party*. University of Arkansas Press: Fayetteville 2006.

11 McKittrick, Katherine: "Mathematics Black Life." *The Black Scholar: Journal of Black Studies and Research* 44 (2), 2014, p. 20.

search of a place in the revolutionary struggle, it becomes possible to trace how the Black Panthers re-oriented the lives of people in their communities.[12]

By centering the Panthers' partnerships with churches, this chapter illuminates how religion continued, albeit in changing ways, to play key roles in Black political organizing following the successes of the civil rights movement. While Black American Christianity provided much of the institutional and ideological infrastructure for the struggles against Jim Crow and voter restrictions in the Southern United States, by the end of the 1960s many Black churches withdrew from direct political organizing. Anthony Pinn laments this turn toward a greater focus on individual salvation and notes that while some Black Christian leaders, like James Cone, continued to connect theology and politics, they did so at an intellectual level and were not able to wield the institutional strength of denominational bodies.[13] Still, the Black Panthers' collaborations with churches show how individual ministers, Black and white, continued to connect their understanding of Christianity to the Black Panthers' radical politics, often despite the desires of their denomination's white leadership.

The Panthers' legacy encourages scholars to reconsider assumptions about the role of religion in Black political organizing. The urban and ostensibly secular Black Panthers are often contrasted with the Southern, Christian-led civil rights movement. Pinn considers the civil rights movement exceptional in how it "developed a persistent and collective cooperation" among religious leaders.[14] Yet as scholars like Barbara Dianne Savage point out, religion held a multifaceted and contested place in the civil rights movement with many participants in Southern actions seeing religion as a marginal aspect of their own identity, yet experiencing churches as "safe havens" for organizing.[15] Further north, the Black Panthers found churches to be crucial, if unanticipated, sanctuaries for their revolutionary work. Scholars like Jeffrey O.G. Ogbar, Joseph Peniel, and Donna Jean Murch point to how the Black Panther Party developed within a dynamic sea of Black Power organizations, and this chapter places churches as key contributors to this milieu.[16]

---

12 Cleaver, Kathleen: "Women, Power and Revolution." In: Kathleen Cleaver/George Katsiaficas (eds.): *Liberation, Imagination, and the Black Panther Party. A New Look at the Panthers and Their Legacy*. Routledge: New York 2001, p. 2.
13 Pinn, Anthony: *The Black Church in the Post-Civil Rights Era*. Orbis Press: Maryknoll, NY 2002, pp. 14–24.
14 Pinn, Anthony: *op. cit.*, p. 13.
15 Savage, Barbara Dianne: *Your Spirits Walk Beside Us: The Politics of Black Religion*. Harvard University Press: Cambridge, MA 2008, pp. 249–252.
16 Ogbar, Jeffrey O.G.: *Black Power: Radical Politics and African American Identity*. Johns Hopkins University Press: Baltimore 2004; Joseph, Peniel H.: *Waiting 'Til the Midnight Hour: A Narrative History of Black Power in America*. Holt: New York 2006; Murch, Donna Jean: *op. cit.*

Getting Breakfast Started

The Black Panthers' breakfast program emerged out of relationships the Panthers built with community members and their pragmatic search for spaces to hold Party functions. One woman from the Oakland community, Ruth Beckford, connected the Panthers with their strongest church ally and also proved crucial to jumpstarting the free breakfast program. Known as the "Mother of Black Dance," Beckford taught Afro-Haitian dance classes in Oakland, and one of her students, LaVerne Williams, was Huey Newton's girlfriend. When Newton was arrested on October 28, 1967, Beckford showed her support of Newton by attending his court hearings. A parishioner at St. Augustine's Episcopal Church, Beckford brought along her pastor and told him that Newton would appreciate if he would visit him in prison.[17] Her pastor, Rev Earl A. Neil, arrived in Oakland in 1967, bringing with him his experiences with Black political organizing and Black self-defense gained during the Mississippi Freedom Summer.[18] Neil began meeting regularly with Newton in prison, and quickly became referred to publicly as Newton's "spiritual adviser."[19] In January 1968 Earl Neil met David Hilliard at a Free Huey rally and learned from him that the Panthers were looking for a regular meeting space. Neil offered the use of his church, and after informing his parish stakeholders of his "action and ... authority" to allow the Panthers to meet at the church, the Black Panthers began regularly meeting on Wednesday evenings and Saturday afternoons at St. Augustine's.[20]

Ruth Beckford was also crucial to the development of the Free Breakfast program. A generation older than most Panthers and a mother figure to "hundreds of young girls" in Oakland, Beckford joined the Black Panthers' newly created Community Advisory Board in 1968 and even sewed them curtains for their new

---

17 Dale, Adrianne: *op. cit.*, p. 83.
18 Raised in the historically Black Rondo neighborhood of St. Paul, Minnesota, as a young priest, Earl Neil contributed to the Mississippi Freedom Summer of 1964 conducting citizenship classes in McComb, Mississippi, where White people bombed or burned forty-eight homes and churches over the course of summer. While in McComb, Neil realized how his daily work was defended by a network of armed locals who kept their community safe. Dale, Adrianne: *op. cit.*, pp. 77–80. Historian Charles Cobb notes: "By September 1964, McComb's black community had begun to take on some of the characteristics of a military camp, with armed patrols protecting homes, businesses, and churches—although even these patrols could not always stop the violence." Cobb, Charles E. Jr.: *This Nonviolent Stuff'll Get You Killed. How Guns Made the Civil Rights Movement Possible*. Duke University Press: Durham, NC 2014, p. 144.
19 Greenlee, Rush: "Newton's Dad: Guilty? That's a Fool Question." *Oakland Tribune*, August 6, 1968, p. 6.
20 Dale, Adrianne: *op. cit.*, pp. 83–84.

office on Grove Avenue.[21] The idea for the Free Breakfast program emerged during a meeting between Panther leadership and the Community Advisory Board in the Fall of 1968 as the Party was seeking ways to institute discipline among its many members.[22] Once she heard about the idea for the Breakfast program, Beckford volunteered to take the lead in organizing it. Beckford approached Rev. Neil about hosting the program and consulted with nutritionists and local health department officials to ensure they were developing a healthy program. After publishing a call for volunteers in the Black Panthers' newspaper, Beckford, Rev. Neil, and the Panthers began hosting breakfasts at St. Augustine's in January 1969. Eleven children arrived on the first Monday of the program, and by Friday, 135 children came.

The Free Breakfast program quickly became the Black Panthers' central programming focus. In April 1969 Bobby Seale ordered all chapters to institute a Free Breakfast program,[23] and with the start of the new school year that fall, the Free Breakfast program expanded to twenty-two cities and fed more hungry children in California than the federal government did.[24] In order to expand this program, the Panthers needed spaces to prepare and serve meals to large groups. Consequently, Black Panthers began connecting with local churches, as many had kitchens that were not otherwise being utilized on weekday mornings.

---

21 The Community Advisory Board consisted of ten members, five of whom were parishioners at St. Augustine's, Dale, Adrianne: *op. cit.*, p. 86; Murch, Donna Jean: *op. cit.*, p. 137; The Community Advisory Board was established in 1968 during the Free Huey Movement, Alkebulan, Paul: *Survival Pending Revolution. The History of the Black Panther Party.* University of Alabama Press: Tuscaloosa 2007, p. 30; Beckford, Ruth: "Interview with Dancer and Performer Ruth Beckford." Interview by Rick Moss, August 7, 2007, retrieved 02.10.2021, from https://californiarevealed.org/islandora/object/cavpp%3A23090. In this interview Beckford connects her decision not to have children to her disinterest in playing with dolls as a child. Her father, a Garveyite, ordered Black dolls to be mailed from New York to Oakland so that his daughters could play with Black dolls. Ruth says she gave her dolls to her sister, who did have children of her own.

Ula Taylor describes this praxis as "community feminism," which she defines as "activism ... focused on assisting both the men and women in their lives ... along with initiating and participating in activities to uplift their communities." Taylor, Ula Y.: "'Negro Women Are Great Thinkers as well as Doers': Amy Jacques-Garvey and Community Feminism in the United States, 1924–1927." *Journal of Women's History* 12 (2), 2000, pp. 104–126, 105.

22 Alkebulan, Paul: *op. cit.*, p. 30; Murch, Donna Jean: *op. cit.*, p. 174.

23 "To Feed Our Children." *Black Panther*, April 27, 1969, p. 3.

24 "Unruh: Panthers Feed More Than the Government." *Fresno Bee*, May 10, 1969, p. 5B.

Bringing People to the Breakfast Table

Not all churches were willing to work with the Black Panthers. In October 1969, Marsha Lovelle Turner, the National Director of the Panther's Free Breakfast program,[25] published an article describing her and her comrades' experiences visiting different churches in the San Francisco Black community and being "treated like hoodlums, like gangsters" by various pastors who refused to allow the Panthers to use their facilities. Turner's article details visits to St. Agnes Catholic Church, First Institutional Friendship Baptist Church, and All Saints Episcopal Church, all located in the Haight-Ashbury area which was, at the time, both largely Black and the center of the San Francisco counter-culture. Outing the pastors of these churches as hypocrites who refused to care for the hungry children outside their doors, Turner called on these pastors to "follow more of the people's example and relate to concrete examples by the people, other than baptizing [San Francisco Mayor Joseph] Alioto and his band of merry hoods." Quoting Matthew 7:9–10, Turner told these pastors, "I'm sure the children of the Black community hope you burn in hell, and that your congregation wakes up to the fact that you are disinterested in them and the community, most of all hungry children."[26]

Despite the rudeness of such "pig pastors," the Panthers did build lasting relationships with at least forty churches across the country. These churches represented a variety of denominational and racial identities, and their support of Panther programs ranged from churches serving as gathering spots for the Panther's Free Busing to Prison program, to hosting press conferences, to, most commonly, providing space for the Free Breakfast Program.[27] Indeed, as historian of the Black Power era, Donna Jean Murch, argues, "Panther community programs would have been impossible without the support of local churches."[28] Through their collaborations with churches across the country, the Panthers fed thousands of children, strengthened their Party, and oriented their broader community toward a socialist world where the people's needs are met.

Some community members found their participation in the breakfast program life-changing. In 1969, Safiya Bukhari, a young Black woman from a middle-class

---

25　Nielsen, Euell A.: "Marsha Lovelle Turner Taylor (1953–1977)." *BlackPast*, April 25, 2020, retrieved 03.10.2021, from https://www.blackpast.org/african-american-history/marsha-lovelle-turner-taylor-1953-1977/.

26　Marsha [Lovette Turner]: "Feeding Hungry Children vs. Men of the Cloth." *The Black Panther*, October 25, 1969, p. 8.

27　See, for example, "Free Busing to Prisons Program." *Black Panther*, October 21, 1972, p. 12; John Seale, "Fighting for Right." *Black Panther*, November 8, 1969, p. 5; I am deeply grateful to Amy Alonso and Elizabeth Moraga who, through their work with Florida State University's Undergraduate Research Opportunity Program, compiled this list.

28　Murch, Donna Jean: *op. cit.*, p. 172.

family, was a college sophomore at City College in New York City with hopes of being a doctor. Having recently pledged a sorority, Bukhari went with her sorority sisters to serve "disadvantaged" children in "the ghettoes of New York." They connected with one of the Black Panthers' free breakfasts in the city, and even though Bukhari did not originally "get into the politics of the Black Panther Party, [...] [she] could volunteer to feed some hungry children." Bukhari developed a daily routine of waking up at 5 a.m. to serve breakfasts, bringing her young daughter with her. Weeks into this routine Bukhari asked one of the Panthers why the number of children attending had begun to trail off, and learned that the police had been spreading rumors that the Panther breakfast served poisoned food. Soon afterward Bukhari found herself arrested for the first time after challenging a police officer harassing a Panther who was selling the Party's newspaper. Realizing she had to make a decision about what sort of approach she would adopt toward the injustice she was experiencing, Bukhari went down to the Harlem Panther headquarters to become an official member. She would go on to lead her own section of the Harlem branch, become a prominent member of the East Coast Panthers following the 1971 schism, and eventually joined the Black Liberation Army being one of its few members who remained aboveground.[29] While not everyone who volunteered at the Panthers' breakfasts went from sorority sister to armed revolutionary, Bukhari's story illustrates the ways Panther breakfasts could reorient volunteers' lives by helping them navigate their experiences of oppression in ways that led toward Black flourishing.

The FBI Attempts to Spoil Breakfast

As the Panthers expanded their Free Breakfast program across the country, the FBI Director distributed an internal memo warning the Panthers would use their breakfast program to indoctrinate children in "anti-white proPagánda."[30] Working with churches did not guarantee that the Panther breakfasts would survive FBI's harassment. The San Diego chapter's breakfast was one such breakfast undone by FBI repression. Shortly after the Panthers began hosting breakfast at Christ the King Catholic Church, FBI agents posing as parishioners called Auxiliary Bishop John R. Quinn to express their displeasure with their pastor's decision to support the Panthers with two agents demanding he be removed as pastor and a third

---

29 Bukhari-Alston, Safiya: "Coming of Age: A Black Revolutionary, 1979." In: Joy James (ed.): *Imprisoned Intellectuals: America's Political Prisoners Write on Life, Liberation, and Rebellion*. Rowman and Littlefield: Lanham, MD 2003, pp. 125–134.
30 Church, Frank, et al.: "Supplementary Detailed Staff Reports on Intelligence Activities and the Rights of Americans. Book III. Final Report of the Select Committee to Study Governmental Operations with Respect to Intelligence Activities." April 23, 1976, p. 210.

threatening to withhold financial assistance. Bishop Quinn transferred the pastor to New Mexico the following month, and Christ the King stopped hosting Panther breakfasts.[31] Still, in the face of repression, some Panther chapters and their pastor supporters did continue to serve children breakfast. At Sacred Heart Catholic Church in San Francisco, Father Eugene Boyle stood with the Panthers despite threats to his job and life.[32]

Sacred Heart was located in the historically Black Western Addition neighborhood of San Francisco.[33] Father Boyle was a middle-aged Irish American priest who, building on the momentum from the Second Vatican council, believed the Church should be deeply involved with struggles for social and racial justice.[34] In the summer of 1968, Boyle joined the "Urban Team" at Sacred Heart and entered a parish whose existing leadership, particularly Sister Margaret Cafferty, had already built strong connections with the surrounding Black community. In fact, Sr. Cafferty arranged for Black Panther Communications Secretary, Kathleen Cleaver, to proclaim offertory prayers during Fr. Boyle's installation Mass.[35] When the Black Panthers, having been rejected by several nearby Protestant churches, reached out to him about hosting a San Francisco location for their breakfast program,

---

31 Church, Frank, et al.: *op. cit.*, pp. 210–211.
32 "S.F. Breakfast Program." *Black Panther*, November 29, 1969, p. 15.
33 The Western Addition, which had been racially mixed, and largely Japanese prior to Japanese Internment, became one of the few areas of San Francisco where Black migrants from the South found landlords willing to rent to Black people. By the 1960s, the Western Addition was one of the centers of Black life in San Francisco and faced the urban renewal efforts of city hall. Kamiya, Gary: "Western Addition: A Basic History." *Found SF*, retrieved 14.09.2021, from https://www.foundsf.org/index.php?title=Western_Addition:_A_Basic_History. Sacred Heart closed in 2004 and is now a roller rink called Church of eight Wheels. Jones, Carolyn: "Old Sacred Heart Church Site Now a Roller-skating Sanctuary." *SF Gate*, April 3, 2014, retrieved 03.10.2021, from https://www.sfgate.com/bayarea/article/Old-Sacred-Heart-Church-site-now-a-roller-skating-5375104.php.
34 More specifically, Boyle threw his support behind Cesar Chavez and the United Farm Workers, protested against the 1964 repeal of California's fair-housing laws, and taught a class of seminarians who published a "little Kerner Report" which applied the findings of the national Kerner Report to the local context of San Francisco. In 1974 he ran unsuccessfully for the California assembly. Burns, Jeffrey M.: "Eugene Boyle, the Black Panther Party and the New Clerical Activism." *U.S. Catholic Historian* 13 (3), 1995, pp. 137–158, 137, 143–149, 157.
35 Harper, Sabrina M.S.: "Jesus Says, 'Power to the People': The Sacred Heart Church Urban Team, 1968–1972," retrieved 02.10.2021, from https://www.smsharper.com/single-post/2020/04/28/jesus-says-power-to-the-people-the-sacred-heart-church-urban-team-1968-1972.

Fr. Boyle, with encouragement from Sr. Cafferty, agreed, and the Panthers began serving breakfast from Sacred Heart's basement kitchen on March 10, 1969.[36]

Weeks after Panther breakfasts started at Sacred Heart, the church received its first visit from local health inspectors. Father Boyle criticized this sudden attention noting, "Untold gallons of spaghetti and pounds of corned beef have passed through that kitchen, onto the plates of Sacred Heart's parishioners and never before had the Public Health Department poked into the refrigerator, checked the stove, or tested the heat of the dishwater." While local health officials adopted a laissez-faire approach to white people gathering together and sharing meals, or flouting state gambling laws by holding church bingo nights, the Public Health Department took notice when Black people gathered to share food.[37] Here the State employed its racialized surveillance system to make hyper-visible the ordinary acts of citizens racialized as Black.[38]

Several months later Father Boyle and the Black Panthers found themselves in a controversy regarding a coloring book allegedly distributed by Panthers to children at the free breakfast at Sacred Heart. The coloring book showed police officers as pigs, showed Black Panthers and Black children killing police officers, and included captions such as "the only good pig is a dead pig."[39] While only three coloring books appeared at a breakfast in late March, controversy erupted in late June when San Francisco Police Chief Ben Lashkoff presented the coloring book to the McClellan Senate committee hearing on "Riots, Civil and Criminal Disorders" as proof the breakfast program was a cover for anti-white and anti-police indoctrination.[40] While Lashkoff wielded this coloring book as evidence that the Black Panthers were instigating anti-police violence, the 1975 Senate Select Committee to Study Governmental Operations with Respect to Intelligence Activities revealed that this coloring book had in fact been designed and planted by FBI agents.[41] Father Boyle stood by the Panthers and refused to apologize for the coloring book.[42] In a press conference he held by himself in his office the day after the 1969 Senate hearing, Boyle described the coloring book as "allegedly given out by the Black Panthers," noting the "Black Panthers themselves indicate that they did not subscribe to this book, they deny that it was a book that they put out or that they

---

36 Harper, Sabrina M.S.: *op. cit.*; Burns, Jeffrey M.: *op. cit.*, p. 137.
37 Rev. Eugene J. Boyle, "An Open Letter." *Black Panther*, October 4, 1969, p. 7.
38 Browne, Simone: *op. cit.*, p. 79.
39 Harper notes this phrase was inspired by U.S. Army General and anti-Indigenous war leader, Philip Sheridan's quote, "the only good Indian is a dead Indian." Harper, Sabrina M.S.: *op. cit.*
40 Williams, Ben: "Father Boyle Discusses Free Breakfast Program." *KPIX*, June 25, 1969, retrieved 04.10.2021, from https://diva.sfsu.edu/collections/sfbatv/bundles/206988.
41 Church, Frank, et al.: *op. cit.*, p. 210.
42 Burns, Jeffrey M.: *op. cit.*, pp. 137–158, 152–154.

sanctioned, or that they okayed." Once Boyle saw the book, the Black Panthers running the breakfast "heeded" his "unequivocal" objection to the coloring book, which was never seen again at Sacred Heart. Perhaps most importantly, Boyle emphasized the Panthers' dedication to serving their community and stated, "[T]he coloring book does not square with our experience with members of the Black Panther Party."[43]

Father Boyle's decision to hold a press conference defending the Black Panthers illustrates how the Black Panthers' activism moved some progressive religious ministers more deeply into a commitment for racial justice. Following the April 28, 1969, raid by the San Francisco Police on the Black Panther's local headquarters, Fr. Boyle held a press conference with other religious leaders from the San Francisco Conference on Race, Religion, and Social Concerns[44] to demand the Mayor "act now" to create an "impartial Citizens Police-Community Relations Committee" that would "be independent and separate from the structure of the police department [...] [and would] develop the means to change the underlying conditions which have brought about today's crisis." While Mayor Alioto had praised groups other than the Panthers who worked with Black youth in the Western Addition, Fr. Boyle said he had talked to one youth leader who said, "The people who cooled the riot and kept it from erupting on Fillmore Street on Monday were the Black Panthers."[45] In addition to defending the Panthers, Boyle amplified their message. Boyle took government officials to task for studying the issue of hunger, instead of feeding children. In doing so he built upon the rhetoric of Panthers like Marsha Lovelle Turner, who declared the Panthers "believe in serving the people wholeheartedly, in a socialistic manner, not spending money like the U.S. to take hunger surveys."[46] For a white Catholic priest to publicly defend the Black Panthers to the press shows how the programs which the Panthers created shaped the lives of people beyond their party membership.

---

43 Williams. Ben: *op. cit.*; Kathleen Cleaver later testified that Bobby Seale also ordered this coloring book destroyed because it "did not correctly reflect the ideology of the Black Panther Party." Church, Frank, et al.: *op. cit.*, p. 210.
44 The Speakers included Father Boyle, Rabbi Saul White of Congregation Beth Sholom, Charles Golden, the Black American United Methodist Bishop for the San Francisco Area.
45 San Francisco Conference on Race, Religion, and Social Concerns: "Press Conference, Police Community Relations." *Archives of the Archdiocese of San Francisco*, 1969, retrieved 03.10.2021, from https://californiarevealed.org/islandora/object/cavpp%3A128478.
46 Marsha [Lovelle Turner]: "Serving the People." *Black Panther*, April 6, 1969, p. 14.

The Youth Make the Revolution

The free breakfast also shaped the lives of the children who enjoyed the free meals. One journalist who visited a Panther breakfast in a Harlem church basement described how the Panthers built "a pleasant oasis within the rampaging storm of the ghetto," creating space for "five-year-olds [...] [to] emit the laughter and cries which can only come from joyful children."[47] By creating spaces of Black joy, the Panthers offered hungry youth an opportunity to imagine, and experience, a world without hunger. In doing so they both sustained these children's bodies and ensured the next generation of Black children might understand, and embody, their socialistic vision of equitably shared resources. The Panthers stated that "the youth make the revolution," and their act of serving breakfast to tens of thousands of school children across the United States was one way to realize the revolution.

The Black Panthers placed the youth at the center of their work in ways that rooted social belonging in the community, not the nuclear family. On May 1, 1969, two Black Panthers, Shelly Sanders and Charles Bursey, got married in what the Black Panthers called a "revolutionary wedding." Those in attendance included both Party members as well as children "who attended the breakfast program." With children from the breakfast program witnessing their wedding ceremony, and "serenading" the couple with the revolutionary song "We want a pork chop, off the pig," the Panthers placed revolutionary marriage as a community commitment.[48]

The Party's coverage of the Sanders-Bursey revolutionary wedding also indicates how the Panthers understood their own relationship to religion. The notice about the wedding in Party's newspaper stated, "[T]he ceremony was performed at the Church of the Minister of Religion of the Black Panther Party, Father Earl Neil." Rather than saying the wedding took place at St. Augustine's Episcopal Church, which Father Neil pastored, the article proposed that for the time of the Sanders-Bursey revolutionary wedding, that space became something else; it became the Church of the Minister of Religion of the Black Panther Party. Marking the church as a sacred space, yet grounding this sacrality in the Black Panther Party, the Panthers enfolded Father Neil into their own work while also revealing their reliance upon St. Augustine's as a pragmatic space for people to gather and mark moments when their lives took new directions.

Like church buildings during the Mississippi Freedom Summer, religion became a necessary requirement for the Black Panther's revolution, not as a moral framework nor a mode of spiritual transcendence, but because it provided spaces for gathering, sharing, and distributing material needs.[49] Religion provided spaces

---

47 "Harlem Breakfast for School Children." *The Black Panther*, September 6, 1969, p. 19, reprinted from *The Daily World*, 23.08.1969.
48 "Black Panther Revolutionary Wedding." *The Black Panther*, May 11, 1969, p. 7.
49 Savage, Barbara Dianne: *Your Spirits Walk Beside Us. The Politics of Black Religion*. Harvard University Press: Cambridge, MA 2008, p. 241.

where the Black Panthers could imagine and build a society that was better than the one they were born into. In the face of harsh government suppression, the Black Panthers survived and managed to feed hungry school children, distribute free shoes and clothing, provide free healthcare, free ambulance services, free rides for families to visit their incarcerated loved ones, free commissary for incarcerated persons, free escorts for senior citizens living in unsafe neighborhoods, free pest control, free plumbing and maintenance, and free education, all while testing thousands for sickle cell anemia. As this work shaped people's lives outside the official Black Panther Party, its impact could not be stopped by the FBI. In 1971, when asked about Kathleen Cleaver's declaration that the Black Panther Party no longer existed, Bobby Seale pointed to the Black Panther Party's food distribution saying, "That food out there in those people's stomachs (35,000 bags of groceries that we've given already) is real."[50] The Panther's work providing sustenance to thousands of people, even while facing repression from the FBI, relied crucially upon church buildings as spaces in which survival programs could develop and thrive.

References

Alkebulan, Paul: *Survival Pending Revolution. The History of the Black Panther Party.* University of Alabama Press: Tuscaloosa 2007.

Austin, Curtis J.: *Up Against the Wall: Violence in the Making and Unmaking of the Black Panther Party.* University of Arkansas Press: Fayetteville 2006.

Beckford, Ruth: "Interview with Dancer and Performer Ruth Beckford." Interview by Rick Moss, August 7, 2007, retrieved 02.10.2021, from https://californiarevealed.org/islandora/object/cavpp%3A23090.

Bloom, Joshua/Waldo E. Martin: *Black against Empire. The History and Politics of the Black Panther Party.* University of California Press: Berkeley 2016.

Browne, Simone: *Dark Matters. On the Surveillance of Blackness.* Duke University Press: Durham, NC 2015.

Bukhari-Alston, Safiya: "Coming of Age: A Black Revolutionary, 1979." In: Joy James (ed.): *Imprisoned Intellectuals: America's Political Prisoners Write on Life, Liberation, and Rebellion.* Rowman and Littlefield: Lanham, MD 2003.

Burns, Jeffrey M.: "Eugene Boyle, the Black Panther Party and the New Clerical Activism." *U.S. Catholic Historian* 13 (3), Summer 1995, pp. 137–158.

Church, Frank et al.: "Supplementary Detailed Staff Reports on Intelligence Activities and the Rights of Americans. Book III. Final Report of the Select Committee

---

50 Keep Chairman Bobby Free!, *The Black Panther*, February 19, 1971, p. 16.

to Study Governmental Operations with Respect to Intelligence Activities." April 23, 1976.

Cleaver, Kathleen: "Women, Power and Revolution." In: Kathleen Cleaver/George Katsiaficas (eds.): *Liberation, Imagination, and the Black Panther Party. A New Look at the Panthers and Their Legacy*. Routledge: New York 2001.

Cobb, Charles E. Jr.: *This Nonviolent Stuff'll Get You Killed. How Guns Made the Civil Rights Movement Possible*. Duke University Press: Durham, NC 2014.

Dale, Adrianne: "Earl A. Neil, African American Civil Rights Reformer: A Profile." *Anglican and Episcopal History* 75 (1), 2006, pp. 69–92.

Farmer, Ashley: *Remaking Black Power. How Black Women Transformed an Era*. University of North Carolina Press: Chapel Hill 2017.

Farnia, Navid: "State Repression and the Black Panther Party: Analyzing Joshua Bloom and Waldo E. Martin's *Black Against Empire*." *Journal of African American Studies* 21, 2017, pp. 172–179.

Foner, Philip S. (editor): *The Black Panthers Speak*. Lippincott: Philadelphia 1970; repr. Haymarket Books: Chicago 2014.

Harper, Sabrina M.S.: "Jesus Says, 'Power to the People:' The Sacred Heart Church Urban Team, 1968–1972," retrieved 02.10.2021, from https://www.smsharper.com/single-post/2020/04/28/jesus-says-power-to-the-people-the-sacred-heart-church-urban-team-1968-1972.

Joseph, Peniel H.: *Waiting 'Til the Midnight Hour: A Narrative History of Black Power in America*. Holt: New York 2006.

Long, Charles H.: *Significations. Signs, Symbols, and Images in the Interpretation of Religion*. Fortress Press: Minneapolis, MN 1986.

McKittrick, Katherine: "Mathematics Black Life." *The Black Scholar: Journal of Black Studies and Research* 44 (2), 2014, pp. 16–28.

Murch, Donna Jean: *Living for the City. Migration, Education, and the Rise of the Black Panther Party in Oakland, California*. University of North Carolina Press: Chapel Hill 2010.

Neil, Earl: "The Role of the Church and the Survival Program." *The Black Panther* 6 (16) 15.05.1971, pp. 10–12.

Nielsen, Euell A.: "Marsha Lovelle Turner Taylor (1953–1977)." *BlackPast*, April 25, 2020, retrieved 03.10.2021, from https://www.blackpast.org/african-american-history/marsha-lovelle-turner-taylor-1953-1977/.

Ogbar, Jeffrey O.G.: *Black Power: Radical Politics and African American Identity*. Johns Hopkins University Press: Baltimore 2004.

Pimblott, Kerry: *Faith in Black Power. Religion, Race, and Resistance in Cairo, Illinois*. University of Kentucky Press: Lexington 2017.

Pinn, Anthony: *The Black Church in the Post-Civil Rights Era*. Orbis Press: Maryknoll, NY 2002.

San Francisco Conference on Race, Religion, and Social Concerns: "Press Conference, Police Community Relations." *Archives of the Archdiocese of San Francisco* 1969, retrieved 03.10.2021, from https://californiarevealed.org/islandora/object/cavpp%3A128478.

Savage, Barbara Dianne: *Your Spirits Walk Beside Us. The Politics of Black Religion*. Harvard University Press: Cambridge, MA 2008.

Self, Robert O.: *American Babylon. Race and the Struggle for Postwar Oakland*. Princeton University Press: Princeton 2003.

Sorett, Josef: *Spirit in the Dark. A Religious History of Racial Aesthetics*. Oxford University Press: New York 2016.

Taylor, Ula Y.: "'Negro Women Are Great Thinkers as well as Doers': Amy Jacques-Garvey and Community Feminism in the United States, 1924–1927." *Journal of Women's History* 12 (2), 2000, pp. 104–126.

Umoja, Akinyele Omowale: "Repression Breeds Resistance: The Black Liberation Army and the Radical Legacy of the Black Panther Party." In: Kathleen Cleaver/George Katsiaficas (eds.): *Liberation, Imagination, and the Black Panther Party. A New Look at the Panthers and Their Legacy*. Routledge: New York 2001.

Van Deburg, William L.: *New Day in Babylon: The Black Power Movement and American Culture, 1965–1975*. University of Chicago Press: Chicago 1992.

Williams, Ben: "Father Boyle Discusses Free Breakfast Program." *KPIX*, June 25, 1969, retrieved 02.10.2021, from https://diva.sfsu.edu/collections/sfbatv/bundles/206988.

Wilmore, Gayraud S.: *Black Religion and Black Radicalism. An Interpretation of the Religious History of African Americans*. 3rd ed. Orbis Books: Maryknoll, NY 1998.

Jajuan S. Johnson

The Fire This Time: Black Church Burnings in the Era of Obama and Black Lives Matter

Abstract: The violent acts perpetrated against Black churches motivated by racial hatred have an extensive history in America that persists. This chapter partly examines the evolution of racialized violence against Black churches in the post-Civil War era across various United States regions and segues into modern cases. The chapter focuses on the resurgence of Black church fires and vandalism during both terms of President Barack Obama. The fires from 2008 to 2016 are examined amid the recent justice movement (Black Lives Matter) centered on the equity of African Americans and the re-emergence of white nationalism. The chapter capitulates that some of the fires represent a new nadir of American race relations and prompts the question: What do the fires symbolize at this juncture of our racist realities? In examining violence against Black cultural spaces, the term "heritage terrorism" is employed to describe the lasting impact of terror against tangible and intangible heritage resources. The chapter uses case studies to illustrate the historical arc of racialized terror on Black churches and draws parallels from past and recent violence against Black churches. In addition to addressing the trauma and terror, the chapter explores how congregations rebuild, analyze the often burden of radical compassion, and expound on ways Black religious institutions continually affirm the value of Black lives.

Keywords: Black Church, Terrorism, Arson, Burning, Heritage, United States

Introduction

The election of the first African American president of the United States of America on November 5, 2008, was a significant change in the country's political landscape. An African American seated in the highest post in a nation with a long history of race-based political disenfranchisement was unprecedented. The undermining of African Americans in the political process started soon after the Fourteenth Amendment to the United States Constitution was ratified on July 9, 1868. The amendment granted citizenship and promised equal rights to formerly enslaved African Americans but garnered several forms of backlash to make full citizenship opaque.[1] Later, impositions of poll taxes, literacy tests, and violence further stymied African Americans' political agency. So, for descendants of citizens who

---

1 Franklin, John Hope/Moss, Alfred, Jr.: *From Slavery to Freedom: A History African*

fought diligently for African Americans to exercise political agency, a dream deferred came to fruition when Senator Barack H. Obama stood in Chicago's Grant Park with his family and throngs of supporters to be announced as president-elect. In the words of singer and musician Sam Cooke, "It was a long time coming."[2] Lions of the civil rights movement, such as Reverend Jesse Jackson and Senator John Lewis, stood witness to this historical moment and recalled the days they risked their lives in the struggle to pass the Voter Rights Act of 1965 and to push for other civil liberties denied African Americans for centuries.[3] During an election night MSNBC interview, United States Congressman John Lewis spoke about the social and political magnitude of Obama's election: "It sends a strongest possible message to all of our citizens and the people of the world that we are prepared to create a truly multi-racial democratic society."[4] As the world watched a seminal moment in U.S. history, dissenters were present, and mounting racial tensions throughout Obama's presidency challenged Senator Lewis' assertion that the nation was ripe for governmental leadership truly reflective of its diverse citizenry. As historian Ibram X. Kendi notes in *The 1619 Project: A New Origin Story*, racist and anti-racist factions will always exist in American democracy: "The singular racial story of the United States is, therefore, a dual racial history of two opposing forces: historical steps towards equity and justice and historical steps toward inequity and injustice."[5] To that end, it was not inconceivable that the election of the first Black president of the United States would be met with racist resistance in the form of violence against African Americans and the places they inhabit—in this case, churches.

One of the purposes of the study resulting in this chapter was to interrogate the notion of racial progress by examining a vintage form of hate used to upend Black communities and invoke fear that sends a message of unbelonging. The ultimate impetus of arson is erasure or removal. The burning of Black churches fits in the extensive conversations on Black citizenship in the United States and how it is thwarted through direct and discursive violence. Following the Civil War, African American churches, schools, benevolence societies, and Freedmen Bureau offices were burned to obliterate any attempt at Black settlement and liberty. This

---

Americans. Alfred Knopf: New York 2000, pp. 252–253.
2   Cooke, Sam: *A Change Is Gonna Come*. RCA: Hollywood, CA 1963.
3   Williams, Juan: *Eyes on the Prize: Americas Civil Rights Years, 1954–1965*. 25th Anniversary ed. Penguin Books: London 2013.
4   Lewis, John: "Speaks About Obama's Victory." *MSNBC*, November 4, 2008. TMP-TV, retrieved 13.02.2022: https://www.youtube.com/watch?v=Oo-ijYnzn1w.
5   Kendi, Ibram X: "Progress." Jones, Nikole Hannah/Roper, Caitlin/Silverman, Ilena/Silverstein, Jake (eds.): *The 1619 Project: A New Origin Story*. One World: New York 2021, p. 425.

antipathy toward Black freedom exists and destroys places deemed sacred by African Americans in current times.

The study is situated in the "Age of Obama." I assert his presidency was partially noteworthy because it was the litmus test for racial progress in the United States of America, and it further revealed enduring systemic racism. In *Making All Black Lives Matter: Reimagining Freedom in the 21st Century*, historian and activist Barbara Ransby offers insight on Obama's election as president and the fledgling activism relating to anti-Blackness: "The honeymoon eventually wore off for many, and Black activists confronted the hard reality that simply having a Black family in the White House was not going to save Black families in general."[6] Ransby further dismisses the idea of post-racialism following Obama's first election: "While no reasonable person could argue that race or racism had been obliterated—that hundreds of years of White supremacy had been swept away in one fell swoop—many wanted to believe that the blatant racism and unapologetic anti-Black racism of the past had been finally put to rest."[7] However, during his presidential terms, Black and non-Black Americans faced the realities of persistent racism that spurred a movement emphasizing the value of Black lives.

During this period, the collective memory of Black church burnings collided with speculated and verified accounts of anti-Black motivated church arson. The cases are often difficult to prove based on current investigative protocols and due to the mysterious nature of church burnings. However, because of these fires, Black churches in the United States re-entered the conversation as a site of terrorization tied to the political struggles of Black people despite its lack of institutional involvement in the recent movement for Black lives. The church fires, proven and unproven as arson, coupled with an anti-Black mass shooting that claimed the lives of eight African American church members and a pastor attending bible study at Emanuel African Methodist Episcopal Church in Charleston, South Carolina, reified anxieties surrounding Black church fires even in the absence of proof of racist hatred. In a spate of Black church burnings following the mass shooting at Emanuel, the National Association for the Advancement of Colored People issued an alert urging Black congregations to take precautions and created the Twitter hashtag #WhoIsBurningBlackChruches.[8] Mystery in this context becomes a form of psyche violence that African Americans and their ancestors have endured from slavery to modern times; thus, this study and chapter partly become an archive of that experience.

---

6   Ransby, Barbara: *Making All Black Lives Matter: Reimagining Freedom in the 21st Century*. University of California Press: Oakland 2018, p. 22.
7   Ransby, Barbara: *op. cit.*, p. 22.
8   Tolbert, Michael, "Who Is Burning Black Churches?" *Black Enterprise Online*, July 2, 2015, retrieved date, 22.02.2022, https://www.blackenterprise.com/who-is-burning-black-churches/.

Some of the Black church burnings from 2008 to 2016 follow similar patterns to those in the wake of anti-Black terror following Reconstruction leading to the 1960s civil rights movement. The arson of Black churches fueled by racial hatred is episodic, and further study is warranted to assess if the fires occur more often during social and political phenomena challenging the racial status quo in the United States or not. The framework of this research is partly informed by Christopher Strain's *Burning Faith: Church Arsons in the American South*. His study of church fires is among the few academic texts solely examining church burnings. Strain focuses on the hundreds of churches burned in the 1990s that led to the enactment of the Church Arson Prevention Act of 1996 and the National Church Arson Task Force (NCAT).[9] The alarming rates of church arsons, particularly in Black churches, led to both sides of the House of Representatives passing the act which resulted in more federal investigations and prosecutions of church arsons.[10] The federal act was propelled by the persistence of Black Church leaders, politicians, and grassroots organizations such as the National Coalition of Burned Churches, who challenged the methodology of local and federal investigations of church arsons.[11] Strain explains the formation of a task force under President William Jefferson Clinton's administration and lists as many incidents as possible based on data collected from 1996 to 2000 by the NCAT. Akin to this study, Strain's query is exploratory but differs in scope. This research focuses on Black church burnings, arsons, and vandalism in different geographic regions of the United States, as anti-Blackness's deleterious effects are boundless. Also, the context of the analysis is civil unrest related to anti-Black violence that spurred the first wave of the Black Lives Matter movement in the year 2015.

The Backstory of Black Church Burnings

Black church fires conjure familiar memories of when Black church burnings by white nationalist operatives were commonplace, particularly during the zenith of the civil rights movement of the 1950s and 1960s. In his book *Parting the Waters: America in the King Years 1953–63*, historian Taylor Branch notes that the

---

9   Strain, Christopher: *Burning Faith Church Arson in the American South*. University of Florida Press: Gainesville 2008.
10 Church Arson Prevention Act of 1996, H.R.3525, 104th Congress (1995–1996), retrieved 02.02.2022, from https://www.congress.gov/bill/104th-congress/house-bill/3525#:~:text=Church%20Arson%20Prevention%20Act%20of%201996%20%2D%20Makes%20Federal%20criminal%20code,%2C%20or%20affects%2C%20interstate%20commerce.
11 Fletcher, Michaelz: "U.S. Investigates Suspicious Fires at Southern Black Churches," *Washington Post*, February 8, 1996, retrieved 22.02.2022, from https://www.washingtonpost.com/wpsrv/national/longterm/churches/reaction.htm.

overall purpose of church burnings during the modern civil rights movement was to subvert the work of activists. He described an account in Birmingham, Alabama, where several churches were bombed following the sentencing of men who were charged with destroying the first Freedom Riders' bus in 1961.[12] According to Branch, terrorist acts against Black churches ensued soon after the news of the convictions was announced. He described how dynamite bombs damaged three Birmingham churches that hosted mass meetings.[13] Of course, there are earlier accounts of attacks against Black churches, particularly during Reconstruction, the period following the United States Civil War where enslaved Black people are emancipated and start building communities. The *Freedmen's Bureau* records bear out thousands of cases of murder and the burning of Black churches and Freedmen Bureau field offices. However, burnings during the modern movements for civil rights are arguably the most deeply etched in American memory.

The details of many early Black church burnings are as shrouded in mystery as are some of the more recent fires. Whether the fires result from an act of nature or malicious intent, the loss nearly always results in grief for those affiliated with the institution that is the bedrock of many African American communities. The array of violence visited on these spaces from arson to murder is a "strike on the identities of the communities."[14] Black churches hold a range of tangible and intangible heritages that tell the story of African American life, history, and culture, that is important given current legislative acts limiting the teaching of Black history in public schools. Amid these circumstances, some Black churches in the U.S. context are repositioning as centers for learning Black history.

Waves of Black Church Burnings

The impetus of the Black church fires, particularly the confirmed arson incidents from 2008 to 2016, prompted further interrogation upon reading the article "Black Church Arson in the United States, 1989–1996" by Sarah Soule and Nella Van Dyke. The two examined the trends of Black church arsons from the late nineteenth to the later part of the twentieth century through the lens of competition theory. The theory partly describes ethnic conflict tied to an actual or perceived scarcity of resources that potentially results in violence against minoritized people groups by a majority group.[15] The authors list four significant waves of African

---

12 Branch, Taylor: *Parting the Waters: America in the King Years, 1954–1965.* Simon & Schuster: New York 1988, p. 570.
13 Branch, Taylor: *op. cit.*, p. 570.
14 Salam, Ziya Us: *Lynch Files: The Forgotten Saga of Victims of Hate Crimes.* Sage Publication India: New Delhi 2019, p. 4.
15 Soule, Sarah/Van Dyke, Nella: "Black Church Arson in the United States 1989–1996." *Ethnic and Racial Studies* 22 (4), 1999, pp. 724–742, retrieved 22.02.2022, https://doi.org/10.1080/014198799329369.

American church burnings as informed by the Center for Democratic Renewal, a defunct organization focused on anti-racist training and organizing. The first wave of Black church burnings occurred during Reconstruction as terrorist organizations such as the Klu Klux Klan (KKK) emerged, inflicting violence on African Americans, and infiltrating every part of American society. The second wave of burnings occurred in the 1920s as the KKK membership swelled and mounting racial tensions resulted in the destruction of Black neighbors and towns such as Rosewood in Levy County, Florida, and massacres in places such as Elaine, Arkansas. The third wave correlates to the civil rights movement of the 1960s. A fourth wave in the 1980s and 1990s led to the Church Arson Prevention Act.[16] The confirmed and unconfirmed Black church arsons from 2008 to 2016 indicate a fifth wave, perhaps not comparable to the numbers of fires in earlier periods, but warrant investigation given similar socio-political dilemmas of the first four waves related to race, ethnicity, class, gender, and economics.

In analyzing the research question about whether church fires increased from 2008 to 2016, the data shows a decrease in church burnings overall; however, the prevalence of the fires raises concern. The number of church burnings ruled as intentional arson and bombings during Obama's two terms as President have ebbed and flowed.[17] According to a *Pew Research* study: "Between 1996 and 2000, an average of 191 intentional fires was reported each year, accounting for 52% of all church fires."[18] However, the study points out that the average number of fires ruled as intentional dropped to seventy-four between 2010 and 2014; this still accounts for 48% of burnings ruled as arson and is only 4% lower than the percentage of the late 1990s.[19] It should also be noted that the data listed in the *Pew Research* study is not only reflective of Black churches.

During the period of increased Black church burnings in the 1990s, grassroots and government-sponsored efforts made assertive strides to investigate church arsons. The data captured by the National Church Arson Task Force (Task Force), a federal entity, was not perfect, given the mysterious nature of church arsons, but it is arguably the most accurate accounting of Black church arsons to date. Numerous factors skew the current data on hate-based or racial hatred-based arsons: the dissolution of Task Force which indicated the racial demographic of churches burned; the National Coalition for Burned Churches and Community Empowerment, an advocacy group that conducted independent investigations also

---

16 Soule, Sarah/Van Dyke, Nella.: *op. cit.*, pp. 727–728.
17 Sandstrom, Aleksandra. *Half of All Church Fires in the Past 20 Years Were Arson.* Washington, DC: Pew Research Center, 2015. retrieved 01.03.2018, http://www.pewresearch.org/fact-tank/2015/10/26/half-of-all-church-fires-in-past-20-years-were-arsons/
18 *Ibid.*
19 *Ibid.*

disbanded, which impacted the data. The most critical aspect resulting in imprecise data is that all states are required to collect data on hate crimes, and many local police departments collecting hate crime data is not required to report numbers to the federal government.[20]

The increased number of church arsons in the early 1990s prompted President Bill Clinton to enact the Task Force in 1995 to offer federal investigative support to state and local law enforcement, particularly on church arsons. The Task Force was successful in opening nearly 1,000 arson cases throughout its five-year duration.[21] In a press release from the U.S. Department of Treasury on the third report of the Task Force's accomplishments, the department reported that it was also effective in its arrest and conviction rates: "The Task Force's arrest rate of 35 percent continues to be more than twice the national average for arson cases and 287 defendants have been convicted in connection with 206 arsons or bombings."[22] The investigation and arrest record of the Task Force yielded noteworthy results in four years of reports detailing the demographic markers of the arsonists, regions, and case outcomes archived at the Clinton Digital Library accessible through the National Archives and Records Administration.[23]

After the Task Force ended at the completion of President Bill Clinton's second term, investigations continued under the Bureau of Alcohol, Tobacco, Firearms, and Explosives (ATF); however, the reports on church arsons are not race specific which makes it impossible to correctly note the number of Black church burnings from 2008 to 2016. Researchers heavily rely on local and national news reports to start inquiry into the burning cases and follow the lengthy process of state and federal investigations. Also, churches are broadly classified as houses of worship in their 2017 report and are categorized as Christian (Protestant, Catholic, and Orthodox), Buddhist, unknown, or not reported. Specific denominations are not mentioned.[24] The National Fire Protection Association (NFPA) also collects data on church burnings, but the organization does not track individual cases of church arson as the Task Force did in the 1990s. The NFPA uses detailed data in

---

20 Schwencke, Ken/Hannah Fresques, "This Is Where Hate Crimes Don't Get Reported." *ProPublica*, November 17, 2017, https://projects.propublica.org/graphics/hatecrime-map.
21 United States Department of the Treasury, "National Church Arson Task Force Issues Third Report: Arsons at Houses of Worship Continues to Decline." Press release no. ls-389, February 10, 2000, https://www.treasury.gov/press-center/press-releases/Pages/ls389.aspx.
22 *Ibid.*
23 *Ibid.* Newton, Michael.: *The Klu Klux Klan: An Encyclopedia*, op. cit., p. 273.
24 United States Bomb Data Center, Department of Justice, *2017 Arson Incident Report*, 2017, https://www.atf.gov/resource-center/docs/report/2017-arson-incident-report-air/download.

the National Fire Incident Reporting System, but each state sets its own reporting requirements ranging from mandatory to voluntary which also distorts the data. In addition, church burnings are included with funeral properties, which makes it difficult to parse the information specifically relating to church arsons and burnings.[25] Perhaps the major success of the Task Force is that it produced the Church Arson Prevention Act of 1996 that possibly curtailed the number of church burnings.

In *The Black Church in the Post-Civil Rights Era*, religion professor Anthony Pinn offers perspective on the burning of Black churches since the 1960s civil rights movement: "Beyond debate over charges of racism vs. more generic explanations for the burnings, the destruction of these churches made a statement. It pointed to the continued understanding of the Black Church as a major nerve for Black life."[26] As with Black church arsons of the late nineteenth and early twentieth century, the fires during this fifth wave warrant further research into the current political symbolism and uses of the Black churches in the United States. As of March 15, 2023, The International Commission to Combat Religious Racism released the report, "Religious Racism in North America: Racially Motivated Attacks Against Places of Worship in the 21st Century." The quantitative study demonstrates the growing scholarly inquiry on attacks against places of worship motivated by racial hatred.[27]

A Brief History of the Black Church and Its Activism

As an institution and collective reality of Black Christians across denominational lines, the Black Church is more than a cultural artifact evolving from slavery and racial segregation, but a living organism that has shaped the socio-political movements of America's past and remains culturally relevant to African Americans and Black people globally. In *Liberating Black Church: Making It Plain*, Professor Juan Floyd-Thomas describes the historic Black Church as a radical institution: "In the years after slavery was abolished, the historic Black Church tradition became the most important cultural institution among African Americans."[28] Of course, the

---

25 Ahrens, Marty: *Background on Church Arson and Related Issues, Fire Analysis and Research Division*. National Fire Protection Agency: Quincy, MA 2005, https://www.nfpa.org/-/media/Files/News-and-Research/Fire-statistics-and-reports/Building-and-life-safety/oschurcharson.ashx.
26 Pinn, Anthony: *The Black Church in the Post-Civil Rights Era*. Orbis Books: New York 2002, p. 36.
27 Boaz, Danielle: "Religious Racism in North America: Racially Motivated Attacks Against Places of Worship in the 21st Century, *International Commission to Combat Religious Racism*, March 15, 2023, retrieved, 30.10.2023, from https://www.religiousracism.org/_files/ugd/bb6958_6a79552988264b64997fe3f76fbf7704.pdf?mibextid=Zxz2cZ.
28 Floyd-Thomas, Juan Marcell: *Liberating Black Church History: Making It Plain*. Abingdon Press: Nashville 2014, p. 44.

Black Church is not a monolith, but possibly an "unwieldy monolith" as by sociocultural anthropologist Todne Thomas in *Kincraft: The Making of Black Evangelical Sociality*; however, its cultural positioning is central in the African American experience even for those who do not identify as Christians.

The Black Church is a historical model of cooperative economics and collective responsibility. As historian Bernard Powers argues in his book *Black Charlestonians: A Social History, 1822–1885*, "The church fostered economic cooperation by pooling the resources of individual members for the construction of buildings and other purposes."[29] Although his book focuses on a much earlier period of history in Charleston, South Carolina, the mutual assistance tradition persists, such as the pooling of resources for community outreach, building fundraisers, benevolence programs for church members, the establishment of credit unions, and private education institutions for youth and young adults. To exercise political and social autonomy beyond the church walls where racism and classism infringed upon nearly every aspect of existence, African Americans created what historian Kidada Williams calls "home places" or racially homogeneous spaces to exercise autonomy.[30] The Church is the nucleus of the home place and provides a sense of protection from racist terrorization. It fosters what bell hooks describes as oppositional thinking in a society where one is constantly dehumanized based on race.[31]

The historical response of the Black churches to social justice issues is hard to ignore. From slave insurrections to voter registration rights and more contemporary topics such as police brutality, the Black Church has been a source of inspiration and, at times, consolation for its parishioners or those culturally connected to it. It is also important to mention that such social justice engagement has ebbed and flowed at different times and on issues ranging from gender equity to sexuality. Of course, no institution is without contradictions, and some scholars consider the Black Church as accommodative to whiteness at specific points in history; however, any critique of the Black Church should consider that it is domiciled in a violent and racially oppressive system: "By assuming that accommodation can never be subversive, scholars neglect how Black churches may have been more accommodative as a survival strategy."[32] To that end, it is crucial to examine the Black Church in the context of the people who make the Church. These are communities

---

29 Powers, Bernard: *Black Charlestonians: A Social History, 1822–1885*. University of Arkansas Press: Fayetteville 1994, p. 217.
30 Williams, Kidada E.: *They Left Great Marks on Me: African American Testimonies of Racial Violence*. New York University Press: New York 2012, p. 21.
31 hooks, bell: *Killing Rage: Ending Racism*. Henry Holt, and Company: New York 1995, p. 57.
32 Barber, Kendra: "Whiter Shall We Go? The Past and Present of Black Churches and the Public Sphere." *Religions* 6 (1), 2015, p. 247, retrieved 22.02.2022, from https://doi.org/10.3390/rel6010245.

of Black people who are often in a liminal space attempting to find coherence amid an incoherence of a system where racial violence abounds. The Black Church, in many instances, becomes their nation as it is often the only environment where soulful expression and spiritual vulnerability are affirmed.

During the Black Power Movement in the early 1970s, some Black Church historians and systematic theologians began to re-assess the role of the Black Church following the civil rights movement of the 1960s. After the assassination of Reverend Dr. Martin Luther King, Jr. on April 4, 1968, in Memphis, Tennessee, a new brand of activists emerged, such as Eldridge Cleaver and Stokley Carmichael: women like Dr. Angela Davis and Elaine Brown were also on the forefront of the changing Black liberation movement after the death of Dr. King. The approach to racial and social inequities by this new generation of resistors contrasted with previous activism primarily underpinned by the Black Church with Black men as the primary leaders.

Arkansas native Dr. James Cone, a professor of systematic theology at Union Theological Seminary, became one of the renowned academics who connected the Black Church and theology to aspects of the Black Power Movement ideology. He also wrote extensively about the historical and contemporary function of the Black Church in a racially oppressive society and critiqued the institution's sometimes passivity.[33] Although Cone is credited as the "father of Black theology," he explains in his book *For My People: Black Theology and the Black Church* that several radical Black organizations influenced the idea of Black theology; and the concept of Black theology was influenced mainly by the National Conference of Black Churchmen who initially called themselves the National Committee of Negro Churchmen. The organization was founded in 1966 and headquartered in Atlanta, Georgia.[34] In detailing Black theology's origins, Cone outlined the bold and radical approach by Black ministers who spoke about the power dynamics in a racist society in their "Black Power Statement." The statement cemented their alignment with the Black Power Movement ideology: "[...] members of the radical black clergy created nearly as much controversy in white churches as secular advocates of Black power did in white society. Once again, white clergy was caught off guard and found it difficult to believe that their trusted Black colleagues were now openly associating with the 'un-Christian' idea of Black Power."[35] Theologian Dwight Hopkins, a contemporary of James Cone, further expanded on being Black and Christian. In *Introducing Black Liberation Theology*, Hopkins pointed out that a theology of liberation has always been present in the lives of Black people in America from slavery to the present:

---

33   Pinn, Anthony: *op. cit.*, pp. 22–23.
34   Cone, James: *For My People: Black Theology and the Black Church*. Orbis Books: New York 1984, p. 1.
35   Cone, James: *op. cit.*, p. 13.

> From the seventeenth to nineteenth century, African and African American enslaved workers constructed a new religion drawing on three sources—memories of African religious beliefs, commonsense wisdom from everyday life, and a reinterpretation of the White-supremacy Christianity introduced to them by their Christian slave masters. The cornerstone of a black theology of liberation was thus a slave religion of freedom.[36]

Black liberation theology is a critical lens to examine the roots of Black Church activism and the current resistance to racial oppression in America. The idea of Black liberation theology is evident in some way in every African American church denomination, and environments of Black spiritual expression, including the streets amid protests centering on the sanctity of Black lives.[37] Although the Black Church is not the epicenter of Black activism during the Black Lives Matter movement as it was during the civil rights movement of the 1950s and 1960s, its presence represents Black autonomy, and it is part of the genealogy of Black activism. This chapter underscores that Black spaces, particularly Black churches, remain critical institutions as African Americans continue what Renaldo Walcott calls the "long emancipation" toward Black freedom.[38]

Where the statistical data fails the inquiry on the actual number of arsons motivated by racial hatred from 2008 to 2016, the cases below reveal details on the loss of these cultural heritage sites, explain the types of community fragmentation leading to and resulting from this type of violence, and demonstrate the process of restoration in one case. The fires at Macedonia Church of God in Christ and Flood Christian Church, and the later mass shooting at Emanuel A.M.E. Church are demonstrative of heightened racial violence during the dawn of a new nadir in American race relations, wherein a new generation of justice activists emerged, and vintage fear tactics in the form of Black church burnings persist.

Fire Amid Hopeful Times

Election day was a mixture of hope and despair for the pastor and members of Macedonia Church of God in Christ, located in Springfield, Massachusetts.[39] The church was burned during the beginning of a more hopeful chapter of U.S. history, and once again, the community was reminded that with racial progress often

---

36 Hopkins, Dwight: *Introducing Black Theology of Liberation*. Orbis Books: New York 1999, p. 15.
37 Hopkins, Dwight: *op. cit.*, pp. 15–16.
38 Walcott, Rinaldo: *The Long Emancipation: Moving Toward Black Freedom*. Duke University Press: Durham, NC and London 2021, pp. 1–3.
39 Barry, Dan: "A Time of Hope, Marred by an Act of Horror." *New York Times*, November 16, 2008, retrieved 22.02.2022, from https://www.nytimes.com/2008/11/17/us/17land.html.

comes racist backlash.[40] Macedonia Church of God in Christ has a nearly eighty-year history in Springfield, Massachusetts. The church grew out of the migration of Black people who left the South and settled in Northern states with hopes of a better life free from the intensity of racial oppression, violence, and political marginalization.

After years of occupying the downtown building, the congregants decided to build a new facility. The pastor and congregation worked for years to raise money and garnered support to secure a loan necessary to start the building process.[41] With the church near completion, the parishioners were ready to move into their new space and celebrate another milestone in the church's history, but the arson temporarily halted that reality.

In their early to mid-twenties, three white men, Benjamin Haskell, Thomas Gleason, and Michael Jacques, seething with hatred, invoked the type of terror reminiscent of the racial trauma endured by their predecessors who migrated from the South. The church pastor, Bishop Bryant, Jr., not only summoned the courage to rebuild, but he also wanted the arsonist brought to justice based on the 1996 Church Arson Prevention Act.

Reporter Jonathan Salzman of the Boston Globe offered a detailed review of the investigation, which revealed the calculated plot of the arsonists: "They walked through the woods behind Gleason's house to back of the church late on November 4, 2008, first to inspect the building."[42] The three men returned to the church hours after Obama's election, doused the building inside and outside with gasoline, and ignited a fire that destroyed the building.[43] Salzman also obtained the affidavit of an undercover FBI agent, which indicated the motive of the arson: "When the associate asked why the men set the fire, the affidavit said, Haskell, replied, 'Because it was a black church.'"[44] The affidavit also indicates the suspects were angry about Obama becoming the first Black president and voiced dissent about his election. The FBI investigation eventually led to the arsonists' prosecution. A press release by the Boston division of the FBI detailed the conviction and sentencing of Michael Jacques on December 22, 2011: "[...] sentenced by U.S. District Judge Michael A. Ponsor to 166 months in prison, to be followed by four years of supervised release. Jacques was also ordered to pay nearly $1.6 million in restitution, including

---

40 Kendi, Ibram: "The Civil Rights Act Was a Victory Against Racism. But Racists Also Won." *The Washington Post*, February 7, 2017, retrieved 04.04.2013, from https://www.washingtonpost.com/news/made-by-history/wp/2017/07/02/the-civil-rights-act-was-a-victory-against-racism-but-racists-also-won/.
41 *Ibid.*
42 *Ibid.*
43 *Ibid.*
44 *Ibid.*

$123,570 to Macedonia Church of God in Christ."⁴⁵ Although justice was partially served, a community was traumatized, and it was reinforced that even during times of progress, the struggle for justice is continual for African Americans. The fire at Macedonia was the beginning of numerous acts of racial terrorism and anti-Blackness occurring over eight years, from 2008 to 2016, where Black churches were sometimes targeted or caught in the crossfire of resistance to racist practices, policies, and procedures.

Black Lives Matter and a Church Fire in Ferguson, Missouri

The arson and burnings, confirmed and undetermined, took place against the backdrop of state-sanctioned violence against Black people during a pivotal point of protest. The mysterious burning of Flood Christian Church in Ferguson, Missouri, again resonated in African Americans' collective memory related to church burnings. The church was caught in the crossfire of an urban rebellion associated with the death of a young man that sparked a new movement for justice. On November 14, 2014, the fire came on the heels of a verdict not to indict Officer Darren Wilson for Michael Brown, Jr.'s murder.⁴⁶

Flood Christian Church was in a community that responded to Brown's murder in a way that changed the international conversation and consciousness of police brutality, especially as it relates to Black men and women. Professor and veteran activist Angela Davis discussed the global impact of the Ferguson uprising in her book *Freedom Is a Constant Struggle: Ferguson, Palestine and the Foundations of a Movement*: "The Ferguson struggle has taught us that local issues have global ramifications. The militarization of Ferguson police and the advice tweeted by Palestinian activists helped to recognize our political kinship with the boycott, divestment, and sanctions movement and with the larger struggle for justice in Palestine."⁴⁷ The tragedy in Ferguson is placed in the broader context of police violence not indicative of one inner city, but a national crisis was impacting every aspect of a community, including faith institutions. Black churches often become sites of healing and, in some cases, a center of resistance when lives are lost due to

---

45 "Springfield Man Sentenced to 166 Months for Arson of African-American Church." FBI press release, U.S. Attorney's Office, December 22, 2011, retrieved 22.02.2022, from https://archives.fbi.gov/archives/boston/press-releases/2011/springfield-man-sentenced-to-166-months-for-arson-of-african-american-church.

46 Saliba, Emmanuela: "Feds Probe Arson of Michael Brown Sr.'s Church," *NBC News*, November 25, 2014, retrieved 02.04.2017, from https://www.nbcnews.com/storyline/michael-brown-shooting/feds-probing-arson-michael-brown-sr-s-church-n255961.

47 Davis, Angela: *Freedom Is a Constant Struggle: Ferguson, Palestine and the Foundations of a Movement*, ed. Frank Barat. Haymarket Books: Chicago 2016, p. 90.

anti-Black violence. Sociologist and Black Church scholar Kendra Barber analyzes the contemporary role of the Black church in responding to racial inequity in "Whither Shall We Go? The Past and Present of Black Churches and the Public Sphere," she asserts; "[...] Black churches are among the few institutions providing race-specific remedies that have been abandoned in a colorblind era."[48] Flood Christian Church and other area Black churches became a place of consolation not only for the Brown family but also for the Ferguson community in the wake of a tragic loss. In *Ferguson and Faith: Sparking Leadership & Awakening Community*, practical theologian and minister Leah Gunning Francis details the interaction between clergy and young protesters during the Ferguson crisis: "For many clergy who responded to the killing of Michael Brown, their rationale was deeply tied to their understanding of God and the mission of the church."[49]

Flood Christian Church was established on March 31, 2013, on Easter Sunday by the late Carlton Lee, a young pastor who became one of the most vocal faith leaders in the community during the Ferguson uprising.[50] Flood was the church home of Michael Brown, Sr., the father of the slain teenager. Lee established a space for communal empowerment and spiritual uplift. The church website indicates that the mission reads: "Flooding Our Community with God's Love."[51] He was thrust into the international spotlight as a clergy-activist following the murder of Michael Brown, Jr. His involvement as a clergy in the movement for Black lives was noble but came with the scrutiny that he believed led to the burning of his church. The pastor and church congregation became increasingly politically active when Lee became a representative for the Ferguson chapter of the National Action Network founded by longtime activist New York City's Reverend Al Sharpton. Lee believed his call for the arrest of Officer Darren Wilson made his church the target of a potential hate crime.[52]

---

48 Barber, Kendra: "Whither Shall We Go? The Past and Present of Black Churches and the Public Square." *Religions* 6 (1), 2015, p. 245. https://doi.org/10.3390/rel6010245.

49 Francis, Leah Gunning: *Ferguson, and Faith: Sparking Leadership and Awakening Community*. Chalice Press: St. Louis, MO 2015, p. 91.

50 Fowler, Lilly: "Federal Officials Investigating Fire at Church Connected to Michael Brown Family." *St. Louis Post-Dispatch*, November 27, 2014, retrieved 23.02.2022 from, https://www.stltoday.com/lifestyles/faith-and-values/federal-officials-investigating-fire-at-church-connected-to-michael-brown/article_e4b41d11-a02d-5956-b396-b67b36302410.html.

51 Flood Christian Center Church: "All About Us," retrieved 17.02.2028, from https://thenewoasis.wixsite.com/the-flood-church/all-about-us.

52 "Obituary: The Rev. Carlton Lee, Pastor of Michael Brown Sr., Dies at 34." *St. Louis American*, June 15, 2017, retrieved 23.02.2018, from https://news.stlpublicradio.org/post/obituary-rev-carlton-lee-pastor-michael-brown-sr-dies-34#stream/0.

In an article by reporter and cultural critic Wesley Lowery, he described the sacrifices made by Lee when purchasing the church: "Buying the church property—which once housed an auto repair shop—took everything Lee had. It cost all his savings and the money he had put away for his children to front the $160,000."[53] During the interview with Lowery, he lamented the loss of his church while describing it as "his baby," but he remained hopeful.[54] Lee felt the church was set afire by arsonists based on the numerous death threats he received after vocalizing his dismay about the grand jury's decision in favor of Officer Darren Wilson.[55]

Flood's burning on November 24, 2014, rapidly resulted in a response from the ATF, resulting from the Church Arson Prevention Act of 196. The Kansas City ATF Field Division not only assigned special agents to the case but also offered a $10,000 reward for tips on the fire that destroyed the church and several area businesses.[56] The ATF's public plea for assistance with details about the burning did not lead to a suspect; however, Lee remained convinced that whoever set fire at the church meant to invoke fear among African Americans.

As a millennial church leader, Pastor Carlton Lee's message resonated with a new generation of Black activists with differing views on how to challenge power structures that were terrorizing their community. Black Church historian Barbara Holmes addressed the necessity of change in resistance movements: "Today, the times require a different approach to oppression and violence against Black bodies."[57] Flood provided a space for a generation with a more radical approach to community action. Unfortunately, the case remains undetermined, and the broader community still mourns the death of Reverend Carlton Lee—a young leader who answered the call to speak truth to power, risking his life. He died of a heart attack at age 34 on June 13, 2017—and will be remembered as a clergy-activist in the movement for Black lives.

---

53 Lowery, Wesley: "The Brown's Family Pastor Tries to Make Sense of the Fire that Gutted his Church." *Washington Post*, November 27, 2014, retrieved 02.02.2018, from https://www.washingtonpost.com/national/the-brown-familys-pastor-tries-to-make-sense-of-fire-that-gutted-his-church/2014/11/28/15520f3e-7711-11e4-a755-e32227229e7b_story.html.

54 *Ibid.*

55 *Ibid.*

56 Bureau of Alcohol, Tobacco, Firearms, and Explosives, Kansas City Field Division, "ATF Offers Reward in Ferguson Fires." Press release, December 5, 2014, https://www.atf.gov/news/pr/atf-offers-reward-ferguson-fires.

57 Holmes, Barbara: *Joy Unspeakable: Contemplative Practices of the Black Church*. Augsburg Fortress: Minneapolis, MN 2017, p. 154.

When Hate Fully Blooms: Emanuel A.M.E. Church

The arc of racial violence continues, but so does resistance to it.[58] From 2008 to 2016, violence and racial tensions escalated with police-citizen violence, the contestation of Confederate iconography, and the further emergence of white nationalism. The murders of eight church members and a pastor at Emanuel African Methodist Episcopal (AME) Church in Charleston, South Carolina, occurred on June 17, 2015. Dylann Roof, a white male, seething with hatred toward African Americans, reveals what happens when hatefully blooms from church arsons to a massacre. The tragedy was partly the impetus of this study, underscoring that racial terror in the United States and other nations has a heritage steeped in the historical subjugation of minoritized people. Professor Maurie McInnis explains the legacy of hate resulting in the murder of parishioners in the essay, "The First Attack on Charleston's AME Church": "The shooting is not simply the action of one deranged and evil individual, but instead springs from our nation's long history of racial prejudice and violence against African Americans."[59] McInnis further invites readers to explore Emanuel's history in the context of the 2015 massacre.

Emanuel is historically rooted in the tradition of Black communal uplift and social justice. The congregation's history dates to 1791 as an assembly of free and enslaved Black people. The congregants were initially members of the Charleston Methodist Episcopal Church but chose to secede from their white counterparts in 1816 after a dispute over burial grounds and later organized under the African Methodist Episcopal denomination founded by Reverend Richard Allen.[60] Emanuel is in many ways the representative of the mythical phoenix consistently rising from the ashes.[61] The church has survived racial violence numerous times since its establishment. In the early 1800s, the church was burned due to accusations of connection to a slave insurrection organized by Denmark Vesey, a formerly enslaved person and well-known Black leader in Charleston. He is also credited as one of the early founders of Emanuel.[62] Nevertheless, members rebuilt their church in 1834 when the South Carolina state legislature outlawed all-Black churches.

---

58 Hasian, Marouf/Paliewicz, Nicholas: *Racial Terrorism: A Rhetorical Investigation of Lynching*. University Press of Mississippi: Jackson 2021.
59 McInnis, Maurie: "The First Attacks on Charleston's AME." *Slate*, July 19, 2015. In: Williams, Chad/Kidada Williams/Keisha Blain (eds.): *Charleston Syllabus: Readings on Race, Racism, and Racial Violence*. University of Georgia Press: Athens 2016, p. 32.
60 Payne, Ed.: "Emanuel African Methodist Episcopal Church: A Storied Church in a Historic City." *CNN*, June 18, 2015, retrieved 23.04.2019, from http://www.cnn.com/2015/06/18/us/charleston-emanuel-ame-church-history.
61 Newman, Richard: *Freedom's Prophet: Bishop Richard Allen, the AME Church, and the Black Founding Fathers*. New York University Press: New York 2008.
62 Robertson, David: *Denmark Vesey: The Buried Story of America's Largest Slave Rebellion and the Man Who Led It*. Vintage Books: New York 1999, pp. 137–139.

The church members adopted the name "Emanuel," which means "God with us."[63] Emanuel is rooted in the conviction of freedom and equity for humanity and kept pace with the social and cultural shifts impacting African American lives, particularly during the first wave of the Black Lives Matter Movement as its pastor championed against police brutality. Emanuel is a testament of Black survival and resilience in the United States; however, the institution remains vulnerable to anti-Black violence.

Emanuel and the nation faced the continued realities of racial hatred as a neo-Nazi opened fire and murdered Reverend Clementa Pinckney, Tywanza Sanders, Susie Jackson, Cynthia Marie, Graham Hurd, Ethel Lee Lance, Depayne Middleton Doctor, Daniel Simmons, Sharonda Coleman Singleton, and Myra Thompson and injured others during Bible study. President Barack Obama gave the eulogy at the memorial service for Reverend Clementa Pinckney and aptly describes *heritage terrorism* as conceived in this study: "It was an act that drew on a long history of bombs and arson and shots fired at churches, not random, but as a means of control, a way to terrorize and oppress."[64] President Obama went further to discuss the dangers of historical denialism and commented on the uses of history: "That history can't be a sword to justify injustice, or a shield against progress, but must be a manual for not repeating mistakes of the past—how to break the cycle."[65] One of the purposes of this study is to create a record of these racial atrocities amid legislative efforts to silence the teaching of past and present facts on the vast and complicated American narrative.

Conclusion: The Fire Is Still Burning

Black church arsons are part of a long historical arc of racial terrorization, and so is African American resistance to oppressive mechanisms. The tragedies of Black church burnings must be seen through the lens of broader racial tensions leading to resistance by activists who have been working in communities for decades to address poverty, food insecurity, gentrification, and heritage terrorism during this new nadir in American race relations. As theologian Anthony Pinn reminded us, beyond the debate about arson motivation or evidence, the burnings continue to illuminate the value of the Black Church in the continued struggle for Black

---

63 Payne, Ed.: "Emanuel African Methodist Episcopal Church: A Storied Church in a Historic City." *CNN*, June 18, 2015, retrieved 23.04.2019, from http://www.cnn.com/2015/06/18/us/charleston-emanuel-ame-church-history.

64 "The White House, "Remarks by the President in Eulogy for Honorable Reverend Clementa Pinckney." June 26, 2015, retrieved 02.02.2022, from https://obamawhitehouse.archives.gov/the-press-office/2015/06/26/remarks-president-eulogy-honorable-reverend-clementa-pinckney.

65 *Ibid.*

freedom in the United States. Through the fire, Black churches remain a prophetic symbol telling the story of people's past and present and is a testament to resilience. And most importantly, it prompts us to craft broader emancipatory visions for the future.

References

Barber, Kendra, "Whiter Shall We Go? The Past and Present of Black Churches and the Public Sphere." *Religions* 6 (1), 2015, p. 247, retrieved 22.02.2022, from https://doi.org/10.3390/rel6010245.

Barnes, Harper: *Never Been a Time: The 1917 Riot That Sparked the Civil Rights Movement.* Walker and Company: New York 2008.

Barry, Dan: "A Time of Hope, Marred by an Act of Horror." *New York Times*, November 16, 2008, retrieved 22.02.2022.

Branch, Taylor: *Parting the Waters: America in the King Years, 1954–1965.* Simon & Schuster, New York 1988.

Butler, Anthea: "Church." In: Nikole Hannah-Jones/Caitlin Roper/Ilena Silverman/Jake Silverstein (eds.): *New Origin Story: The 1619 Project.* One World: New York 2021.

Collins, Jeffery: "Racist Massacre Survivor Urges Hate Crimes Law in S Carolina" *The Charlotte Observer.* April 28, 2022, retrieved 30.04.2022, from https://www.charlotteobserver.com/news/nation-world/national/article260811132.html.

Cooke, Sam: *A Change Is Gonna Come.* RCA: Hollywood, CA 1963.

Cone, James: *For My People: Black Theology and the Black Church.* Orbis Books: New York 1984.

Davis, Angela: *Freedom Is a Constant Struggle: Ferguson, Palestine and the Foundations of a Movement*, ed. Frank Barat. Haymarket Books: Chicago 2016.

Fletcher, Michaelz: "U.S. Investigates Suspicious Fires at Southern Black Churches." *Washington Post*, February 8, 1996, retrieved 22.02.2022, from https://www.washingtonpost.com/wpsrv/national/longterm/churches/reaction.htm.

Floyd-Thomas, Juan Marcell: *Liberating Black Church History: Making It Plain.* Abingdon Press: Nashville 2014.

Fowler, Lilly: "Federal Officials Investigating Fire at Church Connected to Michael Brown Family." *St. Louis Post-Dispatch*, November 27, 2014, retrieved 24.01.2018, from https://www.stltoday.com/lifestyles/faith-and-values/federal-officials-investigating-fire-at-church-connected-to-michael-brown/article_e4b41d11-a02d-5956-b396-b67b36302410.html.

Francis, Leah Gunning: *Ferguson, and Faith: Sparking Leadership and Awakening Community.* Chalice Press: St. Louis, MO 2015.

Franklin, John Hope/Moss, Alfred, Jr.: *From Slavery to Freedom: A History African Americans.* Alfred Knopf: New York 2000.

Gonzales-Tennant, Edward: *The Rosewood Massacre: An Archaeology and History of Intersectional Violence.* University Press of Florida: Gainesville 2019.

Hasian, Marouf/Paliewicz, Nicholas: *Racial Terrorism: A Rhetorical Investigation of Lynching.* University Press of Mississippi: Jackson 2021.

Holmes, Barbara: *Joy Unspeakable: Contemplative Practices of the Black Church.* Augsburg Fortress: Minneapolis, MN 2017.

hooks, bell: *Killing Rage: Ending Racism.* Henry Holt, and Company: New York 1995.

Hopkins, Dwight: *Introducing Black Theology of Liberation.* Orbis Books: New York 1999.

Johnson, Hannibal: *Black Wall Street: From Riot to Resistance in Tulsa's Historic Greenwood District.* Eakin Press: Fort Worth 1998.

Kendi, Ibram: "The Civil Rights Act Was a Victory Against Racism. But Racists Also Won." *The Washington Post*, February 7, 2017, retrieved 04.04.2013, from https://www.washingtonpost.com/news/made-by-history/wp/2017/07/02/the-civil-rights-act-was-a-victory-against-racism-but-racists-also-won/.

Kendi, Ibram X.: "Progress." Jones, Nikole Hannah/Roper, Caitlin/Silverman, Ilena/Silverstein, Jake (eds.): *The 1619 Project: A New Origin Story.* One World: New York 2021.

Lewis, John: "Speaks About Obama's Victory." *MSNBC*, November 4, 2008. TMP-TV, retrieved 13.02.2022, from https://www.youtube.com/watch?v=Oo-ijYnzn1w.

Lowery, Wesley: "The Brown's Family Pastor Tries to Make Sense of the Fire that Gutted His Church." *Washington Post*, November 27, 2014, retrieved 02.02.2018, from https://www.washingtonpost.com/national/the-brown-familys-pastor-tries-to-make-sense-of-fire-that-gutted-his-church/2014/11/28/15520f3e-7711-11e4-a755-e32227229e7b_story.html.

McInnis, Maurie: "The First Attacks on Charleston's AME." *Slate*, July 19, 2015. In: Chad Williams, Kidada Williams, and Keisha Blain, (eds.): *Charleston Syllabus: Readings on Race, Racism, and Racial Violence.* University of Georgia Press: Athens 2016.

Newman, Richard: *Freedom's Prophet: Bishop Richard Allen, the AME Church, and the Black Founding Fathers.* New York University Press: New York 2008.

Payne, Ed.: "Emanuel African Methodist Episcopal Church: A Storied Church in a Historic City." *CNN*, June 18, 2015, retrieved 23.04.2019, from http://www.cnn.com/2015/06/18/us/charleston-emanuel-ame-church-history.

Pinn, Anthony: *The Black Church in the Post-Civil Rights Era.* Orbis Books: New York 2002.

Powers, Bernard: *Black Charlestonians: A Social History, 1822–1885.* University of Arkansas Press: Fayetteville 1994.

Ransby, Barbara: *Making All Black Lives Matter: Reimagining Freedom in the 21st Century*. University of California Press: Oakland 2018.

Robertson, David: *Denmark Vesey: The Buried Story of America's Largest Slave Rebellion and the Man Who Led It*. Vintage Books: New York 1999.

Salam, Ziya Us: *Lynch Files: The Forgotten Saga of Victims of Hate Crimes*. Sage Publication India: New Delhi 2019.

Saliba, Emmanuela: "Feds Probe Arson of Michael Brown Sr.'s Church." *NBC News*, November 25, 2014, retrieved 04.02.2017, from https://www.nbcnews.com/storyline/michael-brown-shooting/feds-probing-arson-michael-brown-sr-s-church-n255961.

Soule, Sarah/Van Dyke, Nella: "Black Church Arson in the United States 1989–1996." *Ethnic and Racial Studies* 22 (4), 1999, pp. 724–742, retrieved 22.02.2022, https://doi.org/10.1080/014198799329369.

Strain, Christopher: *Burning Faith Church Arson in the American South*. University of Florida Press: Gainesville 2008.

Walcott, Rinaldo: *The Long Emancipation: Moving Toward Black Freedom*. Duke University Press: Durham, NC and London 2021.

Williams, Juan: Eyes on the Prize: Americas Civil Rights Years, 1954–1965 25th Anniversary ed. Penguin Books: London 2013.

Williams, Kidada E.: *They Left Great Marks on Me: African American Testimonies of Racial Violence*. New York University Press: New York 2012.

Government Reports

Bureau of Alcohol, Tobacco, Firearms, and Explosives, Kansas City Field Division, "ATF Offers Reward in Ferguson Fires." Press release, December 5, 2014, https://www.atf.gov/news/pr/atf-offers-reward-ferguson-fires.

Church Arson Prevention Act of 1996, H.R.3525, 104th Congress (1995–1996), retrieved 02.02.2022, from https://www.congress.gov/bill/104th-congress/house-bill/3525#:~:text=Church%20Arson%20Prevention%20Act%20of%201996%20%2D%20Makes%20Federal%20criminal%20code,%2C%20or%20affects%2C%20interstate%20commerce.

FBI Releases 2020 Hate Crime Statistics Update: Due to a technical issue, the FBI updated *Hate Crime Statistics, 2020* on October 25, 2021, retrieved 22.02.2022, from https://www.fbi.gov/news/pressrel/press-releases/fbi-releases-2020-hate-crime-statistics.

"Springfield Man Sentenced to 166 Months for Arson of African-American Church." FBI press release, U.S. Attorney's Office, December 22, 2011, retrieved 22.02.2022, from https://archives.fbi.gov/archives/boston/press-releases/2011/springfield-man-sentenced-to-166-months-for-arson-of-african-american-church.

Organization Authored Sources

Boaz, Danielle: "Religious Racism in North America: Racially Motivated Attacks Against Places of Worship in the 21st Century, *International Commission to Combat Religious Racism*, March 15, 2023, retrieved, 30.10.2023 https://www.religiousracism.org/_files/ugd/bb6958_6a79552988264b64997fe3f76fbf7704.pdf?mibextid=Zxz2cZ

Flood Christian Center Church: "All About Us," retrieved 17.02.2028, from https://thenewoasis.wixsite.com/the-flood-church/all-about-us.

Obituary: The Rev. Carlton Lee, Pastor of Michael Brown Sr., Dies at 34." *St. Louis American*, June 15, 2017, retrieved 23.02.2018, from https://news.stlpublicradio.org/post/obituary-rev-carlton-lee-pastor-michael-brown-sr-dies-34#stream/0.

Religion, International Politics, and Global Issues

James L. Guth and Brent F. Nelsen

Religion and Support for the "Trump Doctrine"

Abstract: The "return to religion" in international relations has stimulated interest in how religion shapes public attitudes toward foreign affairs, one channel through which faith influences a nation's international policy. In the American case, analysis has focused on the militaristic posture of evangelical Protestants, but some work reveals distinctive perspectives of other groups, confirming the need for a more inclusive analysis. Here we explore religious constituencies for the "Trump Doctrine's" distinctive blend of nationalism, militarism, and unilateralism. The question of religious support for the "Doctrine" is especially intriguing. Not only did the former president's policies deviate markedly from traditional Republican norms, but he also appealed vigorously for backing from some religious groups and demonized others. We find that religious factors explain a good deal of variation in public attitudes toward Trump's policies and are much more important than many conventionally cited demographic influences. Although largely mediated by other attitudinal and political factors, religion has both direct and indirect influences on Americans' foreign policy attitudes.

Keywords: Trump Doctrine, ethnoreligious tradition, militant internationalism, religious belief

Introduction

The "return to religion" in international relations has sparked interest in how religion shapes public attitudes toward foreign affairs, one key channel through which faith influences a nation's policy.[1] Although early public opinion experts found voters apathetic about global issues, poorly informed, and lacking a coherent perspective, that assessment has changed. In the past two decades, scholars have found that attitudes on foreign policy are shaped by identifiable, coherent, and relatively stable belief systems that allow citizens to be "cognitive misers."[2] The most

---

1 Warner, Carolyn M./Walker, Stephen G.: "Thinking about the Role of Religion in Foreign Policy: A Framework for Analysis." *Foreign Policy Analysis* 7 (1), 2011, pp. 113–135.
2 Holsti, Ole: *Public Opinion and American Foreign Policy*. Rev. ed. University of Michigan Press: Ann Arbor 2004.

influential characterization of these structures has been the "Wittkopf-Holsti-Rosenau" typology of *militant internationalism* and *cooperative internationalism*. Although not incorporating every foreign policy issue, these two orientations have survived many changes in national agendas and may even be useful in cross-national analysis.[3] Scholars have discovered that religious factors influence Americans' position on each dimension[4] or at least on critical components, such as willingness to use the military,[5] Middle East policies,[6] global environmental politics,[7] or the benefits of globalization.[8] Here we review the literature on religious influences on foreign policy views and put the Trump Doctrine in that perspective.

---

3   Wittkopf, Eugene R.: *Faces of Internationalism: Public Opinion and Foreign Policy*. Duke University Press: Durham, NC 1990; Holsti, Ole: *op. cit.*; Eichenberg, Richard: "Citizen Opinion on Foreign Policy and World Politics." In: Dalton, Russell J./Klingemann, Hans-Dieter (eds.): *The Oxford Handbook of Political Behavior*. Oxford University Press: Oxford 2007; Guth, James L.: "Religion and Public Opinion on Security: A Comparative Perspective." In: Seiple, Chris/Hoover, Dennis R./Otis, Pauletta: *The Routledge Handbook of Religion and Security*. Routledge: London 2013; Petrikova, Ivica: "Religion and Foreign Policy Views: Are Religious People More Altruistic and/or More Militant?" *International Political Science Review* 40 (4), 2019, pp. 535–557.
4   Gries, Peter: *The Politics of American Foreign Policy*. Stanford University Press: Stanford, CA 2014; Guth, James L.: "Religion and Public Opinion: Foreign Policy Issues." In: Smidt, Corwin E./Kellstedt, Lyman A./Guth, James L. (eds.): *The Oxford Handbook of Religion and American Politics*. Oxford University Press: New York 2009; Guth, James L.: "Religion and American Public Attitudes on War and Peace." *Asian Journal of Peacebuilding* 1 (2), 2013b, pp. 227–252.
5   Nelsen, Brent F./Guth, James L.: "Religious Influence on American Public Attitudes toward Military Action." Paper presented at the 59th annual meeting of the International Studies Association, San Francisco, 04–07.04.2018.
6   Baumgartner, Jody/Francia, Peter/Morris, Jonathan: "A Clash of Civilizations?" *Political Research Quarterly* 61 (2), 2008, pp. 171–179; Barker, David/Hurwitz, Jon/Nelson, Traci: "Of Crusades and Culture Wars." *Journal of Politics* 70 (2), 2008, pp. 307–322; Roy, Oindrila: "Religious Roots of War Attitudes in the United States: Insights from Iraq, Afghanistan, and the Persian Gulf." *Foreign Policy Analysis* 12 (3), 2016, pp. 258–274.
7   Barker, David/Bearce, David H.: "End-Times Theology, the Shadow of the Future, and Public Resistance to Addressing Global Climate Change." *Political Research Quarterly* 66 (2), 2013, pp. 267–279.
8   Guth, James L.: "Economic Globalization: The View from the Pews." *Review of Faith & International Affairs* 8 (4), 2010, pp. 41–46.

Religious Influences on Foreign Policy Attitudes

Although scholars have identified many social, demographic, and ideological influences on Americans' foreign policy attitudes, much variation remains unexplained. Although political scientists routinely use religious variables in studies of electoral politics and domestic public opinion, their role in shaping foreign policy attitudes has usually been ignored. Indeed, in an extensive review of Americans' views, Kohut and Stokes found nothing to study: "[W]ith the exception of policy toward Israel, religion has little bearing on how they think about international affairs."[9] Despite neglect by political scientists, however, the last two decades have seen an outpouring of work in other disciplines arguing that religion has a profound impact on public attitudes and, hence, on political leaders.[10]

There are two major themes here, each evoking one of Wittkopf's "dimensions."[11] The *hegemonic* theme argues that religion fosters militarism, unilateralism, moralism, and nationalistic assertiveness—clearly a militant internationalist interpretation. The "Trump Doctrine," like most post-World War II GOP policy perspectives, has a militant internationalist flavor, albeit with features peculiar to the former president: certainly more "militant" than "internationalist."[12] An alternative *altruistic* theme has also emerged,[13] focusing on religious campaigns for human rights and religious freedom, fighting climate change, expanding international relief operations, combating AIDS in Africa, and working for economic development—fine examples of Wittkopf's cooperative internationalism. Adherents of this agenda usually deplore the use of military force, except in a few instances such as preventing genocide,[14] and religious groups holding this perspective have typically opposed implementation of the Trump Doctrine.

Unfortunately, many empirical analyses of the linkage with foreign policy perspectives are based on simplistic portrayals of American religion. Studies often emphasize the ideas of religious leaders, despite some enormous opinion gaps between elites and people in the pew. And even the best work is often preoccupied

---

9   Kohut, Andrew/Stokes, Bruce: *America Against the World.* Henry Holt: New York 2006, p. 94.
10 For a review, see Guth, James L.: "Religion and American Public Attitudes on War and Peace," *op. cit.*
11 Wittkopf, Eugene R.: *Faces of Internationalism: Public Opinion and Foreign Policy.* Duke University Press: Durham, NC 1990.
12 Cf.: Dueck, Colin: *Age of Iron: On Conservative Nationalism.* Oxford University Press: New York 2019.
13 Wuthnow, Robert: *Boundless Faith: The Global Outreach of American Churches.* University of California Press: Berkeley 2009.
14 Nelsen, Brent F./Guth, James L.: "Religious Influence on American Public Attitudes toward Military Action," *op. cit.*

with the militaristic propensities of white evangelicals.[15] Few analysts consider the other 80% of the public, creating an analytic dualism arraying evangelicals against "secular" opinion (presumably everyone else). But as Alfred Hero demonstrated long ago, most religious groups have distinctive perspectives.[16] Catholic and Mainline Protestant elites, as well as Jewish leaders, have long sought to sway both their own publics and policymakers, with some success.[17] In addition, the growing ranks of religiously unaffiliated Americans often have their own views.[18] Thus, the literature often overstates the uniqueness of one religious group, ignores the potential influence of others, and treats American religious constituencies simplistically.

Scholars also tend to neglect important dimensions of religion beyond affiliation, such as belief and behavior. In fact, religious affiliation, beliefs, and behavior can all have substantial impact on citizens' location on the militant and cooperative internationalist dimensions, especially the former.[19] Gries found that not only do religious traditions differ in proportions of "hawks and doves"[20] but that religious beliefs also shape attitudes on war and peace. And a groundbreaking

---

15 Barker, David/Hurwitz, Jon/Nelson, Traci: *op. cit.*; Baumgartner, Jody/Francia, Peter/Morris, Jonathan: *op. cit.*; Froese, Paul/Mencken, F. Carson: "A U.S. Holy War? The Effects of Religion on Iraq War Policy Attitudes." *Social Science Quarterly* 90 (1), 2009, pp. 103–116; Page, Benjamin/Bouton, Marshall: *The Foreign Policy Disconnect.* University of Chicago Press: Chicago 2006. This focus is justified by the claim that evangelicals are more influential than other groups (Mead, Walter Russell: "Religion and U.S. Foreign Policy." *Foreign Affairs* 85 (5), 2006, pp. 24–43).
16 Hero, Alfred O.: American Religious Groups View Foreign Policy: Trends in Rank-and-File Opinion, 1937–1969. Duke University Press: Durham, NC 1973.
17 Wald, Kenneth: "Religious Elites and Public Opinion: The Impact of the Bishops' Peace Pastoral." *The Review of Politics* 54 (1), 1992, pp. 112–143; Kurtz, Lester/Goran, Kelly: "Love Your Enemies? Protestants and United States Foreign Policy." In: Wuthnow, Robert/Evans, John H. (eds.): *The Quiet Hand of God: Faith-Based Activism and the Public Role of Mainline Protestantism.* University of California Press: Berkeley 2002; Rock, Stephen R.: *Faith and Foreign Policy.* Continuum: New York 2011.
18 Hansen, Susan B.: *Religion and Reaction: The Secular Political Response to the Religious Right.* Rowman & Littlefield: Lanham, MD 2011; Campbell, David E./Layman, Geoffrey C./Green, John C.: *Secular Surge: A New Fault Line in American Politics.* Cambridge University Press: Cambridge 2021.
19 Guth, James L.: "Militant and Cooperative Internationalism among American Religious Publics." *Politics and Religion Journal* 7 (2), 2013a, pp. 315–343; Guth, James L.: "Religion and Public Opinion on Security: A Comparative Perspective," *op. cit.*; Guth, James L.: "Religion and Public Opinion: Foreign Policy Issues," *op. cit.*
20 Gries, Peter: *op. cit.*

cross-national analysis of eighty-nine countries demonstrated the varying and interacting effects of "religious belief, belonging, and behaviour,"[21] showing the need for careful measurement of multiple religious variables.

Religious Groups in American Politics

To understand the religious context, we draw on two theories on the politics of American religion, each emphasizing different religious variables. *Ethnocultural theory*, formulated primarily by historians, focuses on the numerous ethnoreligious groups that migrated to America and multiplied upon reaching her shores. In this perspective, politics has always been a competition between two uneasy coalitions of ethnoreligious groups. The Republican Party (GOP) long represented historically dominant Mainline Protestants, such as Episcopalians, Presbyterians, and Methodists, with the more recent addition of evangelical Protestants and Latter-day Saints, while Democrats have always spoken for ethnoreligious minorities: Catholics and Jews in the past, and now Black Protestants, Latino Catholics, Muslims, Hindus, Buddhists, and others, including the growing ranks of the religiously unaffiliated or "Nones." Historians argue that these ethnoreligious groups held differing worldviews, cultural preferences, and religious reference groups—all shaping their partisan allegiances and views on public policy.[22]

A few examples illustrate the relevance of ethnoreligious traditions. The hostility of Irish Catholics toward America's alliance with Great Britain and the isolationism of German-American Lutherans and Catholics during World War I are just two cases of ethnoreligious influence. Catholic anticommunism in the 1940s and 1950s was shaped not only by Church condemnation of that "Godless" system but also by solidarity with Eastern European kin under Soviet domination. The persistent concern of American Jews for Israel, the interest of Black Protestants in Africa, and the continuing influence of Armenian Americans on policy toward Turkey are just three examples of patterns characteristic of a host of American "ethnoreligious fragments."[23] Indeed, the late Samuel P. Huntington feared that U.S. policy would be unduly influenced by such "diasporas," especially Latinos.[24] On the other hand, more optimistic observers see the rise of such minorities fostering

---

21 Petrikova, Ivica: *op. cit.*
22 For a review, see Swierenga, Robert P.: "Religion and American Voting Behavior, 1830s to 1930s." In: Smidt, Corwin E./Kellstedt, Lyman A./Guth, James L. (eds.): *The Oxford Handbook of Religion and American Politics*. Oxford University Press: New York 2009.
23 Uslaner, Eric M.: "American Interests in the Balance." In: Cigler, Allan J./Loomis, Burdett (eds.): *Interest Group Politics*. 7th ed. CQ Press: Washington, DC 2007.
24 Huntington, Samuel P.: *Who Are We? The Challenges to America's National Identity*. Simon and Schuster: New York 2004, pp. 285–291.

cooperative internationalism: As America comes to resemble a "United Nations" ethnoreligiously, it should look more favorably on multilateral engagements and cooperation. And some comparative studies do suggest that religious minorities are less militaristic and more "internationalist," especially if part of an ethnic diaspora crossing international frontiers.[25]

An alternative perspective is the *religious restructuring* theory, introduced by sociologist Robert Wuthnow in 1988 to explain growing divisions within American faith traditions. A few years later, James Hunter's *Culture Wars* argued that these theological controversies had created political divides: "Orthodox" believers who accepted "an external, definable, and transcendent authority" adhered firmly to traditional doctrines and gravitated to the political right. Religious "progressives," on the other side, replaced old faith claims with new ones drawn from experience or scientific rationality and moved to the left,[26] joined by the growing ranks of secular Americans who saw morality in a similar vein.[27] Political lines, then, were based on theology rather than ethnoreligious divisions.[28]

There is strong evidence that religious belief influences foreign policy attitudes. Traditionalists and the religiously observant hold more "militant" perspectives than do religious progressives and the less observant, who prefer more "cooperative" approaches.[29] Beyond these general theological orientations, some "specialized" beliefs, such as Protestant dispensationalism, also influence key attitudes, such as support for Israel or willingness to back the UN.[30] Even framing policy in "providential" terms may shape public responses.[31] Whether religious belief

---

25 Petrikova, Ivica: *op. cit.*
26 Hunter, James D.: *Culture Wars: The Struggle to Define America.* Basic Books: New York 1991, p. 44.
27 Hansen, Susan B.: *op. cit.*; Campbell, David E./Layman, Geoffrey C./Green, John C.: *op. cit.*
28 Although Wuthnow (*The Restructuring of American Religion, op. cit.*) and Hunter (*op. cit.*) defined these divides by religious belief rather than behavior, the "orthodox" put more stress on faith and are more observant than "progressives," complicating the task of distinguishing effects of belief and behavior. Indeed, service attendance often serves as a proxy for traditional belief in scholarly analyses.
29 Guth, James L.: "Religion and Public Opinion: Foreign Policy Issues," *op. cit.*; Gries, Peter: *op. cit.*
30 Clark, Victoria: *Allies for Armageddon: The Rise of Christian Zionism.* Yale University Press: New Haven, CT 2007.
31 Glazier, Rebecca: "Divine Direction: How Providential Religious Beliefs Shape Foreign Policy Attitudes." *Foreign Policy Analysis* 9 (2), 2013, pp. 127–142.

has a direct impact, as argued by Taydas, Kentmen, and Olson,[32] or its effects are mediated by partisan and ideological factors[33] is still an open question.

Data and Methods

Although the relationship between religious factors and support for competing foreign policy perspectives is fascinating, empirical analysis suffers from a paucity of surveys with extensive batteries on both policy and religion. The Chicago Council on Global Affairs surveys, for example, are rich in foreign policy items but have only one or two religious measures—and not very sophisticated ones at that.[34] On the other hand, surveys of religion usually lack foreign policy questions. Ideally, then, to test religious influences on the "Trump Doctrine," we need data on central elements of that policy, as well as measures of belonging, behavior, and belief (the "three Bs" of religious analysis).

We use the 2020 American National Election Study (ANES). Long the "gold standard" for political science surveys, the ANES features many tested measures. The large N (over 7,100 in the post-election survey) and fairly precise screens for ethnicity and religious affiliation permit us to examine attitudes of specific ethnoreligious traditions with some accuracy, testing the insights of ethnocultural theory. And the queries on belief, behavior, and identity allow us to assess the value of restructuring theory.

The Trump Doctrine

Our first task is to construct a measure of support for the "Trump Doctrine," a variant of militant internationalism. Although scholars debate whether Trump's foreign policy was built on a coherent "Doctrine," in practice many themes were clear enough: nationalism, unilateralism, militarism, and a preference for breaking international rules and norms.[35] Although not every nuance of Trump's foreign policy is captured by survey questions, we use ten items that tap most of those themes. A principal components analysis (PCA) reveals a powerful first dimension

---

32 Taydas, Zeynep/Kentman, Cigdem/Olson, Laura: "Faith Matters: Religious Affiliation and Public Opinion About Barack Obama's Foreign Policy in the 'Greater' Middle East." *Social Science Quarterly* 93 (5), pp. 1218–1242.
33 Roy, Oindrila: *op. cit.*
34 Page, Benjamin/Bouton, Marshall: *op. cit.*; Guth, James L.: "Religion and American Public Attitudes on War and Peace," *op. cit.*
35 Joffe, Alex: "Explaining the Trump Doctrine." *BESA Center Perspectives Paper No. 1,039*, December 18, 2018, retrieved 08.09.2021, from https://besacenter.org/trump-doctrine/; Council on Foreign Relations: "The World Trump Made." *Foreign Affairs* 99 (5), 2020, pp. 10–56.

that echoes his distinctive emphases: the need to build a wall on the Mexican border (loading = .86), overall approval of Trump's foreign policy (.83), support for enhanced border security spending (.79), approval for more defense spending (.67), skepticism about global warming policy (.62), endorsement of Trump's dealing with the Ukraine (.59), perception that Iran is a major threat to the United States (.41), view that China is a major threat (.40), willingness to use military force in international relations (.31), and opposition to freer global trade (.28). These items have strong face validity, and the PCA score has a *theta* reliability of .84, indicating a robust measure.[36]

Religion

The 2020 ANES religious battery allows us to test the impact of several dimensions of religion: first, it includes the usual ANES religious affiliation questions, permitting us to classify ethnoreligious groups, following the widely used "Reltrad" scheme, emphasizing the theological, social, and organizational settings of religious membership.[37] ANES 2020 also has a "biblicism" item that taps theological orthodoxy, a religious service attendance (religiosity) question, and a religious "importance" score. Although these latter items get at somewhat distinct aspects of religious belief and behavior, restructuring theory suggests that they should be strongly intercorrelated, producing a traditionalism/modernism dimension, with biblical literalists, the observant, and those who see faith as salient in their lives occupying the traditionalist pole, and their opposites dominating the modernist or religiously progressive end of the spectrum. ANES also asked about religious identities, which can also be used to place respondents on the traditionalism/modernism continuum. Finally, ANES queried how warmly respondents felt toward four religious groups ("Christian fundamentalists," "Christians," "Jews," and "Muslims"). These responses probably reflect aspects of belief and identity, but may also reveal "in-groups" and "outgroups," or, as ethnocultural historians might put it, positive and negative reference groups.

All these measures allow us to examine which dimensions of religion shape attitudes toward the Trump Doctrine and how religious factors perform under

---

36 Some might object that the Trump policy evaluation contaminates the score with partisanship, but omission of this score (or any other) has little impact on the results reported below, giving us great confidence in the robustness of the findings. One might wish for inclusion of previous ANES questions on Mideast policy, but other items that might be added would provide little added assistance in measuring support for the president's policy.

37 Steensland, Brian/Park, Jerry/Regnerus, Mark/Robinson, Lynn/Wilcox, Bradford/Woodberry, Robert: "The Measure of American Religion." *Social Forces* 79 (1), 2000, pp. 291–318; Smidt, Corwin E./Kellstedt, Lyman A./Guth, James L. (eds.): *The Oxford Handbook of Religion and American Politics*. Oxford University Press: New York 2010.

A Preliminary Look

controls for other political forces, especially those emphasized by previous studies of American foreign policy attitudes, giving us some perspective on the direct or indirect nature of religious influence.

For a broad overview, we converted Trump Doctrine scores into a hundred-point scale (100 = highest support). In what follows, we report mean scores for members of American ethnoreligious traditions and for respondents to the standard ANES measures of religious belief, behavior, and identity. With the large sample, we can examine twelve ethnoreligious traditions: white evangelical Protestants, white Catholics, Latino Catholics, Latino evangelicals, Latter-day Saints (Mormons), white Mainline Protestants, Eastern Orthodox, Black Protestants, and Jews. We also include the religiously unaffiliated ("the Nones" or "Nothing in Particulars"), of increasing importance to American politics, while separating self-identified agnostics and atheists, quite distinct in attitudes. Finally, we combine Muslims, Hindus, Sikhs, Baha'is, and Buddhists in a "world religions" category. Although obviously different in belief and practice, as ethnoreligious minorities and parts of diasporas, they should be skeptical of the Trump Doctrine's scorn for "non-American" religious traditions.

What do we discover? Confirming previous findings, evangelical Protestants are quite distinctive, exceeding all others in support of the Trump Doctrine (mean score = 70), followed at some distance by Latter-day Saints (61), Latino evangelicals (58), white Catholics (57), Mainline Protestants (56), and Eastern Orthodox (55). On the other side, agnostics and atheists are most critical (26), joined by "world religions" (37), Jews (38),[38] Latino Catholics (42), the unaffiliated "Nothing in Particular" (42), and Black Protestants (45). Clearly, America's major ethnoreligious traditions diverge in willingness to endorse the Trump Doctrine, but those rejecting all religions are most critical.

The starkly contrasting positions of the nonreligious, especially atheists and agnostics, and strongly traditionalist evangelicals buttress restructuring theorists' contention that it is really religious belief and behavior that influence attitudes, not ethnoreligious affiliation. And the Bible item, one measure of theological traditionalism, reveals substantial differences: "literalists" exceed the Doctrine mean (62), while those with "low" views of Scripture are even further *below* that average (35). Those seeing Scripture as the word of God, but not to be read literally, fall a smidgen above the mean (52). Although the Bible item is only a crude measure of

---

38 This figure hides sharp community divisions, as Orthodox and Conservative Jews average 57 on the scale while the larger cohort of Reform and non-affiliated Jews score much lower: 33 and 26, respectively. This gap may well reflect different responses to Trump's Middle East policies.

orthodoxy, these gaps suggest that beliefs may be potent influences—especially when assessed in depth.[39]

Our expectations with respect to religious salience and observance are mixed: some studies suggest that religiosity works against the militarism that pervades the Trump Doctrine, while others find this effect only when other facets of religion are controlled.[40] In our case, those saying religion is "very important" in their lives are more supportive of Trump's policies (59), while those for whom religion is not at all important are equally far on the other side (40). Religious attendance fits the same pattern, with a big gap between the most frequent attenders (63) and those who never go (45).

Does religious identity influence attitudes? Scholars have long sought to use such identities to tap basic religious worldviews, but with mixed results.[41] The recent surge of interest in identity theories and interpretations of American electoral politics has revived interest in religious identities.[42] The 2020 ANES offered a battery of ten religious labels for respondent choice. Although these items are not without conceptual difficulties,[43] they do show some analytic promise. Unfortunately, ANES allowed respondents to choose more than one "traditionalist" identity, but only one "progressive" option. To produce measures roughly comparable for statistical analysis, we created three dichotomous scores: "evangelical/traditionalist" for anyone choosing one or more "conservative" labels, such as "fundamentalist," "evangelical," "both fundamentalist and evangelical," "Pentecostal/charismatic," or "traditional." On the "progressive" side, "Progressive/Nontraditional" includes those selecting either of those labels or "spiritual but not religious." Finally "Secular" includes only that option, which we regard as an indicator of a conscious secularist perspective,[44] as respondents could also select "none"

---

39 Guth, James L.: "Religion and Public Opinion: Foreign Policy Issues," *op. cit.*; Barker, David/Hurwitz, Jon/Nelson, Traci: *op. cit.*; Barker, David/Bearce, David H.: *op. cit.*
40 Petrikova, Ivica: *op. cit.*
41 Leege, David C./Kellstedt, Lyman A. (eds.): *Rediscovering the Religious Factor in American Politics*. M.E. Sharpe: Armonk, NY 1993; Smidt, Corwin E./Kellstedt, Lyman A./Guth, James L. (eds.): *op. cit.*, pp. 17–18.
42 Sides, John/Tesler, Michael/Vavreck, Lynn: *Identity Crisis: The 2016 Presidential Campaign and the Battle for the Meaning of America*. Princeton University Press: Princeton 2018; Jardina, Ashley: *White Identity Politics*. Cambridge University Press: Cambridge 2019. Although Sides, John/Tesler, Michael/Vavreck, Lynn: *op. cit.* repeatedly mention religion as a force in identity politics, they offer virtually no analysis of how religion shapes other social or political identities. Jardina (*op. cit.*) has only a brief discussion.
43 Some labels offered are widely used by religious Americans, while others are more restricted to religious elites. Most labels are more evocative for Protestants, having less resonance for Catholics or non-Christians.
44 Campbell, David E./Layman, Geoffrey C./Green, John C.: *op. cit.*

as an alternative.[45] As expected, "evangelical/traditionalist" identities are linked fairly strongly with favorability toward the Trump Doctrine (62), whereas those choosing "Progressive/Nontraditional" (40) or "secular" (22) labels fell well below the national average.[46]

Finally, thermometer ratings for prominent religious groups also produce strong results. ANES asked for ratings of "Christian fundamentalists," "Christians," "Jews," and "Muslims" from "0" (very cold) to "100" (very warm). The theoretical status of these ratings is unclear, but they probably tap both ethnocultural and restructuring dimensions. The classic ethnocultural theories put considerable stress on both positive and negative reference groups for individual ethnoreligious traditions (e.g., Democratic Irish Catholics were disliked by Republican Scottish Presbyterians and vice-versa). Contemporary scholars have often argued that attitudes on American foreign policy are shaped by positive and negative reference groups, such as "Christians" or "Muslims." Such evaluations may also reflect perceived agreement with or similarity of religious belief, as argued by the restructuring school, evidenced perhaps by the strong positive response of Biblical literalists and evangelical Protestants to "Christian fundamentalists" (r = .531 and .328, respectively). For purposes of illustration, we count those giving a rating of 51 degrees or higher as "warm" toward a group. Although this reduces the variation, we still see clear patterns: those liking fundamentalists support the Doctrine (66), followed distantly by those favorable toward "Christians" (56). Those favoring Jews are just below the national mean (49); those warm toward Muslims are critical of the Doctrine (39).

Thus, we find preliminary support for both ethnoreligious and restructuring theories, as indicators for each show clear patterns.[47] Table 1 formalizes these relationships in a series of OLS regressions, reporting the standardized regression coefficients (b) of each religious measure as a predictor of support for the Trump Doctrine. (Respondents classified in a group not in the table constitute the omitted reference group, scoring close to the sample mean.)

---

45 "Mainline" was picked by very few respondents and showed little impact on Doctrine scores.
46 Those with multiple conservative identities scored higher on Doctrine than those choosing only one, but to maintain symmetry in the analysis, we use the dichotomous measure in the analysis below.
47 These findings are virtually identical to those in our analysis of the 2016 ANES, despite the different items used for Trump Doctrine scores (Nelsen, Brent F./Guth, James L.: "Religious Influence on American Foreign Policy Attitudes: The Case of the 'Trump Doctrine.'" Paper presented at the 60th annual meeting of the International Studies Association, Toronto, 27–30.03.2019).

Table 1. Religion and Public Support for the "Trump Doctrine," 2020 (OLS *betas*)

	Model 1 Religious Affiliation[a]	Model 2 Beliefs and Behavior	Model 3 Religious Identities	Model 4 Religious References	Model 5 All Variables
Ethnoreligious Affiliation					
Evangelical Protestant	.301***				.101***
White Catholic	.115***				.064***
White Mainline	.091**				.046***
Latino Evangelical	.061***				–.010
Latter-day Saints	.050***				.035***
Eastern Orthodox	.024***				.001
Black Protestant	–.029*				–.093***
Latino Catholic	–.038**				–.060***
World Religions	–.047***				–.006
Jewish	–.052***				–.003
Nothing in Particular	–.063***				–.006
Agnostic/Atheist	–.233***				–.028*
Beliefs and Behavior					
Biblical Literalism		.326***			.104***
Religious Guidance		.154***			.027
Service Attendance		–.007			–.064***
Religious Identities					
Evangelical/Traditional			.284***		.024
Progressive/Nontraditional			–.090***		–.065***
Secular			–.151***		–.066***
Thermometers					
Fundamentalists				.373***	.308***
Christians				.134***	.069***
Jews				.032**	.008
Muslims				–.404***	–.337***
Adjusted R squared=	.205	.192	.151	.415	.465

Source: American National Election Study, 2020. $N = 6{,}457$. ***$p < .001$; **$p < .01$; *$p < .05$.

[a] "Other Christians" and many small religious groups constitute omitted reference category as collectively they are very close to the sample mean.

Model 1 summarizes the impact of ethnoreligious membership. Evangelicals stand out as much more favorable toward the Trump Doctrine than any other group, while agnostics and atheists occupy the other end of the continuum. White Catholics, Mainline Protestants, Latino evangelicals, Latter-day Saints, and, finally, Eastern Orthodox provide some additional support for the Doctrine. On the other side, most ethnoreligious "minorities" join atheists and agnostics in opposition. Ethnoreligious affiliation explains over 20% of the variance, a strong performance compared to analyses using a range of other sociodemographic variables.[48]

Model 2 summarizes the impact of belief and behavior, showing that biblicism has the most powerful impact, followed at a distance by the importance of religion. Church attendance, widely used in journalistic parlance (and in some social science) as a marker of conservative religion, actually drops out of the equation when traditionalism and religious salience are accounted for. In any event, these items explain 19% of the variance, close to that of ethnoreligious tradition.[49] We suspect that better religious belief measures would show even greater influence. Religious identities are also solid predictors of attitudes, as Model 3 shows. "Evangelical/traditionalist" choices, as expected, produce backing for the Doctrine, while the other two have negative effects, with "secular" on the opposite pole. Identities, moreover, explain 15% of the variance, slightly less than either ethnoreligious tradition or religious traditionalism. (If we use the full measure of all conservative identities, the *beta* coefficient rises from .284 to .312 and the variance explained by identities goes up to 17%).

Model 4 considers the impact of religious reference groups. Those feeling warm toward fundamentalists are substantially more pro-Trump Doctrine (and, of course, those who feel cold, much less positive). The same is true, though more weakly, for sentiments toward "Christians," while higher ratings for "Jews" produce no significant impact. On the other hand, those with warm sentiments toward Muslims are much more critical. Altogether, the group thermometers predict more than twice as much variance as any other equation: more than 41%, an impressive result.

These first cuts certainly suggest that religious factors have an important bearing on public response to the Trump Doctrine. Of course, religious variables are interrelated in a complex and often powerful fashion. For example, evangelicals typically have high views of Scripture, take conservative religious identities, and

---

48 Cf.: Page, Benjamin/Bouton, Marshall: *op. cit.*
49 As restructuring theorists might predict, these measures are highly correlated: those with orthodox views of Scripture also exhibit high religious salience and attend services frequently; indeed, when combined, they produce a strong traditionalism/modernism scale (*theta* = .81). This measure correlates quite strongly with Trump Doctrine scores (r = .402), but for consistency we use the separate items in the analysis below, illustrating the power of the "belief" measure and revealing a common tendency of observance to "flip" signs in multivariate analysis.

feel warmly toward fundamentalists and coolly toward Muslims. So, it is useful to consider the direct contributions of each variable to support for the Trump Doctrine. Model 5 tests a complete religious explanation.

Although many of the affiliation, belief, and identity measures retain significant effects, their coefficients are substantially reduced, while the thermometer ratings exhibit more staying power. This suggests that the effects of affiliation, belief, and identity are partially mediated by attitudes toward these highly evocative and socially symbolic religious reference groups. A series of regressions confirms that the former religious variables are strong predictors of the thermometer items, especially for "fundamentalists" and "Christians." That the variance explained by all the measures combined rises only slightly to 46.9% (compared to 41.5% for the thermometers alone) supports this interpretation.

Nevertheless, the broader picture is clear: many affiliation, belief, and identity items still move respondents in expected directions: Evangelicals, Mainline Protestants, white Catholics, and Mormons remain more positive toward Trump's posture, while large religious minorities, such as Black Protestants and Latino Catholics, are still significantly less supportive. Note, however, that the strong negative coefficient for "Nothing in Particular" disappears, perhaps mediated by "secular" identity and "non-belief," although professed atheists and agnostics remain slightly more critical of the Doctrine. Biblical literalism retains a notable direct positive influence, but church attendance reverses signs once all the factors are entered, perhaps representing liberal religious activism after conservative belief and identity are controlled for.[50] Similarly, the identity coefficients decline, but all three remain in expected directions and the two "liberal" identities are still strong and significant. Perhaps, the most striking finding is that religious variables combined account for *nearly half* the variance.

Finally, we reran the regression with controls for age, gender, education, income, and veteran status. At the bivariate level, older citizens, men, the wealthy, the less-educated, and military veterans are more likely to favor the Trump Doctrine,[51] and these effects appear in the regression. But the religious coefficients are

---

50 This tendency for church attendance to "flip signs" in multivariate analysis is frequently observed (Petrikova, Ivica: *op. cit.*), but difficult to interpret. Sometimes it may indicate a "liberalizing" effect of attendance on conservative believers, but here it probably taps the impact of (atypical) religiosity among liberals.

51 Cf.: Holsti, Ole: *op. cit.*; Page, Benjamin/Bouton, Marshall: *op. cit.*; Eichenberg, Richard: "Gender Difference in American Public Opinion on the Use of Military Force, 1982–2013." *International Studies Quarterly* 60 (1), 2016, pp. 138–148; *idem*: "Gender Difference in Support for the Use of Military Force in Cross-National Perspective." Paper presented at the workshop on "Public Opinion, Foreign Policy and the Use of Force in Turbulent Times." European Consortium for Political Research Joint Sessions, University of Nottingham, 25–30.04.2017.

virtually unchanged, showing that their influence is largely independent of demographics. Indeed, sociodemographic variables add less than 1% to the variance explained by religion (data not shown), confirming the powerful influence of the "faith factor."

The Trump Doctrine in Ideological and Political Context

We have shown that both ethnocultural and restructuring perspectives provide some analytic tools for understanding religious constituencies for the Trump Doctrine. The historically dominant white religious traditions, but especially white evangelicals, provide much of the public backing for the former president's policies, while religious minorities and nonreligious people constitute the bulk of the opposition. But restructuring factors have influence as well: biblical literalism, traditionalist identifications, and affection for conservative religious groups predict support, independent of ethnoreligious tradition. And all the religious measures account for a great deal of the variation in adherence to the Doctrine.

But do religious influences operate directly? Or are they mediated by other variables more proximate to foreign policy attitudes? In Table 2, we address these questions by including religious factors in successively broader analytic frameworks. First, Model 1 simplifies and summarizes religion's impact by including only the significant variables from Table 1 and combining identities into a single secular-to-evangelical scale.

In Model 2 we add several attitudinal factors to our explanation of support for the Doctrine. We begin with a central tenet of cooperative internationalism, support for multilateral institutions, measured here by a PCA score from thermometer ratings of the UN, NATO, and World Health Organization ($theta = .83$). Although in Wittkopf's pioneering work "militant" and "cooperative" orientations were largely independent of each other, that is no longer true: they increasingly appear as alternatives.[52] As Model 2 shows, *multilateralism* has a strongly negative impact on Doctrine scores, no surprise to anyone observing Trump's denigration of those three international organizations. We also incorporated *generalized threat assessment*,[53] measured by perceptions of dangers to U.S. interests posed by three allies: Mexico, Japan, and Germany ($theta = .76$). As anticipated, those seeing such threats were more supportive of the Trump Doctrine, perhaps echoing his well-known disdain of allies. Finally, we incorporated Page and Bouton's measure

---

52 Wittkopf, Eugene R.: *Faces of Internationalism: Public Opinion and Foreign Policy*. Duke University Press: Durham, NC 1990.
53 Cf.: Dill, Janina/Schubiger, Livia I.: "Attitudes toward the Use of Force: Instrumental Imperatives, Moral Principles, and International Law." *American Journal of Political Science* 65 (5), 2021, pp. 612–633.

Table 2. Religion in Context: Support for the "Trump Doctrine," 2020 (OLS *betas*)

	Model 1 Religion	Model 2 + Attitudes	Model 3 + Politics
Ethnoreligious Affiliation			
Evangelical Protestant	.106***	.101***	.052***
White Catholic	.069***	.055***	.021**
White Mainline	.051***	.057***	.030***
Latter-day Saints	.038***	.020*	−.001
Latino Catholic	−.057***	−.047**	−.028***
Black Protestant	−.088***	−.091***	−.007
Agnostic/Atheist	−.029**	−.002	−.003
Beliefs and Behavior			
Biblical Literalism	.107***	.041***	.018*
Service Attendance	−.056***	−.021*	−.028***
Religious Identities			
Secular to Evangelical	.102***	.034***	−.002
Thermometers			
Fundamentalists	.310***	.138***	.069***
Christians	.073***	.054***	.035***
Muslims	−.332***	−.102***	−.048***
Attitudes			
Multilateralism		−.273***	−.143***
American Exceptionalism		.155***	.093***
Nativism		.146***	.108***
Threat Assessment		.120***	.128***
Authoritarianism		.106***	.086***
Strong Leadership		.098***	.062***
"Active Part"		−.057***	−.060***
Party and Ideology			
Republican ID			.301***
Conservatism			.182***
Adjusted R squared=	.464	.636	.728

Source: American National Election Study, 2020. *N* = 6,421.

***p <. 001; **p <. 01; *p<. 05.

of public preferences for the United States to play an *active part* in international affairs, revealing that isolationism also contributes a little to support for the Doctrine.[54]

Trump's "populist" leadership style and policy positions are common tropes among journalists and scholars. Although usually couched in terms of domestic politics, populist style and orientations might also contribute to public backing for the Doctrine—and they do. *Nativist* attitudes, belief in *American exceptionalism, authoritarianism*, and preference for a *strong leader* "willing to break the rules," all encourage backing for Trump's foreign policy.[55] Once again, none of these findings is terribly surprising.[56]

As we show elsewhere,[57] these "populist" attitudes are shaped by the same religious factors that influence public reception of the Trump Doctrine. Perhaps, then, religion's effects are fully mediated by nativism, exceptionalism, authoritarianism, and other "populist" traits. But as Model 2 shows, most religious coefficients remain significant even after attitudinal factors are added, although some are reduced in magnitude: the ethnoreligious groups largely retain their influence, although the effects of biblicism, service attendance, religious identity, and reference groups are all considerably reduced, hinting that "belief" factors may have more influence on these attitudinal traits than does ethnoreligious affiliation. Nevertheless, the former retains substantial direct influence.

Finally, in Model 3, we add both partisanship and ideology, identified by scholars as the most potent contemporary influences on foreign policy views[58] As religious traits are central to the recent "sorting" of Americans along increasingly polarized

---

54 Page, Benjamin/Bouton, Marshall: *op. cit.*, p. 70. *Active part* is measured by V201349.
55 *Nativism* is a four-item PCA score of items (V202421 to V202424) asking how important to being American is having American ancestry, being born in the United States, speaking English, and accepting American customs (*theta* = .81). *Exceptionalism* is measured by V202273x, asking how much better America is than other countries. *Authoritarianism* is a PCA score derived from the standard four items (V202266 to V202269) (*theta* = .66). *Strong leader* is tapped by V202134.
56 Norris, Pippa/Inglehart, Ronald: *Cultural Backlash: Trump, Brexit, and Authoritarian Populism*. Cambridge University Press: Cambridge 2019.
57 Guth, James L.: "Are White Evangelicals Populists? The View from the 2016 American National Election Study." *Review of Faith and International Affairs* 17 (3), 2019, pp. 20–35; *idem*: "Religion and American Populism." Paper presented to the GIRES International Conference on Religion in American Politics, 17–18.07.2021.
58 See: Holsti, Ole: *op. cit.*; Gries, Peter: *op. cit.* Holsti emphasizes partisan influences on foreign policy opinion, while Gries stresses ideology. Given their increasingly strong correlation (in this sample r = .675), this argument almost seems moot. Indeed, a scale combining ideology and partisanship explains exactly as much variance as the two variables entered separately.

partisan and ideological lines,[59] the religious influences we have seen to this point might ultimately be channeled through ideological and partisan identifications, the variables most "proximate" to electoral choices in the classic "funnel of causality."[60] To test this possibility, we added the standard party and ideological self-identification items in Model 3.

The results suggest some support for the mediation hypothesis. Obviously, both party and ideology matter: Republicans and conservatives are much warmer than Democrats and liberals toward tenets of the Doctrine. Including these variables eliminates most direct effects of ethnoreligious affiliation, although evangelicals, Mainliners, and white Catholics are still a little more inclined toward support and Latino Catholics toward opposition. Biblical literalism retains some impact, as do the three reference groups. Most religious influences, however, are channeled by partisanship and ideology: they are now "baked into" the party system.

Although religion's impact is largely transmitted through partisanship and ideology, the attitudinal factors retain considerable direct effect, showing that the Trump Doctrine drew support from sources beyond those undergirding traditional Republican foreign policy: from citizens skeptical of multilateral organizations and alliances, those seeing threats even from allies, folks liking strong if arbitrary leadership, believers in American exceptionalism, and nativists. In all, Model 3 explains almost three-quarters of the variance. Once again, inclusion of age, education, income, gender, and veteran status hardly changes the coefficients in Model 3, adding only 1% to the variance explained (data not shown).

Discussion and Conclusions

Although the study of religion and foreign policy opinion has a long history, social scientists have just begun to re-examine the relationship in the contemporary era. Although Hero's pioneering work revealed often dramatic ethnoreligious differences on international issues,[61] political scientists have been slow to re-appropriate and expand on his insights. Although leading scholars often stumble upon significant opinion differences among religious groups, these are often downplayed or explained away.[62] This tendency reflects the secular blinders of many social scientists, but also the absence of good data. Recent studies have begun to remedy these defects, often relying

---

59 Kellstedt, Lyman A./Guth, James L.: "Religious Groups as a Polarizing Force." In: Crotty, William (ed.): *Polarized Politics: The Impact of Divisiveness in the U.S. Political System*. Lynne Rienner: Boulder 2015.
60 Cf.: Miller, Warren/Shanks, J. Merrill: *The New American Voter*. Harvard University Press: Cambridge 1996.
61 Hero's (*op. cit.*) pioneering work.
62 Page, Benjamin/Bouton, Marshall: *op. cit.*

on specialized surveys[63] or making best use of studies with limited religious measures but extensive foreign policy items.[64] In either case, such efforts have demonstrated that religion has a powerful influence on foreign policy attitudes, whether with respect to Middle Eastern policies,[65] global environmental politics,[66] international trade, or, most notably, the general structure of foreign policy attitudes.[67]

The present analysis has continued the pursuit by examining the impact of religious factors on a new variant of militant internationalism, "the Trump Doctrine," an amalgam of attitudes consonant with the former president's campaign pronouncements and subsequent official actions. Confirming previous findings, we discover that religious traditionalists, especially evangelical Protestants, whether identified by affiliation, belief, religious identity, or feelings of warmth toward fellow believers, are the strongest defenders of the Trump Doctrine, as they were of earlier versions of militant internationalism. Most ethnoreligious minorities, on the other hand, are less favorable, and the religiously unaffiliated—especially agnostics, atheists, and the consciously "secular"—are even more hostile. Most religious influences, with the notable exception of reference group assessments, are now fully embedded in the partisan and ideological identifications of citizens. But partisanship and ideology are augmented by opposition to multilateral institutions, nativism, perceived threats, authoritarian attitudes, American exceptionalism, and support for a "strong" leader—traits exhibited by Trump himself.

Although the findings here mesh well with the available literature on religion and foreign policy attitudes, many questions require more exploration. First, our assessment of foreign policy viewpoints is still limited by data constraints. Although we have a strong measure of the Trump Doctrine in the 2020 ANES, we have less material to work with in tapping cooperative internationalism, although we have used support for multilateral organizations, an important facet of that orientation. A fuller set of foreign policy questions would allow us to analyze religious support for the broader dimension of cooperative internationalism, providing a portrait of religious influence likely to be almost a mirror image of that exhibited here.[68]

Second, we need more inquiry into the cognitive and other mechanisms underlying these results. What is it about biblical literalism that seems conducive to the Trump

---

63 Gries, Peter: *op. cit.*; Guth, James L.: "Religion and Public Opinion: Foreign Policy Issues," *op. cit.*; Barker, David/Hurwitz, Jon/Nelson, Traci: *op. cit.*
64 Guth, James L.: "Religion and American Public Attitudes on War and Peace," *op. cit.*
65 Baumgartner, Jody/Francia, Peter/Morris, Jonathan: *op. cit.*; Barker, David/Hurwitz, Jon/Nelson, Traci: *op. cit.*
66 Barker, David/Bearce, David H.: *op. cit.*
67 Guth, James L.: "Militant and Cooperative Internationalism among American Religious Publics," *op. cit.*
68 Cf.: Guth, James L.: "Religion and American Public Attitudes on War and Peace," *op. cit.*

Doctrine? Why are ethnoreligious minorities consistently averse to most tenets of that doctrine? Why do secular citizens occupy the most "pacifistic" sector of the opinion spectrum? What explains gaping religious divisions on global environmental policy? We need to understand more about the nature of the linkage between religious factors and foreign policy opinion, but such undertakings will require more consistent use of detailed religious measures in academic surveys.

Some broader implications are quite clear, however. The moral and religious divisions so evident in American electoral and legislative politics on domestic issues clearly pervade foreign policy attitudes as well, reducing the prospects for bipartisan consensus.[69] Contrary to the old adage, politics (including religious politics) does not "stop at the water's edge." If, as seems likely, religious divisions shape a wide range of other foreign policy questions, the ability of decision-makers to resolve such contentious questions may be in doubt, duplicating the ideological and partisan stalemate that afflicts other areas of national policy. And scholars of American foreign policy opinion need to take religious factors much more seriously if they hope to understand fully the nature of these political conflicts.

References

Barker, David/Hurwitz, Jon/Nelson, Traci: "Of Crusades and Culture Wars." *Journal of Politics* 70 (2), 2008, pp. 307–322.

Barker, David/Bearce, David H.: "End-Times Theology, the Shadow of the Future, and Public Resistance to Addressing Global Climate Change." *Political Research Quarterly* 66 (2), 2013, pp. 267–279.

Baumgartner, Jody/Francia, Peter/Morris, Jonathan: "A Clash of Civilizations?." *Political Research Quarterly* 61 (2), 2008, pp. 171–179.

Campbell, David E./Layman, Geoffrey C./Green, John C.: *Secular Surge: A New Fault Line in American Politics*. Cambridge University Press: Cambridge 2021.

Clark, Victoria: *Allies for Armageddon: The Rise of Christian Zionism*. Yale University Press: New Haven, CT 2007.

Collins, Todd A./Wink, Kenneth A./Guth, James L./Livingston, C. Don: "The Religious Affiliation of Representatives and Support for Funding the Iraq War." *Politics and Religion* 4 (3), 2011, pp. 550–568.

Council on Foreign Relations: "The World Trump Made." *Foreign Affairs* 99 (5), 2020, pp. 10–56.

---

69 Collins, Todd A./Wink, Kenneth A./Guth, James L./Livingston, C. Don: "The Religious Affiliation of Representatives and Support for Funding the Iraq War." *Politics and Religion* 4 (3), 2011, pp. 550–568.

Dill, Janina/Schubiger, Livia I.: "Attitudes toward the Use of Force: Instrumental Imperatives, Moral Principles, and International Law." *American Journal of Political Science* 65 (5), 2021, pp. 612–633.

Dueck, Colin: *Age of Iron: On Conservative Nationalism*. Oxford University Press: New York 2019.

Eichenberg, Richard: "Citizen Opinion on Foreign Policy and World Politics." In: Dalton, Russell J./Klingemann, Hans-Dieter (eds.): *The Oxford Handbook of Political Behavior*. Oxford University Press: Oxford 2007.

Eichenberg, Richard: "Gender Difference in American Public Opinion on the Use of Military Force, 1982–2013." *International Studies Quarterly* 60 (1), 2016, pp. 138–148.

Eichenberg, Richard: "Gender Difference in Support for the Use of Military Force in Cross-National Perspective." Paper presented at the workshop on "Public Opinion, Foreign Policy and the Use of Force in Turbulent Times." European Consortium for Political Research Joint Sessions, University of Nottingham, 25–30.04.2017.

Froese, Paul/Mencken, F. Carson: "A U.S. Holy War? The Effects of Religion on Iraq War Policy Attitudes." *Social Science Quarterly* 90 (1), 2009, pp. 103–116.

Glazier, Rebecca: "Divine Direction: How Providential Religious Beliefs Shape Foreign Policy Attitudes." *Foreign Policy Analysis* 9 (2), 2013, pp. 127–142.

Gries, Peter: *The Politics of American Foreign Policy*. Stanford University Press: Stanford, CA 2014.

Guth, James L.: "Are White Evangelicals Populists? The View from the 2016 American National Election Study." *Review of Faith and International Affairs* 17 (3), 2019, pp. 20–35.

Guth, James L.: "Economic Globalization: The View from the Pews." *Review of Faith & International Affairs* 8 (4), 2010, pp. 41–46.

Guth, James L.: "Militant and Cooperative Internationalism among American Religious Publics." *Politics and Religion Journal* 7 (2), 2013a, pp. 315–343.

Guth, James L.: "Religion and American Populism." Paper presented to the GIRES International Conference on Religion in American Politics, 18.07.2021.

Guth, James L.: "Religion and American Public Attitudes on War and Peace." *Asian Journal of Peacebuilding* 1 (2), 2013b, pp. 227–252.

Guth, James L.: "Religion and Public Opinion: Foreign Policy Issues." In: Smidt, Corwin E./Kellstedt, Lyman A./Guth, James L. (eds.): *The Oxford Handbook of Religion and American Politics*. Oxford University Press: New York 2009.

Guth, James L.: "Religion and Public Opinion on Security: A Comparative Perspective." In: Seiple, Chris/Hoover, Dennis R./Otis, Pauletta: *The Routledge Handbook of Religion and Security*. Routledge: London 2013.

Hansen, Susan B.: *Religion and Reaction: The Secular Political Response to the Religious Right*. Rowman & Littlefield: Lanham, MD 2011.

Hero, Alfred O.: *American Religious Groups View Foreign Policy: Trends in Rank-and-File Opinion, 1937–1969.* Duke University Press: Durham, NC 1973.

Holsti, Ole: *Public Opinion and American Foreign Policy.* Rev. ed. University of Michigan Press: Ann Arbor 2004.

Hunter, James D.: *Culture Wars: The Struggle to Define America.* Basic Books: New York 1991.

Huntington, Samuel P.: *Who Are We? The Challenges to America's National Identity.* Simon and Schuster: New York 2004.

Jardina, Ashley: *White Identity Politics.* Cambridge University Press: Cambridge 2019.

Joffe, Alex: "Explaining the Trump Doctrine." *BESA Center Perspectives Paper No. 1,039*, December 18, 2018, retrieved 08.09.2021, from https://besacenter.org/trump-doctrine/.

Kellstedt, Lyman A./Guth, James L.: "Religious Groups as a Polarizing Force." In: Crotty, William (ed.): *Polarized Politics: The Impact of Divisiveness in the U.S. Political System.* Lynne Rienner: Boulder 2015.

Kohut, Andrew/Stokes, Bruce: *America Against the World.* Henry Holt: New York 2006.

Kurtz, Lester/Goran, Kelly: "Love Your Enemies? Protestants and United States Foreign Policy." In: Wuthnow, Robert/Evans, John H. (eds.): *The Quiet Hand of God: Faith-Based Activism and the Public Role of Mainline Protestantism.* University of California Press: Berkeley 2002.

Leege, David C./Kellstedt, Lyman A. (eds.): *Rediscovering the Religious Factor in American Politics.* M.E. Sharpe: Armonk NY 1993.

Mead, Walter Russell: "Religion and U.S. Foreign Policy." *Foreign Affairs* 85 (5), 2006, pp. 24–43.

Miller, Warren/Shanks, J. Merrill: *The New American Voter.* Harvard University Press: Cambridge 1996.

Nelsen, Brent F./Guth, James L.: "Religious Influence on American Foreign Policy Attitudes: The Case of the 'Trump Doctrine.'" Paper presented at the 60th annual meeting of the International Studies Association, Toronto, 27–30.03.2019.

Nelsen, Brent F./Guth, James L.: "Religious Influence on American Public Attitudes toward Military Action." Paper presented at the 59th annual meeting of the International Studies Association, San Francisco, 04–07.04.2018.

Norris, Pippa/Inglehart, Ronald: *Cultural Backlash: Trump, Brexit, and Authoritarian Populism.* Cambridge University Press: Cambridge 2019.

Page, Benjamin/Bouton, Marshall: *The Foreign Policy Disconnect.* University of Chicago Press: Chicago 2006.

Petrikova, Ivica: "Religion and Foreign Policy Views: Are Religious People More Altruistic and/or More Militant?" *International Political Science Review* 40 (4), 2019, pp. 535–557.

Rock, Stephen R.: *Faith and Foreign Policy.* Continuum: New York 2011.

Roy, Oindrila: "Religious Roots of War Attitudes in the United States: Insights from Iraq, Afghanistan, and the Persian Gulf." *Foreign Policy Analysis* 12 (3), 2016, pp. 258–274.

Sides, John/Tesler, Michael/Vavreck, Lynn: *Identity Crisis: The 2016 Presidential Campaign and the Battle for the Meaning of America.* Princeton University Press: Princeton 2018.

Smidt, Corwin E./Kellstedt, Lyman A./Guth, James L. (eds.): *The Oxford Handbook of Religion and American Politics.* Oxford University Press: New York 2010.

Steensland, Brian/Park, Jerry/Regnerus, Mark/Robinson, Lynn/Wilcox, Bradford/Woodberry, Robert: "The Measure of American Religion." *Social Forces* 79 (1), 2000, pp. 291–318.

Swierenga, Robert P.: "Religion and American Voting Behavior, 1830s to 1930s." In: Smidt, Corwin E./Kellstedt, Lyman A./Guth, James L. (eds.): *The Oxford Handbook of Religion and American Politics.* Oxford University Press: New York 2009.

Taydas, Zeynep/Kentman, Cigdem/Olson, Laura: "Faith Matters: Religious Affiliation and Public Opinion About Barack Obama's Foreign Policy in the 'Greater' Middle East.'" *Social Science Quarterly* 93 (5), pp. 1218–1242.

Uslaner, Eric M.: "American Interests in the Balance." In: Cigler, Allan J./Loomis, Burdett (eds.): *Interest Group Politics.* 7th ed. CQ Press: Washington, DC 2007.

Wald, Kenneth: "Religious Elites and Public Opinion: The Impact of the Bishops' Peace Pastoral." *The Review of Politics* 54 (1), 1992, pp. 112–143.

Warner, Carolyn M./Walker, Stephen G.: "Thinking about the Role of Religion in Foreign Policy: A Framework for Analysis." *Foreign Policy Analysis* 7 (1), 2011, pp. 113–135.

Wittkopf, Eugene R.: *Faces of Internationalism: Public Opinion and Foreign Policy.* Duke University Press: Durham, NC 1990.

Wuthnow, Robert: *The Restructuring of American Religion.* Princeton University Press: Princeton 1988.

Wuthnow, Robert: *Boundless Faith: The Global Outreach of American Churches.* University of California Press: Berkeley 2009.

Husam Mohamad

Evangelicals' Influence on U.S. Policy on Israel and the Palestinians in Recent Decades

Abstract: This study reflects on beliefs and conducts relating to modern evangelical groups (i.e., dispensationalists and Christian Zionists), who have, since President Ronald Reagan was elected into office in the 1980s, been involved in promoting unconditional U.S. support for Israel. They have gradually established themselves as a voting bloc whose goals are usually advanced by lobbyists affiliated with the Republican Party. They have utilized their own literal interpretations of the Bible to justify and rationalize the need for stronger U.S. support for Israel, and advance other local and foreign policy goals. Presidents Reagan, George W. Bush, and Donald Trump have embraced evangelicals' efforts to legitimize Israel's control over the Palestinian-occupied territories. In doing so, they have not only hindered the failing Israeli–Palestinian peace process but may have also shifted the politically and territorially oriented conflict into a far more religiously centered one.

Keywords: U.S. evangelical groups, U.S. foreign policy, Israel, and the Palestinians

Introduction

The modern evangelical movement could be difficult to identify due to diversities in the beliefs and conducts of its followers. In general terms, however, the movement embodies within it several Protestant groups and trends that started to emerge in the eighteenth century. Their religious goals were, and largely remain, focused on converting people to Christianity, enticing them to develop personal relationships with Jesus Christ as their savior, and following more literal interpretations of the Bible to guide their faith. In terms of their involvement in politics, there are also diversities among various modern evangelical groups, including, but not limited to, premillennialists, dispensationalists, and Christian Zionists. These groups in the evangelical movement have become increasingly involved in influencing U.S. policy in support of Israel and the end-time prophecies.

Concepts such as the Great Awakening, revivalism, evangelical resurgence, and the like are central to evangelical activists worldwide. The first phase of the Great Awakening began in the 1730s and 1740s. Since then, the movement's focus has been centered on accepting Jesus as one's savior. The second phase of the Great

Awakening emerged in the United States in the 1820s–1840s, where most evangelical trends started to hold a more fundamentalist form of religious beliefs and conducts.[1] Evangelicals generally tried to challenge several scientific advancements and criticisms affecting their Judeo-Christian tradition. For example, the theory of evolution was viewed by most conservative evangelicals as an attempt by secular scientists to undermine the Biblical account of creationism. While evangelicalism and fundamentalism were initially similar, eventually the evangelical movement have become more politicized in the post-fundamentalist era. The most prominent post-fundamentalist evangelical theologian in the United States was perhaps Billy Graham, who played a crucial role in widening the popular appeal of the modern evangelical movement in the United States and abroad.

As indicated earlier, the focus of this chapter is centered on groups within the modern evangelical movement that are actively involved in influencing U.S. policy to favor Israel at all costs. Dispensationalists and Christian Zionists, particularly, have been the most important religious influencers on both UK and U.S. policy concerning Israel and the Palestinians. Contemporary Christian Zionism is a politically oriented group that is rooted in the evangelical tradition, where it views the creation of Israel and the U.S. support for it, as being part of God's eternal plan. For such groups, Israel plays a crucial role in the fulfillment of their prophecies.[2] Similar to Christian Zionists, dispensationalists also recognize Israel and the Jewish people as essential players in the pursuit of the end-time prophecies. Dispensationalists see a close link between the creation of Israel, the return of Jews to the promised land, and God's prophecies that are contingent on Israel's security. As missionaries, modern evangelicals generally caution that the non-born-again Christians must accept Jesus as their savior or be condemned for eternity.[3] Given their rising popular appeal as social movements, dispensationalists and Christian Zionists continue to play a significant role in foreign policymaking, due to their ability to influence the outcome of U.S. national (mainly presidential) elections, in favor of Republican candidates.[4]

---

1 Longhenry, Ethan R.: *A Study of Denominations*. DeWard Publishing: Tampa 2015.
2 Miano, Peter: "Mainstream Christian Zionism." In: Phillip Thomas/Miano Peter/Mitchell Jason (eds.): *Prophetic Voices on Middle East Peace: A Jewish, Christian and Humanist Primer on Colonialism, Zionism and Nationalism in the Middle East*. Claremont Press: Claremont 2016. More about the history of Christian Zionism, its development and organizations representing it: Napierała, Paulina: "The Influence of Religion on American Policy toward Israel: Is FPA a Useful Tool for Analysis?". In: Grabowski Marcin/Pugacewicz Tomasz (eds.) *Application of International Relations Theories in Asia and Africa*. Peter Lang: Berlin et al. 2019, pp. 219–247.
3 Pomper, Miles: "Religious Right Flexes Muscles on Foreign Policy Matters." *Congressional Quarterly Weekly* 13 (3), 2002, pp. 1893–1897.
4 Martin, William: "The Christian Right and American Foreign Policy." *Foreign Policy* 114 (3), 1999, pp. 66–80.

Consequently, today's modern, largely conservative, evangelical movement has, as a religious force and an electoral voting bloc, been able to expand its politics and theology into the heart of U.S. society, institutions, and domestic and foreign policy agendas. Religious involvements in domestic and international affairs are not matters limited to Islamists and/or non-democratic circumstances. Various trends within the modern evangelical movement are playing a vital role in influencing U.S. domestic and foreign policy agendas.[5] Apart from groups that are supportive of Israel and indifferent or hostile toward the Palestinians, such as Christian Zionists, and dispensationalists, it is worth mentioning that other trends in today's Christian Right movement (both in the United States and the West) may also include those affiliated with anti-Semitism, Islamophobia, xenophobia, homophobia, and white nationalism.[6] Regardless of the diversity among and between such evangelical groups and trends, most modern evangelicals have been utilizing their theological, ethical, and political interpretations and justifications of sacred texts, as a means to pressure the United States into backing Israel's claims to the biblical land of Israel (*Ertz Yisrael*). Dispensationalists and Christian Zionists, particularly, believe that the promised land, including the Palestinian territories as identified in the bible—recognized as military-occupied territories by international law and institutions—must remain under Israeli control. Palestinian claims to their homeland have, however, been viewed by groups such as Christian Zionists, dispensationalists, and others as simply false and/or irrelevant to the end-time.

While recognizing the diversity of views and conducts among evangelical groups on domestic and foreign policy matters, most of today's evangelicals accept that the Bible supports the rights of Jews as God's chosen people to have full control over the biblical land of Israel, which includes today's Palestinian-occupied territories. As part of their religious obligations, dispensationalists and Christian Zionists have mainly sponsored missions to entice Jews into immigrating to Israel and establish new settlements in the Palestinian-occupied territories, to help in the fulfillment of God's eternal prophecies. They have always objected to Israel's potential withdrawal from the internationally recognized Palestinian-occupied territories in return for a peace deal with the Palestinians. They believe that Israel must maintain its sovereignty over the site of the old Jewish temple which must be rebuilt on the exact site of the Dome of the Rock (*Al-Aqsa*). They also predict

---

5   Djupe, Paul/Neiheisel, Jacob R./Conger, Kimberly H.: "Are the Politics of the Christian Right Linked to State Rates of the Nonreligious? The Importance of Salient Controversy." *Political Research Quarterly* 71 (4), 2018, retrieved 15.12.2021, pp. 910–922, from https://journals.sagepub.com/doi/full/10.1177/1065912918771526.

6   Sutton, Matthew Avery: "The Capital Riot Revealed the Darkest Nightmare of White Evangelical America." *The New Republic*, January 14, 2021, retrieved 15.12.2021, from https://newrepublic.com/article/160922/capitol-riot-revealed-darkest-nightmares-white-evangelical-america.

that brutal wars will soon escalate at Armageddon (*Megiddo*), where the Antichrist (possibly Muslim) forces will be defeated, leading to the return of Jesus from heaven to Jerusalem. For Christian Zionists, dispensationalists, and those who share their Biblical views, these narratives are absolute facts that will occur in our lifetime or soon thereafter. While believing that the United States must continuously support Israel at all costs, in recent years, however, younger evangelicals, especially those 18- to 29-year-olds are less enchanted with such beliefs or with the need to provide unconditional support for Israel.[7]

Although the security of Israel has never been a partisan issue between Democrats and Republicans in the country, most evangelicals who are usually aligned with Republicans, have emphasized the religious and moral justification for the U.S. backing of Israel. President Trump's pro-Israel policy on Jerusalem, Jewish settlements, Palestinian refugees, and the peace process were, in large part, initiated to satisfy conservative evangelicals who played a crucial role in Trump's election victory in 2016. Most of those evangelicals have also applauded Trump's policy regarding banning Muslims from traveling to the United States and supported his punitive measures against Iran. Trump's inaccurate and misleading statements about President Obama's faith, calling him a Muslim among other things, may have also fueled evangelicals' anti-Muslim sentiments in the country. They endorsed Trump's efforts to establish alliances between Israel and various Arab Gulf states, without expecting Israel to provide territorial concessions to the Palestinians in return for normalizing relations with them. Many of Trump's supporters and activists who are largely affiliated with today's conservative evangelical movement have often expressed double standards about religious liberty in the country. For instance, while they demand that the U.S. government protect their own religious rights and liberties as stated in the U.S. Constitution, they usually express political opposition to providing similar rights to Muslim communities in the country and abroad.

Obviously, the modern, largely conservative, evangelical movement has been candid about the role faith plays in influencing U.S. policy toward Israel and the Palestinians. The support for Israel has been ingrained in the minds of many followers of the modern evangelical movement, who often romanticized biblical narratives taught to them in Sunday schools. Relying on theology, and regardless of the effects of that on the fate of the Palestinians, modern conservative evangelicals continue to view today's Israel as fully entitled to the same promised land given by God to the Jews some two centuries ago. Evangelicals generally consider God's promises as complete and eternally valid.[8]

---

7   Inbari, Motti/Bumin, Kirki/Byrd, Gordon: "Why Do Evangelicals Support Israel." *Politics and Religion* 14 (1), 2020, pp. 1–36.

8   Fea, John/Gifford, Laura R./Griffith, Marie/Martin Lerone A.: "Evangelicalism and Politics." *The American Historian*, November 20, 2018, retrieved 15.12.2021, from https://www.oah.org/tah/issues/2018/november/evangelicalism-and-politics/.

Historical Background

The Protestant movement has over the years experienced transformations and mutations that generally led to abandoning old rigid religious hierarchies linked to the Catholic traditions. Early evangelical groups have embraced a relatively more flexible system of thought and conduct that inspired self-reliance and individualism.[9] However, most supporters of modern conservative evangelical groups have developed more literalist interpretations of their sacred texts, where they have determined, among other things, that Israel was created to play a central role in the end-time prophecies.[10] Most modern conservative evangelical groups have thus utilized their ethical and religious beliefs as a means to justify their support for Israel. For example, dispensationalists and Christian Zionists have placed Israel at the core of their ethical and theological principles. Dispensationalists particularly refer to themselves as born-again Christians who are assisting in God's end-time plans. These plans concern several stages, including the tribulation that consists of a seven-year period of violence leading to catastrophic effects on the world prior to the return of Jesus to earth. Dispensationalists and Christian Zionists have established a close link between their religious interpretations of the Bible, the course of human history, and the end-time which while centered on Israel, is expected to reflect the accounts found in the Books of Genesis, Daniel, and Revelations.[11] Although the United States was not mentioned in those biblical texts, Christian Zionists and dispensationalists along with several other groups believe, based on their renewed vision of U.S. exceptionalism and its superior role in world affairs, that the United States must play a crucial role in securing Israel for the sake of fulfilling God's vision.[12]

In the early phases of its expansion, the evangelical movement, in general, was focused on addressing domestic issues that largely conflicted with Christian values and beliefs. Today, several religious-political conservative organizations that are affiliated with the evangelical movement, notably the Christian Coalition of America, have become deeply involved in domestic political issues, such as protesting against women and abortion rights advocates and homosexuals. They

---

9 Schoenit, Marc: "The Roots of Christian Zionism." *Theological Review* 26 (1), 2005, pp. 3–38.
10 Kurth, James: "Religion in World Affairs: The Protestant Deformation and American Foreign Policy." *Orbis: A Journal of World Affairs* 48 (2), 1998, pp. 221–239.
11 Mayer, Jeremy D.: "Christian Fundamentalists and Public Opinion towards the Middle East: Israel's New Best Friends?" *Social Science Quarterly* 85 (3), 2004, pp. 695–712.
12 Van Engen, Abram: "White Evangelicals and the New American Exceptionalism of Donald Trump." *Religion & Politics*, 2020, retrieved 15.12.2021, from https://religionandpolitics.org/2020/09/29/white-evangelicals-and-the-new-american-exceptionalism-of-donald-trump/.

continue to lobby for conservative judicial appointments at state and federal levels in the hope of outlawing abortion and repressing homosexuality.[13] They also focus on education by highlighting, among other things, the need to teach creationism in science classes, emphasizing abstinence, and securing prayer rights for students in public schools. In the realm of world politics, modern conservative evangelical organizations have also highlighted the centrality of Israel in the political orientation, formulation, and conduct of U.S. foreign policy.[14] Their interest in foreign policy was expanded during Reagan's presidency as evangelicals stood firmly in support of Israel to block the sale of AWACS to Saudi Arabia. They have also, during the George H. Bush Administration, lobbied the president to pressure the UN to overturn the UNGAR 3379 that since the 1970s has equated the Zionist ideology with racism. Dispensationalists, Christian Zionists, and other neo-fundamentalist groups have become, unlike the early liberal Protestant tradition, intensely involved in domestic and foreign policy issues in ways that aim at challenging most, if not all, liberal-oriented policies and silencing all legitimate political criticisms of Israel's policy toward the Palestinians.

Certainly, interest in today's Israel among various conservative evangelical organizations is largely based on theological perspectives concerning Israel's relation to the end-time prophecies. In Genesis, for instance, they believe that God had executed a covenant with Abraham promising him and his successors the land of Israel for eternity. Biblical narratives also illustrate that God's promise to the Jews was then confirmed through Abraham's second son, Isaac, and later by Isaac's son, Jacob. Under the leadership of Moses and Joshua, the Israelites managed to maintain their control of the promised land. Based on the books of Daniel and Revelations, modern conservative evangelical groups also suggest that most, if not all, Jews would be expected to return to the Holy Land and establish their state, thus concluding that Israel's creation in 1948 was in itself an act of God. They point to connections between Jews and Christians, not Muslims, with the promised land. For evangelicals, such as dispensationalists and Christian Zionists, Christ's return, the Apocalypse, Armageddon, and other biblical prophecies cannot occur without the presence of a safe and secure Jewish state of Israel in the entire territory of the promised land.[15] Although Palestinians Christian and Muslim have lived on the same land with no serious disruptions for more than twelve centuries, they remain absent from the evangelical belief system.[16]

---

13 Martin, William: *With God on Our Side: The Rise of the Religious Right in America.* Broadway Books: New York 1996.
14 Durham, Martin: "Evangelical Protestantism and Foreign Policy in the United States after September 11." *Patterns of Prejudice* 38 (2), 2004, pp. 145–160.
15 Schoenit, Marc: "The Roots of Christian Zionism." *Theological Review* 26 (1), 2005, pp. 3–38.
16 Khuri, Fred J.: *The Arab Israeli Dilemma.* Syracuse: Syracuse University Press: New York 1985.

The apocalyptic vision that inspires many evangelical groups in the United States to support Israel has been influenced by similar experiences in Britain. For instance, it was dispensationalist activists in England that first divided world history into seven epochs or dispensations and concluded that the world is currently in its sixth phase. They believed that Christ's return to earth is contingent on Israel's continued control of the promised land. They also assumed that once the second Jewish Temple is built in Jerusalem, which should remain under Israel's authority, and Jesus's return becomes imminent, all of the "born again Christians would fly up to meet him [Jesus] in the air ... leave[ing] behind all non-believers."[17] This view of human history that is based on their scriptural interpretations and ideology has in the end prejudiced British and U.S. policy on Palestine for decades.

For example, leading British politicians such as Winston Churchill and James Balfour, were, although secular, largely influenced by Protestant teachings about Israel and the Jews. They have supported the secular-oriented Zionist movement's efforts to secure a Jewish national homeland in Palestine.[18] Britain's Labour Party, which had close ties with the Methodist Church in the UK, was particularly supportive of the idea of a Jewish national homeland. As a member of the British cabinet and the Labour Party, Balfour succeeded in influencing the Cabinet to endorse the Balfour Declaration in 1917, which officially recognized the idea of establishing a Jewish homeland in Palestine. The Balfour Declaration was then added to the British Mandate of Palestine documents in 1922.[19] These policies, which aided the Zionist project in Palestine and eventually resulted in Israel's creation in 1948, have led to the Palestinians' exodus from their homes. As such, the policies of British governments, and later those of U.S. governments, may have been causally and morally responsible for today's Israeli–Palestinian conflict.[20]

Since the 1970s, and mainly in the 1980s, activists in the United States who have largely been affiliated with dispensationalism and Christian Zionism were able to institutionalize themselves and provide significant support for Israel. Their alliance with Republicans reinforced their ability to influence U.S. politicians through lobbying and campaigning, along with negotiating policies at the domestic and foreign policy levels. Most U.S. evangelicals have, at times, endorsed even secular lobbying groups such as the American Israeli Political Action Committee (AIPAC) because it supported Israel.[21] The appeal of the dispensationalist

---

17 Campolo, Tony: "The Ideological Roots of Christian Zionism." *Tikkun* 20 (1), 2005, pp. 19–20.
18 Anderson, Irvine: *Biblical Interpretation and Middle East Policy, the Promised Land, America and Israel, 1917–2002.* University Press of Florida: Gainesville 2007.
19 Gelvin, James L.: *The Israel–Palestine Conflict: A History.* Cambridge University Press: Cambridge 2021.
20 Mansfield, Peter: *The Arabs.* Penguin Books: New York 1992.
21 Pipes, Daniel: "The Clout of Christian Zionism." *Jewish News: Community Weekly Serving Greater Phoenix and Northern Arizona*, July 18, 2003, retrieved 14.05.2022,

theology among many evangelicals concerning Israel has been triggered by historical turning points—mainly Israel's creation in 1948 and its victory in the 1967 war. The fact that Israel has been created and successfully managed to survive against all odds is viewed by most modern evangelicals as proof of the accuracy of God's promises.[22] While justifying the backing of Israel on religious and moral grounds, many evangelicals have often utilized biblical stories and parallels (i.e., David and Goliath) to portray Israel not only as a victim of Palestinian aggression but also as a force for good versus evil. Ultimately, those evangelicals have also justified and rationalized Israel's violence against Palestinians in the occupied territories. Similar claims were often made concerning the U.S.'s war on terror in the Middle East as examples of good versus evil. Those arguments have been expanded into established narratives that largely demonized Arabs and Muslims across the region. For example, the Bush Administration's use of politically charged phrases such as the axis of evil (concerning Iraq and Iran) and the crusaders in describing post-September 11 conflicts has increased the hatred of Muslims in the country.[23] It also enhanced Israel's centrality in the conduct of U.S. foreign policy and placed Israel's military attacks against Palestinians in the occupied territories on the same side of the U.S. global war on terror strategy. In so doing, and in contradiction with international laws and regulations, Israel and the U.S. tried to effectively delegitimize all forms of Palestinian resistance to Israel's military occupation of the Palestinian territories.

Theology and Politics in Support of Israel

Most U.S. politicians, the media, and the public have largely been oriented to support Israel more than any other country in the region, or perhaps the world. Unlike most Americans though, modern evangelicals' support for Israel has always been guided by a messianic vision that motivates them to act in anticipation of the fulfillment of God's prophecies. Although Christians have been taught that the timing of Christ's return is obscure, modern evangelicals trust that his return may happen in our lifetime. President Reagan, who supported evangelicals largely for electoral reasons, had told a pro-Israeli lobbyist in 1983 that when he "looks back to the ancient prophets," he thinks that the world is coming to an end and that "we

---

      from https://www.jewishaz.com/opinion/the-clout-of-christian-zionism/article_6b29bb21-aecc-51d5-8089-3157eea771b8.html.
22 Carenen, Caitlin: *The Fervent Embrace: Liberal Protestants, Evangelicals, and Israel.* New York University Press: New York 2012.
23 Dart, John: "Bush Religious Rhetoric Riles Critics." *Christian Century* 120 (5), 2003, pp. 10–12.

are the generation that's going to see that come about."²⁴ The significance of this type of messianic rhetoric particularly when held by a U.S. president who carried out policies in support of Israel versus the Palestinians goes beyond theology when translated into actual conduct that affects the lives of millions in the region. President Reagan seemed to have agreed with modern conservative evangelicals that the world was entering the final phase of dispensation, starting with the Rapture and Tribulations, then leading to the defeat of the Antichrist at Armageddon, and ending with Jesus's return to the Jewish Temple. This is when all born-again Christians should begin receiving their eternal salvation. The centrality of Israel in their theology and ideology suggests that all prophecies at the end-time cannot occur without the vital role of Israel.²⁵

Being motivated by theology, modern evangelicals generally insist on rebuilding the Jewish Temple on the exact site of *Al-Aqsa* Mosque, which is revered by Muslims. The prospect of building the Temple next to the Muslim shrine rather than on top of it has been rejected by modern evangelical theologians. Tim LaHaye, for instance, author of the *Left Behind Series*, explained that "some have tried to suggest that perhaps this location [Al-Aqsa] is not the only place in Jerusalem ... [where] the temple could be built." He added, "[T]here is no substitute on the face of the earth for that spot."²⁶ This is reflective of the evangelicals' exclusionary vision, which has been crafted to deny Palestinians' religious and political rights to Jerusalem and the rest of the Holy Land. While today's evangelicals find it suitable to justify their attachment to the ancient Temple based on theology, they, however, deny the validity of Palestinians' religious and political ties to the *Al-Aqsa* Mosque. Modern conservative evangelical leaders such as Pat Robertson, Franklin Graham, and others do not recognize the Palestinian side in the conflict. They generally believe that "the rebirth of Israel" as a Jewish state is the most dramatic event that would lead to Jesus's second coming.²⁷ Being linked to right-wing Israeli politicians and having served as spiritual advisers to Republican presidents, it is

---

24 Lukas, Anthony L.: "The Rapture and the Bomb." *The New York Times*, June 8, 1986, retrieved 15.12.2021, from http://query.nytimes.com/gst/fullpage.html?res=9A0DEFD A153FF93BA35755C0A960948260&sec=&spon=.
25 Lienesch, Michael: *Redeeming America: Piety and Politics in the New Christian Right.* University of North Carolina Press: Chapel Hill 1993.
26 Hanegraaff, Hank: "Rebuild Temple vs. the Dom of the Rock." August 24, 2007, retrieved 15.12.2021, from https://hankhanegraaff.blogspot.com/2007/08/rebuilt-tem ple-vs-dome-of-rock.html. See also Hank Hangraaff, Hank: *The Apocalypse Code: Find Out What the Bible Really Says About the End Times and Why It Matters Today.* Kindle Edition 2010.
27 Gorenberg, Gershom: "Unorthodox Alliance." *The Washington Post*, October 11, 2002, retrieved 15.12.2021, from https://www.washingtonpost.com/archive/opinions/2002/ 10/11/unorthodox-alliance/2bc224d0-2f35-47f5-9ff4-43ae59f2ac34/.

not surprising to any, in Israel or the United States, that those and other similar evangelical views of U.S. policy in the Middle East are based on a biblical promise to Israel.

Much of the modern evangelicals' knowledge of the Israeli–Palestinian conflict has been derived from Sunday school education, where stories about Jewish history and Israel's "rebirth" have resonated in their thoughts since childhood.[28] In their congregations, evangelicals were generally taught inspirational stories about heroic figures in ancient Israel and were coached about battles fought between the forces of good versus evil. The socializing and cultural effects of Sunday schools may have played a central role in strengthening evangelicals' ties with today's Israel. Sunday schools were initially launched to guide troubled children who had lived on the streets.[29] They soon became centers for religious and political indoctrinations that are reflective of the modern evangelical belief system.[30] Having emphasized Israel's central role in their theology, the Sunday schools have been expanded further for the sake of producing similar socializing effects for generations of evangelicals to come. However, given that young evangelicals in the United States are now being exposed to more informative and diversified media sources, especially regarding Israel's policy toward Palestinians, the older and more conservative evangelical groups and activists appear to have less influence on the younger generation.

U.S. evangelicals have established leading universities and seminaries including the Dallas Theological Seminary, Wheaton College, Texas Christian University, Oral Roberts University, Bob Jones University, and Liberty Baptist. On such campuses, students and faculty are taught to internalize the mission of the evangelical tradition, including their support for Israel.[31] Prominent activists such as Dwight Moody, considered the father of the evangelical movement in the United States, have formulated their own biblical accounts that justify the U.S. support for Israel. Evangelicals such as William Blackstone have also succeeded in influencing a wide range of audiences among U.S. politicians and the public to continue supporting Israel.[32] Groups such as the International Christian Embassy

---

28 Robert, Nicholson W.: "Evangelicals and Israel." *Mosaic Magazine—Advancing Jewish Thought*, October 6, 2013, retrieved 14.05.2021, from https://mosaicmagazine.com/essay/uncategorized/2013/10/evangelicals-and-israel/.
29 Anderson, Irvine: *Biblical Interpretation and Middle East Policy, the Promised Land, America and Israel, 1917–2002*. University Press of Florida: Gainesville 2007.
30 *Ibid.*
31 Miller, Paul D.: "Evangelicals, Israel, and US Foreign Policy." *Survival: Global Politics and Strategy* 56 (1), 2014, pp. 7–26, retrieved 15.12.2021, from https://www.tandfonline.com/doi/pdf/10.1080/00396338.2014.882149.
32 Goodman, Walter: "Rise of the Religious Right." *The New York Times*, September 29, 1996, retrieved 15.12.2021, from https://www.nytimes.com/1996/09/28/arts/rise-of-the-religious-right.html.

in Jerusalem, the International Fellowships, the Bridges for Peace, and the 700 Club have invested ample resources in support of Israel. Although the balance of power has always been, and remains, in Israel's favor, evangelicals largely view Israel as the victim of Palestinian and Arab aggression. In their proPagánda campaigns against Palestinians, evangelicals often plan visits and gather donations in support of Israel.[33] While awaiting the end-time prophecies, several U.S. evangelicals and their families have taken residency in various illegal Israeli settlements in Arab East Jerusalem and the West Bank.

U.S. evangelicals and key politicians alike have often explained their backing for Israel as a matter that is sanctioned by God.[34] Oklahoma Senator James Inhofe, for example, a born-again Christian, pointed out that his support for Israel derives from the belief that "God appeared to Abram [Abraham] and said I am giving you this land." The Senator added that "the word of God is true."[35] Although most religions across the board may have intended to play a constructive role in human history, in this regard, however, religious convictions have resulted in denying Palestinians their basic political and religious rights. While most messages of peace, morality, and ethics have often been associated with religious teaching and sentiments, historical and current events revealed that several wars and many acts of terror have been carried out in the name of one religion or another. To evangelicals, peace between Israel and the Palestinians is irrelevant to their end-time prophecies. Evangelical leaders have urged Israel to reject all United Nations mediations because, along with the need to preserve Israel's control of the occupied territories, they believe that the Antichrist might be the head of a world organization.[36] Following the September 11th events, however, evangelicals have implied that the Antichrist might be a Muslim.[37] This type of belief, motivated by anti-Muslim sentiments, was expanded during Trump's presidency, which was overwhelmingly supportive of white evangelicals.

While recognizing Jews as God's chosen people and believing that Israel plays a vital role in the end-time plan, it is not Jews but born-again Christians whom evangelicals believe would be saved to join Christ in heaven. They assume that the

---

33 *Ibid.*
34 Jelen, Ted: "Religion and Foreign Policy Attitudes: Exploring the Effects of Denomination and Doctrine." *American Politics Quarterly* 22 (3), 1994, pp. 382–400.
35 Gershom Gorenberg, Gershom: "Unorthodox Alliance." *The Washington Post*, November 11, 2002, retrieved 15.12.2021, from https://www.washingtonpost.com/archive/opinions/2002/10/11/unorthodox-alliance/2bc224d0-2f35-47f5-9ff4-43ae59f2ac34/.
36 Richardson, Joel: *Mideast Beast*. WND Books: New York 2012.
37 Reagan, David R.: "The Muslim Anti-Christ Theory." Lamb & Lion Ministries: Proclaiming the Soon Return of Jesus Christ. December 2010, from https://christinprophecy.org/articles/the-muslim-antichrist-theory/.

non-born-again Christians, as well as Jews in Israel, along with all Muslims and others, will face deadly wars, famines, and catastrophes.[38] The evangelicals' use of Jews and Israel has been merely for the fulfillment of their own prophecies, which brings no benefit to Jews in the end-time. John Hagee, for instance, an evangelical pastor and a leading Christian Zionist at the Cornerstone Church in San Antonio, has made anti-Semitic remarks by saying the "biblical verses made [it] clear that Adolf Hitler and the Holocaust was part of God's plan to chase the Jews from Europe and drive them to Palestine."[39] Hagee's support for Christian Zionism would not deter him from viewing the Holocaust as being part of God's plan, simply because his main goal is to see Israel's creation for the fulfillment of God's plans. While accepting their policies that are supportive of Israel, Israelis tend to ignore evangelicals' theology that deems Judaism, and other religions, as invalid. The presence of Israel—for evangelicals—is a sign from God about nearing the end of the world. While there have always been Palestinian Christians living in Palestine, evangelicals do not accept them because they are not suited to God's end-time prophecies.

Evangelicals generally agree with right-wing Israelis in believing that the Promised Land is larger than modern-day Israel. They assume that Jordan and other adjacent areas were also included in the Promised Land as revealed in God's promise to Abraham. They also suggest that the Balfour Declaration and the Palestine Mandate documents included Jordan in the twice-promised land.[40] Because of the geopolitical changes that have taken place across the region over the years, most Israelis are no longer supportive of the idea of a greater Israel. Evangelicals and a significant percentage of Israelis remain, however, persistent in their attempts to preserve Israel's control over the Palestinian-occupied territories, which they refer to by the biblical names of *Judea* and *Samaria*. The Jewish settlers' movement—known as *Gush Emunim* (Bloc of the Faithful)—has also, since its creation in the 1970s, called for annexing the entire Palestinian-occupied territories.[41] Israeli Prime Ministers, such as Neftali Bennett, and Benjamin Netanyahu are in favor of annexing the West Bank to avert the two-state solution and block possible shared sovereignty over Jerusalem in favor of the continuation of the status quo. Israeli leaders, supported by today's radical settlers' organizations in the West Bank, also pursued policies that aimed at keeping Palestinians divided

---

38 Halsell, Gracee: *Prophesy and Politics: Militant Evangelists on the Road to Nuclear War.* Lawrence Hill: Westport, CT 1986.
39 "McCain Rejects Hagee Backing as Nazi Remarks Surface." *The New York Times*, May 22, 2008.
40 Friedman, Isaiah: *Palestine: A Twice Promised Land.* Routledge: New York 2018.
41 Javadikouchaksaraei, Mehrzad: "Religion and Politics in Israel: The Mythology of Jewish Nationalism." *International Journal of Multicultural and Multireligious Understanding* 4 (3), 2017, pp. 35–45.

and isolated along different geopolitical lines in the Gaza Strip, the West Bank, and Arab East Jerusalem.

For Democrats and Republicans alike, the support for Israel is a non-partisan matter. Evangelicals usually align themselves more with Republicans and tend to be skeptical of Democrat's policy toward Israel as being less genuine.[42] In rhetoric, President Joe Biden supports the two-state vision, which Israeli right-wingers and U.S. evangelicals have rejected on religious and political grounds.[43] Prominent politicians and evangelical activists including Pat Robertson, Gary Bauer, John Hagee, John Bolton, Douglas Feith, John Ashcroft, James Inhofe, and Tom DeLay have, along with many others, exerted significant influence on successive U.S. governments to refrain from pressuring Israel to withdraw from the Palestinian territories. At their media outlets, evangelicals tried to influence U.S. public opinion in support of Israel against Palestinians. Until his death in 2007, evangelical leader Jerry Falwell was among key activists who lobbied officials to transfer the U.S. embassy to Jerusalem. In speeches and rallies supportive of Israel, Falwell reflected on the religious and political significance of Israel by asking: "Can you love Jesus without loving Israel?" He also stated that the U.S. role toward Israel is part of "God's design."[44] Pat Robertson also indicated that Israel has no better friends than evangelicals. He was among those who pressured the Reagan Administration to reevaluate the status of the occupied territories, which are recognized as colonized by international law. However, President Reagan named them—under the evangelicals' influence—as disputed land to be decided in peace talks. This labeling also allowed Israel to expand its settlements in defiance of existing international laws.

Israeli Prime Minister Benjamin Netanyahu is known in evangelical circles as "the Ronald Reagan of Israel."[45] Over the years, strong alliances have been made between right-wing Israeli politicians, prominent U.S. evangelicals, and neo-Conservative trends linked to Reagan's presidency. Netanyahu's appeal among evangelicals may shed light on the type of alliances that existed between evangelicals and Israeli officials. According to one source, "there is perhaps no Israeli Prime Minister who has grasped the passion and political potential of folks like

---

42 Phillip-Fein, Kim: "Conservatism: A State of the Field." *The Journal of American History*, 2011, pp. 723–745.

43 Balmer, Randall: "Pro-Israel and Anti-Semitic: Understanding Evangelicals Support for Israel." *Palestine–Israel Journal* 25 (1&2), 2020, pp. 100–104.

44 "Is the Modern Nation of Israel Important?" *La Vista Church of Christ*, June 28, 2005, retrieved 15.12.2021, from https://www.lavistachurchofchrist.org/cms/is-the-modern-nation-of-israel-important/.

45 Wagner, Donald: "Reagan and Begin, Bibi and Jerry: the Theo-political Alliance of the Likud Party with the American Christian Right." *Arab Studies Quarterly* 20 (4)1998, pp. 33–52.

[evangelicals] [...] better than Netanyahu." He has been and remains well connected to U.S. politicians from both political parties.[46] The George W. Bush Administration was also closely linked to evangelicals and Israeli right-wing politicians. Former Congressional member Tom DeLay visited Israel during the Bush Administration, and while visiting a Jewish settlement in the West Bank stated: "I don't see occupied territory, I see Israel."[47] Richard Armey, another former Republican member of Congress at the time, also indicated that the post-1967 territories must remain part of Israel. As a contributor to the United Jewish Appeal organization which supports Jewish settlements, John Hagee stated: "I am a Bible scholar and a theologian and from my perspective, the law of God transcends the law of the United States." He continued to say that "in the Bible, there is not a Green Line but there is a 'Promised Land.'"[48] To preserve Israel's control of the Palestinian-occupied territories, increase its dominance across the region, and expand settlements to sustain a Jewish demographic majority in the Promised Land, evangelicals, and their supporters continue to back Israel.

Trump's Presidency: The Evangelicals' Dream President

As a payback for the role evangelicals had played in ensuring Trump's election in 2016 and to preserve their support for his agenda, the Trump Administration pursued a narrow view of the relationship between religion and politics to satisfy evangelicals' domestic and foreign policy goals. While establishing a strong connection with white evangelicals, Trump's policies were particularly harmful to religious minorities.[49] Although Trump's popular appeal across the board has not been high enough compared to his predecessors, evangelicals have provided him with consistent support that at times reached over 70% approval. Evangelicals felt vindicated as they began to achieve many of their vital goals during Trump's presidency, such as the appointment of three pro-life Supreme Court justices and the

---

46 Prusher, Ilene: "Israel's Unlikely Ally: American Evangelicals." *Christian Science Monitor* 90 (104), 1998, retrieved 15.12.2021, from https://www.csmonitor.com/1998/0424/042498.intl.intl.2.html.

47 Daniel, Benjamin/Simon, Steven: *The Next Attack: The Failure of the War on Terror and a Strategy for Getting It Right*. Times Books: New York 2005.

48 Wagner, Donald: "The Interregnum: Christian Zionism in the Clinton Years." *Daily Star* October 10, 2003, retrieved 15.12.2021, from https://www.dailystar.com.lb/Opinion/Commentary/2003/Oct-10/93261-the-interregnum-christian-zionism-in-the-clinton-years.ashx.

49 Rubin, Jennifer: "Should Religion and Politics Mix?" *The Washington Post*, December 15, 2019, retrieved 15.12.2021, from https://www.washingtonpost.com/opinions/2019/12/15/should-religion-politics-mix/.

transfer of the U.S. embassy to Jerusalem. They were also pleased by Trump's opposition to abortion rights activists and the rights of homosexuals. While praising Trump's policies, the then president of Liberty University Jerry Falwell Jr. referred to Trump as the evangelicals' dream president.[50] David Brody, an evangelical activist, also branded Trump as the most evangelical-friendly.[51] However, there were others, including young evangelicals and liberal protestants, who objected to Trump's policies as being racially biased and criticized his mishandling of family separation, undocumented immigrants, people of color, women, and the LGBTQ community. They were also critical of Trump's view of science and his exit from the Paris Climate Accord.

Other challenges to Trump's presidency have come from new social movements such as Black Lives Matter (BLM). The rising popular appeal of the BLM came about because of police brutality and violent events often launched by white nationalists at many cities across the country, including but not limited to Charlottesville in 2017, which became a flash point for resistance in the country. The Family Separation Policy, enacted by Trump in 2018, has particularly increased public criticism of the administration. In response, Attorney General Jeff Sessions and White House Press Secretary Sarah Huckabee Sanders invoked biblical justifications for the separation policy. At the foreign policy level, as a candidate, Trump pledged to recognize Jerusalem as Israel's united capital and to transfer the U.S. embassy to Jerusalem. Trump delivered on his promises, and by reallocating the embassy, he revised a long-held legacy in U.S. foreign policy toward Israel and the Palestinians. He also reinforced the same regular Israeli approach to negotiations with the Palestinians, where the U.S. role is to remain confined to providing help in the process. This approach falsely assumes the presence of equality in the structure of negotiations between Israel and the Palestinians. In terms of the negotiation's content, like many of his predecessors from both parties, Trump has overlooked key issues that matter the most to Palestinians including, Jerusalem, Israeli settlements, Palestinian statehood, and refugees. Additionally, the Trump Administration failed

---

50 Showalter, Brandon: "Jerry Fallwell Jr.: Evangelicals Have Found 'Dream President' in Donald Trump," *Christian Post*, April 30, 2017, retrieved 15.12.2021, from https://www.christianpost.com/news/jerry-fallwell-jr-evangelicals-dream-president-donald-trump.html.
51 Christopher, Tommy: "Christian Broadcasting Reporter Grills Trump Whether He Thinks God Put Him in Office." June 27, 2020, retrieved 15.12.2021, from https://www.mediaite.com/news/watch-christian-broadcasting-reporter-grills-trump-on-whether-he-thinks-god-put-him-in-office/.

in its peace plan, widely known as the deal of the century, where the administration attempted to determine the future of the Palestinians without consulting them.[52]

The former U.S. ambassador to the UN, Nikki Haley, an evangelical herself, played a key role in Trump's decision to transfer the location of the U.S. embassy.[53] Trump's selection of David Friedman as the U.S. ambassador to Israel despite his support for Jewish settlements in the West Bank, and the choice of Jason Greenblatt as the U.S. special envoy in the region, along with appointing David Kushner as the key negotiator, reveals the depth of the administration's pro-evangelical and pro-Israeli agendas. The transfer of the U.S. embassy to Jerusalem on May 14 (the day of the Palestinian *Nakba* that was followed by Israel's creation) has offended Palestinians even at the symbolic level.[54] Trump's policy in the region also concluded agreements between the Arab countries of Bahrain, Oman, the UAE, and Morocco, who, having deserted the Palestinian cause, started an era of normalizing ties with Israel without demanding its withdrawal from the Palestinian-occupied territories.[55]Contrary to their expectations, subsequent events, including the ongoing war against Palestinians in Gaza and the West Bank, reveals, among other things, the centrality of the Palestinian issue in regional and world affairs.

Critics of Evangelicals' Theology and Politics

While evangelicals have invested ample resources and pressure on the United States to support Israel, mainstream Christians' view of Israel is mostly limited to the historical ties that connect Christians and Jews together within the framework of the Judaic-Christian tradition. American public support for Israel has also been motivated by a spiritual connection within the Judeo-Christian tradition. However,

---

52 Entous, Adam: "Donald Trump New World Order." *The New Yorker*, May 11, 2018, pp. 1–38, retrieved 15.12.2021, from https://www.newyorker.com/magazine/2018/06/18/donald-trumps-new-world-order.

53 Fisk, Robert: "This Is the Aim of Donald Trump's Visit to Saudi Arabia." *The Independent*, May 19, 2017, retrieved 15.12.2021, from http://www.independent.co.uk/voices/donald-trump-saudi-arabia-iran-iraq-kurdish-population-shia-muslims-a7742276.html.

54 Hassan, Zaha: "Despite Two Years of Hostility, Palestinians Will Thank Trump One Day." *Haaretz*, October 22, 2018, retrieved 15.12.2021, from https://www.haaretz.com/us-news/.premium-despite-two-years-of-hostility-palestinians-will-thank-trump-one-day-1.6575581.

55 Thrull, Nathan: "Israel-Palestine: The Real Reason There's Still No Peace." *The Guardian*, May 16, 2017, retrieved 15.12.2021, from https://www.theguardian.com/world/2017/may/16/the-real-reason-the-israel-palestine-peace-process-always-fails.

U.S. evangelicals and their supporters' backing of Israel is more motivated by their belief that "the key to [God's] plan is the re-founding of Israel as a nation." They also believe that "without Israel, the whole plan falls apart."[56] To generate more support for Israel, evangelicals have emphasized that "God will bless those who bless the Jewish people."[57] To most evangelicals, except perhaps for the younger generation, U.S. support for Israel has also been intended to enact God's foreign policy agenda.

In contrast with evangelicals though, other Christian groups, namely those subscribing to the replacement theology, have challenged the evangelicals' vision that has dominated U.S. foreign policy toward Israel for decades. Replacement theologians have simply decided to remove Israel's role from the end-time prophecy. The support for the replacement theology derives mainly from Eastern Orthodox, Catholic, and liberal Protestant groups. Replacement theologians generally believe that today's Christians should no longer consider the Jews as God's chosen people. They assume that "the Christian Church is the continuation and heir of biblical historical Israel."[58] As such, to them, "the church is the new Israel."[59] Replacement theologians also suggest that since God's prophecies are no longer contingent on Israel's control of the Promised Land, the United States should start practicing a more evenhanded approach to settling the Israeli–Palestinian conflict. Their belief that God's "new covenant in Jesus has replaced the previous one with Israel" has created a major rift between evangelicals and those who uphold the replacement theory.[60] Some of those who support the replacement theology and Catholic's liberation theology suggest that the Palestinian Christians, not Israel, should now be considered as the "lineal successor of the Israelites of the Exodus."[61] Replacement theology activists also question and at times reject evangelicals' beliefs concerning the statement that says, "[W]hoever curses you I will curse; and all people on earth will be blessed through you."[62]

From a more secular perspective, social scientists have largely been skeptical of the value of literalist interpretations of sacred texts. Advances in scientific

---

56 Weber. Timothy P.: "How Evangelicals Became Israel's Best Friend." *Christianity Today*, October 5, 1998, p. 40, retrieved 13.05.2022, from https://www.christianitytoday.com/ct/1998/october5/8tb038.html.
57 Genesis 12:3.
58 Ariel, Yaakov: "An Unexpected Alliance: Christian Zionism and its Historical Significance." *Modern Judaism* 26 (1), 2006, pp. 74–100, p. 87.
59 McCall, Thomas S.: "Israel and the Church: The Differences." *Levitt Newsletter* 18 (5), 1996, retrieved 13.05.2022, from https://www.levitt.com/newsletters/1996-05.html.
60 Perko, Michael F.: "Contemporary American Christian Attitudes to Israel Based on the Scriptures." *Israel Studies* 8 (2), 2003, p. 5.
61 *Ibid.*, p. 14.
62 Genesis 12:3.

discoveries and analytical approaches have motivated scholars and students to pursue critical studies of religious texts. New and accelerated findings in the fields of evolution, archaeology, and geology also led to more critical reviews and interpretations of religion. However, such developments in methods and technology may have ignited backlashes against science and intelligentsia. Evangelicals have, for instance, managed to drift more toward religiosity to counterbalance the expanded secularization of today's Western societies.[63]

Critical analysis of evangelicals' beliefs and conduct have also come from secular young Jews, many of whom believe that evangelicals are deepening the Israeli–Palestinian conflict and leading to a new rise in Antisemitism in the West.[64] They argue that evangelicals may "have simultaneously catalyzed total love for the Jewish State while unwittingly unleashing a wave of anti-Semitism against the Jewish people."[65] Aside from Jewish secular voices of criticism, other groups in the ultra-Orthodox Jewish community in Israel and the United States have expressed opposition to Israel and Zionism. For instance, the ultra-Orthodox Jewish group known as Neturei Karta has not only supported Palestinians' claim to statehood but also considered today's Israel and Zionism as inconsistent with the teaching of the Torah.[66] They warn that the current State of Israel, based on its exclusionary ideology and conduct, may lead to devastating effects on Jews.

Conclusions

Early evangelicals highlighted the need for expanding religious liberty and freedom in the new American colonies. However, as their beliefs have changed and morphed into ideological doctrines associated with dispensationalism, Christian Zionism, and other fundamentalist beliefs, they became less associated with the values of early evangelicalism and liberal Protestantism. They began reinterpreting the ideas and ideals of sacred texts to serve their theology and politics at the domestic and global levels. As a consequence, many groups and trends in the modern conservative evangelical movement, while utilizing their theology and politics, have placed themselves in opposition to anything that could hinder what they view as God's eternal plan for Israel and the world.

---

63 Niebuhr, Gustav: "Christian Split: Can Nonbelievers Be Saved?" *New York Times*, August 22, 1996, retrieved 15.12.2021, from https://www.nytimes.com/1996/08/22/us/christian-split-can-nonbelievers-be-saved.html.
64 Balmer, Randall: *Evangelicalism and America*. Baylor University Press: Waco, TX 2016.
65 Shindler, Colin: "Likud and the Christian Dispensationalists: A Symbiotic Relationship." *Israel Studies* 5 (1), 2000, p. 178.
66 Epafras, L.: "Unhoming Homeland: Jewish Diaspora and Neturei Karta Community." *Melintas: An International Journal of Philosophy and Religion* 26 (3), 2010, pp. 255–270, retrieved 15.12.2021, from https://core.ac.uk/download/pdf/235702078.pdf.

Evangelicals' ultimate objective has mainly been centered on "advancing the Kingdom of God" domestically and globally. The feeling that they were and remain victimized has strengthened their resolve to align themselves with Trump's policies and helped them to defend their Christian way of life. For today's evangelicals, there is little or no separation between most aspects of everyday life and religious life. Evangelicals view their opponents, including women's and abortion rights advocates, homosexuals, and Muslims, as hostile to their Christian way of life. While they continue to idealize Israel for the sake of fulfilling their religious prophecies, evangelicals are now facing other challenges coming from progressives and liberals who are critical of Israel's policy toward the Palestinians. The support for Israel among young evangelicals has also been slipping away, given that the youth are no longer easily influenced by old-style indoctrinations and conspiracies.[67]

Furthermore, unlike liberal Protestants, today's evangelicals' support for Israel has not been motivated by guilt derived from the crimes of the Nazi holocaust against Jews, nor because of the presence of resemblances between the United States and Israeli political cultures. Liberal Protestants who have supported the Zionists' goals have indeed been influenced by remorse about the Holocaust. As a result, they tried to amend those crimes by supporting the creation of a Jewish homeland in Palestine without considering the impact of that on the native inhabitants of Palestine.[68] Today's evangelicals' support for Israel is largely inspired by their messianic theology concerning the end-time prophecies. Along with derailing the peace process from moving forward, evangelicals may have also highlighted the religious dimension of the current Israeli–Palestinian conflict. Today's Israeli–Palestinian conflict may be experiencing a transformation from its early phase as a nationalist-oriented conflict between two competing nationalist movements (i.e., political Zionism vs. Palestinian nationalism) into a more religiously dominated conflict between devout fundamentalists (i.e., Islamists, Jewish, and evangelical extremists) on all sides.

While not conclusively demonstrating religion as the only underlying factor in the United States or British alliances with Zionism and Israel, the support for Israel has been at the forefront of the U.S. foreign policy agenda. This support has placed Israel at an advantage as a leading force in the region. Other factors, such as geopolitics, security, and economy, have also played an important role in the U.S. support for Israel. On issues surrounding Israel's security, there are no significant disagreements between Republicans and Democrats where both sides

---

67 Brog, David: "The End of Evangelical Support for Israel: The Jewish State International Standing." *Middle East Quarterly* 21 (2), 2014, retrieved 15.12.2021, from https://www.meforum.org/3769/israel-evangelical-support.

68 Mohamad, Husam: "US Policy and Israeli-Palestinian Relations." *Journal of Middle East and South Asian Studies* 43 (1), 2019, pp. 26–56.

have committed themselves to safeguarding Israel's security needs. For their part, Republican presidents (such as Reagan, Bush, and Trump) may have often based their support for Israel on behalf of U.S. evangelicals who play a crucial role in Presidential and Congressional elections.[69] Democrats' support for Israel on the other hand is usually more influenced by geopolitical factors. Democrats are also more influenced by secular-oriented lobbying groups such as AIPAC and J-Street, not evangelicals. The support for Israel among younger progressive Democrats, including young Jewish activists, is also on the decline in part because of Israel's policies against the Palestinians in the Occupied-Territories.[70]

Finally, it must be noted that all messianic messages, including those associated with Judaism, Christianity, and Islam, have presented serious challenges within their own societies and against each other. The messianic messages associated with the Abrahamic traditions predict a violent end to the world, and the extremist elements among them welcome, in their own and separate ways, these end-time prophecies as fulfillments of their own doctrines. Extremists associated with the three religious orientations have made it particularly difficult for mediators to try to resolve the conflicts (i.e., on the basis of territorial, nationalist interests, etc.). However, Jewish, Christian, and Islamist fundamentalists have been, and remain, focused on the religious and messianic dimensions that connect each of them separately, or in their own way, with the same Promised Land.

References

Anderson, Irvine: *Biblical Interpretation and Middle East Policy, the Promised Land, America and Israel, 1917–2002.* University Press of Florida: Gainesville 2007.

Ariel, Yaakov: "An Unexpected Alliance: Christian Zionism and its Historical Significance." *Modern Judaism* 26 (1), 2006, pp. 74–100.

Balmer, Randall: "Pro-Israel and Anti-Semitic: Understanding Evangelicals Support for Israel." *Palestine-Israel Journal* 25 (1&2), 2020, pp. 100–104.

Balmer, Randall: *Evangelicalism and America*, Baylor University Press: Waco, TX 2016.

---

69 Djupe, Paul/Neiheisel, Jacob R./Conger, Kimberly H.: "Are the Politics of the Christian Right Linked to State Rates of the Nonreligious? The Importance of Salient Controversy." *Political Research Quarterly* 71 (4), 2018, pp. 910–922, retrieved 15.12.2021, from https://journals.sagepub.com/doi/full/10.1177/1065912918771526.

70 Fandos, Nicholas/Edmondson, Catie: "Democrats Growing More Skeptical of Israel, Pressure Biden." *The New York Times*, May 17, 2021, retrieved 15.12.2021, from https://www.nytimes.com/2021/05/18/us/politics/israel-gaza-democrats-biden.html.

Brog, David: "The End of Evangelical Support for Israel: The Jewish State International Standing." *Middle East Quarterly* 21 (2), 2014, retrieved 15.12.2021, from https://www.meforum.org/3769/israel-evangelical-support.

Campolo, Tony: "The Ideological Roots of Christian Zionism." *Tikkun* 20 (1), 2005, pp. 19–20.

Carenen, Caitlin: *The Fervent Embrace: Liberal Protestants, Evangelicals, and Israel.* New York University Press: New York 2012.

Christopher, Tommy: "Christian Broadcasting Reporter Grills Trump Whether He Thinks God Put Him in Office." June 27, 2020, retrieved 15.12.2021, from https://www.mediaite.com/news/watch-christian-broadcasting-reporter-grills-trump-onwhether-he-thinks-god-put-him-in-office/.

Daniel, Benjamin/Simon, Steven: *The Next Attack: The Failure of the War on Terror and a Strategy for Getting it Right.* Times Books: New York: 2005.

Dart, John: "Bush Religious Rhetoric Riles Critics." *Christian Century* 120 (5), 2003, pp. 10–12.

Djupe, Paul/Neiheisel, Jacob R./Conger, Kimberly H.: "Are the Politics of the Christian Right Linked to State Rates of the Nonreligious? The Importance of Salient Controversy." *Political Research Quarterly* 71 (4), 2018, pp. 910–922, retrieved 15.12.2021, from https://journals.sagepub.com/doi/full/10.1177/1065912918771526.

Durham, Martin: "Evangelical Protestantism and Foreign Policy in the United States after September 11." *Patterns of Prejudice* 38 (2), 2004, pp. 145–160.

Entous, Adam: "Donald Trump New World Order." *The New Yorker*, May 11, 2018, pp. 1–38, retrieved 15.12.2021, from https://www.newyorker.com/magazine/2018/06/18/donald-trumps-new-world-order.

Epafras, L.: "Unhoming Homeland: Jewish Diaspora and Neturei Karta Community." *Melintas: An International Journal of Philosophy and Religion* 26 (3), 2010, pp. 255–270, retrieved 15.12.2021, from https://core.ac.uk/download/pdf/235702078.pdf.

Fandos, Nicholas/Edmondson, Catie: "Democrats Growing More Skeptical of Israel, Pressure Biden." *The New York Times*, May 17, 2021, retrieved 15.12.2021, from https://www.nytimes.com/2021/05/18/us/politics/israel-gaza-democrats-biden.html.

Fea, John/Gifford, Laura R./Griffith, Marie/Martin Lerone A.: "Evangelicalism and Politics." *The American Historian* 20, 2018, retrieved 15.12.2021, from https://www.oah.org/tah/issues/2018/november/evangelicalism-and-politics/.

Fisk, Robert: "This Is the Aim of Donald Trump's Visit to Saudi Arabia." *The Independent*, May 19, 2017, retrieved 15.12.2021, from http://www.independent.co.uk/voices/donald-trump-saudi-arabia-iran-iraq-kurdish-population-shia-muslims-a7742276.html.

Friedman, Isaiah: *Palestine: A Twice Promised Land.* Routledge: New York 2018.

Gelvin, James L.: *The Israel–Palestine Conflict: A History.* Cambridge University Press: Cambridge 2021.

Genesis 12:3.

Gershom Gorenberg, Gershom: "Unorthodox Alliance." *The Washington Post*, October 11, 2002, retrieved 15.12.2021, from https://www.washingtonpost.com/archive/opinions/2002/10/11/unorthodox-alliance/2bc224d0-2f35-47f5-9ff4-43ae59f2ac34/.

Goodman, Walter: "Rise of the Religious Right." *The New York Times*, September 29, 1996, retrieved 15.12.2021, from https://www.nytimes.com/1996/09/28/arts/rise-of-the-religious-right.html.

Gorenberg, Gershom: "Unorthodox Alliance." *The Washington Post*, October 11, 2002, retrieved 15.12.2021, from https://www.washingtonpost.com/archive/opinions/2002/10/11/unorthodox-alliance/2bc224d0-2f35-47f5-9ff4-43ae59f2ac34/.

Halsell, Gracee: *Prophesy and Politics: Militant Evangelists on the Road to Nuclear War.* Lawrence Hill: Westport, CT 1986.

Hanegraaff, Hank: *The Apocalypse Code: Find Out What the Bible Really Says About the End Times and Why It Matters Today.* Kindle ed. 2010.

Hanegraaff, Hank: "Rebuild Temple vs. the Dom of the Rock." August 24, 2007, retrieved 15.12.2021, from https://hankhanegraaff.blogspot.com/2007/08/rebuilt-temple-vs-dome-of-rock.html.

Hassan, Zaha: "Despite Two Years of Hostility, Palestinians Will Thank Trump One Day." *Haaretz*, October 22, 2018, retrieved 15.12.2021, from https://www.haaretz.conews/.premiumdespite-two-years-of-hostility-palestinians-will-thank-trump-one-day-1.6575581.

Inbari, Motti/Bumin, Kirki/Byrd, Gordon: "Why Do Evangelicals Support Israel." *Politics and Religion* 14 (1), 2020, pp. 1–36.

"Is the Modern Nation of Israel Important?" *La Vista Church of Christ*, June 28, 2005, retrieved 15.12.2021, from https://www.lavistachurchofchrist.org/cms/is-the-modern-nation-ofisrael-important/.

Javadikouchaksaraei, Mehrzad: "Religion and Politics in Israel: The Mythology of Jewish Nationalism." *International Journal of Multicultural and Multireligious Understanding* 4 (3), 2017, pp. 35–45.

Jelen, Ted: "Religion and Foreign Policy Attitudes: Exploring the Effects of Denomination and Doctrine." *American Politics Quarterly* 22 (3), 1994, pp. 382–400.

Khuri, Fred J.: *The Arab Israeli Dilemma.* Syracuse: Syracuse University Press: New York 1985.

Kurth, James: "Religion in World Affairs: The Protestant Deformation and American Foreign Policy." *Orbis: A Journal of World Affairs* 48 (2), 1998, pp. 221–239.

Lienesch, Michael: *Redeeming America: Piety and Politics in the New Christian Right*. University of North Carolina Press: Chapel Hill 1993.

Longhenry, Ethan R.: *A Study of Denominations*. DeWard Publishing: Tampa 2015.

Lukas, Anthony L.: "The Rapture and the Bomb." *The New York Times*, June 8, 1986, retrieved 15.12.2021, from http://query.nytimes.com/gst/fullpage.html?res=9A0DEFDA153FF93BA35755C0A960948260&sec=&spon=.

Mansfield, Peter: *The Arabs*. Penguin Books: New York 1992.

Martin, William: "The Christian Right and American Foreign Policy." *Foreign Policy* 114 (3), 1999, pp. 66–80.

Martin, William: *With God on Our Side: The Rise of the Religious Right in America*. Broadway Books: New York 1996.

Mayer, Jeremy D.: "Christian Fundamentalists and Public Opinion towards the Middle East: Israel's New Best Friends?" *Social Science Quarterly* 85 (3), 2004, pp. 695–712.

"McCain Rejects Hagee Backing as Nazi Remarks Surface." *The New York Times*, May 22, 2008, retrieved 14.05.2022, from https://thecaucus.blogs.nytimes.com/2008/05/22/mccain-rejects-hagee-backing-as-nazi-remarks-surface/.

McCall, Thomas S.: "Israel and the Church: The Differences." *Levitt Newsletter* 18 (5), 1996, retrieved 13.05.2022, from https://www.levitt.com/newsletters/1996-05.html.

Miano, Peter: "Mainstream Christian Zionism." In: Phillip Thomas/Miano Peter/Mitchell Jason (eds.): *Prophetic Voices on Middle East Peace: A Jewish, Christian and Humanist Primer on Colonialism, Zionism and Nationalism in the Middle East*. Claremont Press: Claremont 2016.

Miller, Paul D.: "Evangelicals, Israel, and US Foreign Policy." *Survival: Global Politics and Strategy* 56 (1), 2014, pp. 7–26, retrieved 15.12.2021, from https://www.tandfonline.com/doi/pdf/10.1080/00396338.2014.882149.

Mohamad, Husam: "US Policy and Israeli-Palestinian Relations." *Journal of Middle East and South Asian Studies* 43 (1), 2019, pp. 26–56.

Napierała, Paulina: "The Influence of Religion on American Policy toward Israel: Is FPA a Useful Tool for Analysis?". In: Grabowski Marcin/Pugacewicz Tomasz (eds.) *Application of International Relations Theories in Asia and Africa*. Peter Lang: Berlin et al. 2019, pp. 219-247.

Niebuhr, Gustav: "Christian Split: Can Nonbelievers Be Saved?" *New York Times*, August 22, 1996, retrieved 15.12.2021, from https://www.nytimes.com/1996/08/22/us/christian-split-cannonbelievers-be-saved.html.

Perko, Michael F.: "Contemporary American Christian Attitudes to Israel Based on the Scriptures." *Israel Studies* 8 (2), 2003, pp. 1–17.

Phillip-Fein, Kim: "Conservatism: A State of the Field." *The Journal of American History*, 2011, pp. 723–745.

Pipes, Daniel: "The Clout of Christian Zionism." *Jewish News: Community Weekly Serving Greater Phoenix and Northern Arizona*, July 18, 2003, retrieved 14.05.2022, from https://www.jewishaz.com/opinion/the-clout-of-christian-zionism/article_6b29bb21-aecc-51d5-8089-3157eea771b8.html.

Pomper, Miles: "Religious Right Flexes Muscles on Foreign Policy Matters." *Congressional Quarterly Weekly* 13 (3), 2002, pp. 1893–1897.

Prusher, Ilene: "Israel's Unlikely Ally: American Evangelicals." *Christian Science Monitor* 90 (104), 1998, retrieved 15.12.2021, from https://www.csmonitor.com/1998/0424/042498.intl.intl.2.html.

Reagan, David R.: "The Muslim Anti-Christ Theory." *Lamb & Lion Ministries: Proclaiming the Soon Return of Jesus Christ*, December 2010, from https://christinprophecy.org/articles/the-muslim-antichrist-theory/.

Richardson, Joel: *Mideast Beast*. WND Books: New York 2012.

Robert, Nicholson W.: "Evangelicals and Israel." *Mosaic Magazine: Advancing Jewish Thought*, October 6, 2013, retrieved 14.05.2021, from https://mosaicmagazine.com/essay/uncategorized/2013/10/evangelicals-and-israel/.

Rubin, Jennifer: "Should Religion and Politics Mix?" *The Washington Post*, December 15, 2019, retrieved 15.12.2021, from https://www.washingtonpost.com/opinions/2019/12/15/should-religion-politics-mix/.

Schoenit, Marc: "The Roots of Christian Zionism." *Theological Review* 26 (1), 2005, pp. 3–38.

Shindler, Colin: "Likud and the Christian Dispensationalists: A Symbiotic Relationship." *Israel Studies* 5 (1), 2000, pp. 153–183.

Showalter, Brandon: "Jerry Fallwell Jr.: Evangelicals Have Found 'Dream President' in Donald Trump." *Christian Post*, April 30, 2017, retrieved 15.12.2021, from https://www.christianpost.com/news/jerry-fallwell-jr-evangelicals-dream-president-donald-trump.html.

Sutton, Matthew Avery: "The Capital Riot Revealed the Darkest Nightmare of White Evangelical America." *The New Republic*, January 14, 2021, retrieved 15.12.2021, from https://newrepublic.com/article/160922/capitol-riot-revealed-darkest-nightmares-white-evangelical-america.

Thrull, Nathan: "Israel-Palestine: The Real Reason There's Still No Peace." *The Guardian*, May 16, 2017, retrieved 15.12.2021, from https://www.theguardian.com/world/2017/may/16/the-real-reason-the-israel-palestine-peace-process-always-fails.

Van Engen, Abram: "White Evangelicals and the New American Exceptionalism of Donald Trump." *Religion & Politics*, 2020, retrieved 15.12.2021, from https://religionandpolitics.org/2020/09/29/white-evangelicals-and-the-new-american-exceptionalism-of-donald-trump/.

Wagner, Donald: "The Interregnum: Christian Zionism in the Clinton Years." *Daily Star*, October 10, 2003, retrieved 15.12.2021, from https://www.dailystar.com.lb/Opinion/Commentary/2003/Oct-10/93261-the-interregnumchristian-zionism-in-the-clinton-years.ashx.

Wagner, Donald: "Reagan and Begin, Bibi and Jerry: The Theo-political Alliance of the Likud Party with the American Christian Right." *Arab Studies Quarterly* 20 (4), 1998, pp. 33–52.

Weber, Timothy P.: "How Evangelicals Became Israel's Best Friend." *Christianity Today*, October 5, 1998, retrieved 13.05.2022, from https://www.christianitytoday.com/ct/1998/october5/8tb038.html.

Lyman A. Kellstedt and James L. Guth

Religion and American Public Attitudes on Global Warming, 2020

Abstract: Few contemporary issues have garnered more international attention than the climate crisis. The problem of global warming has been addressed not only by political leaders and environmental advocates but by religious leaders and faith communities as well. Here we continue a long tradition of social science research into the impact of religious factors on public environmental attitudes. Despite the much-discussed "greening of religion," we find considerable differences among members of American religious groups on environmental policy, differences that have remained quite consistent over the past three decades. Although ethnoreligious affiliation, religiosity, and religious beliefs all have substantial relationships with environmental views, we find that theological traditionalism is the strongest religious influence on environmentalism in multivariate analysis, largely absorbing the effects of affiliation and religiosity. We also discover that political and ideological variables mediate part, but not all, of the influences of religion.

Keywords: climate change, ethnoreligious tradition, theological traditionalism, science skepticism, conservative media use

Introduction

Climate change is in the news. Firestorms on the West Coast, hurricanes in the South, droughts in the West, and floods in the East are all linked to global warming. In late 2021 the United Nations implored its members to take action to counter the negative effects of climate change.[1] Although this plea was quickly echoed by President Biden, Democratic legislators, and environmental interest groups, effective governmental action in the United States will depend in large part on strong public support, shaped by a confluence of demographic, ideological, and partisan influences.

Although scholars have investigated a wide range of factors influencing public attitudes, one of the oldest and most intriguing line of inquiry has assessed the

---

1 United Nations Intergovernmental Panel on Climate Change: *Climate Change 2021: The Physical Science Basis*. United Nations: New York 2021. www.un.org/en/climatechange/reports.

impact of religion, a research tradition sparked by the "Lynn White thesis" of the late 1960s.[2] Although researchers have invariably disagreed about which facets of religion have the greatest impact on attitudes, almost all attest to their influence, direct or indirect. And religious leaders and organizations have contributed to the dialogue, from Pope Francis to a multitude of local ministers, priests, rabbis, and imams. Indeed, one major trend of this century, according to some observers, is the "greening of religion." This chapter considers contemporary religious influences on Americans' views on global warming and how those views are mediated politically. Just how "green" is American religion?[3] And which religious communities are "greenest"?

To answer these questions, we proceed as follows: first, we briefly summarize the central findings of past studies on religion and environmental attitudes, especially on global warming. Then we use the 2020 American National Election Study (ANES) to illustrate the divergent responses of different ethnoreligious traditions to climate change and governmental policies to address it. Next, we calculate a robust measure of public support for action on climate change to consider the influence of religious factors on that support. Finally, we examine how religion interacts with demographics, media attention, and related political issues, as well as partisan and ideological variables, in shaping environmental responses.

Religion and Environmentalism

The body of empirical research on religion and environmentalism is truly massive, representing work by sociologists, political scientists, anthropologists, economists, and scholars from other disciplines.[4] The content and quality of this work vary in many ways: in the geographical focus of the survey (local, national, or international); in the composition and size of the sampled population; in the content, number, and validity of environmental questions; and, finally, in the variety and sophistication of religious items.[5] Like this chapter, most research has focused

---

2   White argued that adherents of "Judeo-Christian" traditions accepted the Biblical injunction to "take dominion over the Earth" and thus neglected the environment. White, Lynn, Jr.: "The Historical Roots of Our Ecological Crisis." *Science* 3767, 1967, pp. 1203–1207.
3   Squally, Jay: "Is Religiosity Green in the United States?" *Economic Analysis and Policy* 63, 2019, pp. 11–23.
4   We cannot assess here this complex body of work. For an extensive review, see Taylor, Bron/Van Wieren, Gretel/Zaleha, Bernard: "The Greening of Religion Hypothesis (Part 2): Assessing the Data from Lynn White, Jr, to Pope Francis." *Journal for the Study of Religion, Nature and Culture* 10 (3), 2016, pp. 306–378.
5   For a survey of some of these questions, see Berry, Evan: "Religious Environmentalism and Environmental Religion in America." *Religion Compass* 7 (10), 2013, pp. 454–466.

on the American case, although a growing body of cross-national studies also addresses these issues.[6]

In both the American and comparative literature, there is considerable divergence of opinion on which facet of religion is most influential in shaping environmental attitudes. Some scholars argue that the most significant differences are between religious traditions. Originally this was often expressed in the classic "Lynn White" formulation of "Judeo-Christianity" versus other world religious traditions, with the latter supposedly more solicitous toward the environment. In the American context, however, the focus has usually been on intra-"Judeo-Christian" differences. Some early comparisons spotlighted divergences between "Protestants" and "Catholics,"[7] but later research has usually relied on more nuanced definitions of ethnoreligious traditions—albeit with considerable variation in the groups examined. Such studies often find substantial gaps between traditions: white evangelical Protestants are quite skeptical about environmentalism; Catholics, Jews, and religious "minorities" are more supportive, and the unaffiliated are most enthusiastic of all about environmental policies.[8]

Another influential stream in the literature emphasizes religious beliefs. Many studies have examined the impact of specific aspects of "Protestant" theology: beliefs in Biblical authority, dispensationalism ("End-Times" theology), "fundamentalism," or—harking back to Lynn White, "dominion theology" versus

---

[6] See, for example, Hagevi, Magnus: "Religion and the Environmental Opinion in 22 Countries: A Comparative Study." *International Review of Sociology* 24 (1), 2014, pp. 91–109; Tsimpo, Clarence/Wodon, Quentin: "Faith, Religiosity, and Attitudes towards the Environment and Climate Change." *Review of Faith and International Affairs* 14 (3), 2016, pp. 51–64.

[7] Greeley, Andrew: "Religion and Attitudes toward the Environment." *Journal for the Scientific Study of Religion* 32 (1), 1993, pp. 19–28. For a more recent comparison, see Leiserowitz, Anthony/Maibach, Edward W./Roser-Renouf, Connie/Rosenthal, Seth: *Climate Change in the American Christian Mind.* Yale Project on Climate Change Communication: New Haven, CT 2015. For a comparative example, cf. Hagevi, Magnus: *op. cit.*

[8] Taylor, Bron/Van Wieren, Gretel/Zaleha, Bernard: "Lynn White Jr. and the Greening-of-Religion Hypothesis." *Conservation Biology* 30 (5), 2016, pp. 1000–1009; Arbuckle, Matthew B./Konisky, David M.: "The Role of Religion in Environmental Attitudes." *Social Science Quarterly* 96 (5), 2015, pp. 1244–1263; Jones, Robert P./Cox, Daniel/Navarro-Rivera, Juhem: *Believers, Sympathizers, & Skeptics: Why Americans Are Conflicted About Climate Change, Environmental Policy, and Science.* Public Religion Research Institute (PRRI): Washington, DC 2014; Pudio, Jason: "Public Opinion and Religion: Environmental Attitudes in the United States." In: *Oxford Research Encyclopaedia of Politics.* Oxford University Press: New York 2019 (online) https://doi.org/10.1093/acrefore/9780190228637.013.790.

"stewardship theology."[9] Much less attention has been paid to the influence of competing currents in Catholic belief or theological differences in Judaism. Nevertheless, there seems to be a common theme, not always articulated, that there is a negative relationship between most "traditionalist" theologies and concern for the environment—or at least willingness to support government policies protecting the environment.[10]

Finally, many studies consider the impact of "religiosity" on environmental attitudes. This concept is usually tapped by survey items on attendance at religious services, frequency of personal prayer, propensity to read scripture, or the subjective importance of religion in one's life. Here the divergence of findings is most striking, with some investigators finding high religious behavior contributing to support for environmentalism, others revealing a negative relationship, and yet others discovering that religiosity has a negative effect at the bivariate level, but a positive one when religious beliefs or attitudes are controlled for. To complicate matters even further, a few studies find interactive effects, where the differing propensities of each tradition are enhanced by high religious engagement.[11]

To summarize: Despite the expansive body of research on religion and environmental attitudes, the relative influence of religious traditions, religious beliefs, and religiosity remains unsettled. Another important question is whether religion influences environmental attitudes directly, or if its effects are fully mediated by other variables. Although we cannot resolve any of these questions definitively by analyzing a single survey, we can provide a broad "lay of the land" picture of religious environmentalism in 2020, just as struggles over a "Green New Deal" seemed poised to erupt onto the top of the American political agenda.

Religious Groups in American Politics

To understand the American religious context, we draw on two theories interpreting the politics of American faith communities, each emphasizing a different configuration of the religious variables commonly employed in

---

9   For examples, see Barker, David/Bearce, David H.: "End-Times Theology, the Shadow of the Future, and Public Resistance to Addressing Global Climate Change." *Political Research Quarterly* 66 (2), 2013, pp. 267–279; Guth, James L./Kellstedt, Lyman A./ Smidt, Corwin E./Green, John C.: "Theological Perspectives and Environmentalism among Religious Activists." *Journal for the Scientific Study of Religion* 32 (4), 1993, pp. 373–382.

10 For a more skeptical perspective on the role of religious beliefs, see Djupe, Paul A./ Hunt, Patrick Kieren: "Beyond the Lynn White Thesis: Congregational Effects on Environmental Concerns." *Journal for the Scientific Study of Religion* 48 (4), 2009, pp. 670–686. Djupe and Hunt argue for the importance of congregational influences.

11 For a good review of these varied findings, see Pudio, Jason: *op. cit.*

environmental studies. *Ethnocultural theory*, formulated primarily by historians, focuses on the numerous ethnoreligious groups that migrated to America and multiplied upon reaching her shores. In this perspective, politics has always been a competition between two uneasy coalitions of ethnoreligious groups. The Republican Party (GOP) long represented historically dominant Mainline Protestants, such as Episcopalians, Presbyterians, and Methodists, with the more recent addition of evangelical Protestants and Latter-day Saints, while Democrats have always spoken for ethnoreligious minorities: Catholics and Jews in the past, and now Black Protestants, Latino Catholics, Muslims, Hindus, Buddhists, and others, including the growing ranks of the religiously unaffiliated or "Nones." Historians argue that these ethnoreligious groups held differing worldviews, cultural preferences, and religious reference groups—all shaping their partisan allegiances and views on public policy.[12] Although most sociologists of religion argue that ethnoreligious attachments have been weakened by assimilation and the wide "choices" now available in religion, political analysts continue to think at times in "ethnoreligious" terms, discussing the preferences of "Black Protestants," "Latino Catholics," or "white evangelicals."

An alternative perspective is *religious restructuring* theory, introduced by sociologist Robert Wuthnow in 1988 to explain growing divisions within American faith traditions.[13] A few years later, James Hunter's *Culture Wars* argued that these theological controversies had created political divides: "Orthodox" believers who accepted "an external, definable, and transcendent authority"[14] adhered firmly to traditional doctrines and gravitated to the political right. Religious "progressives," on the other side, replaced old faith claims with new ones drawn from experience or scientific rationality and moved to the left, joined by the burgeoning ranks of secular Americans who saw morality in a similar vein.[15] Political lines, then, were based on theology, rather than ethnoreligious divisions. Thus, theological divisions should influence environmental attitudes across all ethnoreligious traditions, eclipsing the influence of affiliation and religiosity.[16] In other words, "culture wars" should shape responses to the "climate wars."

---

12 For a review, see Swierenga, Robert P.: "Religion and American Voting Behavior, 1830s to 1930s." In: Smidt, Corwin E./Kellstedt, Lyman A./Guth, James L. (eds.): *The Oxford Handbook of Religion and American Politics*. Oxford University Press: New York 2009, pp. 69–94.

13 Wuthnow, Robert: *The Restructuring of American Religion*. Princeton University Press: Princeton 1988.

14 Hunter, James D.: *Culture Wars: The Struggle to Define America*. Basic Books: New York 1991, p. 44.

15 Campbell, David E./Layman, Geoffrey C./Green, John C.: *Secular Surge: A New Fault Line in American Politics*. Cambridge University Press: Cambridge 2021.

16 Although Wuthnow (*op. cit.*) and Hunter (*op. cit.*) defined these divides by belief rather than behavior, the "orthodox" put more stress on faith and are more observant

As a review of the literature on environmentalism suggests, scholars have drawn somewhat haphazardly from among the religious variables central to either the ethnoreligious or restructuring perspectives, often without much thought about which should dominate explanations. For White, world religious traditions varied greatly in environmental sensitivity, with "Judeo-Christians" coming out worst. Although scholars still investigate his grand scheme, most recent work on the United States has considered differences among "Christians," or even among "Protestants," finding specific faith traditions more or less sensitive to environmental issues. Others have argued for the power of religious belief, central to the restructuring argument, while a few studies find religious behavior most significant, with the highly committed either more—or less—likely to support environmental action.

Guiding Hypotheses

Although our ability to assess all these claims is limited somewhat by our data, we can examine American attitudes at a critical point in time. Based on our own previous work and reading of the literature, we offer several guiding hypotheses about religion's impact on environmental attitudes in 2020:

H_1 Ethnoreligious groups will differ considerably on climate change. White evangelicals will be most skeptical, while most religious minorities as well as atheists and agnostics will anchor the environmentalist pole.

H_2 Theological traditionalism, measured in several ways, will have a strong negative relationship with environmentalism.

H_3 High religious commitment, as evidenced by ritual attendance and importance of religion, will work against environmentalism at the bivariate level.

H_4 In multivariate analysis, theological traditionalism will dominate the explanation, with some residual effects from religious affiliation. Religious commitment will have only a very small direct impact in either direction.

We also anticipate that other factors will mediate or perhaps modify the impact of religion in multivariate analysis:

H_5 Conservative media attention will foster climate change denial.

H_6 Individuals with anti-science views, those who oppose government intervention in economic life, and those who disapprove of international organizations will oppose efforts to deal with global warming.

H_7 Conservatives, Republicans, and those approving Donald Trump's job performance will be less supportive of policies to fight climate change.

---

than "progressives," complicating efforts to distinguish effects of belief and behavior. Indeed, service attendance often serves as a proxy for traditional belief in analyses.

H_8 Demographic variables such as age, education, and gender, all tied to environmental concerns in previous research, will have limited independent impact in multivariate analysis.

Data and Methods

In the following analysis, we use data from the 2020 American National Election Study (ANES), a widely used source favored by political scientists.[17] The final post-election iteration of the survey included numerous environmental questions, detailed religious measures, and a host of other variables, with a weighted sample size of 7,453 respondents. We begin by examining responses of ethnoreligious groups[18] to seven questions that tap (directly or indirectly) attitudes toward climate change (Table 1).[19] In addition, we report the results of a principal components analysis (PCA) of these seven items: the factor loadings are at the bottom of each column, and mean factor scores for each group are in the right-hand column (the highest positive scores are most "pro-environmental").

As many national surveys have shown, the proportion of Americans concerned about climate change and wanting to do something about it is quite substantial.[20] And the 2020 ANES is no exception: as the top line in Table 1 shows, Americans tend to express positive views toward environmental policies: solid majorities favor spending more on the environment, regulating greenhouse gases, and doing more to fight rising temperatures. Narrower majorities are strongly convinced that global temperatures are rising and that such climate change explains extreme weather events. Finally, large pluralities prioritize the environment over economic concerns and regard the climate issue as very important. As the factor loadings at the bottom show, these responses form a powerful single dimension of opinion

---

[17] American National Election Studies: *ANES 2020 Time Series Study Preliminary Release: Combined Pre-Election and Post-Election Data* [dataset and documentation]. March 24, 2021 version. www.electionstudies.org.

[18] Our classification of ethnoreligious traditions follows the RELTRAD coding strategies outlined in Smidt, Corwin E./Kellstedt, Lyman A./Guth, James L. (eds.): *The Oxford Handbook of Religion and American Politics.* Oxford University Press: New York 2009, and Steensland, Brian/Park, Jerry/Regnerus, Mark/Robinson, Lynn/Wilcox, Bradford/Woodberry, Robert: "The Measure of American Religion." *Social Forces* 79 (1), 2000, pp. 291–318.

[19] Although two of the items do not address global warming directly, the dominance of climate change discussions in 2020 suggests they tap such attitudes indirectly, as do their strong correlations with the explicit climate items.

[20] See, for example, the summary of survey findings from the Yale Center for Climate Change at https://climatecommunication.yale.edu/visualizations-data/ycom-us/.

Table 1. Ethnoreligious Traditions and Environmental Attitudes (in percent)

	Spend More	Regulate Gases	Fight Rising Temps	Temps Are Rising	Climate Affects Weather	Environ Over Business	Climate Issue Vital	Factor Score**
All=	60.0	58.6	57.1	52.4	52.3	49.9	47.3	.000
White Evangelical	34.5	38.5	29.5	34.6	27.3	26.4	23.7	−.668
Latter-day Saints	34.8	49.1	37.6	50.6	30.9	31.0	24.6	−.515
Orthodox/Cons. Jews	60.6	53.8	48.2	54.8	44.8	45.1	42.5	−.223
Eastern Orthodox	52.0	51.0	52.4	50.9	53.5	47.3	45.6	−.096
White Catholic	55.4	59.9	52.0	55.0	49.5	45.4	45.9	−.070
Latino Evangelicals	54.2	54.2	54.0	49.0	54.4	42.9	47.3	−.069
White Mainline	54.7	60.4	51.7	51.2	48.4	49.3	43.4	−.067
Black Protestants	72.5	53.7	67.8	44.5	57.4	50.3	51.1	.113
Nothing in Particular	71.3	60.4	65.6	51.9	55.9	52.7	49.8	.171
Latino Catholics	65.4	58.4	67.9	49.6	64.3	52.9	57.6	.182
World Religions	74.7	71.2	70.6	66.0	67.3	59.2	61.7	.294
Atheist/Agnostic	82.2	83.6	83.2	76.7	74.7	81.3	73.1	.646
Reform Jews	86.1	79.8	82.0	72.9	76.3	80.4	68.9	.676
**Factor Loading=	.775	.797	.832	.593	.854	.801	.865	

Source: American National Election Study, 2020. N = 7,453.

**Mean factor score derived from a principal components analysis (PCA) of these seven variables, producing a single component with an eigenvalue of 4.386, accounting for 62.7% of the variance.

(*theta* reliability = .90), showing that at least in the present era, climate change has been fully assimilated into the larger realm of environmental politics.

Despite this general public support for pro-environment perspectives, ethnoreligious groups are quite divided: on each measure, white evangelicals are the least "environmentalist," approached only by Latter-day Saints (Mormons). Orthodox and Conservative Jews also hold more skeptical views, albeit inconsistently. Eastern Orthodox, white Catholics, Latino evangelicals, and white Mainliners are also slightly more conservative than the national average, although not on all items. Other groups fall on the "pro-environment" side, with Reform and unaffiliated Jews just beating out atheists and agnostics for the pole position, followed at a distance by "world religions" (Muslims, Hindus, Buddhists, Sikhs, and others), Latino Catholics, the religiously unaffiliated ("Nothing in Particular"), and Black Protestants.[21]

Thus, climate change attitudes track broader environmental orientations and ethnoreligious traditions differ rather sharply on such questions. But what explains the differences? As the literature review showed, scholars have posited religious observance, theological orientations—and ethnoreligious affiliation itself—as the governing factor. We consider all these possibilities: Table 2 presents five OLS regression models that examine the relationships between ANES religious measures and environmental attitudes. We start with ethnoreligious affiliation, which basically reprises the order seen in Table 1's last column: white evangelicals are at one end of the scale, with agnostics and atheists at the other. Mormons join white evangelicals on the conservative side, while Black Protestants, Latino Catholics, world religions, unaffiliated respondents, and Reform and unaffiliated Jews hold more environmentalist views. Other ethnoreligious groups do not differ significantly from the sample mean. Religious affiliation accounts for 13.3% of the variance in attitudes.[22]

Model 2 tests the impact of four religious beliefs and practices, critical to restructuring perspectives. As many earlier studies found, belief variables seem to have the strongest ties to environmental attitudes. In this case, Biblical literalism stands out: at the bivariate level, this three-point measure has about an equal number of "literalists" and those that believe that the Bible is *not* the word of

---

21 Smaller ethnoreligious groups not in the table include Black Catholics ($N = 47$; mean score = .138); all Asian evangelicals ($N = 34$; mean = −.086); Asian Mainline ($N = 20$; mean = .444); Asian Catholics ($N = 52$; mean = .208); "other" Christians ($N = 290$; mean = .076); and "Other Religions" ($N = 221$; mean = .138). These respondents and the unclassified constitute the omitted reference group in regressions, slightly on the positive side of the environmental score.

22 Religious affiliation measures account for twice as much variance as a combination of demographic variables: age, education, gender, income, marital status, and urban/rural residence ($R\ squared$ = .067) (data not shown).

God; the mean environmental score is −.464 for the former and .495 for the latter. And in the regression, literalism has the strongest coefficient, with a *beta* of −.252. Those who say they are "born-again" and those who see religion as extremely important are also less sympathetic to environmentalism, but neither relationship is as substantial as that with Bible item. Finally, although the bivariate correlation between religious service attendance and environmentalism is negative and moderately strong ($r = -.207$), that coefficient is insignificant in the regression. Thus, the analysis strongly suggests the primacy of theology, as tapped by the Bible item, with some contribution from born-again status and religious salience. The *R squared* for this package of religious variables is .124, very slightly less than that for ethnoreligious affiliation.

Another way of tapping basic theological orientations is through religious identities.[23] In the American context, a series of traditionalist movements has sought to restore religious bodies to "orthodoxy," most notably in the major white Protestant traditions, while "progressive" movements have produced competing "modernist" theological perspectives. Similar divisions have appeared elsewhere, most notably among Roman Catholics, although the terminology of their "restructuring" has somewhat differed. Labels of "fundamentalist," "evangelical," and "Pentecostal" have mostly Protestant origins, while Catholics tend to respond more to "traditional" (on the orthodox side) and "progressive," "nontraditional," and "spiritual," on the other (the same is true for Jewish respondents).[24] Thus, to be inclusive of all major traditions, we add "traditional" to the three "evangelical" labels in our "Conservative identity" measure, and combine the other three in a "progressive/nontraditional" category. Finally, we add a separate variable for those claiming a "secular" identification to the analysis. All three measures are significant predictors: conservative identity works strongly against environmentalist views, while the other two identities produce more support. The *R squared* of .119 is only marginally lower than that for affiliation and for beliefs and practices.

Finally, we consider sentiments toward religious reference groups, using ANES thermometer ratings for "fundamentalist Christians" and "Christians." The former item no doubt captures a strong component of theological traditionalism, especially for Protestants, while the latter may have the same effect, if more weakly (but more broadly) for all Christians. Both have strong negative correlations with environmentalism ($r = -.442$ and $-.303$, respectively). But only fundamentalism really

---

23 On the utility of using religious movement identifications as a measure of theological orientation, see Leege, David C./Kellstedt, Lyman A. (eds.): *Rediscovering the Religious Factor in American Politics.* M.E. Sharpe: Armonk NY 1993, chapter 4.

24 In the 2020 ANES data, 58% of white Catholics take at least one "conservative" label, while 27% choose a "progressive" one. As we expected, the former group says religion is more important, attend services more frequently, have a higher view of scripture, and are much more skeptical about global warming policies.

matters in the regression, as the coefficient for "Christians" is greatly reduced, if still statistically significant. Together, these two items account for one-fifth of the variance, more than any of the first three models.

Of course, all these religious variables are related in complex ways. To sort out their effects, Model 5 includes them all in one regression. Although ethnoreligious groups are characterized by different beliefs, practices, and identities, many of the group coefficients retain statistical significance, even with those other religious variables included. White evangelicals still lead the opposition to environmental initiatives, even when theological traditionalism is in the equation, followed again by Latter-day Saints. The coefficients for Orthodox Jews, Eastern Orthodox, white Catholics, the unaffiliated, and world religions drop out, but Latino Catholics, atheists and agnostics, and Reform Jews remain somewhat more environmentalist than their other religious traits would suggest.

Biblical literalism also maintains a significant impact, while the other belief and behavior variables drop out of the equation. All three identification measures remain significant in the expected direction, but "Progressive/Nontraditional" has the greatest impact. Finally, the "fundamentalist Christian" thermometer emerges as the most powerful religious predictor: those warm toward fundamentalists are staunch opponents of measures to combat global warming and climate change—and those cold, of course, are most environmentalist. The religious factors explain over 26% of the variance, a striking performance. Indeed, adding important demographic controls leaves the religious coefficients virtually unchanged and adds only about 2% to the variance explained.[25]

In sum, Table 2 shows the importance of some religious variables in understanding attitudes toward climate change and the insignificance of others. As in other studies, white evangelical Protestants hold negative attitudes even when controls for other religious variables are instituted. Nor is it unexpected to find Biblical literalists in the same camp as well as those who identify religiously with a "conservative" religious movement or feel warmly toward fundamentalist Christians. On the whole, these results suggest that the basic force underlying religious reactions to the global warming crisis is the "restructuring" division between the "orthodox" and the "progressive," whether gauged by religious affiliation, "traditional" belief, "traditional" identities, or sentiments toward "traditionalist" believers.

Do these results hold up when we introduce political and ideological factors into the equation? To simplify matters, we reduce our beliefs, practices, identities, and group assessment measures to two variables; first, we use a "religious traditionalism" measure produced from a principal components analysis of several

---

25 The highly educated, women, singles, and urbanites are all slightly more environmentalist in this analysis of religious variables (data not shown).

religious items in Table 2.[26] Note the very high negative correlation of this composite measure with environmental views ($r = -.436$). To create a religious commitment score, we combined items for attendance at services and subjective importance of religion (Cronbach's *alpha* = .77). As Table 3 shows, this religious commitment score is also negatively related to environmental views, but at a considerably lower level than theological traditionalism.

To put the religious analysis in the context of ideological and partisan perspectives, we added several potential mediating factors. First, we included a conservative media index that captures respondents' attention to major radio and online conservative commentators, invariably critical of environmentalism. And as the correlation shows, those listeners do indeed have negative attitudes toward liberal environment proposals.[27] We have also added three ideological stances that some scholars have found important. First, we include attitudes toward bigger government providing more services, tapping generic opposition to expansion of government functions. Second, we consider favorable attitudes toward science and, finally, evaluations of multilateral organizations, major actors in climate change politics.[28] Indeed, as *The Economist* puts it, "Environmentalism is driven by populists' two big bogeymen, scientific experts and multilateral institutions."[29] These are "bogeymen" for many religious conservatives as well and

---

26 The four "restructuring" items produced a single PCA component with an eigenvalue of 2.849 and these loadings: views of the Bible (.81), "Christian fundamentalist" thermometer (.81), "Christian" thermometer (.78), religious identification scale (.70), and "born-again" status (.67). *Theta* reliability = .81. (The identification scale was created from ANES items as follows: (3) "Traditionalists" include anyone taking "evangelical," "fundamentalist," "Pentecostal/charismatic," or "traditional" identities; (2) "None" includes all not responding or choosing "none" as a response; (1) *Progressive* includes "progressive," "spiritual but not religious," or "nontraditional"; and (0) *Secular*.

27 Interestingly, attention to the conservative TV network, Fox News, does not produce the same effect. Heavy Fox viewers share slightly more pro-environment attitudes with other members of the attentive public, although they do not come close to matching those watching CNN, MSNBC, or PBS (data not shown).

28 For historic and contemporary evangelical opposition to multilateral organizations, see Ruotsila, Markku: *The Origins of Christian Anti-Internationalism: Conservative Evangelicals and the League of Nations*. Georgetown University Press: Washington, DC 2008; Page, Benjamin/Bouton, Marshall: *The Foreign Policy Disconnect*. University of Chicago Press: Chicago 2006, p. 243; Guth, James L.: "Economic Globalization: The View from the Pews." *Review of Faith & International Affairs* 8 (4), 2010, pp. 41–46; Guth, James L.: "Religion and American Public Attitudes on War and Peace." *Asian Journal of Peacebuilding* 1 (2), 2013, pp. 227–252.

29 Bagehot: "Dirty Politics." *The Economist*, September 25, 2021, p. 48. Scholars have confirmed these tendencies among religious traditionalists: see Ecklund, Elaine Howard/Scheitle, Christopher P./Peifer, Jared/Bolger, Daniel: "Examining the Links

Table 2. Religious Variables and Support for Action on Global Warming (OLS *betas*)

	Model 1 *Affiliation*	Model 2 *Beliefs/ Behavior*	Model 3 *Religious Identities*	Model 4 *Reference Groups*	Model 5 *All Variables*
Ethnoreligious Affiliation					
White Evangelical	−.241***				−.137***
Latter-day Saints	−.062***				−.050***
Orthodox/Cons. Jews	−.017				−.001
Eastern Orthodox	−.016				.003
White Catholic	−.027*				−.015
Latino Evangelicals	−.012				.028*
White Mainline	−.025				−.018
Black Protestants	.026*				.078***
Nothing in Particular	.051***				−.018
Latino Catholics	.038**				.055***
World Religions	.039***				.008
Atheist/Agnostic	.202***				.052***
Reform Jews	.081***				.034**
Beliefs/Behavior					
Biblical Literalism		−.252***			−.115***
"Born-again"		−.072***			−.002
Importance		−.062***			.028
Attendance		−.025			.012
Religious IDS					
Conservative IDS			−.244***		−.034*
Progressive/Nontraditional			.119***		.116***
Secular			.121***		.049***
Reference Groups					
Fundamentalists				−.420**	−.319***
Christians				−.036**	.025
R squared=	.133	.124	.119	.196	.265

Source: American National Election Study, 2020. *N* = 7,453; "Other religions" constitute the omitted reference category in the regressions.

***p <. 001; **p <. 01; *p <.05.

attitudes toward them might well mediate the relationship between religion and environmental skepticism. All three measures have strong correlations with environmentalism in the expected direction, showing that advocates of small government, skeptics about science, and critics of multilateral agencies all tend to oppose environmental measures.

Finally, given the infusion of religious factors into the American party system, we expect that partisanship and ideology will also mediate the influence of religion on global warming perspectives.[30] And, in fact, Republicans, conservatives, and those who approve of Donald Trump's job performance oppose action on climate change, with strong bivariate correlations.

How do all these factors fit together? And do the other variables mediate completely the effects of religion? Model 1 reprises our look at the religious variables alone: our "religious traditionalism" measure has a very strong impact, greater than that of any of the ethnoreligious categories. On the other hand, religious commitment has little independent impact, and actually changes signs, becoming a very mild positive influence on environmental attitudes. (The apparently modest impact of religiosity may also reflect the fact that involvement has different effects in varied religious contexts, largely canceling out or muting its overall influence. If instead of using a single religiosity score, we use interaction terms for the larger ethnoreligious groups, we find that greater religiosity *intensifies* anti-environmental attitudes among white evangelicals, bolsters them significantly among white Catholics, and nudges them upward among Mainliners. At the same time, greater commitment *enhances* pro-environment sentiments among Black Protestants, Latino Catholics, and some other groups.) In any case, when theological traditionalism is added to the equation, the effects of religiosity disappear for white Catholics, but remain substantial, if somewhat reduced, for other ethnoreligious traditions—in the expected directions (data not shown).

Incorporating traditionalism reduces the coefficient for the highly traditionalist white evangelical community, and for Latter-day Saints, although both coefficients remain significant in the expected direction. The strong positive correlation for atheists and agnostics is naturally reduced a great deal by this operation, although

---

between Religion, Evolution Views, and Climate Change Skepticism." *Environment and Behavior* 49 (9), 2017, pp. 985–1006. Also: Collins, Harry/Evans, Robert/Durant, Darrin/Weinel, Martin: *Experts and the Will of the People: Society, Populism and Science*. Palgrave Macmillan: London 2020.

30 Kellstedt, Lyman A./Guth, James L.: "Religious Groups as a Polarizing Force." In: Crotty, William (ed.): *Polarized Politics: The Impact of Divisiveness in the U.S. Political System*. Lynne Rienner: Boulder 2015, pp. 157–186; Kellstedt, Lyman A./ Guth, James L.: "Religion and Electoral Behavior in the United States, 1936–2016." In: Malici, Akan/Smith, Elizabeth (eds.): *Political Science Research in Practice*. 2nd ed. Routledge: New York 2019, pp. 117–136.

Table 3. Religious, Media, Issue, and Political Influences on Support for Action on Global Warming (OLS *betas*)

	Pearson's r=	Model 1	Model 2	Model 3	Model 4
Ethnoreligious Affiliation					
White Evangelical	−.277	−.120***	−.096***	−.050***	−.015
Latter-day Saints	−.062	−.048***	−.045***	−.028***	−.016*
Orthodox/Cons. Jews	−.017	−.025*	−.022*	−.022**	−.015*
Eastern Orthodox	−.015	.006	.008	.018*	.017*
White Catholic	−.028	−.031*	−.017	−.020*	.010
Latino Evangelicals	−.011	.037***	.034***	.020*	.021**
White Mainline	−.026	−.015	−.015	−.012	.010
Black Protestants	.030	.089***	.066***	.011	−.047***
Nothing in Particular	.060	−.049***	−.048***	−.013	−.011
Latino Catholics	.042	.039***	.030**	.001	−.011
World Religions	.040	.001	.001	−.016*	−.018*
Atheist/Agnostic	.231	.036**	.045***	−.014	−.015
Reform Jews	.084	.032**	.031**	−.001	−.010
Belief and Commitment					
Traditionalism	−.436	−.439***	−.388***	−.209***	−.099***
Commitment	−.269	.050***	.056***	.038***	.028**
Conservative Media Use	−.375		−.286***	−.115***	−.079***
Issues					
Favor More Government	.523			.244***	.146***
Multilateralism	.575			.196***	.133***
Favorable to Science	.633			.349***	.261***
Party and Ideology					
Trump Job Approval	−.665				−.215***
Conservatism ID	−.641				−.150***
Republican ID	−.611				−.058***
R squared=		.226	.303	.597	.655

Source: American National Election Study, 2020. $N = 7,453$; "Other religions" and the unclassified constitute the omitted reference category in the regressions. Mean substitution for missing values.

***$p < .001$; **$p < .01$; *$p < .05$.

those taking either label are more environmentalist than their lack of traditional beliefs and practices would predict. Note that the coefficients for Latino evangelicals and Black Protestants become larger and more positive: both groups become more environmentalist once their theological traditionalism is accounted for. Overall, in this specification, the religious variables explain almost 23% of the variance in environmental attitudes.[31]

We know that religious traditionalists and progressives have distinct media preferences. How much do these preferences influence the distribution of attitudes? Adding conservative media attention to the religious variables in Model 2 does bolster the total variance explained but does not erase the effects of religious traditionalism. The coefficient for white evangelicals is reduced somewhat but remains quite strong, and the coefficients for most of the other ethnoreligious traditions hardly budge. This does suggest that some part of evangelical anti-environmentalism is explained (or mediated) by evangelicals' conservative media choices, but that effect still pales in comparison with that of basic theological orientations.

Model 3 adds the scope of government, support for multilateral organizations, and respect for science to the equation, greatly increasing the variance explained and reducing the coefficients for most of the ethnoreligious groups, many to insignificance. On the other hand, the *beta* for theological traditionalism is reduced substantially but remains strong. These findings are expected: previous studies have found that theological traditionalism is associated with preferences for smaller government, dislike of international organizations, and suspicions about science—and that is true in this sample as well. Thus, some religious anti-environment thinking reflects these attitudes but is hardly restricted to them. And finally, Model 4 shows that another portion of religious influence is translated through partisanship and ideology, as Trump supporters, conservatives, and Republicans are global warming skeptics.[32] This result is hardly surprising: these political measures are "close" to final choices in the political world.[33] But traditionalism remains a significant predictor at almost the same magnitude as the conservative media index, albeit far below that of the three issues, ideological conservatism, and Trump job approval. It is not surprising that ideology and partisanship transmit much of the

---

31 Use of the traditionalism and religiosity scores reduces very slightly the variance explained by religious variables alone in Table 2's Model 5, but clarifies the analysis conceptually. If we employ the alternative specification using interactive religiosity terms for each ethnoreligious group, we add another 1% to the variance explained.
32 Cf. this finding with the careful longitudinal analysis in Schwadel, Philip/Johnson, Erik: "The Religious and Political Origins of Evangelical Protestants' Opposition to Environmental Spending." *Journal for the Scientific Study of Religion* 56 (1), 2017, pp. 179–198.
33 Miller, Warren/Shanks, J. Merrill: *The New American Voter*. Harvard University Press: Cambridge 1996.

influence of religious factors, but it is still clear that traditionalism in belief retains significant direct effects.[34]

Conclusions

Our look at religious influences on American attitudes toward climate change has revealed a great deal of continuity with the findings in earlier studies of environmental concerns. Although climate change was just reaching a modest level of public consciousness when we wrote on religion and the environment in 1995,[35] the patterns of religious response remain very much the same. As we conjectured above, white evangelical Protestants and other religious traditionalists remain the "skeptical squad" when considering the need for strong environmental policies, while secular citizens and religious progressives are the vanguard of the environmental movement in public opinion. Most ethnoreligious groups are closely divided, with the "older," white European traditions leaning toward the conservative side, and ethnoreligious "minorities" more sympathetic to environmentalism.

Although specific ethnoreligious traditions may harbor unique "pro-" or "anti-" environmental theological traits that go unmeasured in the ANES, generalized theological perspectives are probably the primary influences: in every major ethnoreligious group, the theologically "traditionalist" are most skeptical about vigorous policies to address climate change (or even about its existence). Religiosity, on the other hand, has little independent effect; the solid negative bivariate correlation is largely spurious, an artifact of the greater "devotionalism" of theological conservatives. Indeed, the positive effect of religious commitment appears only in multivariate analysis when theological perspectives are controlled—and appears primarily among members of a few large ethnoreligious traditions such as Black Protestants and Latino Catholics (and a scattering of smaller groups). Elsewhere, religious commitment often works in the other direction.

Thus, despite the much-discussed "greening of religion" in recent decades, this tinting has occurred primarily at elite levels and has not shifted the attitudes of those in the pew. This finding raises a number of questions for further research. One of the most important is an analysis of the "cues" on environmental measures that believers receive in religious settings, especially from local faith leaders. We suspect that part of the strong environmental skepticism of white evangelicals comes from the pulpit. In a 2017 study of ten major Protestant denominations,[36] we

---

34 At this point in the analysis, demographic variables are all insignificant or nearly so, and add nothing to the variance explained in Model 4 (data not shown).
35 Guth, James L., et al. 1995: *op. cit.*
36 Smidt, C.E.: *The Cooperative Clergy Project of 2017.* Association of Religious Data Archives, August 13, 2020. https://www.thearda.com/Archive/Files/Descriptions/COOPCL17.asp.

found mixed sentiments on climate change. When asked whether "global warming is a serious threat to the future of our planet," 40% of evangelical pastors "disagreed strongly," and another 31% "disagreed." Mainline clergy were on the other side, with 49% "agreeing strongly," and 21% "agreeing." Even more than among laity, these differences were largely theological: conservative Protestant theology correlated at $r = -.740$ with the global warming question, and at $r = -.425$ with frequency of addressing the issue. Although we do not have recent data on clergy in other religious traditions, we expect similar theological divisions there.[37]

Nor did we find a universal sense of urgency among Protestant clergy. When asked how frequently they addressed environmental issues in their work, the results varied by tradition: Evangelical pastors were quite unlikely to talk about environmental concerns: only 3% said they talked about such issues "very often" and another 19% said "often," compared with 13% and 37% for Mainline clergy. In another vein, only 3% of Evangelicals reported an educational session on the environment in their parish, compared to 19% of Mainline ministers. Of course, the very infrequency of evangelical talk on the environment raises questions about clergy influence: if evangelical clergy doubt global warming and oppose action to solve the problem, but say nothing about the issue, how do congregations pick up the critical "cues"? In a slightly different vein, why are Mainline Protestants, who obviously hear a good bit more from pro-environment clergy, not the vanguard of the religiously "green"?

Of course, religious believers receive cues from secular sources, as our findings on conservative media reliance suggest. And politicians also provide opinion leadership, as conservative and Republican officials offer very different assessments of the climate change issue. And although some have argued that much religious environmental skepticism is political, not religious in origin, the task of separating those influences is daunting in an era where religious and cultural factors have thoroughly infused the American party system. Nevertheless, scholars will have plenty of work in the future sorting out the interactions of religious and political influences in the shaping of environmental attitudes.

References

Arbuckle, Matthew B./Konisky, David M.: "The Role of Religion in Environmental Attitudes." *Social Science Quarterly* 96 (5), 2015, pp. 1244–1263.

---

[37] For observations on the importance of religious elites, especially among evangelicals, see Veldman, Robin G./Wald, Dara M./Mills, Sarah B./Peterson, David A.M.: "Who Are American Evangelical Protestants and Why Do They Matter for US Climate Policy?" *Wiley Interdisciplinary Reviews: Climate Change* 12 (9), 2020. https://wires.onlinelibrary.wiley.com/doi/10.1002/wcc.693.

Barker, David/Bearce, David H.: "End-Times Theology, the Shadow of the Future, and Public Resistance to Addressing Global Climate Change." *Political Research Quarterly* 66 (2), 2013, pp. 267–279.

Campbell, David E./Layman, Geoffrey C./Green, John C.: *Secular Surge: A New Fault Line in American Politics*. Cambridge University Press: Cambridge 2021.

Collins, Harry/Evans, Robert/Durant, Darrin/Weinel, Martin: *Experts and the Will of the People: Society, Populism and Science*. Palgrave Macmillan: London 2020.

Djupe, Paul A./Hunt, Patrick Kieren: "Beyond the Lynn White Thesis: Congregational Effects on Environmental Concerns." *Journal for the Scientific Study of Religion* 48 (4), 2009, pp. 670–686.

Ecklund, Elaine Howard/Scheitle, Christopher P./Peifer, Jared/Bolger, Daniel: "Examining the Links between Religion, Evolution Views, and Climate Change Skepticism." *Environment and Behavior* 49 (9), 2017, pp. 985–1006.

Guth, James L.: "Economic Globalization: The View from the Pews." *Review of Faith & International Affairs* 8 (4), 2010, pp. 41–46.

Guth, James L.: "Religion and American Public Attitudes on War and Peace." *Asian Journal of Peacebuilding* 1 (2), 2013, pp. 227–252.

Guth, James L./Green, John C./Kellstedt, Lyman A./Smidt, Corwin E.: "Faith and the Environment: Religious Beliefs and Attitudes on Environmental Policy." *American Journal of Political Science* 39 (2), 1995, pp. 364–382.

Guth, James L./Kellstedt, Lyman A./Smidt, Corwin E./Green, John C.: "Theological Perspectives and Environmentalism Among Religious Activists." *Journal for the Scientific Study of Religion* 32 (4), 1993, pp. 373–382.

Hagevi, Magnus: "Religion and the Environmental Opinion in 22 Countries: A Comparative Study." *International Review of Sociology* 24 (1), 2014, pp. 91–109.

Hunter, James D.: *Culture Wars: The Struggle to Define America*. Basic Books: New York 1991.

Jones, Robert P./Cox, Daniel/Navarro-Rivera, Juhem: *Believers, Sympathizers, & Skeptics: Why Americans Are Conflicted About Climate Change, Environmental Policy, and Science*. Public Religion Research Institute (PRRI): Washington, DC 2014.

Kellstedt, Lyman A./Guth, James L.: "Religion and Electoral Behavior in the United States, 1936–2016." In: Malici, Akan/Smith, Elizabeth (eds.): *Political Science Research in Practice*. 2nd ed. Routledge: New York 2019, pp. 117–136.

Kellstedt, Lyman A./Guth, James L.: "Religious Groups as a Polarizing Force." In: Crotty, William (ed.): *Polarized Politics: The Impact of Divisiveness in the U.S. Political System*. Lynne Rienner: Boulder 2015, pp. 157–186.

Leege, David C./Kellstedt, Lyman A. (eds.): *Rediscovering the Religious Factor in American Politics*. M.E. Sharpe: Armonk, NY 1993.

Miller, Warren/Shanks, J. Merrill: *The New American Voter*. Harvard University Press: Cambridge 1996.

Page, Benjamin/Bouton, Marshall: *The Foreign Policy Disconnect*. University of Chicago Press: Chicago 2006.

Ruotsila, Markku: *The Origins of Christian Anti-Internationalism: Conservative Evangelicals and the League of Nations*. Georgetown University Press: Washington, DC 2008.

Schwadel, Philip/Johnson, Erik: "The Religious and Political Origins of Evangelical Protestants' Opposition to Environmental Spending." *Journal for the Scientific Study of Religion* 56 (1), 2017, pp. 179–198.

Smidt, C.E.: *The Cooperative Clergy Project of 2017*. Association of Religious Data Archives, August 13, 2020. https://www.thearda.com/Archive/Files/Descriptions/COOPCL17.asp.

Smidt, Corwin E./Kellstedt, Lyman A./Guth, James L. (eds.): *The Oxford Handbook of Religion and American Politics*. Oxford University Press: New York 2009.

Steensland, Brian/Park, Jerry/Regnerus, Mark/Robinson, Lynn/Wilcox, Bradford/Woodberry, Robert: "The Measure of American Religion." *Social Forces* 79 (1), 2000, pp. 291–318.

Swierenga, Robert P.: "Religion and American Voting Behavior, 1830s to 1930s." In: Smidt, Corwin E./Kellstedt, Lyman A./Guth, James L. (eds.): *The Oxford Handbook of Religion and American Politics*. Oxford University Press: New York 2009, pp. 69–94.

Taylor, Bron/Van Wieren, Gretel/Zaleha, Bernard: "The Greening of Religion Hypothesis (Part 2): Assessing the Data from Lynn White, Jr, to Pope Francis." *Journal for the Study of Religion, Nature and Culture* 10 (3), 2016, pp. 306–378.

Taylor, Bron/Van Wieren, Gretel/Zaleha, Bernard: "Lynn White Jr. and the Greening-of-Religion Hypothesis." *Conservation Biology* 30 (5), 2016, pp. 1000–1009.

Tsimpo, Clarence/Wodon, Quentin: "Faith, Religiosity, and Attitudes towards the Environment and Climate Change." *Review of Faith and International Affairs* 14 (3), 2016, pp. 51–64.

United Nation's Intergovernmental Panel on Climate Change: *Climate Change 2021: The Physical Science Basis*. United Nations: New York 2021. www.un.org/en/climatechange/reports.

White, Lynn, Jr.: "The Historical Roots of Our Ecological Crisis." *Science* 3767, 1967, pp. 1203–1207.

Wuthnow, Robert: *The Restructuring of American Religion*. Princeton University Press: Princeton 1988.

Notes on Contributors

ELAD BEN DAVID (Ph.D., the Department of Middle Eastern Studies at Bar Ilan University in Israel). His Ph.D. research dealt with Da'wa (call to Islam) in America, emphasizing Muslim preachers and Islamic organizations, focusing on the doctrine of Yasir Qadhi. Ben David is also a research associate at the Forum of Regional Thinking (FORTH), an independent Jewish and Arab research institute, and the Middle East Network Analysis Desk at Tel-Aviv University. His studies have appeared at many academic conferences and scholarly platforms, and he also executes as a board member of the Israeli Association for the Study of Religions (IASR).
eladbd608@gmail.com

EMILY R. GILL is Caterpillar Professor of Political Science Emerita at Bradley University. In addition to a number of articles and book chapters, she has written three books: *Becoming Free: Autonomy and Diversity in the Liberal Polity* (Kansas 2001); *An Argument for Same-Sex Marriage: Religious Freedom, Sexual Freedom, and Public Expressions of Civic Equality* (Georgetown 2012); and *Free Exercise of Religion in the Liberal Polity: Conflicting Interpretations* (Palgrave Macmillan 2019). Along with Jason Pierceson and lead editor Gordon A. Babst, she has also co-edited *Moral Argument, Religion, and Same-Sex Marriage: Advancing the Public Good* (Lexington 2009). She is the past president of the American Section, International Association for Philosophy of Law and Social Philosophy.
gill@fsmail.bradley.edu

JAMES L. GUTH (Ph.D., Harvard University) is William R. Kenan, Jr., Professor of Politics and International Affairs at Furman University. A specialist in American and European politics, his recent work has assessed the impact of religion on the electoral process and public policy issues. He is the coauthor or coeditor of several books, including *The Bible and the Ballot Box: Religion in the 1988 Election* (1991), *Religion and the Culture Wars* (1996), *The Bully Pulpit* (1997), *The Oxford Handbook on Religion and American Politics* (2009), and *Religion and the Struggle for European Union: Confessional Culture and the Limits of Integration* (2015). In 2023 he was a co-recipient of the inaugural Lifetime Achievement Award of the Religion and Politics Section of the American Political Science Association.
jim.guth@furman.edu

JAJUAN S. JOHNSON (Ph.D. Arkansas State University) is the Mellon Postdoctoral Research Associate for The Lemon Project at William & Mary. As a public historian and heritage studies scholar, his research explores the power of places of difficult histories to cultivate public emotion and generate a collective sense of community in the aftermath of traumatizing events of the distant and recent pasts. He was a 2022-2023 Cultural Vistas DAICOR Fellow, a transatlantic network of experts who promote an inclusive and progressive culture of remembrance in public spaces in

Germany and the United States. He has been published in *Ethnohistory*, *Southern Cultures*, and the *Arkansas Review: A Journal of Delta Studies*.
writejajuan@gmail.com

LYMAN A. KELLSTEDT (Ph.D., University of Illinois) is Professor of Political Science (emeritus) at Wheaton College, Illinois. He has authored or coauthored numerous articles, book chapters, and books in the field of religion and politics, including *Rediscovering the Religious Factor in American Politics* (1993), *Religion and the Culture Wars* (1996), *The Bully Pulpit* (1997) and *The Oxford Handbook on Religion and American Politics* (2009), and *Evangelicals and Immigration* (2019). In 2023 he was a co-recipient of the inaugural Lifetime Achievement Award of the Religion and Politics Section of the American Political Science Association.
lyman.kellstedt@gmail.com

SEBASTIAN KUBAS (Ph.D., Jagiellonian University) works at the Faculty of Law and Administration, Jagiellonian University, Kraków, Poland. He is a specialist in constitutional law. Current research concerns the judicial review procedures in the United States. He has recently published a book devoted to the myth of the *Marbury v. Madison* case and to the figure of Chief Justice John Marshall (*Warta na obrzeżach Konstytucji: dekonstrukcja mitu założycielskiego amerykańskiej sądowej kontroli konstytucyjności prawa*).
sebastian.kubas@uj.edu.pl

MICHAEL MCLAUGHLIN (Ph.D., Florida State University) is an Assistant Teaching Professor of religious studies at the University of Missouri where he teaches courses on religion and race in the United States. His ongoing research traces the religious roots of the Black Power movement.
mmclaughlin@missouri.edu

HUSAM MOHAMAD (Ph.D., University of Cincinnati) is Professor of Political Science at the Department of Political Science of the University of Central Oklahoma. He previously taught at Zayed University in the UAE, Qatar University, the Eastern Mediterranean University in Cyprus, and the Junior State of America Foundation. Husam was the recipient of the Fulbright Scholar Award in 2008, and the Brandeis University Fellowship in 2009. He has published several journal articles, book chapters, reviews, and short communications addressing Middle East politics, Israeli–Palestinian relations, U.S. policy toward the Arab and Muslim world, democratization in Arab politics, and Islamist movements across the Arab region.
hmohamad@uco.edu

PAULINA NAPIERAŁA (Ph.D., Jagiellonian University) is a political scientist, and Assistant Professor at the Institute of American Studies and Polish Diaspora, Jagiellonian University. Her research explores the intersection of religion and politics in the United States. She has published two books on this topic (2013, 2015), two edited volumes (2013, 2016), and a number of articles and book chapters. Currently, she is focusing on the socio-political role of the Black Church. She was a grantee of the Kosciuszko Foundation (2015, 2022), the Fulbright Commission

(2007–2008), and the National Science Centre Poland (NCN 2019), which allowed her to conduct research and consultations at Boston College, Harvard University, CUNY, and Valdosta State University.
p.napierala@uj.edu.pl

BRENT F. NELSEN (Ph.D., University of Wisconsin-Madison) is Jane Fishburne Hipp Professor of Politics and International Affairs and Director of the Tocqueville Center at Furman University where he has taught since 1990. His teaching and scholarship focus on Europe and the European Union with an emphasis on religion and politics. He is the co-author of *Religion and the Struggle for European Union: Confessional Culture and the Limits of Integration* (2015). His most recent book is *The North Sea System for Petroleum Production* (2024).
brent.nelsen@furman.edu

KÁROLY PINTÉR (Ph.D., Eotvos Lorand University, Budapest) is Associate Professor and currently Chair of the Institute of English and American Studies, Pazmany Peter Catholic University, Budapest, Hungary. He has published a book on literary utopias of Thomas More, H.G. Wells, and Aldous Huxley. His other major interest is American studies, particularly the U.S. Constitution, the American Presidency, and church-state relations in the United States. He was Visiting Scholar at the Nanovic Institute of Notre Dame University in 2017.
pinterk@gmail.com

CRISTÓBAL SERRÁN-PAGÁN Y FUENTES (Ph.D., Boston University) is Full Professor in the Department of History, Philosophy, Religious Studies, and Interdisciplinary Studies at Valdosta State University, GA. He is the author of *Saint John of the Cross: His Prophetic Mysticism in the Historical Context of Sixteenth-Century Spain* (Pacem in Terris Press, 2018). He is currently serving as the editor of a special issue entitled "Mysticism and Social Justice" for *Religions*, an international journal. He has presented papers on King at different international conferences and has published articles on King and the Civil Rights Movement. At Valdosta State University, he was a member of the Martin Luther King Planning Committee and was part of the MLK Annual Celebration Week of events.
cserranPagán@valdosta.edu

JEROLD WALTMAN (Ph.D., Indiana University) is the R.W. Morrison Professor of Political Science Emeritus at Baylor University. He taught at Louisiana College and the University of Southern Mississippi before coming to Baylor. His past research has ranged over tax policy, minimum wage policy, and American and comparative constitutional law. Currently, his research concentrates on comparative constitutional law. He has published a number of articles, book chapters, and books, including *Principled Judicial Restraint* (Palgrave, 2015) and *Congress, the Supreme Court, and Religious Liberty: The Case of City of Boerne v. Flores* (Palgrave, 2013). He also served as editor of the *Journal of Church and State*.
jerold_waltman@baylor.edu

Index

A
accommodation of religion 95, 109, 110
African American churches 193, 280
African American 52, 55, 56, 190–195, 197, 198, 204, 212, 213, 216, 218, 220, 224, 226, 227, 233, 241–243, 248–250, 253, 255, 258, 264–267, 279–281, 283, 284, 286, 287, 289, 291, 293–295
Al-Aqsa Mosque 335
Alfred Daniel Williams 201, 202, 214
American civil religion (ACR) 8, 31, 32, 34, 35, 37–39, 44, 46, 47, 56, 62, 63
American exceptionalism 36, 44, 46, 57, 318–321, 331
Antichrist 330, 335, 337
Anti-Semitism 131, 329, 344
Arlene's Flowers v. State of Washington 138
arson 279–286, 289–291, 293–295

B
Balfour Declaration 333, 338
Bellah, Robert N. 31–33, 35, 36, 38–40, 46, 63
The Beloved Community 241, 245
Birmingham 213, 214, 219, 227, 248, 249, 283
Black Church activism 16, 227, 289
Black Church studies 16, 189
Black Church 7–9, 16, 25, 189–198, 202, 204, 207, 212, 213, 215, 218, 220, 224–228, 230–234, 279–296, 374
Black Lives Matter 9, 224, 279, 281, 282, 289, 291, 295, 341
Black Panther Free Breakfast for Schoolchildren Program 9, 263–265, 268–271, 273, 275
Black Panther Party 9, 263–267, 269, 271, 272, 274–276
Black people 195, 205, 216, 251, 264, 272, 273, 281, 283, 286, 288, 290, 291, 294
Bobby Seale 264, 265, 269, 274, 276
burning 16, 205, 254, 279–286, 289, 291–293, 295
Bush, George W. 42–45, 48, 49, 103, 106, 327, 332, 334, 340, 346

C
Carter, Jimmy 39, 41, 42, 196, 215, 223
Christian nationalism 75, 84, 96–98, 100, 101, 120, 124, 143
Christian Right 8, 16, 24, 26, 33, 42, 95–101, 103–106, 110, 113, 117, 120, 124, 328, 329, 335, 339, 346
Christian Zionism 308, 328, 331–333, 338, 340, 343, 344
church 7–9, 13, 16, 19, 20, 22, 24, 25, 40–42, 45–48, 101–103, 107–109, 111, 112, 114–116, 118, 132, 135–137, 144, 167, 168, 174, 179, 181–183, 189–210, 212–222, 224–234, 241–243, 247–249, 252, 253, 263, 264, 266–276, 279–296, 305, 307, 315, 316, 333, 338, 339, 343, 374, 375
civil marriage 148, 150, 157–159, 161
civil religion 8, 24, 31–40, 44–47, 56, 62, 63, 131
Civil Rights Movement 25, 52, 193, 197, 198, 200, 203, 209, 226, 241–243, 249, 250, 254–258, 267, 268, 280, 282–284, 286, 288, 289, 375
climate change 259, 304, 305, 353–356, 358, 359, 361, 363, 364, 366, 369, 370

Index

conservative populism 8, 24, 71–77, 79, 81, 83, 85–87, 89
cooperative internationalism 304–306, 308, 317, 321
Coretta Scott King 213, 259
COVID-19 pandemic 83, 95, 96, 117, 118, 120–122, 224
cultural resentment theories 71
culture wars 15, 33, 34, 41, 77, 90, 99, 109, 304, 308, 357, 373, 374

D

David Hilliard 263, 265, 268
declinism 74, 81–83, 87
Defense of Marriage Act 150, 156
discrimination 84, 102, 110, 112–116, 130, 133–138, 140, 148–151, 155–157, 169, 190, 191, 218, 228, 259
Dispensationalism 308, 333, 344, 355
distrust of experts 74, 83
dominion theology 355
due process 107, 130, 153–155, 158, 167

E

The Ebenezer Baptist Church in Atlanta 9, 189, 190, 193, 194, 201, 219, 225
economic stress theories 71
Employment Division of Oregon v. Smith 129
environmental attitudes 353–358, 360, 361, 366, 368, 370
equal protection 151, 153, 155–158, 161
Establishment Clause 8, 95, 102, 107, 108, 110, 111, 113, 117, 122, 133, 167, 168, 177
ethnoreligious traditions 8, 71, 73, 77–79, 83, 87, 89, 307, 309, 311, 313, 354, 355, 357, 359–361, 366, 368, 369
evangelical Protestants 48, 71, 73, 133, 134, 303, 307, 311, 313, 321, 355, 357, 363, 368–370

F

Federal Bureau of Investigation 265
First Amendment 8, 95, 102, 105–108, 110, 116, 118, 119, 122, 123, 130, 138, 143, 153, 167, 169, 174, 176, 180, 182, 183
Fourteenth Amendment 107, 130, 153–155, 161, 181, 279
Free Exercise Clause 107, 108, 111–113, 118, 122, 134, 138, 143, 167, 168
freedom from interference 143, 144, 147–149, 152–154, 158
freedom from Religion Foundation 133
Freedom of Religion 169, 174
Fulton v. City of Philadelphia 114, 115, 118, 136, 139
fundamentalism 204, 207, 210, 229, 328, 355, 362

G

Goliath 334
Great Awakening 190, 202, 327

H

heritage 16, 36, 40, 53, 189, 218, 279, 283, 289, 294, 295, 373
Holocaust 338, 345
Hosanna-Tabor Lutheran Church v. EEOC 135
Howard Thurman 212, 221, 245, 257
Huey Newton 264, 265, 268

I

ideology 24, 34, 52, 74, 82, 84, 85, 87–90, 100, 120, 173, 233, 274, 288, 318–321, 332, 333, 335, 344, 366–368
Immigration and Nationality Act of 1965 132
Islam 8, 167, 169–183, 346, 373
Islamophobia 84, 167, 169–171, 181, 182, 329

Index

J

Jerusalem 57, 330, 333, 335, 337–339, 341, 342
Joseph L. Roberts, Jr. 216–218
Judicial review 95, 104–106, 110, 118, 374
justice 37, 38, 46, 49, 52, 104–106, 111–113, 115–120, 122, 124, 129, 131, 135–139, 146–154, 158, 159, 176, 178, 193, 195, 196, 201, 206, 211, 213, 215, 219, 222, 231, 232, 241, 244, 246–250, 252, 253, 255, 257, 258, 260, 271, 272, 274, 279, 280, 285, 287, 289–291, 294, 340, 374, 375

L

LGBTQ rights/Homosexuality 76, 105, 129, 133, 136, 139, 145, 178, 182, 221, 332
LGBTQ 76, 109, 113, 114, 129, 133, 134, 136, 137, 139, 181, 182, 341
Liberal Theology 210–212, 214, 221, 222, 229–231
Lynn White thesis 354, 356

M

majoritarian rough politics 74, 79–81, 83, 87, 89
Malcom X
marriage equality 8, 143–153, 156–161
Marsha Lovelle Turner 270, 274
Martin Luther King Jr. 9, 189, 190, 193, 201, 204, 207, 209, 211, 212, 214, 215, 223, 241, 244–247, 249–259, 264, 288
Martin Luther King, Sr. 205, 218, 222
media use 353, 367
Memphis 180, 214, 243–245, 250, 252, 253, 288
militant internationalism 303, 304, 309, 321
ministerial exception 112, 113, 135, 136, 139

Mohandas K. Gandhi 241
Montgomery 209, 212, 213, 227, 242, 243, 248, 249
Muslim community 167, 169–171, 178–182

N

nativism 51, 72, 75, 84, 318, 319, 321
negative liberty 143, 144, 147–149, 151, 153, 154, 158, 161
nonviolence 214, 241, 242, 246–249, 251, 255, 257, 258, 260

O

Obama, Barack 9, 16, 37, 45–47, 55, 57, 100, 109, 133, 215, 223, 279–281, 284, 290, 295, 309, 330
Obergefell v. Hodges 8, 143, 144, 148, 152–155, 157, 159–161
opiate or inspiration debate 199
Otis Moss, Jr. 215
Our Lady of Guadalupe School v. Morrisey-Berru 134

P

partisanship 62, 83, 87, 89, 90, 310, 319–321, 366, 368
party polarization / political polarization 63
Personalism 211, 212, 229, 242
police violence 264, 266, 273, 291
political church 199
political distrust 80, 83
political mobilization of Black churches 16, 190
Poor People's March to Washington 251
populist attitudes 71, 73, 77, 78, 89, 319
populist style 74, 89, 90, 319
positive liberty, rights 8, 143, 144
post-9/11 era 167, 169, 173, 182

presidency, US presidency 31, 38, 39, 42, 43, 47, 51, 54, 56–58, 62, 63, 89, 95, 96, 103, 106, 280, 281, 332, 337, 339–341, 375
presidential rhetoric 31
Promised Land 243, 328–330, 332, 333, 336, 338, 340, 343, 346
Prophet Muhammad 177, 180
"Proposition 8" Case 178, 180, 181

R

racism 9, 51, 102, 195, 204, 205, 223, 241, 243, 244, 247, 248, 250, 251, 254, 255, 258–260, 281, 286, 287, 290, 294, 332
radical secularism 36, 37
Raphael G. Warnock 189, 190, 219
Reagan, Ronald 39, 41–43, 48, 49, 102, 103, 133, 259, 265, 327, 332, 334, 335, 337, 339, 346
religion 7–9, 11–24, 26, 31–40, 42–48, 56, 62, 63, 71–73, 76–89, 95–97, 99–124, 130–136, 143, 144, 147–149, 153, 158, 168–172, 174–176, 179, 182, 190–193, 195, 197, 198, 206, 210, 224, 230, 232, 233, 245, 246, 263, 264, 266, 266, 274, 275, 286, 287, 289, 292, 303–312, 315, 317–321, 328, 330, 331, 337, 338, 340, 344, 345, 353–370, 373–375
religious belief 14, 15, 26, 41, 80, 96, 108, 109, 111, 113, 117, 120, 124, 143, 153, 168, 289, 303, 306–308, 310, 311, 313, 315, 328, 331, 353, 355, 356, 358, 361
religious clauses 8, 167–169, 174, 180, 182
religious exemptions 95, 114, 116, 117, 120, 124, 153
Religious Freedom Restoration Act (RFRA) 130
religious nationalism 35–38, 44

religious restructuring 15, 77–79, 89, 308, 357
Religious Right 25, 33, 42, 99–103, 105, 120, 306, 328, 330, 332, 336, 337
resistance 89, 96, 114, 153, 154, 192, 195, 198, 248, 251, 258, 266, 280, 289, 291, 293–295, 304, 334, 341, 356
Reverend Earl Neil 268, 275
Reverend Eugene Boyle 272
revolution 12, 36, 49, 98, 99, 109, 170, 175, 191, 215, 247, 248, 251–254, 257–259, 263, 265, 267, 269, 271, 275
Robert F. Kennedy 244
Roe vs. Wade case 176, 178
Rosa Parks 248, 258, 259
Ruth Beckford 268, 269

S

same-sex marriage 144–148, 150–153, 155–158, 161, 178, 181, 373
science skepticism 353
Second Coming 50, 210, 335
Selma 213, 215, 217, 243, 249
sexual orientation 130, 133, 136, 147, 149, 150, 156, 157, 161
Sharia 175–177, 179, 181
social gospel 189, 192, 197, 198, 203, 204, 207, 210–215, 219, 221, 228–234, 242
social justice 37, 46, 201, 211, 213, 215, 219, 222, 231, 232, 241, 260, 287, 294, 375
State of the Union addresses 62
stewardship theology 356

T

terrorism 43, 57, 170, 279, 291, 294, 295
theological traditionalism 8, 9, 26, 71, 311, 353, 358, 362–364, 366, 368
"thin populism" 71, 74, 79
traditional marriage 145, 148, 151, 160, 162

Tribulation 331, 335
Trump Doctrine 9, 303–305, 309–321
Trump, Donald 8, 9, 31, 42, 47–63, 71–75, 82, 85, 87, 89, 95–97, 101, 103–106, 110, 114, 119, 120, 140, 224, 303–305, 309–321, 327, 330, 331, 337, 340–342, 345, 346, 358, 366–368

U

The United States 7–9, 11, 16, 17, 19, 23, 24, 31, 32, 34, 36, 37, 43, 44, 46, 50, 53, 55, 57, 61, 71–76, 84, 90, 95–97, 104, 117, 131, 132, 140, 143, 144, 147–150, 153, 158, 167–170, 173–175, 177, 180, 182, 183, 194, 198, 203, 220, 223, 224, 241–244, 247, 250–259, 265, 269, 275, 279–283, 286, 294–296, 304, 310, 319, 328–333, 336, 340, 342–345, 353–355, 358, 366, 374, 375

V

violence 9, 59, 61, 180, 192, 206, 212, 214, 218, 241, 242, 246–249, 251, 255, 257, 258, 260, 264–266, 268, 273, 279–284, 287–295, 331, 334

W

War in Vietnam 241, 243, 251, 253–255, 258
white evangelicals 31, 42, 47, 48, 50, 51, 72, 79, 80, 83, 84, 96, 97, 101, 134, 306, 317, 319, 331, 337, 340, 357, 358, 361, 363, 366, 368, 369
white nationalism 31, 52, 53, 72, 75, 84–87, 89, 279, 294, 329

Y

Yasir Qadhi 167, 169, 172–182, 373

INTERNATIONAL RELATIONS IN ASIA, AFRICA AND THE AMERICAS

Edited by Andrzej Mania & Marcin Grabowski

Vol. 1 Olga Barbasiewicz (ed.): Postwar Reconciliation in Central Europe and East Asia. 2018.

Vol. 2 Adam Nobis: A Short Guide to the New Silk Road. 2018.

Vol. 3 Radka Havlová (ed.): Untangling the Mayhem: Crises and Prospects of the Middle East. 2018.

Vol. 4 Marcin Grabowski / Paweł Laidler (eds.): Global Development Policy in the 21st Century. New Challenges. 2018.

Vol. 5 Andrzej Mania / Marcin Grabowski / Tomasz Pugacewicz (eds.): Global Politics in the 21st Century. Between Regional Cooperation and Conflict. 2019.

Vol. 6 Marcin Grabowski / Tomasz Pugacewicz (eds.): Application of International Relations Theories in Asia and Africa. 2019.

Vol. 7 Адам Нобис. Краткий путеводитель по Новому Шелковому Пути. 2019.

Vol. 8 Olga Barbasiewicz / Marcin Grabowski / Ewa Trojnar (eds.): Security Dilemmas and Challenges in 21st Century Asia. 2020.

Vol. 9 Marcin Gabryś / Magdalena Marczuk-Karbownik / Magdalena Paluszkiewicz-Misiaczek (eds.): Canadian Political, Social and Historical (Re)visions in the 20th and 21st Centuries. 2020.

Vol. 10 Agata Wiktoria Ziętek / Grzegorz Gil (eds.): ASEAN in a Changing World. 2021.

Vol. 11 Maciej Kurcz: Urban Now. A Human in the Face of Borderliness and Urbanisation in Juba, South Sudan. 2021.

Vol. 12 Olga Barbasiewicz / Maciej Pletnia (eds.): Internal and External Aspects of Japanese Security. 2021.

Vol. 13 Olga Barbasiewicz / Michał Lipa / Karolina Rak (eds.): Historical and Collective Memory in the Middle and Far East. 2021.

Vol. 14 Tomasz Pugacewicz / Marcin Grabowski (eds.): Great and Small Games in Central Asia and the South Caucasus. 2022.

Vol. 15 Anna Pruska: Swiss Banking Secrecy and the US-Swiss Conflict Over Holocaust Claims. 2022.

Vol. 16 Łukasz Gacek / Rafał Kwieciński / Ewa Trojnar: Taiwan under Tsai Ing-wen. Democracy Diplomacy. 2023.

Vol. 17 Magdalena Musiał-Karg / Natasza Lubik-Reczek (eds.): The War in Ukraine. (Dis)information – Perception – Attitudes. 2023.

Vol. 18 Bogdan Góralczyk: China in the Xi Jiping's Era. 2024.

Vol. 19 Paulina Napierała (ed.): Religion and American Politics. Domestic and International Contexts. 2024.

www.peterlang.com